# JEFFERSON'S SPY

# Other Books by Tony L. Turnbow

### Non-fiction

*Hardened to Hickory: The Missing Chapter in Andrew Jackson's Life*

### Young Adult Historical Fiction

## FIGHTING DEVIL'S BACKBONE TRILOGY

Book 1  *The Shadow of E. Z.'s Fear*
Book 2  *E. Z. and the Chikasha Warrior*
Book 3  *E. Z. in the Den of Thieves*

For more information, visit tonyturnbow.com

# JEFFERSON'S SPY

## VOLUME 1
## THE SECRET LIFE OF MERIWETHER LEWIS

By
Tony L. Turnbow

Copyright 2026 by Tony L. Turnbow.

All Rights Reserved.

No part of this publication may be reproduced, distributed, or transmitted in any form or by any means, including photocopying, recording, or other electronic or mechanical methods, or by any information storage and retrieval system without the prior written permission of the publisher, except in the case of very brief quotations embodied in critical reviews and certain other noncommercial uses permitted by copyright law.

ISBN:
978-1-7362608-3-8 (hardcover)
978-1-7362608-5-2 (paperback)

Library of Congress Number (LCCN): 2025922412

Cover design by Michael Hutzel and FoxFuel Creative, LLC, Nashville, Tennessee

Interior design by booknook.biz

Map illustrations by Daniele De Vecchi

Cover image includes Thomas Jefferson's cipher for Meriwether Lewis.

# CONTENTS

Author's Note     vii
Prologue: Shooting Star     1

1. Protégé and Patron     5
2. Soldier to Spy     19
3. Agent 13 in Command     31
4. Nest of Spies     41
5. Mission to Legend     53
6. Adventure of a Lifetime     67
7. Aaron Burr and the Lure of Santa Fe     77
8. Hero's Pedestal     93
9. Stepping Off the Pedestal in St. Louis     105
10. Honor Among Spies     117
11. Hero Weakened     127
12. Secret Service Revealed     135
13. Hero Shattered     149
14. Journey to the Nest of Hornets     163
15. Perfect Storm     179
16. Necessary That He Be Stopped     193
17. Stalled     205
18. Fateful Decisions     213
19. Ride into the Storm     223
20. Crossing the River to the Unknown     233
21. Long Roads to Monticello     245

| | |
|---|---|
| Image Credits | 266 |
| Maps | 267 |
| Preview of Volume Two | 273 |
| Acknowledgments | 275 |
| Abbreviations | 277 |
| Selected Bibliography | 279 |
| Notes | 303 |
| Index | 429 |
| About the Author | 439 |

# AUTHOR'S NOTE

The cause of explorer Meriwether Lewis's sudden death in 1809, is one of the most intriguing and enduring mysteries in American history. Lewis was said to have died from multiple gunshot and knife wounds on one of the bloodiest roads of his era. No eyewitnesses came forward to admit to seeing Lewis receive—or inflict—his fatal wounds.

Ten days after Lewis's death, a narrative began to emerge: Meriwether Lewis, who had co-led the most important cross-continental expedition in American history had committed suicide. The claim was first made in letters and then repeated in newspapers across the nation. Hearsay witnesses came forward to provide statements to support it.

At the same time, however, a counter-narrative emerged, suggesting that Lewis was murdered. Hearsay witnesses also came forward with statements to support that theory. A civil investigation four decades later by a State of Tennessee commission concluded that it was more likely Lewis died at the hands of an assassin.

But the first individuals to interpret a historical event have the advantage of setting public perception. Thomas Jefferson accepted the suicide narrative in his letters, though he was not present when Lewis died. Until recently, a majority of historians who have written about Lewis's life also concluded Lewis's biography with a retelling of the suicide narrative.

Growing up in the area where Lewis died, I frequently visited the national park where he is buried. Like other visitors, I walked the grounds where he took his last breath, studied the remains of the tavern chimney where he lodged, and tried to make sense of the competing narratives. My interest was further piqued by older generations who enjoyed telling the stories their ancestors had passed down—stories about the Natchez Trace and the death of the national hero buried beneath the stone cairn topped by a single broken column.

Despite biographers' reasoned opinions, the suicide narrative has never provided a satisfactory explanation. Like Jefferson, historians have generally based their views on the shaky assumption that hearsay accounts from the scene of Lewis's death are reliable. I have no strong belief about whether Lewis was the type of person who would or would not have committed suicide, if such a trait can be known with reasonable certainty. What will not let the matter rest is that the known accounts are contradictory. And the limited incontrovertible evidence does not fit together neatly to close all gaps, which I have learned is not uncommon in the investigations of even open-and-shut cases.

Historians have reexamined a limited set of known facts. Some studies even analyze the views of historians who believe Lewis committed suicide versus those who think he was murdered. Still, none of this reexamination has settled reasonable questions surrounding Lewis's death.

In 1996, I had the opportunity to serve as the alternate juror on a formal coroner's inquest convened by the District Attorney for Lewis County, Tennessee, to examine the evidence known then about Lewis's death and to make a recommendation on whether his remains should be exhumed for further investigation. The proceedings were public, and a transcript was later published. Several historians who had written about Lewis's death over the previous two decades testified to their opinions and experts demonstrated possible effects of gunshots. One fact that became clearer was how little incontrovertible evidence exists in Lewis's case.

I approached this study with as open a mind as possible to reexamine every piece of the limited evidence to determine whether a different perspective might offer a more convincing explanation. I also searched archives for additional evidence that previously had not been considered.

Although I have always found reliable evidence more persuasive that Lewis was murdered, there is hearsay and circumstantial evidence suggesting he died by his own hand. What may prevent some of us who have studied Lewis's death from reaching a satisfactory conclusion is that the story we think we know may prevent us from considering facts that would otherwise be clear.

This book, and the one to follow, will not attempt to prove or disprove a historian's thesis. Rather, they are offered as part of a search for the truth of how Lewis died—or as much of the truth as the evidence that remains will reveal. They offer a slightly different perspective along with some additional facts to consider.

It became clearer during this search that some of the individuals who helped shape the narrative of Lewis's death in 1809, were not disinterested parties. Understanding their earlier roles in Lewis's life helped explain their involvement at the time of his death. It was enlightening to see how their vested interests and personal conflicts may have colored the statements they offered as well as how they attempted to cover up their involvement.

What also became clearer—intriguing enough to merit this separate first volume—is a fascinating story of how Thomas Jefferson used Meriwether Lewis as his point man, agent, or spy from the time Lewis was twenty years old; how Lewis was given opportunities to develop his talents as an agent and informant; and how Lewis was still performing that work at the time of his death.

The concept of spying was broader in Lewis's day. Spies were not concentrated in agencies specifically organized for that purpose. Army commanders were given authority to organize small companies of scouts they called "spies." Members of a company of spies provided intelligence on the enemy's strength and performed strategic missions. Not surprisingly, commanders learned that they could use their spies intended for an external enemy to gather intelligence on fellow commanders and government officials for their own career advancement.

Beyond the military, governments have long utilized their employees and agents to covertly advance their objectives and execute missions out of public view. It should not be surprising that Lewis was expected to promote secret government objectives in his role as territorial governor. One question is whether Lewis's work as a spy for his country—or for Jefferson—contributed to his death.

I initially planned to rely solely on unquestionable evidence to see where that analysis would lead. But realizing how little evidence exists that reasonably cannot be questioned, I came to understand that it would be impossible to tell the story without including some hearsay and speculation to fill the gaps. The result in this first volume is a narrative of Lewis's life and the immediate reaction to his death based on sources of mixed reliability, intended to set up an examination of the facts surrounding Lewis's death in the second. Readers can use the endnotes to assess for themselves the reliability of the sources and the conclusions I draw from them.

Men engaged in clandestine activities rarely created a permanent record. When they found the need to write letters detailing their actions, the recipients often burned them. When they recorded their actions in journals, they later ripped out the pages. It is known, for example, that as John Overton, one of the men included in this account, lay on his deathbed, he supervised the burning of letters he never wanted to enter into the historical record. What bits of evidence that remain, then, must be pieced together to tell the story.

This narrative is presented as one interpretation of the limited and murky written evidence, much like a lawyer might present a view of conflicting evidence to a jury. Correlation is not always causation, but I suggest that the most reliable interpretation of ambiguous facts should be based upon how they fit into a succession of events that produced a known result. As such, I add events that could have occurred merely by coincidence or, to the contrary, that could have conveniently furthered a motive. At some point, the reader may conclude that the number of coincidences would be improbable unless they furthered a larger event. I also presume that it is more likely that the people took the actions described in this narrative in their own self-interest, regardless of how they professed their motives.

Permit me to acknowledge the near certainty that other researchers will draw different conclusions from the same facts and will discover additional sources that may lead to different conclusions. But that is an admission every writer should make. While I will offer comments and assessments, I invite readers to base their own conclusions on an examination of the reliability of the facts rather than on my opinion.

With those points in mind, please note the following as you read:

- The focus of these two volumes is to examine the evidence to attempt to provide a more satisfactory explanation of how Lewis died; therefore, the thread of the story told relates to that subject. For example, I briefly describe portions of the Lewis and Clark Expedition—a fascinating story told best by Stephen Ambrose—in just a few pages to explain its influence on Lewis's life and death without attempting to retell the story. I also describe actions Lewis took in response to Jefferson's directions related to tribal nations to demonstrate how Lewis dealt with the challenges he was given, without discussing the merits or effects of his actions. Those topics have been the subjects of other books.
- Most individuals mentioned by name are those critical to understanding the events surrounding Lewis's death. Others are described more generally to help the reader focus on the narrative.
- The main narrative in the first two-thirds of the book is written to interest a broader audience in the Lewis story. Additional details of interest mainly to historians, such as names of the person generally described, are reserved for the endnotes in the last third.

- General James Wilkinson and Aaron Burr played such an important role in the events in Lewis's life—and possibly his death—that it is necessary to focus attention on their activities to understand Lewis's actions.
- To avoid repeatedly describing three key sources, I will refer to the letter that U.S. Agent to the Chickasaw Nation, James Neelly supposedly wrote to Thomas Jefferson on October 18, 1809, as "**The Neelly Letter**," the letters William Clark received purporting to have been written by Fort Pickering commander Gilbert C. Russell as "**The Suspicious Russell Letters**;" and a copy of a statement that Gilbert C. Russell supposedly gave to army officer and scribe Jonathan Williams in November 1811, as "**The Russell Statement**."
- Historians avoid repetition in expository writing; narrators use repetition for effect. This narrative nonfiction blends the two approaches. Although the narrative is generally written in chronological order, some facts are best combined by topic and used out of order to make it easier to compare facts. Some repetition of facts or points is intentional to make an analysis of the facts easier or to prevent a gap in the story.
- Most books about Lewis's death focus heavily on the three contradictory hearsay statements attributed to the innkeeper Priscilla Grinder, who was said to be one of the last people to see Lewis alive. Except for a brief reference, this first volume intentionally omits those statements to make the examination of the other circumstances clearer. The supposed "Grinder" accounts will be included as part of the narrative and discussion of evidence in the second volume.
- Quotations often intentionally retain the misspellings and unique capitalizations of the original writing.
- As I have explained in earlier books, I sometimes use the word "Indian" to refer to tribal members because that was the appellation

used at the time of the subject and because members of tribes that I know prefer the use of that description over "Native American" or "indigenous person." I use the word "Indian" to be clear and to avoid offense rather than to offend.

This first volume primarily focuses on Lewis as a person and the characteristics of his relationship with Thomas Jefferson that may have contributed to the circumstances of his death. The second, *Jefferson's Spy: The Mysterious Death of Meriwether Lewis*, will focus on the physical evidence, witness statements, and circumstantial evidence related to his death.

Tony L. Turnbow

George Washington, as painted by James House, who helped create the narrative that Meriwether Lewis took his own life.

[T]here are some Secrets, on the keeping of which so, depends, oftentimes, the salvation of an Army: Secrets which cannot, at least ought not to, be intrusted to paper; nay, which none but the Commander in Chief at the time, should be acquainted with.

—George Washington[1]

Thomas Jefferson

## PROLOGUE

# SHOOTING STAR

> prey do not mention this about the Govr. excupt Some unfavorable or wrong Statement is made __ I assure you that he has done nothing dis honorable, and all he has done will Come out much to his Credit __ as I am fully pursuaded.
>
> —William Clark regarding Governor
> Meriwether Lewis, August 26, 1809[2]

One of the few certainties in the mystery surrounding Meriwether Lewis's death at age thirty-five is that its gruesome details shocked the Nation. Only three years earlier, Lewis had returned from leading the Lewis and Clark Expedition over the North American continent to be celebrated as one of the first American popular heroes. Across the Atlantic, *The London Times* praised the American who would be known even two centuries later as one of the world's greatest explorers.[3] It seemed inconceivable that such a bright star could flame out so soon.

Eulogies for Lewis summed up his extraordinary success. Several newspapers lauded: "A new world had been explored—additional knowledge in all the sciences obtained, at a trifling expense of blood and treasure—The voice of fame echoed the glad tidings thro' the civilized world—the name of Lewis was the theme of universal praise."[4]

In less than a decade, the young soldier had been propelled on a meteoric rise—becoming personal secretary to the president of the United States, leader of the historic Lewis and Clark Expedition, and governor of the vast Upper Louisiana Territory, which stretched from the Mississippi River to the Rocky Mountains. His future appeared boundless.

Lewis could have combined his fame with experience as governor of the western territory to become an eventual contender for the presidency. He enjoyed connections in both political parties of the time: his mentor, Thomas Jefferson, was a leader of the Republican Party, and his grandfather's brother was married to the sister of the leader of the opposing Federalist Party, George Washington.[5]

Until the time came to decide on a presidential run, Lewis stood to amass a fortune. He and co-explorer William Clark had entered the fur trade business in the Northwest to capitalize on the growing demand for pelts in Europe. The company they helped found eventually succeeded in opening the fur trade in the Rockies.[6] Based in part on Lewis and Clark's exploration discoveries, the fur trade would later make their new competitor, John Jacob Astor, one of the wealthiest in the world.[7] Just the names "Lewis" and "Clark" alone in connection with their St. Louis Missouri Fur Company should have given the duo a significant advantage in a business to be built in the largely undiscovered West.[8]

It was poignant, then, that Lewis's abrupt end was rooted in fulfilling the very mission that had fueled his success. His sudden rise to fame and power had not been by chance. From his teenage years, Lewis's life had been orchestrated by Thomas Jefferson.

On February 23, 1801, Jefferson accelerated Lewis's ascent by inviting the soldier to become personal secretary to the president and to swap his army quarters for the East Room of the President's House—later known as the "White House."[9] Unlike other administrators who spent hours bogged down in mundane letter writing and recordkeeping, Lewis was told he would serve more like a general's aide-de-camp.[10] In reality, his role would be to carry out special assignments for the president—some official, others Jefferson hoped would never come to light.[11] It would be no secret that Lewis was Jefferson's man—the secret would be the actions Lewis took on his mentor's behalf.

The twenty-six-year-old was elated. The offer appeared to be a once-in-a-lifetime opportunity from a father figure Lewis could expect to act in his best interest. Without appearing to consider all the ways the decision would change his life, he readily accepted.[12]

Meriwether Lewis, however, was not selected for his political or administrative acumen—Thomas Jefferson needed a spy.

One of the teenage Meriwether Lewis's classmates later was said to have remarked that Lewis's face reminded him of an image he had seen of Napoleon. This illustration of a young Napoleon from an 1803 painting by Jean Baptiste Greuze bears a remarkable resemblance to Lewis in Charles Willson Peale's 1807 painting.

# CHAPTER 1

# PROTÉGÉ AND PATRON

> presumeing that as you were once his Patron, you still remain'd his friend.
> —Gilbert C. Russell to Thomas Jefferson, on Lewis's death

Meriwether Lewis was one of the few army officers whom Thomas Jefferson believed he could trust with his life. Lewis drew Jefferson's attention from the beginning. Stories of the eight-year-old boy stalking the woods at night, hunting barefoot, even in winter, when ice cut his feet and left a bloody trail in the snow, intrigued Jefferson so much that he recalled them years later in his brief biography of Lewis.[13] He may have heard the story of when Meriwether, no older than ten, stood his ground and calmly fired a heavy gun as an angry bull charged him.[14] Or perhaps he heard the tale of young Meriwether extinguishing a campfire to evade an approaching hostile tribe while the adults around him hid.[15]

By the time the boy became a man, Jefferson reflected that Lewis was "early remarkable for intrepidity, liberality & hardihood."[16] Curiosity for exploration was a trait Jefferson could harness and develop in the boy; heroic courage was an inborn strength he needed in a spy.

Jefferson's plantation, "Monticello," was located about ten miles from Lewis's parents' farm, "Locust Hill," near Charlottesville, Virginia.[17] The two families shared the close bonds of early settlers who relied on one another for survival in the foothills of the Blue Ridge Mountains. As was common in small communities, the families intermarried.[18] In fact, Lewis's mother, Lucy, knew the Jeffersons well enough to supply information about Jefferson's early years to one of the president's first biographers.[19]

When Meriwether was five, his father died of apparent pneumonia after crossing a river at flood stage in winter. At his father's dying suggestion, Meriwether's mother soon married his father's friend, Captain John Marks. The couple moved to Georgia along with other Virginia families looking to speculate in cheaper land. It is unclear whether Meriwether remained behind with the extended family in Virginia or briefly moved to Georgia.[20]

When Meriwether was eight, his uncle, William Meriwether, was appointed as his legal guardian in Charlottesville. Jefferson later wrote that Meriwether was "taken from his mother" when he was eleven.[21] The boy inherited the family home and plantation, subject to his mother's dowry, and it was rented to a caretaker until he became old enough to manage it.[22] He spent time on his grandparents' farm, "Cloverfields," where his father was buried and where he often explored the woods.[23] Meriwether could have been expected to join the ranks of Virginia planters and live out his life, never traveling farther than a few miles from home.

But Charlottesville was Jefferson's sphere of influence. Meriwether's uncle, Nicholas Meriwether, who lived on land that adjoined Monticello, served as Jefferson's land agent and Meriwether's unofficial guardian.[24] Jefferson spent much of Meriwether's early years in Paris as U.S. Minister to France and returned to Virginia when the boy was fifteen. Though Jefferson was soon off to Philadelphia to serve as Washington's secretary of state, his occasional visits back to Charlottesville provided opportunities to interact with Lewis. Jefferson had lost his own father when he was in his teens, and he could appreciate the difficulties of growing up without a father's support.[25]

Whether Jefferson sparked Lewis's interest in geography, natural science, and exploration or whether Lewis approached Jefferson with a thirst for knowledge is not documented. Lewis credited his family for what he described as his "governing passion for rambling." Even his use of that phrase may have revealed the influence of Jefferson, who described an explorer on the famed Cook Expedition as having a "roaming disposition."[26] Meriwether's mother could also have been an inspiration. As a medicine woman, Lucy often searched the woods for plants to cure her neighbors' illnesses. She fostered Lewis's interest in exploration, natural science, and health from an early age. However it began, Jefferson mentored Meriwether, likely lending him books from his library. Given Jefferson's interest in expanding knowledge, it can also be assumed that the two discussed Meriwether's readings and that Jefferson enjoyed shaping the boy's mind.

Jefferson may have influenced Meriwether's formal education. Lewis had studied in the common schools until his uncle took over his education. At that point, he began his studies under Episcopal minister Reverend Matthew Maury at the Albemarle Classical School. Maury's father had been Jefferson's teacher, and Jefferson encouraged his own family to study under Maury.[27] At sixteen, when Lewis left school to work on his farm, he revealed his interest in distant lands by expressing disappointment that he would not have an opportunity to learn about geography in school.[28]

The boy made a mixed impression on his classmates. One student was said to have recalled that Meriwether's face bore a resemblance to images he later saw of a young Napoleon. But unlike Napoleon, the teenage Meriwether was bowlegged and awkward. The classmate saw Lewis's courage and a military character at even a young age, yet he thought Lewis stifled himself with so much self-control that he appeared "stiff and without grace."[29] Growing up without a father and being sent to live with an uncle and cousins to attend school may have stunted Meriwether's self-confidence in his social abilities.

Jefferson returned to Charlottesville full-time when Lewis was nineteen. By that time, Lewis struggled to turn tobacco crops on his farm into cash.[30] The future president had a similar interest. He would fixate on details of how to produce a profit on his larger plantation, Monticello.

Lewis later recalled that he was twenty when he heard about Jefferson's plans to promote an expedition to the Pacific and that he offered to lead it. If so, Jefferson did not take such an offer from the inexperienced farm boy seriously enough to remember it.[31]

Leaders of society at the time followed a form of the Roman patrician model, mentoring young men of extraordinary talent who lacked the means to reach their full potential. Mentors' motives were not entirely altruistic. When protégés later assumed positions of influence, they were expected to add to their patron's base of political and social support.[32]

Jefferson's influence over Lewis's development would become obvious. Lewis adopted Jefferson's republican—and later Republican Party—views to the point that one army officer would remember them as one of Lewis's defining characteristics.[33] In fact, Lewis's party views became so strong that co-explorer William Clark would later suggest that they would interfere with Lewis's relationship with a prospective girlfriend whose father did not share them.[34] It was the beginning of a time when, as Winfield Scott would observe, "party spirit ... knew no bounds."[35]

As an impressionable teenager, Lewis also undoubtedly latched onto Jefferson's stories of France and mirrored Jefferson's love for the French Revolution. In Paris, French citizens seized control of their country from the monarchy to reorganize their government around ideals of self-government in a republic that fostered "liberty, fraternity, and equality." Jefferson could provide a first-hand account, adding the glow of his own thoughts on the virtues of self-government.[36]

Young people who supported the French cause hoped it would spark a political revolution that would sweep across Europe, overthrow all the old monarchies, and grant people the freedom to govern themselves. Lewis became captivated with the movement to the point of once even addressing his mother as "Citizen Lucy Markes," like other impressionable young men who wanted to be identified with their support for the French revolutionaries.[37]

Yet, each generation finds a way to mark its independence from its elders. During Lewis's youth, the Romantic Movement emerged in Europe as a reaction against the Enlightenment Era of Jefferson's generation. The older generation believed that dispassionate reason could solve any problem and that a stoic demeanor, which reflected reason, demonstrated the height of human perfection—minds that used logic to overcome emotion. In reaction, it became fashionable among young men of Lewis's generation to show that the whole person included emotion or sensibility as well as reason. Realism would be viewed through the senses. The movement gained traction early in the United States among young people who supported the French Revolution and sought ways to model French ideals.

Meriwether was receptive. Not only did the movement allow young Americans to participate peacefully in revolution with their counterparts in France, but romanticism also incorporated the geography he loved. It provided spatial anchors and cultural context to ideas.[38] Or, as with other ideas, Jefferson may have been ahead of his time as an early fan of the poetry and expressions of the Romantic Movement. He could have unwittingly passed those ideas on to Lewis.[39]

When Lewis received the president's offer to become private secretary, he said he accepted Jefferson's confidence in him with "lively sensibility," a phrase popular among the Romantics to affirm the use of their senses.[40] Growing numbers of young Romantics demonstrated their sensibility by intentionally appearing contemplative, moody, and even melancholy. Jefferson noticed that Lewis sometimes appeared melancholy but passed off the affectation as "sensible depressions of mind" that Lewis may have inherited from his family rather than from his own mentorship or the trend of the day.[41]

The young Lewis reveled in the times of change. Marveling at the notion that a small-town farm boy could even be considered for the position of the president's private secretary, he gushed, "nothing is extraordinary in these days of revolution and reform."[42]

If Meriwether's penchant for fads was an act of rebellion against his elders, it would be insignificant. Like a son, Lewis craved Jefferson's approval, and he would obediently follow Jefferson's direction for the remainder of his life. Jefferson, on the other hand, assured affection for Lewis in his letters as he often did for friends, but his letters to Lewis rarely expressed the emotions of a surrogate father.[43]

In the fall of 1794, the twenty-year-old Lewis—as Jefferson described being in "the ardor of youth" with a "passion for more dazzling pursuits"—took the first opportunity to escape a confining life on the farm by volunteering to march as a private with about 2,000 fellow Virginia militiamen to Western Pennsylvania.[44] Their mission was to support the U.S. Army in suppressing a rebellion by farmers who refused to pay what amounted to the first internal federal tax.[45] For both sides of the conflict, it was the first post-revolution fight for the soul of the Nation. For Lewis in particular, it was a chance to engage in a fight between his mentor Jefferson and Jefferson's political enemy, Alexander Hamilton, and their opposing visions for the Republic.

Unlike Jefferson, who envisioned a small, decentralized federal government that controlled little of its citizens' lives in a new experiment of liberty and self-representation, Hamilton was understood to propose a strong central government, run by an elite bureaucracy. At best, Hamilton hoped to centralize federal control over the states to harness the fledgling nation into an economic power that could compete with other nations. Opponents saw Hamilton's goals as a threat to create a new monarchy and feudal aristocracy, supported by citizen serfs. His dream, as one early historian said, was "to make America a larger and better England."[46]

Republicans branded Federalists as "pro-British," an insult so soon after the Revolution.[47] Like his love for all things French, Jefferson passed his Revolution-era hatred of the British on to his protégé. In fact, Lewis held such contempt for the British that he would be unable to mask his views even years later when attempting to gain intelligence from a British trader.[48]

As treasury secretary, Hamilton had persuaded Congress to enact the first federal excise tax to help pay off Revolutionary War debt. The tax of up to thirty percent on distilled liquors particularly burdened western and southeastern farmers who produced whiskey for income from surplus farm products.[49] Everyone who distilled alcohol would be required to register with the federal government. Each county would be required to have a federal excise tax office to collect the tax; therefore, federal enforcement officers would have a local presence. Western farmers feared that once the tax collection system was in place, it could be expanded to other functions, enabling the distant eastern government to regulate the lives of western citizens.[50] The tax would create a controlling federal bureaucracy that was as far from Jefferson's ideals, literally, as the East was from the West.

Early Americans were still primarily loyal to their states. The federal government under the new Constitution was barely six years old, and memories of the contentious ratification process were still fresh. Westerners had only reluctantly agreed to the Constitution with the assurance that a federal government of the states would be used solely for the common defense and to promote a general welfare. All other powers were reserved to the states.[51] Americans would not begin to think of themselves as one united nation until after the War of 1812. During Lewis's time, the boundaries of federal power were mainly untested. Hamilton saw an opportunity to expand them.

Western Pennsylvania, on what was then the edge of the frontier, had resisted federal control. Prior to the time that voters divided themselves into political parties, farmers and laborers in Western Pennsylvania and bordering Virginia counties began to organize themselves by forming democratic societies to oppose the governing Federalist policies. The farmers correctly assessed that Hamilton directed the new tax toward them to punish them for their populism. Despite Hamilton's professing that his actions were solely to benefit the government, farmers noticed that the tax would have the effect of enriching Hamilton's friends and supporters at the expense of his opponents.[52]

Farmers objected that they had not voted for the tax. Many opponents were Revolutionary War veterans who argued that the tax was a form of taxation without representation, much like the one that sparked the Revolutionary War. After all, it was the Federalist Washington who had given as justification for the Revolution that Parliament had "no more Right to put their hands into my Pocket, without my consent, than I have to put my hands into your's, for money."[53] But the majority of federal representatives had approved the tax.

In defiance, farmers erected liberty poles as political statements, as they had during the first Revolution, for the new conflict that some rebels called "The Second Revolution." Easterners would call it "The Western Insurrection," and Hamilton would ridicule it as "The Whiskey Insurrection."[54] Elite Federalists only stiffened the resistance by branding their western opponents as an "ignorant herd."[55]

Westerners' acts of political resistance led to excesses of anarchy. Some tax rebels claimed their fight to be in the spirit of the French Revolution, which by that time had devolved into attacks on French government facilities and the building of guillotines to chop off officials' heads. Like their Parisian heroes, western farmers built mock guillotines to intimidate federal officials.[56] As anger boiled, a few westerners humiliated and violently attacked Hamilton's tax collectors by stripping them in public and pouring hot tar and feathers over their bodies.[57]

At the same time, President Washington's reluctance to support the French Revolution led to thousands of people demonstrating for days outside his house and threatening to drag him into the streets.[58] Hamilton's followers feared that violent attacks on authority through the western democratic societies were creating instability that threatened to destroy the infant federal government. A few Federalists even suggested that connections between citizens who supported the French and their opposition to Federalist policies proved that a sinister foreign influence was at work.[59]

American supporters of the French Revolution, like Lewis, may have overlooked the excesses and violence of their own side. This fight was their chance to participate in a global awakening against the old European monarchists. They feared that Federalists who supported the European system would prevent Jefferson's ideals of liberty from ever being realized.[60]

Under Hamilton's European vision for the new government, taxpaying serfs would be held in check by the military. He argued that coercing citizens to obey laws through force of arms is among "the great and essential principles necessary for the support of government."[61] An exasperated Washington finally agreed with Hamilton that if the federal government did not act, "there is an end of, and we may bid adieu to, all government in this country, except mob, or club government, from whence nothing but anarchy and confusion can ensue."[62] With the cover of Washington's support, Hamilton jumped at his opportunity to establish federal power over the states. As treasury secretary and Washington's former aide-de-camp, he persuaded Washington to allow him to assume some of the duties of the secretary of war to call up troops under the guise of putting down an insurrection.[63]

Jefferson viewed Hamilton as a dangerous man, claiming, "Hamilton was not only a monarchist, but for a monarchy bottomed on corruption."[64] And Hamilton did not disappoint his expectations. On what westerners would long remember as "The Dreadful Night," Hamilton-led militias broke into farmers' homes in the middle of the night, pulled more than

150 men and boys from their beds, and arrested them on the mere suspicion of supporting insurrection. Doubling down on the "ignorant herd" insult, Hamilton's soldiers dragged Pennsylvanians in their nightshirts through the snow to unroofed cow pens that served as makeshift jails.[65]

If there was any doubt that Hamilton triggered the conflict to use military force against citizens for the purpose of establishing the supremacy of federal laws over citizens of states, he confided to a relative that "the insurrection will do us a great deal of good and add to the solidity of everything in this country."[66] Coincidentally, in addition to denying the civil rights of his grassroots political opposition, Hamilton took the opportunity to attempt to extort locals into providing testimony he could use to arrest his chief critic, Albert Gallatin, and other western opponents in Congress.[67]

Jefferson concluded that "Our citizens are divided into two political sects. One which fears the people most, the other the government," bragging that he had no fear of the people.[68] He opposed the federal tax as a top-down affront to his view that the nation should be controlled from the bottom up by citizen farmers. He especially opposed the use of arms to enforce the tax, as a "war on our own citizens to collect it."[69]

Though Jefferson recognized the need for a militia, he also was thought, as Winfield Scott observed, to have a "low estimate of, or rather contempt for the military character" as a general principle because most military commanders of the Revolution became Federalists.[70] Jefferson was more of a bookish philosopher than a warrior. No doubt, the mentor shared his views with his patron before Lewis set out for his first military service.

With Jefferson's help, Lewis could have taken advantage of a provision in the militia law that allowed him to hire a substitute to serve in his place rather than submit to Federalist officers.[71] If he joined as a volunteer, he would march under the orders of Virginia general Daniel Morgan, a Federalist, stopping briefly to be reviewed in a grand ceremony by

President Washington. Once perceived as the father of a unified nation, Washington had stepped off his hero's pedestal to make decisions as president that could not please everyone. Westerners who did not support his decisions had come to view him merely as the leader of the Federalist political party.[72]

On the surface, then, Lewis's volunteering to support Hamilton's militias might appear to be a more serious act of rebellion against Jefferson and a contradiction of Lewis's own firmly held values of the French Revolution and Anti-Federalism—except that Jefferson could use Lewis's militia service to gain information to fight the Federalists.

When Lewis's militia company arrived in Pennsylvania, he searched for alliances with the Anti-Federalist rebels, even joking to his mother that he might bring home an "Insurgent Girl to se them next fall bearing the title of Mrs. Lewis."[73] Most fellow Virginia troops began returning home after a few days, when it became apparent that the conflict had been quelled before they arrived. Lewis instead volunteered to remain behind for another six months as part of a detachment of about 600 militiamen.[74] He later defended the decision to his mother, writing that the "insurgiants are at the same at heat as they ever were."[75] However, the returning militia revealed that he had overstated the threat, possibly as an excuse to continue his mission for Jefferson.

Lewis's detachment was assigned to patrol the western area to ensure that rebels would remain calm. Washington would describe their mission as a success because it "terrified the insurgents."[76] Westerners saw the soldiers' presence, however, as military intimidation designed to suppress protected political speech in their democratic societies that were becoming political opposition to the Federalists. Hamilton's noble cause was undermined further when undisciplined troops took license to create noisy and bloody disturbances in the taverns at night and rob houses in Pittsburgh.[77]

Before Lewis arrived in Pennsylvania, federal troops shot and killed rebel ringleader Major James McFarlane, a Revolutionary War hero and local militia captain, after one of the rebels had raised a white flag to surrender. Perhaps more significantly, McFarlane was a leader in one of the democratic societies that opposed Federalist policies.[78] Lewis's commander, Morgan, chose to build winter huts for his soldiers' camp near the late McFarlane's ferry operation on the Monongahela River. In addition to controlling a strategic transportation point, the location of the camp made a statement of force by poking a thumb in the eye of local rebels.[79] Yet, even Morgan eventually appreciated that his soldiers had turned their forces on fellow Americans, writing, "we ought to make these people our friends."[80]

And Lewis did, but for Jefferson's purposes. Morgan's outreach provided cover for Lewis to gain information from rebels who wandered into the camp to surrender and to seek pardons. He developed close friendships with the rebel McFarlane's nephew, James, and the nephew's brothers, Andrew and Lewis.[81] The McFarlane brothers likely knew fellow Pennsylvania rebels who refused to surrender to the traveling judges that Hamilton hired to dispense his justice and who instead chose to escape to the western frontier to seek refuge in enemy Spanish territory.[82] Fourteen years later, Governor Meriwether Lewis would place the McFarlane brothers in positions to renew those relationships when he selected them as his agents in the West.

Hamilton used the populist rebellion as part of the justification to create a "New Army," the nation's first standing army. Federalist officers would serve as its commanders, with one mission to tamp down political dissent and preserve federal authority, or, as Republicans would see it, Federalist control of federal authority.[83] It was a main reason a standing army had never been authorized. James Madison assessed that it was "the old trick of turning every contingency into a resource for accumulating force in the government."[84]

By the time Lewis's militia service ended in the spring of 1795, Jefferson had obtained enough information to argue that the Whiskey Rebellion "answered the favorite purposes of strengthening government and increasing the public debt; and therefore an insurrection was announced and proclaimed and armed against, and marched against, but could never be found."[85]

Hamilton had gone too far. Anti-Federalists used information about Hamilton's violent suppression of western farmers and their democratic societies to help stoke voters' fears of Hamilton's abuse of the army as a political weapon.[86] Their arguments found support among farmers in Kentucky, North Carolina, and Maryland, among others, who had also engaged in acts of civil disobedience to protest the tax. Together, their Anti-Federalist opposition transformed the political landscape, and, as one historian said, laid the foundation for Jefferson's Republican Party that presented the first formidable national opposition party and led to the creation of a two-party system.[87]

Jefferson decided to test the power of his new party by running for president in 1796 against Federalist John Adams. Jefferson failed to receive the highest number of votes. He was relegated to serving as vice president under his opponent—the Constitution at the time provided that the candidate who received the second-highest number of electoral votes would serve as vice president. But opposition to Hamilton's use of the army continued to simmer. Four years later, as the political pendulum inevitably swung to the opposite direction, it became one issue that created Jefferson's political revolution. His new opposition party won the presidency, House, and Senate. Jefferson's win, followed by Aaron Burr's duel, would prevent Hamilton from returning to the federal government.[88]

To whatever extent Jefferson used Lewis's time in the militia to gather information about Hamilton's abuses of power to help define his new party and win the presidency, Lewis was off to a successful start in fulfilling his role as a spy for his patron.[89]

William Clark

## CHAPTER 2

# SOLDIER TO SPY

> Where-ever their Army lies it will be of the greatest advantage to us to have spies among them...
> 
> —George Washington[90]

Lewis's brief stint in the militia changed his life as he found the adventure of military service, friendships among soldiers, and an abundance of provisions to his liking.[91] He assured his mother, "I am quite delighted with a soldier's life," bragging that the soldiers shared "mountains of beef and oceans of whiskey."[92] And like other military men of his time, he wrote home to deny rumors that soldiers led a "life of debauchery."[93]

Cementing Lewis's interest, reports arrived from the Ohio Frontier that General "Mad" Anthony Wayne had won a significant victory over tribes in what would be called the "Battle of Fallen Timbers." Settlers in the Western Pennsylvania area celebrated that they could rest from the constant fear of attack from neighboring tribes. The news sparked a surge of excitement and a renewed sense of patriotism.[94] Soldiers who had helped remove the threat of attack became the new American heroes.

As Lewis's Virginia militia service was coming to an end, he was encouraged to enlist in the regular U.S. Army, and like most men in his company, he accepted. He entered the army with the rank of ensign, the lowest commissioned officer rank at the time.[95] For the moment, rank seemed to be of little importance. His military adventure would continue as army duties presented opportunities to explore new territory. It also may have been more than a coincidence that the military training and information he acquired through his connections with army officers would be used to benefit his patron, Jefferson.

Lewis fed his wanderlust as he crossed the Appalachian Mountains to what then was the Northwest Frontier. Only a small percentage of U.S. citizens lived west of the Appalachians, and few had ever seen the new territory. At the end of Lewis's 500-mile trek down the Ohio River or through the wilds to a point about fifty miles north of Cincinnati, his destination, Fort Greeneville, added to his awe for the army. As the largest fort in the U.S., its ten-foot palisade walls enclosed approximately fifty acres. The amazing spectacle could be seen from a distance. Trees had been cleared all around to give soldiers a clear view of any potential attackers.[96]

Inside the walls, the army had built a small city that served as headquarters for commanding general Wayne, the victor of the battle everyone was talking about. But the massive fortification would not protect Wayne from his rival General James ("Jimmy") Wilkinson. South on the Ohio River at Cincinnati, Wilkinson commanded the smaller Fort Washington and plotted to take Wayne's command.[97] Of the two generals, Wilkinson would play a larger role in influencing Lewis's life.

Just before Lewis's twenty-first birthday, representatives of regional tribes defeated in the battle assembled at Fort Greeneville to sign a treaty ending their fight against the army. Wayne began the treaty process by making a show of pointing to the arrows held by an eagle on a carved U.S. seal. Tribal leaders acknowledged their defeat by ceding territory that would become parts of Ohio, Indiana, Illinois, and Michigan. For Lewis, the event provided an opportunity to study the treaty process that he would lead fourteen years later to acquire territory for additional states.[98]

The army's victory over the confederation of tribes that controlled the frontier along the Ohio was a tipping point. Lewis had arrived west of the Appalachians at a moment when the United States was poised to push forward with western exploration and settlement, aiming to stave off further colonization by Europe.

The next year, Lewis was chosen to become part of a select sharpshooter unit known as the "Chosen Rifle Company."[99] Shooting posed no challenge for a boy who had spent endless hours hunting in the woods.[100] The new commander and trainer of the unit was one of the victors of the Battle of Fallen Timbers—William ("Billy") Clark. The opportunity to be trained by a soldier with Clark's family reputation and talents was a boon for Lewis. Clark's older brother, George Rogers Clark, had earned renown for his daring capture of large swaths of western territory from the British during the Revolution.

Billy Clark was four years older than Lewis, and like General Washington, he was tall, red-haired, and stood out in a crowd.[101] As Lewis's commander, the older Clark had a duty to help shape Lewis's views of the army and its leaders. The infectious enthusiasm Lewis would have heard from Clark sounded in Clark's description of a soldier's life at Fort Greeneville as:

> all is gaiety, good humer & Devertion. The eye is constantly enterained with the Spledour of Dress and equipage, and the year [ear] with the Sounds of Drums, fifes, Bugles, Trumpets, and other Intrementeals. We have Daily Parades, & Manuvers, when we are amused by the roreing of the Connon, and the yells of the Guards that perform those manuvers daily.[102]

Outgoing and a natural influencer, Clark no doubt became a role model.

The two soldiers developed a friendship that Lewis later described as "long and uninterupted."[103] Lewis and Clark had different talents that made the duo an effective team: Lewis was reserved and detail-oriented. In contrast, Clark enjoyed the details of mapmaking but was an extrovert who influenced others through persuasion. In addition to military life, the friends shared an affinity for hunting, exploration, adventure, and danger. Writer Samuel Clemens, known to many as "Mark Twain," would later observe through dialogue that the average man does not like trouble and danger.[104] The duo were not average, and they would become two of a select group of men the early U.S. government would rely on to conduct clandestine military missions.[105]

From the time of General Washington's command in the Revolution, the U.S. depended on spies for survival. As president, Washington approved the use of government funds for spying by government agents known as "secret service."[106] The practice continued once he became president, and it was followed by subsequent presidents, including Jefferson.[107]

The young nation occupied only a fraction of the North American continent, and all the territory it controlled lay east of the Mississippi River. Enemies and competitors surrounded: Spain controlled most of the territory west of the Mississippi, Florida, the Gulf Coast, and New Orleans; Britain still held a foothold in Canada, maintained forts on the Great Lakes, and retained control of the Atlantic and Caribbean; Russians were exploring Alaska with an eye to the northwest fur trade; and French emperor Napoleon threatened to invade and reclaim territory France had ceded.

The fight for eventual control of the continent was not viewed at the time as a conflict between European settlers and native tribes, but rather as a contest between the newly formed American states and European powers.[108] The Americans' goal was exclusive control of the continent, separated from the rest of the world by two oceans, so that, as Jefferson said, Americans would never have to "jostle with other nations" and face endless wars.[109] As European countries and the U.S. vied for control of the North American continent, each worked to gain the loyalty of tribes to use as proxies against the other on a figurative chessboard.

Jefferson revealed his vision for the Americas as early as 1786 when he said, "Our confederacy must be viewed as the nest from which all America, North and South is to be peopled."¹¹⁰ The practical military aspect of removing potential enemies from the hemisphere was one goal. But Jefferson also envisioned the spread of his ideals of liberty and self-government, which later formed into the republican ideals that Lewis would adopt.¹¹¹ Even as Washington's secretary of state, Jefferson proposed the eventual acquisition of the territory west of the Mississippi. His stated vision was that the U.S. eventually acquire both continents "peice by peice"[sic].¹¹² That acquisition would first require spies to enter occupied territory to discover the best means of conquering it.¹¹³

The army of the day relied on rivers to move large numbers of troops; therefore, Jefferson said that one of the spies' first missions would be to "delineate with correctness the great arteries of this great country."¹¹⁴ Much of the "great country" Jefferson described was part of the continent claimed by European and tribal nations.

Military conquest and defense were intertwined. At a time when the U.S. relied mainly on local militias for defense, the more settlers the government could persuade to occupy settlements near the borders, the easier those borders were to defend with citizen militias. Conversely, the farther the government could extend the borders, the safer those established settlements became. The continuous cycle pushed settlements westward. The use of spies as a first incursion into enemy territory was as common a practice for the U.S. military in Early America as it had been for centuries in the rest of the world.

The U.S. lacked the military strength to risk war with the European powers along its borders; therefore, Jefferson needed to find alternative means to fulfill his vision. One enemy weakness he could exploit was the population imbalance. European colonials had populated their colonies with only small numbers compared to those of native tribes. If tribes could be persuaded to shirt their loyalty from the Europeans to the U.S., territory could be acquired without firing a shot.¹¹⁵

General Wayne had already used Clark as an envoy to take presents under the noses of Spanish officials to the Chickasaw at the Chickasaw Bluffs in Tennessee to persuade them to shift their loyalty from Spain to the United States. Chickasaw clans had divided into factions that supported Spain versus those that hoped to use the U.S. as leverage to gain power within the Chickasaw Nation. Clark's mission proved a success and led to an alliance among the Chickasaw, the U.S. Army, and Tennessee settlers that Jefferson would eventually use as a springboard for his westward expansion.[116] The Spanish governor, recognizing Clark as a "youth of enterprise and extraordinary activity," suspected that he might also be at work on a clandestine mission, but Clark covered his boat to prevent Spanish spies from seeing the goods he was transporting to the Chickasaw.[117]

After training in the Chosen Rifle Company for a few months in the summer of 1795, Clark was tagged again for a critical mission as a spy and diplomat. The U.S. had negotiated a treaty in which Spain agreed to allow U.S. citizens to navigate the Mississippi River and to relinquish control of its forts in American territory east of the river; however, Spain was slow to vacate the east banks.[118] Wayne appointed Clark as an official envoy to travel down the Mississippi to warn Spanish officials that they no longer had authority to build or maintain forts on the east side. As Clark floated downriver to deliver his message under the guise of a diplomat, he covertly sketched Spanish military installations on the west bank that could be used to develop an attack plan if necessary. Clark also spied the Spanish governor's boat that navigated the Mississippi River and drew its advanced design.[119]

While Clark was traveling down the Mississippi, Lewis followed General Wayne east to Pittsburgh, where headquarters were being established under Hamilton's reorganization of the New Army. Lewis's new direct supervisor at headquarters was considered one of Wilkinson's army "spies" he used to gain information on Wayne as part of his plot to take his command.[120] Although now stationed in the East, Lewis was assigned the duties of Paymaster of the First United States Infantry, a position that still allowed him to spend much of his time on the western frontier. According to one historian, as paymaster, Lewis frequently rode a circuit "through the wilderness and up and down the Ohio River between Detroit and Pittsburgh," before returning to the quartermaster general's depot in Pittsburgh.[121]

Because paymasters did not keep a set schedule, the new position allowed Lewis to take on special assignments. Early on, he was tasked to escort a Wyandot tribal leader from Detroit to Pittsburgh.[122] It was a learning experience. The future transcontinental explorer lost his way in the woods but managed to assure the tribal leader's safe arrival at his destination. Wayne also trusted Lewis to transport the official records for the army headquarters to Philadelphia.[123] The general used Lewis to courier confidential dispatches to the secretary of war, and it is certainly possible that Lewis was assigned other sensitive duties that were not, as Washington said, entrusted to paper.[124]

By 1796, hostilities with a second U.S. enemy, France, began to escalate with a series of provocations that would later be known as the "Quasi-War." France had first established its own settlements along the Mississippi River, including St. Louis, St. Genevieve, Natchez, and New Orleans, before ceding control of that territory to Spain. Hamilton, who then served as Major General of the Army, suggested that because the public was already primed for war, the U.S. should use the pretext of war with France to take additional American territory from Spain.[125] Such an action would require military intelligence of the best points for attack and defense. General Wilkinson would later claim that he had "traversed a trackless wilderness four times, from the borders of Louisiana to the frontiers of Georgia."[126] But Wilkinson was known for his excessive weight, one enemy ridiculing him a "mammoth of iniquity."[127] Certainly, he delegated those duties to younger and fitter men.

Interestingly, during the same period, Lewis received a furlough to travel home to Charlottesville. He took the time to become a Mason in the lodge at Staunton, Virginia, and advanced to the position of Past

Master Mason in just three months.[128] Second to the military, Masonic membership offered the quickest means to political and social advancement in the early United States. However, instead of remaining in the East, Lewis traveled south and west into Ohio, Kentucky, and Georgia for three and a half months for the stated purpose of attending to family land matters. He, in fact, used some of that time to purchase land in Kentucky in April 1799.[129]

One of the reasons Jefferson later gave for selecting Lewis as private secretary was that he had gained knowledge of the "Western country."[130] He certainly developed a knowledge of the Northwest Territory through his duties as paymaster. However, during his time on furlough, Lewis had the opportunity to gain information about the U.S. Southwestern Frontier if he chose to take it.

In 1796, Clark also took a furlough and then resigned from the army, supposedly to assist with his aging parents. However, after returning to his parents' home in Kentucky, Clark again traveled down the Mississippi River in early 1798.[131] The public purpose of Clark's voyage was to transport tobacco for Kentucky family members for sale in New Orleans.[132] But during the voyage, Clark covertly drew detailed maps of the river as he traveled toward Spanish territory. Mapmaking was a skill Clark would employ five years later on the transcontinental expedition. Eventually, it became significant that Clark's maps of the Mississippi noted points in ascending order from New Orleans, providing directions a mercenary army could use to march northward to invade the U.S. rather than southward in defense.[133]

After Lewis's trip to the western country, he returned to official army duty as a recruiter in the Charlottesville and Staunton, Virginia areas. He was said to be stationed out of Camp Allegheny along with future explorer and spy, Zebulon Pike.[134] It was during that period that Lewis learned that Jefferson had renewed an interest in sending an expedition across the continent if he won the presidency. The public purpose of the expedition was to gain scientific knowledge for commercial use in the Pacific Ocean, specifically to locate the elusive Northwest Passage. The true purpose, however, would be to discover a river route that the military could utilize to help expand the nation's western boundaries.[135]

Jefferson discussed the expedition with Lewis, likely to get his perspectives on the use of the army, among other reasons. It was a time when the public assumed that explorers of the Far West risked encountering human giants and massive mastodons. Jefferson later remembered that Lewis reacted with his characteristic "courage undaunted" and offered to lead the expedition.[136]

Lewis again may have appeared overconfident in his own abilities that a twenty-three-year-old paymaster and recruiter could lead a transcontinental intelligence-gathering and diplomatic mission through hostile territory and return his team safely home. More logically, this time Lewis's offer revealed that he had gained experience in missions on a smaller scale in the Northwest Territory and possibly on the Southwestern Frontier.[137] And this time, Jefferson did not reject Lewis's offer outright. Instead, he pondered that Lewis had gained "the firmness of constitution & character, prudence, habits adapted to the woods, & the familiarity with the Indian manners & character, requisite for [the] undertaking."[138]

When Jefferson later invited Lewis to work as his personal secretary, he reached out to Wilkinson to forward the invitation to Lewis, if Wilkinson knew Lewis's location.[139] The request followed a chain of command to the army commander. But Jefferson may have contacted Wilkinson regarding Lewis's whereabouts because Wilkinson was already using Lewis for projects as a way of earning Jefferson's future support.

It may have been more than a coincidence that, as Jefferson prepared for his second run for the presidency, Lewis, who had served in the army for four years at the rank of ensign without any promotion, was appointed lieutenant in 1799 and then promoted to captain the following year.[140] Lewis was also promoted to District Paymaster and assigned to Detroit, where, as a captain, he technically was placed in command of a company that bore his name. That promotion would enable him to serve as captain of the special army company that would conduct Jefferson's transcontinental expedition.[141] Jefferson assured Lewis that he would retain the rank of captain even if he served as his private secretary.[142] The promise seemed to be for Lewis's benefit, but the ultimate beneficiary would be Jefferson.

Even Lewis's brief time as District Paymaster would provide training he would use on the expedition. The position allowed him to travel from post to post on the Ohio River in a bateau and pirogue similar to the boats he would command up the Missouri River three years later.[143]

Once Lewis moved into the President's House, his appointment as Jefferson's private secretary elevated his role as a spy. The open-ended nature of the job allowed Jefferson to use Lewis's services without public scrutiny. Many days, Lewis hunted in the woods near the new Washington City to provide wild game for the president's table and then joined Jefferson, Senators, Congressmen, and some of the best minds in the nation for conversation over a dinner prepared by Jefferson's French cook.[144] At one later dinner, Jefferson displayed a bottle of water from the Mississippi River. He perhaps served it as a delicacy to excite legislators over the possibility of settling western lands.[145]

The public saw Lewis performing official functions such as serving as a scribe on several of Jefferson's letters or formally hand-delivering Jefferson's written State of the Union to Congress. Privately, however, Jefferson tasked Lewis with missions such as delivering money to a blackmailing writer who described the payment as "hush money."[146] Lewis and Jefferson also likely spent hours in Jefferson's office in the southwest corner of the President's House or down in its basement planning the secret nature of the expedition to the Pacific.[147]

It may have been merely by chance that events aligned to place men with Lewis and Clark's talents and experience in command of the expedition to the Pacific Ocean, the most significant intelligence-gathering expedition of their time. More logically, Jefferson and Wilkinson did not leave such a critical mission to chance. Perhaps the explorers had been selected, tested, and trained years earlier in the skills needed, ready whenever the opportunity for such a mission arose.[148]

General Wilkinson would later refer to Philip Nolan, the young protégé he helped raise, as "a powerful instrument in our hands, should occasion offer."[149] Similarly, for the remainder of his life, Meriwether Lewis would find himself in all the right positions to take on missions of risk for his mentor, Thomas Jefferson.

And like Nolan, Lewis would die young.

General James Wilkinson

## CHAPTER 3

# AGENT 13 IN COMMAND

[Wilkinson is] the only man that I ever saw who was from the bark to the very core a villain.
—Congressman John Randolph[150]

The master spy was Lewis's eventual U.S. Army commander, General James Wilkinson. Wilkinson was a double agent. At the same time that Jefferson used Lewis to push the boundaries of the nation west of the Mississippi River into territory controlled by the U.S. enemy Spain, Wilkinson agreed to work as an agent for Spain to confine the U.S. to the east. Jefferson knew of the general's double-dealing, but Wilkinson marshaled his masterful powers of persuasion to turn his corruption into an asset. He convinced Jefferson that with his unique knowledge of the West and contacts with Spain, he was the only general who could secure U.S. control of the Mississippi River and New Orleans.

It is unclear how much Jefferson concerned himself with Wilkinson's history as a traitor—or whether he believed he had any alternatives.[151] Wilkinson had utilized his unparalleled talents in deception, flattery, and intelligence gathering to convince George Washington to promote him to the rank of general at the age of nineteen. The appointment angered seasoned military men who had earned their ranks in battle, and it created a division in the army that grew into a contest between Wilkinson and Wayne to become Washington's successor in command.[152]

When Congress first reorganized the Army in 1792 into a type of legion to reduce reliance on militias, Wilkinson and Wayne were the primary candidates for the position of commanding general. Congress chose Wayne because of suspicions that Wilkinson could not be trusted. In one of the great ironies of the early Republic, the man who later would become its commanding general doubted that the new nation would last. Though the eastern states held an advantage from earlier development and established connections with European shipping interests and money, Wilkinson believed that the future lay in the West.

Like his British military counterparts, Wilkinson viewed a map of North America from a military and strategic perspective. One fact was unmistakable: control of the mighty Mississippi River, which bisects much of North America, was crucial for controlling the continent. As Wilkinson may have surmised, more than forty percent of the waters of the portion that would become the United States drains into the Mississippi.[153] In an era when most goods were shipped by water, most future North American inhabitants would be expected to transport their farm produce and other products to the Mississippi River to market. In Jefferson's time, those waters also would support the largest movement of troops. The Mississippi flowed into the Gulf of Mexico near New Orleans; therefore, New Orleans became the strategic objective. Jefferson held the same opinion, adding to his vision for the continent, "The navigation of the Mississippi we must have."[154]

For Spain, its western North American territory, including Texas, which some called "New Spain" or "New Mexico," was simply one of its distant colonies. The former conquerors could not afford to send an army large enough to hold it.[155]

The Spanish colonial governor attempted to create a buffer of people who would oppose westward expansion by encouraging sympathetic U.S.

settlers to become Spanish citizens and move to new settlements on the Mississippi River, at New Madrid and across from Chickasaw Bluffs, at Camp Esperanza, which later became Hopefield. He further attempted to turn the Mississippi River into a firewall to stop expansion by ordering that only people who pledged loyalty to Spain would be permitted to transport goods to market on the Mississippi.[156]

Wilkinson saw opportunity. He briefly resigned from the army and persuaded investors to fund his new Kentucky settlements of Frankfort and Lexington.[157] He then led a flotilla of boats loaded with hams and other Kentucky products down the Mississippi River and brazenly asked to meet with the Spanish governor. Rather than petitioning the governor to open river shipping to support his Kentucky neighbors, Wilkinson advised the governor to continue to block U.S. shipments—except those that Wilkinson controlled. Wilkinson would be one of the few Americans permitted to ship goods to New Orleans. He could purchase goods cheaply in Kentucky, and the Spanish governor could sell them at higher prices in New Orleans.[158]

Wilkinson assured the Spanish governor that he had concluded the United States would never allow him to use his talents to his full potential, and he offered them to Spain. In what would become known as the "Spanish Conspiracy" in Kentucky, Wilkinson agreed to use his influence to persuade Kentucky and Tennessee to secede from the U.S. and pledge allegiance to Spain as an additional buffer.[159] Conditions seemed ripe. Western states, such as Kentucky and Tennessee, needed access to the Mississippi River to transport farm goods to market. Eastern states had eagerly bargained away those rights to protect their own shipping interests on the Atlantic when negotiating with Britain.[160] Tennesseans had already revealed their sympathies by naming the central portion of their state "The Mero District" to flatter Spanish Governor Esteban Miró.[161]

As Clark's drawings revealed, the Spanish built a string of forts along the Mississippi River to enforce their blockade, creating a panic in U.S.

commercial and political circles. Land speculators and government officials sought to sidestep their dependency on the Mississippi by developing plans to build canals and roads from Kentucky and Tennessee southward through the Chickasaw and Choctaw nations to transport farm products directly to the Gulf Coast. President Washington proposed the construction of a federal wagon highway from Kentucky to the Gulf. That project came to a halt when Wilkinson alerted Spanish agents. They persuaded tribal warriors to kill U.S. troops sent by Washington to negotiate with the tribes for the project.[162] U.S. officials never guessed that Wilkinson had sold the lives of his own troops or that Spain had only built its forts along the Mississippi River at Wilkinson's urging.[163]

Wilkinson's dreams of riches were short-lived. Miró lacked the soldiers even to stand between scores of enterprising boatmen and markets at Natchez and New Orleans. When Miró relented and allowed farmers to resume shipping, Wilkinson's finances dried up.[164] He was forced to return to the army for income.

But Wilkinson's experiences in working with the Spanish had given him insight into new intrigues. Much of the vast land west of the Mississippi, generally known as "Louisiana," was the target. It offered what seemed to be unlimited land for settlement and cultivation, as well as valuable fur trapping and the lure of gold and silver mines.

As Wilkinson warned, the Spanish colonial capital Santa Fe enchanted adventurers as the ultimate prize. They had long circulated tales that Santa Fe might hold the lost mines of the Aztecs.[165] The fact that Mexico exported so much silver that the Spanish silver dollar served as a global currency seemed to confirm the legends.[166]

Additionally, trails from Santa Fe led to Los Angeles to the west and San Antonio to the east, offering lucrative trade with several tribes. Even the unknown Arkansas River land generated rumors of what a Congressional committee would describe as "masses of virgin silver and gold that glitter in the veins of the rocks... offer themselves to the hand of him who will gather, refine, and convert them to use."¹⁶⁷ There was little regard for Spain's prior claims—it was believed that the distant European government had sent explorers, followed by soldiers and colonial officials, to America for the sole purpose of seizing gold from wealthy tribes.¹⁶⁸ No river was wide enough to keep ambitious or greedy adventurers from crossing, especially when it appeared they would be met with little resistance.

The Adams administration that preceded Jefferson's hoped to secure possession of a portion of Louisiana.¹⁶⁹ But by 1801, France controlled the Spanish government and considered retaking possession of Louisiana.¹⁷⁰ The smaller U.S. army was thought not to be a match for Napoleon's troops.

Wilkinson persuaded his superior, Alexander Hamilton, that he was the general who could take Louisiana.¹⁷¹ First, Wilkinson needed to gain control of the army. By his own admission, Wilkinson set out to take Wayne's position by undermining his command at every turn.¹⁷² He began by establishing his own base of support among impressionable young officers and then leveraged that base to peel off Wayne loyalists. Wilkinson also abused the court-martial system as officers loyal to Wayne found themselves more likely to be charged for infractions than officers who supported Wilkinson. Even Lewis was hauled before a court-martial on charges that he threatened to duel a superior officer while drunk. The conduct likely arose from Lewis arguing his republican views with a staunch Federalist officer.¹⁷³ He was acquitted at trial.¹⁷⁴

Perhaps worse in the eyes of young soldiers, Wilkinson thwarted Wayne's battle plans to make it appear that Wayne was an ineffective commander.¹⁷⁵ The Wilkinson faction turned their contempt toward Wayne instead of Wilkinson, who was willing to sacrifice their lives for his personal gain.

The personable William Clark was one of several junior officers Wilkinson targeted to attract others to his base of support.¹⁷⁶ Wilkinson began by inviting Clark to ride with him on excursions into tribal territory to build a personal relationship.[177] Soldiers carefully considered their riding companions, and the young Clark would have been flattered. Wilkinson then selected Clark to courier messages from Fort Washington to Kentucky, giving Clark the privilege of visiting with his family, who lived there.[178] Wilkinson's favors produced the intended effect. As the rivalry between Wayne and Wilkinson heated up, Clark followed Wilkinson's orders to maintain a private journal of Wayne's actions that Wilkinson could use as evidence to have Wayne removed.[179]

Even in 1795, when Wayne assigned Clark to deliver messages to the Spanish governor, one of Clark's party found it odd that rather than praising his commander, Wayne, to the Spanish, Clark praised Wilkinson. Clark, he said, presented to the governor a "grand tribute to his [Wilkinson's] concept of the Army."[180] And when Clark returned from the mission, he chose not to disclose to Wayne all the intelligence he had obtained about the Spanish.[181] Wilkinson's recruitment of Clark proved to be a success.

Wayne was too late in discovering the depths to which Wilkinson was willing to sink to take his position. He suspected that Wilkinson was an agent of Britain and that he was also receiving money as an agent of Spain to separate western territory from the Union.[182] When Wayne began to gather evidence to have Wilkinson prosecuted for treason, he narrowly survived a tree sawed by a soldier crashing on his tent, only to die suddenly in 1796, with severe stomach pains.[183] Wilkinson publicly insisted that he wanted an investigation to clear his name as an alleged traitor, but with crocodile tears, he gloated, "prosecution is in the grave with General Wayne."[184] Suspicions arose that Wilkinson arranged for Wayne's assassination. Andrew Jackson later repeated the allegation to the secretary of war.[185]

By the time of Wayne's death, Hamilton had resigned from the army, and Wilkinson remained as the sole general in charge.[186] As commander of the U.S. Army at last, Wilkinson could convince Spain that he was in a unique position to serve its interests. Spanish officials agreed and placed him on their payroll as their agent. They assigned him the code name "Agent 13" to hide his identity.[187]

Wilkinson's most difficult challenge as a double agent was smuggling his traitorous payments of silver out of Spanish territory without raising suspicions. Shipments of silver transported by mule along the Spanish Trail, El Camino Real, near the New Spain town of Nacogdoches, were reported to be his.[188] To move the silver beyond that point, Wilkinson recruited trusted men to hide the payments in barrels of sugar, which were then transported by boat from the lower Mississippi.[189]

Clark was one of those boatmen. During his 1798 trip down the Mississippi River, Clark noted in his journal that he picked up 670 Spanish dollars for a man he named "Mr. Riddle." Though Spanish colonial law prohibited removing Spanish silver dollars from its territory, Clark nevertheless assisted in hiding the silver in barrels of sugar bound for Kentucky to smuggle it out. Clark's receipt of Mr. Riddle's silver coincided with a Wilkinson collaborator's delivery of papers to the Spanish. However, there is no evidence that Clark was aware of the true purpose of the shipment.[190]

Likely unknown to Clark, two of his fellow passengers were traveling to New Orleans to gather intelligence on Wilkinson's Spanish intrigues. One was Sam Houston's first cousin, John McKee, who, like a good double agent, would also attempt to convince Wilkinson of his loyalty. If McKee noticed Clark's work for Wilkinson, he did not include it in his report.[191]

When some of Wilkinson's payments of Spanish dollars were discovered, he convinced his supporters in Congress that he was collecting old debts for his sale of Kentucky farm products. The organization of the federal bureaucracy in the early republic was still finding its way. Many offices, including those in the military, acted as a type of subcontractor with a guaranteed salary. Higher-ranking officers and government officials were expected to pay the expenses of their offices out of their own funds and then seek reimbursement from the federal government.[192] Several army officers were forced to maintain side businesses during their service to make ends meet.[193] Appointment to a government position was seen not only as the assurance of a steady income but also as an opportunity to use that position to generate income through a side venture.

Once Wilkinson was firmly in command of the army, he began moving parts of his headquarters from Pittsburgh to the southwestern-most point of U.S. territory on the Mississippi River north of New Orleans. In 1798, Wilkinson made the case to the secretary of war that construction of a fort on the Loftus Heights bluff overlooking the lower portion of the river was crucial to protect navigation and to prevent invading armies from traveling north. To assure support, he named the installation "Fort Adams" in honor of the president.

However, many troops assigned to Fort Adams would be quartered instead five miles southeast at a new military cantonment, Columbian Springs. There, rather than preparing for defense, Wilkinson used the troops to help build what his successor would consider luxurious houses for his top aides.[194] Soldiers at Columbian Springs filled out the ranks of Wilkinson's own military bureaucracy that would control the network of U.S. forts in the Southwest. Major Amos Stoddard would characterize Wilkinson's southwestern conglomerate of headquarters as a "nest of hornets."[195]

The more than a thousand miles between Columbian Springs and the federal capital served Wilkinson's power struggle by allowing him to avoid direct oversight from the War Department. It took a month to six weeks for an order from the secretary of war to arrive at Columbian Springs to counter Wilkinson's actions—too late to have a direct effect. Additionally, many government officials in the new republic established their own standards until they were reprimanded by their superiors.

Wilkinson could plead ignorance of wrongdoing. Given all the problems the new country faced, there was little will for his superiors to devote time to holding him accountable.[196]

What made Wilkinson even more dangerous was that his nest of hornets was also a nest of spies.

Remains of c. 1798 house at Fort Adams

## CHAPTER 4

# NEST OF SPIES

[T]here are spies everywhere.
—General James Wilkinson, February 6, 1797[197]

The independence Wilkinson enjoyed on what was then the Southwestern Frontier, near the border with New Spain, allowed him to develop a separate headquarters fifty miles north, near Natchez, for men willing to perform spy operations. One group of spies operated out of scientist William Dunbar's home, known as "The Forest." One historian described The Forest as "the headquarters of Southwestern exploration."[198]

Before the Revolutionary War, Dunbar had purchased plantations in British Natchez and Spanish Baton Rouge, and he found himself entangled in intrigues with merchants who tried to pass intelligence to the British to help them maintain control of the Mississippi River.[199] After the war, Dunbar and his associates frequently ventured west into enemy Spanish territory under the guise of trading horses and other goods with tribes before returning to Natchez with maps and other intelligence they had gathered.[200]

Wilkinson's most active spy was his protégé, Philip Nolan.[201] Like Lewis, Nolan began performing missions for his mentor by age twenty. Natchez townspeople knew Nolan for his athletic feats in capturing wild horses in New Spain and bringing them back to sell in the Mississippi

Territory. The fact that Nolan once returned to Natchez from one trip with 1,000 horses he had rounded up speaks to his talents.[202] Of course, the spectacle everyone remembered served to mask his true mission. Out of public view, in addition to transporting bribe payments for Wilkinson, Nolan mapped Spanish territory.[203]

Wilkinson's work with the Spanish enemy was abetted by New Orleans businessman Daniel Clark, Jr., who also served as U.S. Consul to New Orleans. Clark, Jr. was a Spanish immigrant who had recently become a U.S. citizen. His uncle had been one of Wilkinson's business partners in Kentucky when Wilkinson sold farm produce to the Spanish.[204] Jefferson appointed Clark, Jr. to provide intelligence on activities in New Orleans, which was then still under the control of Spain.[205] The new agent belonged to a group of men in the New Orleans area known as the "Mexican Society" that secretly supported efforts to help gain independence for Texas from Spanish control.[206] Because of Clark, Jr.'s wealth and connections, Wilkinson chose to build his Columbian Springs compound on land adjoining Clark Jr.'s plantation.[207]

At the U.S. border town Natchitoches—about 120 miles west of Natchez and ninety miles east of the New Spain town Nacogdoches—Dr. John Sibley's home provided a second base for spy operations. Major Amos Stoddard noted that the small Natchitoches village of forty families "will always preserve some importance, particularly as it is the usual thoroughfare over land from settlements east of the Mississippi to the Mexican dominions."[208] From American settlements northeast to Natchitoches, Nolan's trail ran through the town to connect with the old east-west Spanish El Camino Real at Nacogdoches in New Spain. As a border town, Natchitoches was a natural haven for spies, land pirates, freebooters, and others escaping the legal system in the East.[209]

The Spanish side was an easy target. Most of the colonial New Spain population, which consisted of only about 4,000 non-tribal people, lived hundreds of miles south, toward San Antonio and the coast.[210]

In between, the land was sparsely occupied by tribes that, for the time, showed allegiance to Spain. Sibley worked with traders willing to venture into the Spanish Texas area, trade with the tribes, and gather intelligence to bring back to Natchitoches.[211] Like Dunbar, he sometimes continued to make excursions himself to win the confidence of area tribes. Jefferson would later provide official cover for Sibley's actions by appointing him as Indian agent for the Orleans Territory.[212] The U.S. Army built a fort at Natchitoches, which provided Wilkinson with the intelligence he needed to monitor and direct the spies' activities.

Before Wilkinson constructed Fort Adams, President Washington sent surveyor Andrew Ellicott to Natchez to survey the agreed boundary between Spain and the United States at Natchez. That job provided Ellicott with an official cover to have contact with local tribes, as well as Spanish officials and traders. Philip Nolan, no doubt under Wilkinson's orders, met Ellicott upriver to escort him through Spanish watches down the Mississippi and to test him. He noticed that Ellicott stood his ground even when Spanish officials refused to let him pass. And when Ellicott arrived in Natchez, he held firm against Spanish officials who refused to turn over control of the town to the U.S. in violation of their treaty. Ellicott passed the spies' test, and he seemed to have been welcomed into the confidences of The Forest network.[213] But Ellicott also served double interests—President Washington had assigned him to Natchez to gather intelligence on Wilkinson's activities.[214] It should have been no surprise when Ellicott later submitted reimbursement requests to the government for work for "secret services."[215]

Ellicott hired immigrant engineer Thomas Freeman to assist in surveying the boundary with Spain. Freeman had demonstrated talent in surveying the District of Columbia, which would serve as the new national capital, and Wilkinson quickly recognized Freeman as a valuable resource. He persuaded Ellicott to fire Freeman, and once Freeman was desperate for a position, Wilkinson hired him to help oversee the construction of Fort Adams.[216] Not realizing Wilkinson's role in his firing,

Freeman, who would play a critical role in events after Lewis's death, became a Wilkinson loyalist. He must have frequented The Forest during the time he worked on projects for Wilkinson.[217]

Clark's trip to Natchez in 1798 would have placed him in a position to meet with Wilkinson and the men that Wilkinson, and later Jefferson, would use to plan intelligence probes into New Spain. If Lewis ventured as far southwest as Natchez during his army furlough, he would have had the same opportunity.[218]

The future explorers' absences from official duty and their travels to the Southwest followed the failed attempt by Tennessee Senator William Blount to use state militias to seize Texas from Spain and establish a new country west of the Mississippi.[219] When news of the plot leaked, it imploded and became a political scandal known as "The Blount Conspiracy." Some historians concluded that both Jefferson and Wilkinson supported Blount's mission as a means to gain control over Texas and that Wilkinson's knowledge of Jefferson's involvement gave him additional leverage over Jefferson.[220]

Wilkinson knew that Jefferson wanted to control the western continent, but he also knew that the Washington administration had created a major hurdle. Either to prevent private individuals from engaging in activities that might pull the country into war—or politically to maintain Federalist power by concentrating the population in the East—Federalists passed the Neutrality Act of 1794, which made it a crime to participate in any actions hostile to neighboring foreign powers at peace with the United States.

Wilkinson's continued influence over both U.S. officials and Spanish colonials depended on his continuing as commanding general, no matter which party controlled the presidency. Wilkinson was likely a Federalist to the extent he had any fixed principles. A consummate bureaucrat, Wilkinson began hedging his bets in case the most visible Anti-Federalist, Jefferson, won the presidency in 1800. He could prey on Jefferson's disdain for a law passed for what Jefferson would consider corrupt political reasons and one that undermined the future security of the country.

Like the techniques Wilkinson used to gain Clark's trust, he first worked to establish a personal relationship with Jefferson based on shared interests. Wilkinson likely knew that Jefferson nurtured his passion for natural science, in part, by serving as president of the American Philosophical Society, the nation's first scientific society, headquartered in Philadelphia.[221] Wilkinson joined the society and arranged to serve alongside Jefferson on a committee focused on collecting the natural history of the American continent.[222]

Wilkinson's plans might have been too obvious if he had contacted Jefferson directly. He is not known to have corresponded directly with Jefferson during that period, but his nucleus of southwestern spies did.

In 1798, a Wilkinson collaborator, U.S. Senator John Brown from Kentucky, approached Jefferson with information that Philip Nolan was exploring Spanish territory in search of horses to trade. Jefferson wrote to Nolan, vaguely expressing an interest in obtaining information about "the horses" in their wild state, adding that it would not be necessary to specify the facts he would welcome.[223]

Rather than Nolan, Wilkinson's associate Daniel Clark, Jr. responded a few months later and offered to provide Jefferson with the information he requested. By way of introduction, Clark, Jr. mentioned that Andrew Ellicott, who was engaged in surveying the line between the U.S. and Spain, was a guest in his home, and the two had discussed the information Jefferson needed. He also made a point to state that if Nolan met his end in New Spain, Clark, Jr. had possession of Nolan's papers, "which are confided to me & a mutual Friend now in the Spanish Service, shall be carefully examined, and every thing relating to that Country shall be forwarded to you with [such] other remarks as both of us from our own Knowledge & information have acquired."[224] Clark, Jr. suggested that Jefferson meet with Nolan to answer his questions as to horses and as to the "manners Customs, situation of the Country Strength, Population &ca" of the Spanish territory.[225] It was clear that Clark, Jr. understood Jefferson's interest in the Far Southwest to be broader than its horses.

Daniel Clark Jr. informed Jefferson that William Dunbar who had settled near Natchez, was a man of science.[226] Jefferson reached out to Dunbar in 1799.[227] The owner of The Forest intrigued the future president by discussing the natural science of the Southwest that he had observed during his excursions. Jefferson replied, and their correspondence continued over matters related to the natural features of the Spanish Texas.[228]

Perhaps Jefferson's interest in Nolan's information related solely to the natural science of horses in the West as he suggested, but Jefferson was not yet president. Without the cover of authority, he had to carefully word letters that could be used as evidence. Given the fact that Nolan's maps and information would eventually be used to meet Jefferson's military objectives in the West, Jefferson's words could be seen as having more than one meaning to the men in possession of that information.

Jefferson agreed to a meeting, and Nolan set off for Charlottesville. Wilkinson provided a letter of introduction, describing Nolan simply as a "Mexican traveler."[229] Before Nolan reached Virginia, however, something changed his plans. He suddenly turned back and crossed over the border into New Spain. In March 1801, Spanish patrols suspected Nolan's spying activities and killed him.[230]

When Spanish officers took Nolan's remaining party prisoner, one adventurer was identified as Thomas House from Dandridge, Jefferson County, Tennessee—a region that produced several figures who would later play a role in the final days of Meriwether Lewis. Jefferson County attracted military men due to its proximity to the U.S. fort Southwest Point, which had once marked the limits of U.S. settlement in the Southwest.[231] Wilkinson may have recruited House. After his release, House persuaded the Spanish colonial government to give him a passport to hunt on the Natchitoches River, then ran west into New Spain. There was evidence that his true mission was to persuade tribes in the area to accept gifts and shift their loyalty to American officials in general—perhaps Wilkinson in particular.[232]

Once Jefferson was fully engaged with Wilkinson's spy network, Wilkinson joined the conversation to sink the hook. In 1800, Wilkinson wrote to Jefferson, professing that he was simply doing his friend Dunbar the favor of passing along scientific information.[233] The two began corresponding, and Wilkinson used the intelligence he gathered from the Southwest to gain Jefferson's confidence.

Andrew Ellicott, perhaps in his double agent role, reached out to Wilkinson to suggest that he had a "thousand things" he needed to discuss with the general.[234] Ellicott subsequently recommended Dunbar for membership in the American Philosophical Society and began his own correspondence with Jefferson on astronomical observations.[235] Ellicott would later unconvincingly deny that he was aware that Nolan was engaged in any of Wilkinson's double-dealing with Spain.[236]

Dunbar followed up by writing to Jefferson about a reputed long river that ran toward New Spain and that would support a large population. Then, dangling potential natural science discoveries, Dunbar suggested that an expedition sent west up the river toward Texas would likely find a strange water creature, unicorns, and, more importantly, silver ore.[237] Jefferson would eventually take the bait, and as president, authorize Dunbar and Thomas Freeman to organize expeditions up the Red River near the border with Spain.[238]

Wilkinson's second tactic to win Jefferson's confidence was to stoke his fears of Federalists in the army. Contrary to what Jefferson and other founders had envisioned, the U.S. Army played an oversized role in the new republic.[239] The ever-present enemy just over the horizon and the early nation's reliance on volunteer militias kept frontier leaders indebted to generals.

The military also provided a stable bureaucracy to carry out government tasks before the federal government established its own agencies. Army forts dotted the landscape, particularly near the frontier. The small community of army officers was among the few privileged to travel the western country from fort to fort. That contact gave them the ability to influence town leaders in between. No national institution rivaled its political influence, and Jefferson viewed the army led by Federalists as a threat to his Republican administration.

Hamilton had proposed more than doubling the size of the standing army while his Federalist party controlled the government. As Jefferson suspected, some historians believe that Hamilton planned to use the force of the army to intimidate Jefferson's opposition party into perpetual submission.[240] For their part, Federalists worried that if Jefferson won the presidency, their Republican opponents would destroy the government with their new powers, or worse, exercise federal powers to punish their political opponents just as the Federalists did when they were in office.[241] To make certain the army would support Federalist laws and suppress dissent, Hamilton was careful to fill the upper army officer corps with Federalists.[242]

Wilkinson knew Jefferson feared that Federalists could call on their loyalists in the army to stage a coup.[243] He could suggest that he would be the only person who could protect Jefferson.[244]

Another reason Jefferson said that he appointed Lewis as personal secretary was that he had gained knowledge "of the army and of all it's interest & relations."[245] But Jefferson needed to know more than how the army functioned—he needed intelligence. As paymaster, Lewis gained first-hand information on many of its officers. One of the first private assignments Jefferson gave Lewis was to evaluate a list of all U.S. Army officers and determine who should be dismissed as being too loyal to the opposing political party, just as Alexander Hamilton had done in the prior Adams administration.[246]

Clark's support of Wilkinson no doubt influenced Lewis, but Lewis's initial service under Wayne and his own Republican sentiments may have tainted his support. Whatever Lewis's personal views, Jefferson certainly talked with Lewis about his need for Wilkinson's support within the army and to carry out his vision for the West. Still, when Lewis later marked the names of Federalist officers who should be dismissed, he left an uncommitted blank beside Wilkinson's name.[247]

Wilkinson moved to Washington City, and after Jefferson's inauguration ceremony in March 1801, attended a small victory dinner for the new president at a tavern in Alexandria.[248] The general took the opportunity to influence Jefferson's policies to gain even more control over the West.[249]

Knowing that Jefferson's western supporters favored any effort to make their settlements safer, Wilkinson picked up on Washington's earlier idea and proposed construction of a federal military road from Fort Adams to Nashville, where it would connect with primitive roads north into Kentucky and east to Virginia. A wagon highway could be justified to move supply wagons to march Tennessee and Kentucky militias to fend off an invasion of New Orleans and the Mississippi River. Jefferson could also use the road, along with improvements to other roads, to encourage settlers to move southwest, where they would provide militias to defend those borders. Of course, if Wilkinson were successful in establishing a new country centered in New Orleans, such a road would also make it easier for him to assert military control over western states. As Jefferson's advisor on the army, Lewis likely advised Jefferson on the army's role in building the road as well as using the army for other internal improvements.

When Jefferson met with his advisors in May 1801 to set directions for his new administration, Wilkinson's success in winning Jefferson's support shone. Jefferson's plan would first be a two-pronged advance of military power across the continent, as he later detailed in his January 18, 1803, "Confidential" letter to Congress. The government would send an exploratory party to the Northwest to find a military passage for troops, and it would take peaceful military action southwest along the Mississippi River to secure New Orleans.[250] At the same time, Jefferson approved the acquisition of land from the Chickasaw, Choctaw, and Cherokee tribes in the Southwest and the construction of a military road from Nashville through their nations to Fort Adams, aimed at securing control of the Mississippi River.[251] He later would credit the plans approved at that planning meeting with helping secure the vast Louisiana Purchase territory.[252]

What Jefferson would not disclose to Congress for another two years was that he was also engaged in unofficial discussions to send spies and soldiers southwest to Spanish Texas and Santa Fe. One historian suggests that Jefferson put the need for a Santa Fe expedition on equal footing with the planned Northwest Passage expedition. In both cases, spies would map rivers and encourage tribes to shift their support from Spain to the United States to help the U.S. acquire the territory.[253]

Confirming Wilkinson's influence in developing the plans, Jefferson appointed Wilkinson to negotiate with the southeastern tribes for authority to build the military road. A former congressman thought the selection of an army general as negotiator made no sense—except that he knew Wilkinson. Wilkinson must have sought the position to utilize the negotiations to enhance his own influence over the southwestern tribal territories.[254]

It may have been Wilkinson's power play that prompted Andrew Ellicott to reveal his role in gathering intelligence on the general. Daniel Clark, Jr. later claimed that Ellicott met with Jefferson in June 1801 with evidence that Wilkinson was receiving a salary from the Spanish government. It made no difference. Jefferson would unconvincingly deny that anyone informed him that Wilkinson was a spy during the period he thought he needed his services.[255]

Having made his mark on Jefferson's plans—and confident the president would not oppose him—Wilkinson took license to exercise his new power. During the last year of the Adams administration, Wilkinson had begun construction of a large army camp or cantonment on the Ohio River, only twelve miles from the already established U.S. Fort Massac. He may have won Hamilton's support for the project to defend against a possible invasion by Napoleon, but he continued construction without any apparent approval after Hamilton resigned. He named his new installation "Wilkinsonville."

Fifteen hundred soldiers were sent to the camp, the largest quartering of U.S. troops to that point. The military presence had the effect of settling conflicts with the northern tribes, and perhaps Wilkinson wanted to use the amassing of force as a threat against the southern tribes he would meet to negotiate with for the right to build the new military highway.[256] Given the timing and Jefferson's fear of Federalists in the military, however, Wilkinson may also have used the troop presence as leverage in his negotiations with Jefferson for his new powers as general.

Only a few months into the Jefferson administration, the secretary of war ordered the cantonment abandoned, in part, due to the deaths of troops from fever at the camp. Although newspapers reported the presence of the military installation, typical military records detailing fort activities do not appear in the archived records, leading historians to speculate about Wilkinson's true objectives.[257] Though his namesake cantonment was short-lived, Wilkinson had declared himself a force to be reckoned with by both Spain and the United States on the western frontier.

Wilkinson was so eager to begin work on the military highway from Nashville that companies of soldiers left Wilkinsonville in August 1801, to travel to Nashville and Franklin, Tennessee, to start construction.[258] Because treaties with the tribes had not been signed or ratified, Wilkinson assured that troops would work only outside the Chickasaw Nation boundary. However, when the Senate delayed approval of the treaties for months, Wilkinson's troops crossed over the boundary to begin work prior to ratification without fearing any consequences from Jefferson.[259] In short order, Wilkinson would write at the bottom of an official survey for the new highway: "this road being compleated I shall consider our Southern extremity [sec]ured, the Indians in that quarter at our feet. and the adjacent province [la]id open to us."[260] "Province" was how Spanish territory was described. The years of work by Wilkinson's spies to expand the borders into the Far Southwest would now have the backing of a military threat.

Jefferson and Wilkinson never acknowledged their terms in writing, but from all appearances, they had come to an accommodation. Wilkinson would remain in command of the army as Jefferson ignored his contacts with the enemy, Spain. In return, Wilkinson would protect Jefferson from a coup by Federalist army officers and help Jefferson pursue his quest for New Orleans and the West by means that would allow Jefferson plausible deniability. Or as one historian put it, "In short, the general's sinuous morality made him the ideal candidate for the dirty and deniable work that an upright president needed doing without knowing how it was done."[261] Like George Washington and countless leaders before their noble experiment in self-government, Thomas Jefferson determined it necessary to sacrifice some of his noble ideals for the ugly practicalities of governing.

The half of the army that remained loyal to the late General Wayne considered Jefferson's accommodation with Wilkinson as a deal with the Devil. Jefferson did not foresee that the price of his Faustian bargain would be the future of his protoge, Meriwether Lewis.

## CHAPTER 5

# MISSION TO LEGEND

> The object of your mission is single, the direct water communication from sea to sea formed by the bed of the Missouri & perhaps the Oregan.
> —Thomas Jefferson to Meriwether Lewis,
> November 16, 1803

As Wilkinson went to work to build Jefferson's military highway southwest toward the lower Mississippi, Lewis planned the organization of his military expedition to the Far Northwest. Jefferson warned Lewis that his small military team—to be known as the "Corps of Discovery"—would "encounter considerable dangers from the Indian inhabitants" who could see the military company as hostile.[262] Other deadly challenges loomed: disease, limited food supplies, weather extremes, and unknown wild animals. While such hazards were no different from those other military men had faced and overcome on shorter excursions, it would take intense planning to prepare to support and defend an expedition that would travel more than 3,500 miles into unknown terrain and back. There would be little room for error.

Jefferson's first attempts at sending an expedition to the Pacific Ocean had suffered from false starts. He had approached Clark's brother, George Rogers Clark, with the idea years earlier, only to be rebuffed.

Later, in 1793, Jefferson was likely supportive of an expedition led by French explorer André Michaux that dissolved when it became entangled in one of the first movements to separate the western states from the United States.[263] It was expected that Federalist politicians would attempt to scuttle the latest attempt, and if it failed, Jefferson's dream would become his embarrassment. The president undoubtedly assured that the mission was well thought out by the time he asked Congress to fund the enterprise.

Jefferson requested that the Spanish colonial government provide Lewis's party a passport to travel through its territory, assuring that the sole purpose of the expedition was to discover a Northwest Passage for commerce. Spanish officials were not fooled. One Spanish diplomat noted that explorer Alexander Mackenzie had already traveled across the northern continent (through present-day Canada) to the Pacific a decade earlier and found that there was no Northwest Passage. Jefferson's real purpose, he astutely surmised, was to "discover the way by which the Americans may some day extend their population and their influence up the coasts of the South Sea [Pacific]."[264]

Then, to the consternation of Spain's colonial North American government, Napoleon unexpectedly claimed the right to take back a vast portion of Spain's territory west of the Mississippi and sell it to the United States. The area that would be called the "Louisiana Purchase" nearly doubled the size of the nation, providing land for what eventually became fifteen new states. Although Jefferson's representatives in Paris quickly accepted Napoleon's offer and completed the purchase terms, it was unclear whether Spain would accept the sale. Even if it did, the agreement identified the boundaries vaguely as "the Colony or Province of Louisiana with the Same extent that it now has in the hand of Spain, & that it had when France possessed it."[265] No one knew those boundaries. The vagueness of the terms necessary to seal the deal would require investigations to establish what territory France had previously occupied.

Spanish Texas was a central point of contention. Jefferson claimed that the Louisiana Purchase contained land as far south as the Rio Grande River and that most of Texas and Santa Fe should belong to the United States. Spain was just as adamant that the new U.S. border ran north of Texas and Santa Fe, closer to the Red River.[266] Uncertainties over which country had the right to claim much of Texas, Santa Fe, and West Florida to the east set up conflicts ultimately to be challenged by military force. Wherever the southern boundary would eventually be established, the Louisiana Purchase did not extend as far as the Pacific, and the Corps would still need to travel through disputed areas, which would raise the ire of Spanish officials and put the Corps of Discovery at risk of attack. Jefferson pushed forward anyway.

Federalist opponents claimed that the president who argued for limited government had exceeded his authority—the U.S. Constitution gave Jefferson no power to extend the nation's boundaries. Hamilton declared that if the Louisiana Purchase turned out to benefit the U.S., Jefferson simply got lucky, and that it was Hamilton who deserved credit for bringing France to the bargaining table through his earlier threats to increase the size of the army.[267] Hamilton's real Federalist concern was that the opening of vast new land for settlement could depopulate the East and make it more difficult for the government to regulate its citizens.[268] Similarly, another Federalist complained that the territory was far too large, objecting that it would be "impossible to govern."[269]

A separate element of the Jeffersonian-Hamiltonian battle for the soul of the nation was whether the U.S. would become an industrial nation or remain agrarian. Hamilton's vision of developing the country into an economic power required that much of the population concentrate in cities where they could work for manufacturing industries. Jefferson feared that citizens who depended on an industry for their income would become its subjects and those who depended on foreign trade would become slaves to foreign interests. He envisioned a nation of citizen farmers whose independence was guaranteed by their ability to support themselves from their own land.[270] For Jefferson, making it difficult for a central government or business interests to overregulate the citizens' lives was a plus.

Wilkinson stirred political division by spreading rumors that Jefferson's unstated goal was to force U.S. citizens to move west of the Mississippi by point of bayonet, if necessary, to spread out the population and enforce his limited government ideals.[271] Lesser wits claimed that Jefferson had saddled the country with a "Wild Land" and "a wilderness unpeopled with any beings except wolves and wondering Indians." One more humorously boiled it all down to, "We are to give money of which we have too little for land of which we already have too much."[272]

Jefferson also hoped that if the Louisiana Purchase land eventually became several states, the combined power of those state governments would counter federal power, helping to assure that the federal government would never be able to assert dominance over the states.[273] The Purchase suddenly added political value to Lewis's expedition to discover what the nation had bought. Jefferson staked much of his political capital on the Louisiana Purchase, and for him, a successful expedition across the new Purchase could prove the wisdom of his risk. He transferred much of that responsibility squarely to Lewis's shoulders.

Once Congress approved funding, Jefferson honed his final instructions for the mission.[274] There were no training academies for spies. Early American schools taught by Christian ministers used the Bible as a foundation for daily readings. The story of Moses sending spies into Canaan to spy out the land for conquest would have been familiar to both Jefferson and Lewis from Reverend Maury's school. Moses instructed his spies to determine the strength of the armies in the land he planned to conquer. Jefferson instructed Lewis to assess the strength of the tribal nations he encountered, making detailed maps that the military could use for future troop movements to navigate the Missouri River to the Pacific Ocean.

Moses also directed his spies to observe the fertility of the soil for growing food and to bring back samples that he could examine and use to help motivate his soldiers.[275] Similarly, Jefferson directed Lewis to note soil conditions, minerals, plants, and other interesting characteristics of the land, as well as the availability of furs that could be harvested. Although Jefferson did not provide Lewis with written instructions to gather samples of what he found, Lewis would collect samples of plants, animals, and minerals and assign a Corps member to send them back to Jefferson at government expense.

A third goal would be to gain support from tribal leaders to secure influence over the new Purchase land. Like Washington, Jefferson hoped that tribes would eventually assimilate into Western culture, but first, he hoped they would provide support for removing the presence of Spanish and British troops. Jefferson instructed Lewis to invite influential tribal leaders to travel to Washington City to meet with him. He also directed him to bring back with the party any tribal young people the leaders wished to have educated in American academies.[276]

What unrecorded objectives Jefferson discussed with Lewis in their months of private planning in the President's House can only be surmised by the actions Lewis took to accomplish the mission. As Jefferson's protégé, Lewis held the president's confidence, and he would report directly to the president. Extraordinary in American history for such an undertaking, Lewis was given sole authority to create his expedition and plan every detail, subject only to the president's instructions and War Department procedures and regulations. It was no small matter that any reports to the secretary of war would be perfunctory or at Lewis's discretion.[277] Lewis would answer to no committee of second-guessing armchair bureaucrats—at least so long as Jefferson was president.[278]

Before embarking on the mission, Lewis underwent intense training. Jefferson provided Lewis with the most detailed maps of the American continent that the government had acquired. He then sent Lewis to Philadelphia to meet with his friends in the American Philosophical Society and to be trained by some of the best minds in natural science, anatomy, and medicine in the U.S. for the particulars he would need for the mission.[279] Dr. Benjamin Rush provided Lewis a condensed list of the most modern medical treatments for anticipated ailments.[280] And because new mapping would be crucial, and the most certain means of determining locations at the time was by astronomical measurements, Lewis acquired the necessary instruments. Andrew Ellicott, who had moved to Pennsylvania, taught him how to use them. If Lewis was interested in developing his spy craft, Ellicott could teach him what he had learned from his time in the lower Mississippi. It would also have been an opportunity for Ellicott to warn Lewis about Wilkinson.

Lewis's Corps of Discovery would not be able to transport all the food supplies they would need, and there was no way to know whether they would find game in the uncharted wilderness. To reduce the risk of starvation, Lewis purchased portable soup—a concentrated beef gelatin that could be reconstituted with hot water when needed.[281]

Lewis next traveled to the army's new armory and laboratory at Harper's Ferry, Virginia, where he would help oversee the development and collection of new equipment worthy of a spy expedition: a modified short rifle, an air gun that could fire bullets without gunpowder; and a collapsible boat frame that could be carried over dry land and then reassembled and covered with bark or animal hides.[282] He requisitioned tomahawks and knives designed to survive the expected conditions.[283]

Lewis wrote to Tennessee Congressman and Andrew Jackson loyalist, William Dickson, to ask for the name of a "confidential" boat builder he might use in the Nashville area to build a boat and canoe for the expedition.[284] Lewis may have meant the request for Jackson. Eight months later, Jefferson would award Jackson a contract to build boats for a separate military expedition to Natchez.[285] In any event, if Dickson received the letter, he likely shared its contents with Jackson. When Lewis did not receive a reply, he arranged for a boat builder in Pittsburgh to craft a boat that met his specifications.

Jefferson instructed Lewis to recruit a backup expedition leader in the event he became disabled or died. A second-in-command could also share the burdens of logistics and discipline. Wisely, Lewis realized the importance of selecting a leader with strengths he lacked. Among the small number of men with experience in similar missions, Billy Clark seemed the obvious choice. Lewis had first-hand knowledge of Clark's ability to command a company, and he knew how Clark had successfully outwitted Spanish operatives and influenced tribal leaders during his time in the army. The two friends had remained in contact after Clark resigned from the army.[286]

Lewis based his offer to Clark on the foundation of their friendship. Rather than a second-in-command, Lewis favored a co-captain model. After describing the proposed mission, Lewis wrote: "If therefore there is anything under those circumstances, in this enterprise, which would induce you to participate with me in it's fatiegues, it's dangers and it's honors, believe me there is no man on earth with whom I should feel equal pleasure in sharing them as with yourself."[287]

Clark accepted, assuring Lewis of his friendship, and anticipating the dangers as well as the "honors & rewards" that would be theirs if they accomplished their mission.[288] Jefferson promised to promote Clark to the rank of captain to make his rank the same as Lewis's. When Congress objected, Lewis suggested that no one under their command be told. For their purposes, they would share equally in the responsibilities of command as well as the rewards.[289] Clark would demonstrate the benefits of his experience and contribute to the expedition's creation. Early on, he modified Lewis's boat design by adding side panels that could be raised to provide shields from bullets, arrows, and spears in the event of an attack.[290]

Jefferson's official request to Congress proposed funds to form an expedition of about a dozen men.[291] Lewis and Clark set out to recruit soldiers from forts where their absences would not cause a disruption.[292] Given the length of the expedition and rigors expected, only select soldiers would qualify. Clark searched for "the best woodsmen & Hunters, of young men in this part of the Countrey."[293] Lewis would later assess that they were, "robust, active young men, accustomed to fatiegue and danger; most of them good hunters & all of them good boatmen, and above all who feel equally with myself, an enthusiasm in accomplishing the objects of this enterprise."[294] Every man would be required not only to carry his own weight but also to help support the others when needed.

The Corps additionally needed men with specialized talents, including boatmen and a blacksmith. Because the true purpose of the mission had to be kept confidential, the captains were circumspect in how much information they provided in their recruiting activities.

One observer was not sure that Lewis met his own recruitment standards, describing him as "a stout young man but not so robust as to look able to fully accomplish the object of his mission."[295] No one expressed doubt of the towering Clark's physical abilities in the outdoors.[296]

Part of a spy's stock in trade was the ability to deceive and to divert attention away from the strategic actions performed to complete the mission. Clark's backcountry speech and notoriously creative spelling belied a strategic mind that observed details as reflected in his military mapmaking. And his boyish enthusiasm deflected from the threat of his overpowering size. For Lewis, his average size and more polished mannerisms masked his rugged abilities as a seasoned woodsman—and the threat he posed to his enemies. Inside Lewis's average frame was a scientific mind and an unrelenting drive to push his physical limits. Like many men in history who lost their fathers at a young age, Lewis seemed propelled by a need to prove something—to himself, or to his mentor—which motivated him to attempt what few others were willing to risk.

Among the list of instructions Jefferson gave Lewis in June 1803 was a direction "to communicate to us, at seasonable intervals, a copy of your journal, notes & observations, of every kind, putting into cypher whatever might do injury if betrayed."[297] One writer who described the history of code observed, "CIPHER IS THE LANGUAGE OF SPIES."[298] Though Jefferson had developed a cipher device using a cylinder made of letters on wheels, by 1802, he had discarded that technique for a simpler method of lining letters in columns on a piece of paper based on a common source, such as a literary work that could be used as a key to decode the message.[299] The message would appear to be gibberish without the key. The president used his new method to create a special code for Lewis to send highly sensitive messages.[300]

It was common practice for military men to record their actions in the event their decisions were challenged. Most soldiers' journals of the period were bound with a simple pasteboard cover, and Lewis purchased a few for his notes on the expedition. But aware of the significance of the record of his observations in the West, Lewis also purchased pocket journals covered in red Moroccan leather, as well as other leatherbound notebooks. The explorers would plan to record working notes in the field on loose papers and later transfer their notes to the leather journals to create an official record.[301]

On August 31, 1803, after assembling equipment and a few crew members, Lewis boarded his specially designed boat and set off down the Ohio River. He stopped to pick up Clark in Louisville, Kentucky, and recruited additional men along the way. Perhaps revealing unwritten directions from Jefferson, Lewis quadrupled the size of his Corps from the proposed dozen to about forty-eight men.[302]

He planned to travel up the Mississippi to access the Missouri River and make a final launch upstream. But it had already become clear that the Corps would miss their expected September launch on the Missouri. Boat builders had fallen behind schedule, and then low water stalled his descent to the Mississippi.[303] The approaching winter would further delay their launch until spring to avoid ice floes and other winter hazards that could unnecessarily endanger the Corps and equipment.[304]

The staging time near St. Louis could be put to good use. There were still supplies to be purchased for the additional men, and the new company needed to be trained into a dependable unit that would act predictably in a crisis. The success of the mission depended on a flawless launch.

It was astonishing, then, that Lewis changed plans at the eleventh hour. Earlier, as his boat reached Cincinnati, Lewis wrote to Jefferson that he planned to spend the upcoming winter months taking an excursion on horseback south of the Kansas River toward Santa Fe. He also planned to send Clark toward Spanish territory, but on a different route.[305] Presumably, Lewis planned that the captains would divide the Corps and take them on their excursions rather than leaving them for months at a winter camp training under a subordinate's command.

The lure of Santa Fe had suddenly seemed more significant to Lewis than assuring the success of the Northwest Passage expedition, though he had spent at least a year in preparation. He might have justified the side trip as a training exercise for the longer expedition. But side excursions increased the risk that the Corps could be captured or that a mishap could scuttle the entire expedition before it began, which would have defeated the purpose of waiting until spring. Lewis argued that the side trips would provide "information relative to that Country" toward Santa Fe that would show the importance of the expedition to the Pacific and silence Jefferson's critics.[306] He did not state what information he proposed to obtain to justify the side excursions—he presumed Jefferson knew. It is doubtful that Lewis would have boldly altered the expedition plan by beginning with Santa Fe, unless Jefferson had already discussed that the acquisition of Santa Fe and Texas was a greater goal.

What suddenly drew Lewis's attention to Santa Fe is unknown. He later submitted blank pages for that portion of his journals.[307] The president rejected Lewis's plan quickly and without equivocation. He reminded Lewis of treaties between the U.S. and Spain and advised him that he would likely encounter even greater dangers toward Santa Fe than toward the Northwest. Jefferson's order left no room for misinterpretation: "you must not undertake the winter excursion which you propose."[308]

Jefferson's reply did not deny that Santa Fe was an objective. In fact, he assured Lewis that he would proceed to send a separate expedition in that direction. But at that moment, with all attention focused on their expedition to the Pacific, the Northwest Passage was Lewis's primary objective. Jefferson was already feeling the heat of criticism. Fulfilling the mission the public expected was politically expedient, even if another had suddenly become more promising.

As to the mission to the Pacific, if there was any doubt about its true purpose—the public one of gathering scientific data or searching for a water route for commerce as Jefferson stated in his formal written instructions—Lewis's threatened side excursions forced Jefferson to prioritize it emphatically to one: "The object of your mission is single, the direct water communication from sea to sea formed by the bed of the Missouri & perhaps the Oregon."[309] Wilkinson would also disclose that the secondary objective was to persuade the tribes to shift their loyalties from Spain to the U.S. through trade.[310] Still, the overriding objective of locating routes to move troops to the West was one of the types of secrets Washington had advised should never be put in writing.

Lewis complied with Jefferson's order, and the Corps built their winter camp, which they named "Camp Dubois," on the east side of the Mississippi River upstream from St. Louis, which Spain still controlled. It was common for captains to make camps far enough from towns that soldiers would not be tempted to break curfew and engage in activities that dishonored their company. Clark generally remained in camp, hunted, and drilled the men, while Lewis often traveled across the river to the St. Louis area to make additional preparations for their departure.[311]

Conveniently, Lewis arrived at St. Louis in time to witness the handover of the town to the United States. Major Amos Stoddard, whom the U.S. government had appointed as its agent to take control of the new Upper Louisiana at St. Louis, arrived in March 1804.[312] Lewis met Stoddard and was given the honor of signing the transfer document as a witness.[313] Stoddard would become the first commandant of the territory, a role comparable to the future territorial governor's office that Lewis would hold at the time of his death.[314]

Lewis and Clark visited with Stoddard several times over the following two months, and Stoddard won Lewis's trust. Lewis gave Stoddard and a few other prominent men in St. Louis his power of attorney to serve as his agent to take care of his business affairs there while he was away on the expedition.[315] As a government agent in the West, Stoddard would have been informed of the government's objective of extending its borders. He and Lewis no doubt discussed intelligence about New Spain.

While in St. Louis, Lewis took the opportunity to speak with hunters and trappers to gather descriptions of the immediate region through which the Corps would be traveling. He persuaded them to share their maps and journals.[316] Lewis also hired additional boatmen who were familiar with the portions of the river that had been traveled. The final number of team members had grown to about fifty-one men.[317]

Lewis initially estimated that the expedition would cost $2,500, but his final expenses totaled more than fifteen times that amount.[318] Jefferson had given him an authorization—essentially a line of credit—to purchase whatever supplies he needed for the expedition. He purchased most of the additional supplies from the local French Chouteau family.[319] Lewis would learn later that, despite Jefferson's assurance of government backing for any obligation that he incurred, he would become personally liable for expedition obligations that the War Department refused to reimburse.

The St. Louis Chouteau family gave Lewis a piece of silver and other metals that the Osage had discovered at some point farther west. The metals lent credibility to the rumors that the West was rich in ore. Prior to departing St. Louis, Lewis sent the samples to Jefferson.[320]

By May 1804, the Missouri River was free of winter ice floes, and Clark set out with the Corps upriver to the town of St. Charles, where they would make their final departure. Stoddard and prominent men of St. Louis accompanied Lewis overland to St. Charles to see them off.[321] Citizens of St. Charles assembled to witness the historic departure, waving their well-wishes to the Corps of Discovery.[322]

The intrepid team that set off up the Missouri River exemplified the bravery of the earliest explorers, facing the risk of death with stoic determination. In fact, the Far West was so remote and its dangers so unknown that it could be easy to conceal the actual cause of the explorers' deaths.

For Wilkinson, the timing was perfect. He had determined that the expedition, in general, or Lewis, in particular, had become a threat to his control over Jefferson and the West. It cannot be discounted that Wilkinson may have suggested that Lewis take his proposed winter excursions toward Santa Fe to make it easier for the Spanish to capture Lewis and Clark before the expedition began.

The double agent reached out to his Spanish contacts to take advantage of the opportunity to see that Lewis and Clark never returned.

Meriwether Lewis

# CHAPTER 6

# ADVENTURE OF A LIFETIME

O! the joy.

—William Clark, upon his view of the
Pacific Ocean, November 16, 1807

All the expected hazards awaited. According to Lewis's calculations, the Corps of Discovery had traveled 1,609 miles when it reached the Mandan Nation in November 1804. Near the northern point where the Corps would begin to turn due west, they stopped to build winter quarters, which they named "Fort Mandan."[323]

To that point, they had followed in the footsteps of a few hunters and trappers. Now, they would no longer have the assurance of knowing what to expect.[324] As they set out for the next leg in April 1805, Lewis took the liberty to imagine his party as comparable to that of the explorers Columbus or Cook, even as he looked at the Corps' small boats and summed up the challenge:

> we were now about to penetrate a country at least two thousand miles in width, on which the foot of civilized man had never trodden; the good or evil it had in store for us was for experiment

yet to determine, and these little vessels contained every article by which we were to expect to subsist or defend ourselves.[325]

While the explorers were encamped at Fort Mandan, they met a tribal woman, "Sacagawea," who was familiar with local tribes and recognized landmarks. She would play a pivotal role as an interpreter and diplomat. Lewis's extensive planning had not anticipated recruiting a member of a western tribe, particularly a tribal woman, to serve as a type of spy among her people. But on more than one occasion, Sacagawea's native skill and assistance helped the party obtain resources they needed to survive.[326]

Winter blizzards were followed by severe heat and then blizzards. Over the next thousands of miles, Lewis faced down a Brown Grizzly, treated sick Corps members, and pulled out the portable soup as a last resort to keep the Corps from starving in the Bitterroot Mountains in winter.[327] Along the way, western tribes sometimes threatened to attack the outnumbered party.

Lewis and Clark carefully charted the rivers by measuring their width and depth and used field notes to document the suitability of the rivers for transporting soldiers, traders, and, later, settlers. They noted locations of fresh drinking water for advancing troops and the availability of game that army hunters could kill for food for their units. The explorers highlighted good locations for a fort near the Independence River and a trading post near the Yellowstone River.[328] As Jefferson ordered, the co-captains often copied each other's entries to create a complete account if the journals of one of the captains were lost.

With their focus on the wonders of the West, the duo was unaware of the danger they faced from within the army. Wilkinson provided his Spanish contacts with intelligence about the Corps' expected locations. He even urged the Spanish governor to force Lewis and Clark to retreat or "take them prisoners."[329] One historian suggested that the Spanish paid Wilkinson handsomely for the confidential information.[330]

Giving credence to the theory that Lewis's proposal to take an early excursion to Santa Fe was more than a whim, one Spanish official noted that Americans were already "making themselves masters of our rich possessions, which they desire. It is painful to acknowledge it and to experience it, but it will be much more painful not to use all our forces while there is still time to remedy it."[331]

Another suggested that the true purpose of the Lewis and Clark Expedition was to advance to Santa Fe. He concluded, "The only means which presents itself is to arrest Captain Merry Weather and his party, which cannot help but pass through the nations neighboring New Mexico, its presidios or *rancherias*."[332] In the meantime, the Spanish colonial government sent select patrols to intercept the explorers. At two points, the patrols came within a "several days' march" of the expedition party.[333]

Unaware they were being pursued, the Corps of Discovery reached the Pacific on November 7, 1805. Clark wrote, "we are in view of the opening of the Ocian, which Creates great joy."[334] The company built a second camp, "Fort Clatsop," for the second winter, 1805-1806, before returning east. The elusive Northwest Passage did not exist, but expedition reports of rich resources nevertheless spurred western settlement and ultimately fulfilled Jefferson's goal.

As Lewis and Clark mapped the Far Northwest, Jefferson sent inquiries in the form of questions to his associates in the Southwest to help him establish the southern boundary of the Louisiana Purchase. When no one could provide the credible information he needed to convince Spain that the boundary lay much farther south than Spain acknowledged, he pressed harder to gather intelligence.[335]

To journey to Santa Fe, Jefferson selected Wilkinson loyalist Thomas Freeman to serve in the "Meriwether Lewis" role to lead the expedition. After working under Wilkinson, Freeman had gained experience interacting with tribes while surveying boundaries in the Mississippi Territory.

Reminiscent of the invitation he extended to Lewis, Jefferson invited Freeman to dinner at the President's House to present his proposal.[336]

The president gave Freeman instructions for his mission up the Red River similar to the ones he had given Lewis and Clark for the Northwest. He also sent Freeman to Philadelphia to be trained by the same experts who had trained Lewis.[337] Freeman was equally excited, writing, "a Great many difficulties, and some personal danger will attend the expedition, but, I will —'Stick or go through' The more danger more honor."[338]

After preparations in the East, Freeman traveled down Jefferson's new military highway on the Natchez Trace to begin assembling his team near Natchez and Fort Adams. Along the way, he met with John McKee, who now at times served as Choctaw agent and Chickasaw agent. Freeman provided McKee with details of the expedition and tried to recruit him.[339] It is not clear how much Freeman had been informed of McKee's prior spying on Wilkinson.

Coincidentally, Wilkinson sent McKee a letter promising him a "splendid enterprise" in Mexico if the U.S. went to war with Spain.[340] McKee may have understood Jefferson's policy as Orleans governor Claiborne described it: "The interest of the U. States requires that all European influence should be banished [from] the Continent of America."[341] Like Stoddard, it was not unreasonable to expect McKee to be aware of the government's policies for expansion and to double as a spy or agent to further those policies.[342] What was uncertain was whether Wilkinson's proposed mission was to support Jefferson's or to create a separate mission to rival it.

Bird illustrator, or ornithologist, Alexander Wilson, who would play a role in supporting the suicide narrative about Lewis's death, lobbied to be included in Freeman's Santa Fe expedition. Wilson had immigrated to America after being sued for slander in his native Scotland. Deep in debt, Wilson admitted that he saw the expedition as an opportunity to earn much-needed income and advance his career.[343] He began corresponding with Jefferson in 1805 to offer unsolicited information on birds. Wilson flattered Jefferson as he shamelessly worked through a mutual ornithologist friend to gain Jefferson's attention.

Wilson told Jefferson that he had heard of his plans to send explorers up the Red River, the Arkansas River, and others, adding, "I beg leave to offer myself for any of these expeditions; and can be ready at a short notice to attend to your Excellency's orders."[344] Jefferson did not record that he received the letter.[345] But he subscribed to Wilson's first book, *American Ornithology*, compensating Wilson only with the price of his subscription and words saluting him with "great respect."[346] Perhaps at Wilkinson's prodding, Wilson would not give up attempting to interject himself into Jefferson's and Lewis's affairs.

In early 1806, Freeman's team traveled to Natchitoches, where they met with Dr. Sibley and area explorers before setting out west. A few months later, the Freeman-Custis Expedition launched up the Red River to map the river to help establish the location of the southern boundary with Spain and, more importantly, to try to discover a southern river route to Santa Fe.[347] Unknown to Freeman, Wilkinson had also provided intelligence to the Spanish about his Freeman-Custis Expedition. Spanish patrols were more successful in locating his team and turned them back east.[348] Undeterred, Jefferson made plans to send former soldier John McClallen on a separate mission up the Missouri River and then toward Santa Fe.[349]

The several American expeditions into its territory in 1806, outraged the Spanish to the point that they threatened war. Spanish colonials tested the U.S. Army by crossing over the unofficial boundary on the Sabine River west of Natchez.

But war with Spain may have been Wilkinson's goal. Those who wanted to take Texas and Santa Fe could use attacks by the Spanish colonials as a pretext for starting a fight that would allow the U.S. to occupy their land. By summer 1806, Wilkinson further stoked war fires by sending Lieutenant Zebulon Pike, Wilkinson's son, James Biddle Wilkinson, and Alexander Hamilton's nephew, Dr. John Hamilton Robinson, on a separate expedition toward Santa Fe.[350] Wilkinson had previously sent Pike on a shorter mission up the Mississippi in 1805, to scout locations for military and trading posts.[351] Wilkinson favored the Pike family after he had persuaded Pike's father not to arrest the boatmen couriering Wilkinson's bribe money when their boat was intercepted at Fort Massac.[352]

Pike said that he understood that his mission was to obtain coordinates to map the southern boundary of the United States with Spanish Mexico; however, from the intelligence he gathered, he mapped a route that could be used for the movement of artillery and baggage wagons to seize Santa Fe.[353] After Pike's party separated from the one led by Wilkinson's son, it was captured by Spanish patrols and taken to Santa Fe. Chameleon-like Robinson pretended to be a territorial debt collector, and then, when discovered to be a U.S. spy, he brazenly offered to march to the Northwest to secure that territory for the Spanish if they would release his party.[354]

When knowledge of Pike's capture became public, Wilkinson claimed that Jefferson knew nothing of the Pike Expedition.[355] Nevertheless, the public speculated that Jefferson's Freeman-Custis expedition was operating in coordination with Pike's and that Jefferson had approved the Pike mission despite Wilkinson's denials.[356] Jefferson claimed plausible deniability on the technicality that Pike reported the purpose of his mission to be solely the exploration of the geography of the Red River, and no one had formally told Jefferson otherwise.[357]

From the intelligence Wilkinson gathered from his spies, an invasion of Santa Fe appeared achievable. He assessed that soldiers would only be required to march 900 miles and cross one mountain range to reach their target. Troops would find enough food to make the march if they could persuade tribes to shift their loyalty.[358]

Lewis and Clark did not account for the increased risk of capture by Spanish patrols as they led their company back home across the continent in 1806. They certainly had not prepared for war with Spain.[359]

As the Corps of Discovery returned by way of the Missouri about 180 miles west of St. Louis, they unexpectedly encountered spy John McClallen, who was just setting out west on Jefferson's latest mission to Santa Fe. McClallen was a friend of Lewis's. Though anxious to make their final return, the co-captains halted for twelve hours to discuss details of McClallen's mission with him.[360]

Clark wrote that McClallen told the explorers he was sent "to Santa Fee where he will apear in a stile calculated to atract the Spanish government in that quarter and through the influence of a handsome present he expects to be promited to exchange his merchindize for Silver & gold of which those people abound."[361] Clark thought the plan a good one; however, after narrowly escaping an attack by a regional tribe, McClallen's party never arrived at its destination.[362]

Before separating, McClallen informed the co-captains that so many months had passed without any communication from the Corps of Discovery, the public had given them up for lost. Rumors had spread that they had been killed by Spanish troops or had been forced to work as slaves in Spanish gold and silver mines.[363] In a rare expression of emotion for an Enlightenment man, Jefferson later admitted to his protégé that he had worried about his safety, writing, "The unknown scenes in which you were engaged, & the length of time without hearing of you had begun to be felt awfully."[364]

The Corps, still dressed in buckskins sewn from hides of animals encountered on the expedition, marched back into St. Louis to a cheering crowd and dined with St. Louis trader Auguste Chouteau. A more formal banquet at William Christy's tavern served as the town's official celebration of their return.[365] Lewis spoke highly of Clark to share the praise for their success.[366]

The maps Lewis and Clark produced accomplished Jefferson's purpose of collecting strategic information. Lewis was so anxious to deliver them to Jefferson that he sent them ahead through couriers. Jefferson wasted no time delivering surveys of the rivers to the secretary of war.[367]

One of the rewards Lewis and Clark hoped to enjoy was the publication of their expedition narrative in several volumes. After dutifully noting military intelligence, they often followed Jefferson's instructions to document the unexplored country and describe the characteristics of the tribes, plants, and animals they observed along the way, details that would intrigue Jefferson, his scientific peers, and, ultimately, the general public. Lewis deepened his own growing interest in natural history, which may have been another reason he gathered and returned samples of plants and animals. He planned to publish a separate volume focused solely on his observations of the "Botany, Minerology and Zoology" of the western territory.[368]

The final version of the explorer's journals would be expected to be viewed by the generations that followed them.[369] Historians still debate whether the explorers cleanly transferred their field notes into red leather journals in the field or sometime later. Lewis and Clark never claimed to have transcribed all their field notes into the journals. Whether copied or not, some loose field notes remain. [370]

More significantly, no sensitive expedition documents that Jefferson had directed Lewis to cipher in code have been found. Lewis could have included any such documents in the package of maps he sent to the War Department from St. Louis or retained them to hand-deliver.

Most of Lewis's journal entries were technical listings of facts and details, formatted for scientists and military men—perfect for an Enlightenment man like Jefferson. Yet occasionally, as a man of the budding Romantic Era, Lewis recorded how his sensibilities were stirred by the beauty of a landscape few had seen. As he viewed the Great Falls in what is now Montana, he wrote:

> here the river pitches over a shelving rock, with an edge as regular and as streight as if formed by art, without a nich or brake in it; the water decends in one even and uninterrupted sheet to the bot-

tom wher dashing against the rocky bottom rises into foaming billows of great hight and rappidly glides away, hising flashing and sparkling as it departs the sprey rises from one extremity to the other to 50 f. I now thought that if a skillfull painter had been asked to make a beautifull cascade that he would most probably have pesented the precise immage of this one.[371]

Another Lewis journal entry stood out for its introspection. On August 18, 1805—his thirty-first birthday—Lewis, unable to perform duties due to rain, recorded a midlife epiphany similar to one written years earlier by his mentor, Jefferson:

This day I completed my thirty first year, and conceived that I had in all human probability now existed about half the period which I am to remain in this Sublunary world. I reflected that I had as yet done but little, very little indeed, to further the hapiness of the human race, or to advance the information of the succeeding generation. I viewed with regret the many hours I have spent in indolence, and now soarly feel the want of that information which those hours would have given me had they been judiciously expended. but since they are past and cannot be recalled, I dash from me the gloomy thought and resolved in future, to redouble my exertions and at least indeavour to promote those two primary objects of human existence, by giving them the aid of that portion of talents which nature and fortune have bestoed on me; or in future, to live for *mankind*, as I have heretofore lived *for myself.*[372]

Lewis expressed his melancholy "gloomy thought" that showed he was a man of his time—one shaped as much by the emerging Romantic sensibility as by Enlightenment ideals. On one level, this may have been a calculated move, a wager that romanticism would triumph in posterity's eyes, and that his work would be judged incomplete if he failed to show the emotional awareness expected in such moments.[373]

Success is an intoxicating elixir. In a rare moment for a man focused on the details of his mission, Lewis freed his thoughts from the chains of daily duties and human limitations. If he survived the expedition, led his Corps of Discovery to the Pacific Ocean, and then safely back home, what could he not accomplish over the following three decades?

In a less contentious time in America, Lewis might have reached the highest levels of success. But as the explorer sat alone in the Far West, contemplating his post-expedition goals, on the other side of the continent, Wilkinson worked tirelessly, orchestrating his marionettes like a puppet master. And through Wilkinson's influence, conflicts back home further divided both the army and the government, creating challenges that Lewis would not overcome.

Meriwether Lewis misjudged the amount of time he would remain on earth.

## CHAPTER 7

# AARON BURR AND THE LURE OF SANTA FE

[P]laying at treason is a dangerous game!
—Winfield Scott[374]

Newspaper accounts of Lewis and Clark's surprising, triumphant return in late 1806 competed with stories that Wilkinson had joined with Aaron Burr to plot a rebellion against the United States. Some newspaper editors openly viewed Wilkinson's gathering of intelligence in the Southwest and interactions with colonial Spanish officials from a new perspective—Wilkinson had been working all along for his own interests rather than those of the country he was sworn to defend.

Wilkinson was an astute reader of people. He assessed that Burr imagined himself destined to become a ruler, and, as Andrew Jackson would conclude, that Burr could easily be fooled.[375] Wilkinson had needed a front man to execute his plan to create a new empire in the West, and Burr was the politician he had awaited.

Burr initially helped the Republicans manage Jefferson's election as president in 1800, with the expectation that Burr would receive the second-highest number of votes and become vice president. After thirty-six ballots in the House of Representatives, Jefferson finally prevailed, and Burr succeeded in winning the second-highest number.

During the process, however, political turmoil and close votes seemed to present Burr with the chance to step ahead of Jefferson and claim the presidency for himself. Jefferson suspected that Burr's ambitions overtook him. Burr seemed to confirm that suspicion when, in his dual role as president of the Senate, he voted to break a tie in favor of the opposing Federalists.[376] Jefferson lost all trust in Burr and did everything in his power to exclude him from a meaningful role in his administration.[377] To prevent Burr's reelection, Jefferson spearheaded the passage of the Twelfth Amendment to the U.S. Constitution to ensure that the candidate with the second-highest number of electoral votes would no longer become vice president. There was no question that Burr would be out of office at the end of Jefferson's first term in 1805.

Burr next attempted a run as Governor of New York. During the heat of the campaign, Alexander Hamilton stated that Burr was "a dangerous man." It was a time when a gentleman felt duty-bound to defend his reputation or risk being branded a coward, and the two founders of the Republic fought their infamous duel. Hamilton threw away his shot, as gentlemen often did during duels, but Burr's shot hit and killed Hamilton.[378] Losing the election for governor and facing charges of murder in New York, the vice president avoided prosecution simply by remaining out of the state at a time when states did not extradite fugitives. But Hamilton was popular with Federalists in the East, and Burr's hopes of ever winning Easterners' support for another national office were dashed.

As Wilkinson guessed, Burr was determined to become ruler of a country, even if it was not the United States. He was still wildly popular west of the Appalachians, where the Federalist Hamilton was despised.[379] Burr concluded that westerners might be ripe for dissolving their attachment to the new constitution of states and joining a separate nation. He reached out to the British minister to the U.S. to test whether the British navy might provide military support for a new western nation.[380] Wilkinson would have learned of Burr's overtures.

In May 1804, Wilkinson seized the opportunity from Burr's defeat. He wrote to Burr, reminding him of the days they shared in the army during the Revolution, when Burr's job was to gather intelligence as a scout or spy. Wilkinson directed Major James Bruff, the military commander in the Louisiana Territory near St. Louis, to send additional information he had gathered about the trade route to Santa Fe.[381] Wilkinson offered to introduce Burr to his "particular," or close, friends and show him his maps.[382] The two met for days behind closed doors, where they apparently pored over the maps Wilkinson had obtained of New Spain from Nolan and others. He also reached out to Kentucky Senator James Adair to test his interest in supporting a seizure of Santa Fe. Adair responded enthusiastically, "Mexico glitters in our Eyes—the word is all we wait for."[383]

Given the actions that followed, Wilkinson convinced Burr that they could combine their resources to conquer New Spain. Burr could become emperor of the new country, Wilkinson would command the troops, and Santa Fe would provide wealth beyond their dreams. Once Santa Fe was in their control, all of Latin America could be theirs for the taking.[384]

Timing worked to their advantage. Burr was still vice president, and Jefferson needed his support in the Senate to impeach a Supreme Court justice who opposed his administration's policies. The president was forced to negotiate with Burr. Burr's price was that Jefferson appoint Wilkinson as Governor of the Upper Louisiana Territory, all of the Louisiana Purchase north of New Orleans.[385] Burr's brother-in-law, Robert Wescott, would be appointed Secretary, the second-highest office.[386] Wilkinson would not be the first to hold the position of general and the office of territorial governor at the same time, but Jefferson knew that the dual role would give Wilkinson extraordinary power to influence events in the West.[387] Wilkinson would even have the temerity to order that the army headquarters be moved west of the Mississippi to St. Louis.[388] To the average citizen, it made no sense that the president would give a general so much unsupervised power that far from the Capitol. But given their accommodation, Jefferson may have preferred to have Wilkinson in that position.

Wilkinson arranged for Burr to travel to New Orleans to meet with Daniel Clark, Jr., and the Mexican Society that was plotting to take Texas and Mexico.[389] Burr first stopped in Nashville to pay a visit to Andrew Jackson.[390] Jackson then served as Major General of the Western Division of the Tennessee Militia, the largest number of troops in the states closest to the southwestern border. It was known that Jackson supported the taking of Spanish territory in the Floridas and Texas to extend the frontiers and make the western states safer for settlement.[391] Jackson could be persuaded to supply the military forces for the conquest. The plotters also likely knew that Jackson had lobbied Jefferson for the position of Governor of the Orleans Territory, and that Jefferson's appointment of W. C. C. Claiborne instead had made Jackson his political enemy.[392] It may have explained why Dickson never replied to Lewis's request to build boats for the expedition.[393]

Burr, who had supported the admission of Tennessee as a state into the Union, could expect a good reception.[394] Jackson welcomed him with militia cannon salutes and agreed to stable his horses while the vice president traveled to New Orleans. Jackson then met privately with him to hear of his confidential plans.[395]

After securing Jackson's support, Burr traveled north to Fort Massac on the Ohio River and reported to Wilkinson.[396] Major Amos Stoddard was present. Wilkinson ordered Fort Massac commander Daniel Bissell to crew a large army boat to transport Burr to New Orleans in the style of a future emperor, as Bissell followed behind in a smaller boat.[397]

Wilkinson traveled on to the Upper Louisiana territorial capital, St. Louis, to take his office as governor. He soon began testing his officers to see who might support his plan for a new empire. The general approached local military commander Bruff with the suggestion that the American republic was not the best form of government for the continent and revealed a "great secret" that he was plotting "a large enterprise."[398] The details were vague, but the goal was to make their fortunes from Santa Fe.[399] At the same time, Wilkinson informed his Spanish handlers of Burr's plans to take military action in the West with the ruse that the whole purpose was to detach the western states from the U.S. and tie their loyalty to Spain.[400] Spanish officials in Louisiana at first grew anxious that they might have to defend against an American invasion.[401]

Burr used Wilkinson's letter of introduction to meet with Daniel Clark, Jr. and his associates. When Burr left New Orleans, Clark, Jr. traveled on to Latin America to spy out Spanish defenses and to make possible plans for a military expedition there.[402] Apparently unknown to Burr, Clark, Jr. supported an alternate action to wrest control of Latin America from Spain through his friend Francisco de Miranda in what would become known as "The Miranda Expedition."[403]

Encouraged by the support he received in New Orleans, Burr returned overland up the Natchez Trace. He stopped at the Chickasaw Agency village, where he met John McKee, who was serving as Chickasaw agent. McKee understood that Burr planned to gain popularity and power in the West, but he grew suspicious of what Burr might do with that power once he had it.[404]

Burr needed money and supplies for his invasion. He met with Jackson again to lay the groundwork for taking the riches of Santa Fe as an incentive for Jackson's soldiers.[405] Burr then proceeded north to Kentucky and Ohio, where he recruited businessmen, mainly Wilkinson's friends, to support the effort. In September 1805, Burr then traveled to St. Louis, where he provided a progress report to Wilkinson.[406]

Burr's troops would need lead bullets, and the Missouri area contained some of the largest lead mines in the nation. The owner of one of the largest lead claims was John Smith T, whose mother was a Wilkinson of the same family as the general.[407] At some point, Wilkinson recruited Smith T and his associates to support Burr.

But Burr's momentum was thwarted in St. Louis when Wilkinson received a letter from Daniel Clark, Jr. informing him that someone had leaked news of the plot. It was Wilkinson's Spanish handlers. They had come to believe that he had created the plot to separate western states for their advantage and had begun to worry that he was getting cold feet. They began publishing rumors of the conspiracy in newspapers to force him to act.[408]

Wilkinson worried whether he could rely on continued support from the Spanish.[409] He decided it was time to lay the groundwork for an escape, depending on how events unfolded. When Burr left St. Louis to continue his preparations in the East, Wilkinson sent a letter to the secretary of the navy to warn that Burr was developing a nefarious plot and that he should be watched.[410]

Wilkinson's opponents in Kentucky took advantage of the Spanish rumors and began publishing stories that he and Burr were plotting some type of military action in the West. By late autumn 1805, newspapers across the country reprinted the stories. When Burr returned to Washington for a dinner with Jefferson in November 1805, the president could no longer claim ignorance of the rumors.[411] But he ignored the warnings. Jefferson even followed through to give Wilkinson a three-year extension on his term as Governor of the Upper Louisiana.[412]

In St. Louis, Major Bruff grew suspicious of Wilkinson's intentions toward Spain and told colleagues that Wilkinson's days as governor were numbered.[413] A few months later, when the conflicts with Spain erupted along the contested border between Louisiana and Texas on the Sabine River, Wilkinson received the secretary of war's orders to leave St. Louis and travel to the New Orleans area to prepare a defense.[414] Wilkinson may have wanted war with Spain, but he also wanted to remain governor to control events west of the Mississippi. He concluded that he had been ordered to give up the governor's office because Bruff had alerted the War Department that Wilkinson was plotting his own invasion in the West. Wilkinson wrote an angry reply, outrageously suggesting that Bruff be investigated for treason, because anyone who would accuse Wilkinson of being a traitor could not be trusted with military secrets.[415]

The outbreak of hostilities with Spain gave Burr new hope that the plotters might have the war they needed after all, and he increased his momentum. He wrote to Jackson that the plans had changed; that Jefferson was proposing to buy the Florida territory from Spain; and that if Spain refused, the president would need Jackson to command troops to take Florida by force. Jefferson, he said, would disavow any knowledge of the invasion to avoid war with Spain.[416] Jackson had longed for a military conquest that would give credence to his rank as a general and may have seen the proposition as an olive branch from Jefferson. Burr then sent Wilkinson a letter to set their plan in motion: "The people of the country to which we are going are prepared to receive us… The gods invite us to glory and fortune. It remains to be seen whether we deserve the boons."[417]

At the same time, Daniel Clark, Jr.'s friend Miranda held public functions to raise financial support in New York for his own invasion of Venezuela. Miranda claimed that Jefferson told him he could not openly support the expedition because it might lead to war with Spain but assured him that the government would "wink" at the results. Later, when the financial backers of the expedition were prosecuted for violation of the Neutrality Act of 1794, they successfully argued that they had acted with full knowledge of Jefferson's administration.[418] More than a few later believed that Jefferson also reacted to Burr and Wilkinson's conspiracy to take Texas and Santa Fe with a similar wink.[419]

Burr returned to Nashville to meet with Jackson. Far from keeping the meeting secret, Jackson held a ball in Burr's honor and entered the room arm in arm with Burr.[420] Jackson associates Judge John Overton and William P. Anderson attended the festivities and invited Burr to their houses.[421] Privately, Burr told Jackson that Miranda's Expedition might lead to war with Spain. He revealed that Spanish troops had driven back an expedition exploring the Red River. Burr made it clearer that Jackson's troops might be needed to help obtain the independence of Texas and Santa Fe.[422]

Burr told Jackson he needed him to build boats to transport soldiers for the expedition down the Mississippi River. Because Jefferson had previously awarded Jackson the contract to build boats for an earlier expedition, Jackson could assume the request came from Jefferson. And Wilkinson would have known that Jackson was strapped for cash due to bad land investments, which would make him even less eager to question the offer. Burr would also need Jackson to recruit soldiers.

Jackson readily agreed.[423] Burr provided notes payable to himself and endorsed them to Jackson as payment for the boats and soldiers to join the venture, providing written proof of Jackson's involvement with his scheme.[424] As further evidence of his participation, Jackson published orders in the newspapers for his militia to stand ready to march against Spanish forces.[425] Convinced that Burr was acting with Jefferson's approval, Jackson wrote to the president to assure his support.[426] Jackson not only relished the thought of taking Texas and Santa Fe, but he proclaimed that "Mr. Burr would eventually prove to be the savior of this Western country."[427]

Despite his accommodation with Jefferson, Wilkinson had already begun to doubt the president's continued support when one of his contacts informed him that Jefferson would end his command during the next session of Congress.[428] He determined that it was time to turn on Burr publicly, expose him as a traitor, and salvage his own position by defending the nation against a plot he could blame on Burr. Wilkinson sent a soldier to deliver a message to Jefferson that he had received from Burr, ciphered in code. Wilkinson left out a portion of the message that would have implicated himself.[429] Fearing interception, the soldier hid the message in a space in the sole of his shoe until he met with Jefferson in private.[430] As part of Wilkinson's report, he warned Jefferson that a conspiracy in the West had recruited up to 10,000 men.[431]

Another soldier traveling east from New Orleans stopped at Jackson's home, The Hermitage, and casually revealed the plot during dinner. He said that the insurrection would begin by inciting a slave rebellion in New Orleans, robbing the Bank of New Orleans, and then using the stolen funds to hire additional soldiers to march to Washington and disband Congress.[432] Jackson realized that he was implicated. He and Wilkinson had earlier clashed over the location of Jefferson's new military highway and control of military personnel. Jackson suspected that Wilkinson had used Burr as his puppet to entangle him in the plot to eliminate him as a rival general. But for Jackson, it was too late to salvage his credibility in Washington.

It was only when Jefferson heard rumors that Burr planned to have him assassinated that Jefferson sent out messengers with orders for the former vice president's arrest.[433] It did not matter that the president lacked the authority to arrest Burr. Jefferson would stretch the law to remove him as a threat. Jefferson first dispatched government spies to determine the extent of the plot, then issued an official proclamation stating that a treasonous conspiracy threatened the government.[434]

The public reacted to the news with panic. The War Department ordered Amos Stoddard to take troops to the main federal arsenal in the Southwest at Newport, Kentucky, to prevent Burr supporters from stealing federal weapons to use against the government. In the Nashville area, men whom Jackson had encouraged to support Burr suddenly distanced themselves from him and declared their loyalty to the Union.[435]

Oblivious to Wilkinson's turning, Burr led his small band of invaders south to Nashville to take control of the boats and begin his march by river. Now aware of the plot, Jackson refused to meet with Burr and refunded his payments for all the boats except for two, which he arranged to have delivered to Burr.[436] Or, perhaps, Jackson refunded the money because he had not mustered the 2,000 volunteers Burr had requested. Only Jackson's nephew and sixty to seventy-five mercenaries boarded the boats at Jackson's Clover Bottom boat dock to join Burr.[437]

Someone had recruited the mercenaries, who were typically paid in advance for their military service. Jackson's records would reveal that about one-third of his account with Burr—for boats and mercenaries—was for payments that Jackson made to his militia aide-de-camp, William P. Anderson.[438] The evidence suggests that it was Anderson who used Burr's funds to recruit mercenary soldiers to join Burr.[439] Jackson later claimed that he sent his nephew on the mission only to keep an eye on Burr. The nephew kept a journal of his trip, or rather his return, leaving out the portion when he travelled with Burr.[440]

Jackson's provision of two boats and support of mercenaries was all the evidence the secretary of war needed to accuse Jackson of being a traitor in league with Burr.[441] The U.S. Attorney considered charging Jackson with treason.[442]

Setting out just prior to the delivery of Jefferson's proclamation to Nashville, Burr's flotilla followed the Cumberland River to the Ohio, where he stopped at Fort Massac, met with commander Daniel Bissell, and asked him to supply troops he could spare. Bissell apparently cooperated, and a few men agreed to join Burr's flotilla.[443] Burr's next stop was New Madrid to load supplies on the Mississippi River. While there, he attempted to recruit the townspeople to join him.[444]

Burr's boats continued downstream to Fort Pickering on the Chickasaw Bluffs. Arriving after dark, Burr introduced himself and asked if he and his men could spend the night. The fort commander, Jacob Jackson, readily agreed. Burr reported that he was headed to Spanish territory and implied that once there, he would relieve that territory from Spanish government control.

Burr told the fort commander that the upper levels of government and the army approved his mission, but warned that it had to be kept confidential. Fort Pickering commander Jackson declined to supply Burr with arms but allowed Burr's men to melt lead for bullets at the fort.

Burr coordinated with the commander to send a letter by express rider to the then-former Chickasaw and Choctaw agent John McKee, asking him to recruit Chickasaw men to support the expedition.[445] Wilkinson had also communicated through intermediaries to McKee to ask him to support the plot. McKee traveled to Natchez to join the effort when Wilkinson's agent told him that the government would "wink at" the legality of the excursion, but once he discovered that the plans were to separate the western territory rather than join it to the United States, he bowed out. He said Wilkinson must have thought he was a Burrite, but professed, "as yet, I am not." He wanted more information before committing.[446]

As Burr prepared to depart, he attempted to recruit Commander Jackson and his men. The commander replied that serving under Burr while still serving as a U.S. Army officer would be a violation of his duty. Nevertheless, the commander accepted Burr's payment of $150 to help recruit men for Burr as soon as the commander resigned from the army.[447]

John Smith T, St. Genevieve Sheriff Henry Dodge, Wilkinson's brother-in-law, territorial secretary Robert Wescott, and others Lewis would later encounter in the territory, gathered arms, ammunition, and volunteers south of St. Louis in St. Genevieve before launching down the Mississippi to join Burr. Smith T had purchased a large amount of dry goods from Andrew Jackson, which some thought might have been intended to supply Burr's troops.[448] By the time that Smith T's party arrived at New Madrid, however, they learned that Jefferson had ordered Burr's arrest, and they returned home.[449]

Wilkinson imposed virtual martial law in New Orleans despite Governor W. C. C. Claiborne's refusal to make it official.[450] Exerting the same military authority, he ordered that witnesses who could implicate him in the conspiracy be taken prisoner and held on a ship offshore.[451] He also paid New Orleans police officers to spy on people arriving in the city and report their intelligence to him.[452]

On the Mississippi, still several miles north of Natchez, Burr learned that Wilkinson had implicated him in a rebellion. Fearing that Wilkinson would use his military authority to have him assassinated to prevent him from testifying, Burr stopped his descent downriver. He left his boat, surrendered to the arrest of the proper Mississippi Territory authorities, and traveled by land to Natchez to appear before judges he thought would be friendly to his cause.[453]

As Burr suspected, Wilkinson sent an offer to pay the Choctaw agent $5,000 to capture Burr, implying that the sum would be paid regardless of whether Burr was dead or alive.[454] In case Burr's expedition made it as far as Baton Rouge, Wilkinson hired a foreign agent to kidnap Burr and bring him to New Orleans.[455] At the same time, Wilkinson dispatched a party of five men from New Orleans, one civilian and four military officers, disguised as civilians, to enter the Mississippi Territory and capture Burr. It made no difference to Wilkinson's spies that their actions were illegal. They traveled to Natchez with a plan to seize Burr from the jurisdiction of the courts and either take him to Wilkinson or assassinate him.[456] Either way, Burr would be silenced. Reading a letter in which Wilkinson confided, "… its best *to take him* [Burr] *off*," Congressman and Jefferson opponent John Randolph marveled, "The plain english of which is That Wilkinson has men in pay to *assassinate* Burr!"[457]

Natchez townspeople seemed to care little that Jefferson had ordered Burr's arrest. They welcomed the former vice president by holding balls in his honor. Local judges at first refused to find him guilty of any crime.[458]

When Burr heard rumors that Wilkinson had sent out assassins, he devised an escape plan. Burr arranged to exchange clothes with his servant before sending him as a decoy to ride away from Natchez to courier a note to Burr's friends.[459] Any assassins would be expected to follow the servant dressed as Burr. Then, disguising himself in a servant's clothes, Burr rode east into the Mississippi Territory. When Burr reached what is now Southern Alabama, a federal land agent noticed that the quality of Burr's boots and horse did not match the old clothes he was wearing. Figuring out that the vagabond was Burr, the agent acted under Jefferson's illegal order to arrest him. The agent was tasked to escort Burr as a prisoner to Richmond for trial.[460]

Jefferson selected Richmond, Virginia, as the trial venue, reasoning that a jury from his home state would be more likely to prosecute Burr. Winfield Scott attended the trial as a spectator. He wryly observed that the two political parties descended on Richmond and turned the post-courtroom hours into a political circus, stating, "It was President Jefferson who directed and animated the prosecution, and hence every Republican clamored for execution. Of course, the Federalists… compacted themselves on the other side."[461] Federalist newspapers derided the trial as political theater, branding it "King Tom's Puppet Show."[462]

Andrew Jackson and William P. Anderson were subpoenaed to testify.[463] Anderson ignored the subpoena from an out-of-state court, but Jackson took the opportunity to travel to Richmond to clear his name. He testified that Wilkinson and Burr established their plan to attack Mexico while Burr was in St. Louis in 1805.[464] Outside the courtroom, Jackson stood on the statehouse steps and loudly proclaimed that Jefferson was prosecuting an innocent Burr rather than Wilkinson, who had masterminded the conspiracy.[465]

Wilkinson was called as a witness. Unfortunately for Jefferson's prosecution, his political enemy, John Randolph, was selected foreman of the grand jury. The jury broke the cipher code that Wilkinson and Burr had used to communicate and discovered that Wilkinson had failed to disclose evidence that he was to serve as Burr's second-in-command. The grand jury came within one vote of indicting Wilkinson.[466]

While the witnesses were still in Richmond, a false rumor spread that Randolph had shot Wilkinson.[467] It was true that Wilkinson challenged Randolph to a duel. Randolph rejected the challenge with the insult that "I cannot descend to your character," arguing Wilkinson was not a gentleman worthy of shooting. In response, advertisements were plastered throughout Washington proclaiming, "John Randolph is a prevaricating poltroon—signed 'James Wilkinson.'" Randolph followed up by introducing a letter to Congress claiming that Wilkinson was on the payroll of enemy Spain and suggested that it begin an inquiry into the general.[468]

Congress took no action. Both grand jury foreman Randolph and future general Winfield Scott claimed that Wilkinson would have been prosecuted if Jefferson had not prevented it.[469] At the least, Jefferson would be held politically responsible for failing to supervise Wilkinson. At worst, opponents might claim that Jefferson encouraged Wilkinson's and Burr's actions to send soldiers into neutral foreign territory in violation of the Neutrality Act. It would not be the first time that the government could claim ignorance of the actions of rogue soldiers that ultimately served its policies.

The jury found that the prosecution had not proven its case that any overt act of treason had occurred in Virginia. Burr objected and asked for complete vindication. Additional attempts to prosecute Burr failed.[470]

In those uncertain times, Jefferson's supporters were unsure which government and military officials still secretly supported Burr. Meriwether Lewis followed Jefferson's lead and reacted personally to the plot that might have cost his mentor's life. Lewis would make fighting Burr's enablers and copycats, the "Burrites," one of his main goals for the brief remainder of his life. He assured Clark, "I can never make any terms with traitors," underlining the statement for emphasis.[471] Just as adamantly, Lewis would not be able to abide the country he loved branding him another Aaron Burr.

After Burr's trial, Andrew Jackson returned to Nashville humiliated, but not defeated. He set out to clear his reputation by searching for evidence that Wilkinson was a spy for Spain, as he had proclaimed in Richmond.[472]

Two years later, Lewis's fatal journey through Tennessee may have provided Jackson with the opportunity to gain the proof he needed.

Meriwether Lewis, painted by Charles Willson Peale in 1807 on his return from the Lewis and Clark Expedition.

## CHAPTER 8

# HERO'S PEDESTAL

> [T]he information of captain L[ewis] will not merely gratify literary curiosity, but open views of great and immediate objects of national utility; and it will be seen that he has rendered very important services to his country.[473]
> —*The Wilmington Gazette*, January 27, 1807

Fame briefly boosted Lewis and Clark to new heights as newspapers heralded the explorers' unexpected return. Articles recited toasts offered at the banquet held in their honor in St. Louis: "Captains Lewis and Clark—their perilous services endear them to every American heart."[474]

The Washington elite honored Lewis with a banquet at which he was hailed as a "favorite of fortune, who has thus successfully surmounted the numerous and imminent perils of a tour of nearly four years, through regions previously unexplored by civilized man." Normally jaded Washingtonians admitted to being elated merely to sit at the same table with a man they would toast as "Patriotic, enlightened, and brave, who had the spirit to undertake, and the valor to execute an expedition, which reflects honor on his country."[475]

Lewis introduced the Mandan chief Sheheke and the Osage, whom he and Clark had invited to return with them under Jefferson's instructions. Members of the Mandan tribe who accompanied the chief were persuaded to perform a native dance at a Washington theater.[476] Tribal representatives were presented as a cultural curiosity that provided visual confirmation of the success of the expedition. Like Jefferson, the public was eager to learn about the people who inhabited the West.

Eastern socialites and politicians were not the only ones impressed by the explorers' feat. One young man who was inspired to follow in Lewis and Clark's footsteps wrote that accounts of their journey across the continent "excited a spirit of trafficking and adventure among the young men of the West."[477]

Jefferson reported to Congress, "The expedition of Messrs. Lewis & Clarke, for exploring the river Missouri, & the best communication from that to the Pacific ocean, has had all the success which could have been expected."[478] The explorers had successfully mapped future military routes. Administration critics had been deprived of the ammunition of a failure, and a grateful Congress gave Lewis and Clark an immediate financial boost. In addition to approving double pay for their time on the expedition, it awarded each 1,600 acres of land by issuing land warrants to be redeemed in government land offices.[479]

Lewis next was off to the nation's social center, Philadelphia, where he attended parties and met adoring ladies from America's new aristocracy. It was an opportunity for the military hero to win the heart of a daughter of an influential family who could boost his political and business ambitions. But none of the "bewitching gipsies," as he described them, matched the qualities he later saw in a striking, and perhaps more authentic, Letitia Breckinridge, a young woman in the rural hometown of Clark's future bride. Unfortunately for Lewis, Miss Breckinridge did not share the attraction and ran away to avoid the bowlegged hero.[480]

The official purpose of Lewis's Philadelphia trip was to meet with publisher C & A Conrad to make plans to publish the co-captain's narrative of the harrowing adventure.[481] Once Lewis approved the publisher's prospectus, it would appear in newspapers across the country, continuing to keep his name in the public eye. Lewis and Clark planned to maintain control over the first publication of their narrative to maximize profits and provide each of them with the income to support their new social status.

That goal, however, would prove unattainable. The public was so eager for details that counterfeit narratives began to appear.[482] By January 1809, even the popular river travel guide *The Navigator* claimed to contain new information gathered by Lewis and Clark.[483] Nevertheless, the much-anticipated volumes featuring Lewis's personal narrative were expected to secure his legend in exploration and extend his legacy into the realms of natural science, history, and literature.

Lewis had achieved an elevated status in society. Artists sketched his portrait—an honor typically bestowed on the wealthy or powerful.[484] One portrait of Lewis would eventually hang in the historical gallery of Independence Hall.[485] A wax figure of him was added to the collection of other national notables at Charles Willson Peale's museum in Philadelphia, where the public could gawk at the hero's likeness.[486]

Alexander Wilson, who had been rejected from Freeman's Santa Fe expedition, hoped to take advantage of Lewis's public aura to improve his flailing career. In addition to publishing bird illustration books, Wilson earned his regular income from penning articles for periodicals and seasoned his own writings with the fashionable Romantic Movement words "gloomy" and "melancholy" to fit the artistic times.[487] According to Wilson, Lewis allowed him to make use of bird specimens brought back from the expedition to create drawings in future volumes of Wilson's books.[488] Images of exotic birds from the Far West could be expected to boost sales.

As Lewis basked in the praise heaped on him, President Jefferson offered what appeared to be the crowning reward: governorship of the Upper Louisiana Territory. Lewis would replace Wilkinson and complete the remainder of the three-year term that Jefferson had just renewed. As territorial governor, Lewis would also serve as Commander-in-Chief of the Militia and Superintendent of Indian affairs, with an annual salary of

$2,000.[489] The governorship could serve as an essential stepping stone to a higher office where Lewis could continue to support Jefferson's Republican policies long after the president's retirement.

Rather than a reward, however, the appointment was simply Jefferson's next mission for Lewis. Like his selection of Lewis as his private secretary, Jefferson did not appoint him as governor for his political or administrative skills—Jefferson needed a spy, if not an agent, in the West. Jefferson's goal of the acquisition of Texas and Santa Fe remained, and Lewis had more work to do before he could rest on the personal rewards of his success. Lewis's servant would later summarize the explorer's work of territorial governor as "exploring the Louisiana."[490]

Jefferson had said that he considered the new Upper Louisiana territorial government "not as a civil government, but merely a military station."[491] In addition to expanding boundaries to the Far Southwest, part of Jefferson's legacy would rest on the successful assimilation of the Louisiana Purchase territory into the United States. Enforcing the U.S. claim required settlers to move to the territory, establish settlements, and form militias to defend it. First, prospective settlers had to be convinced that it was safe. A well-known military leader should serve that purpose.[492]

In one of the first major settlements west of the Mississippi River, St. Louis settlers lived in proximity to Osage, Cherokee, Sac, Fox, and eighteen other tribes whose territory they threatened. Any tribe could attack a lone farmstead. Although the army had begun to build forts, the limited number of troops could not offer sufficient protection. Within the settlements, law enforcement was limited and sometimes no match even for private armies that mine operators hired for security.[493] It was understood that settlers who chose to move to the territory would be expected to defend themselves.

Burr's conspiracy had demonstrated the fragility of the federal government's control over events in the West, where Spain and Britain still vied for control, and where U.S. citizens thought they could make vast fortunes under a different government structure. The territory west of the Mississippi could easily come under the influence of an enemy power or rebels when the small federal government was hundreds of miles away to the east. Men who had supported Burr's conspiracy still held power in Missouri and could be expected to undermine federal control.

Further evidence that Jefferson did not appoint Lewis for the routine duties of governor is that he gave him special assignments that detained him in the East for a year after his gubernatorial term began. Certainly, Jefferson encouraged Lewis to complete the publication of his expedition narrative when Lewis was not sought out to tell his expedition stories at private dinners.[494] Lewis even took time in Philadelphia to have Jefferson's ring and watch repaired, as if he were still a personal secretary.[495] Possibly with an eye to the dangers he would face on the frontier, Lewis also took time to purchase a pair of pistols.[496]

More significantly, Lewis remained in the East while Burr was still in the East, and a related and more critical assignment may have been to travel to Richmond, Virginia, for Burr's trial for treason.[497] Lewis's personal Memorandum Book, which he used to document his business transactions, provides a few clues to his activities. Memos confirm his arrival in Philadelphia in April 1807, where he worked into July to prepare his narrative of the expedition for publication. No additional transactions appear until October 8, 1807—during Burr's second trial—when Lewis wrote a draft for an advance on his salary as governor and "transmitted" it to "Mr. Wirt at Richmond" to be negotiated. The evidence of whether Lewis was in Richmond for the trial hinges on whether he meant the "at" to identify Mr. Wirt or to describe where Lewis was at the time the draft was transmitted.

The "Mr. Wirt" at Richmond was no doubt William Wirt, the Richmond lawyer whom Jefferson hired as chief federal prosecutor against Burr.[498] Lewis's draft was negotiated, and twelve days later, he received the funds, less the payment on a debt that he owed to an estate.[499]

Ironically, the wealthy Richmond businessman who had posted Burr's bond for trial apparently advanced the funds for Lewis's salary. It is possible that Wirt represented Lewis on the debt in Richmond and that Lewis transmitted the draft from another location. Otherwise, the most likely reason Lewis would have selected Wirt to negotiate his draft in Richmond during Burr's trial, whether or not Wirt represented him, is that Lewis was also in Richmond at the time. The fact that Lewis did not record how he transmitted the draft to Richmond or how the large sum of money was forwarded to him from Richmond suggests that he was in Richmond at the time of Burr's trial. If so, as witnesses from across the country gathered to testify against Burr, Lewis would have had a unique opportunity to gather information to determine Burr's true motives in the West, how far his supporters had infiltrated state and local governments, and how best to thwart any remaining influence.[500]

Other than Lewis's cryptic references to Richmond in his Memorandum Book, his activities during the time of Burr's trial are unknown. If Lewis was in Richmond, he maintained such a low profile that no newspaper reported his presence there. Witnesses who would have seen one of the most famous men in the U.S. did not mention him in letters, and Scott did not list Lewis among the notables he saw at the trial.[501] The attention of the nation was focused on Richmond in the summer of 1807, and if Lewis was there, the secrecy surrounding his presence raises questions about Jefferson's mission for him and why such secrecy was needed.

In any event, Lewis's notations in his Memorandum Book reveal that at the time Jefferson was using every means in his power to jail Burr for treason, his protégé Lewis was in contact with the prosecutor. Even if Wirt represented Lewis as an attorney, Lewis would have been just as interested in matters related to Burr.

Though Lewis's term had begun months earlier, he did not set out for his new home in St. Louis until after Burr's trial had ended. Lewis's Memorandum Book noted that he cleared up personal business in Charlottesville in late October 1807, before traveling west. Because Jefferson had pressing objectives for Lewis in the West, the timing suggests that he detained Lewis in the East until Burr's fate was settled.[502]

In retrospect, it was a miscalculation. In addition to Lewis's military obligations, dealing with normal administrative duties for a new territory would be challenging for any neophyte politician: new laws would have to be codified and enforced; an administrative system would need to be created; roads would have to be built; conflicting claims of ownership of valuable mining lands would have to be sorted out; and conflicts among warring western tribes would have to be settled.[503]

Wilkinson had compounded those challenges by attempting to seize power from other officeholders during his tenure as governor. St. Louis lawyer William C. Carr assessed, "There is probably no part of the United States so much torn to pieces by dissention and partyism as St. Louis and whose government is so unsettled [,] the laws of which are so few, vague, and uncertain."[504] Wilkinson's brief administration and battle with the judges left Carr with the opinion, that "with General W. as governor this territory… Louisiana will never be restored to tranquility…"[505] Some complained that his administration was not the "Government of the United States, but the Government of General Wilkinson."[506] Eventually, even the territorial militia refused to serve under him.[507] Lewis's future territorial secretary would observe that Wilkinson had stirred up so much conflict, there was hardly anyone in the territory who had not been charged with committing a crime.[508]

But general military and civil administrative duties were neither Jefferson's main assignment for Lewis, nor his measure of success. Lewis understood the latest Jefferson assignment—he confided to Clark that one of his goals would be to remove from power those who had "the infection of Burrism."[509] The objective was not to prevent westward expansion but to keep it under Jefferson's control. By that point, Burrism had grown larger than Aaron Burr. Burr was simply the face of shadowy networks of adventurers working to take Texas and Santa Fe for their own interests. Lewis may not have understood, at first, that Wilkinson was at the center of Burrism.

Three days after Lewis's appointment, Clark was appointed as the Agent of Indian Affairs for the tribes of the Upper Louisiana Territory.[510] Lewis needed his own man whom he could trust in St. Louis, and he quickly appointed Clark as Brigadier General of the Militia of Louisiana. Lewis wasted no time alerting Clark of a report that three or four Burrites presented a present danger to the civil government."[511] Clark responded by requesting deposits of gunpowder in case he needed to use force against them.[512]

Military commanders at the time referred to their staff as their "family," reflecting the trust they developed in the men they could depend on, far from their natural families at home. At first, the two explorers would share the rented governor's house with Clark's new bride, Julia.[513] Lewis was joined by a newly hired servant who had worked for Jefferson in the President's House. The servant spelled his own name "Jeau Peerny," the "Jeau" likely a phonetic corruption of "Jean," French for "John," a common practice in parts of France. Peerny may have been a mulatto immigrant from French colonies in the Caribbean.[514] In addition to performing official duties, Clark could also have served as an informal bodyguard for Governor Lewis.

The office of Territorial Secretary was filled by thirty-year-old Frederick Bates, who had the power to carry out many administrative duties of the governor until Lewis arrived.[515] Bates's commercial business of making high-interest loans to frontier soldiers at Detroit had fallen with the economy, and he needed a salary.[516] As the brother of a Lewis army friend, Bates must have concealed the fact that he was a Federalist who opposed Jefferson's policies.[517] If Lewis influenced Jefferson to have Bates appointed as Territorial Secretary, either Lewis overestimated Bates's loyalty, or the position fed his ambition. Bates soon found that he enjoyed the power he wielded as temporary governor. He finagled his new position into several government offices in which he would earn more income than Lewis. With that income, Bates bought up land warrants from Corps of Discovery members, soon owning 960 acres in what appeared to be an acquisition of land to qualify as a future territorial governor and rival to Lewis.[518]

As a rival, Bates would have learned that Wilkinson was angry that he lost his office to Lewis. He would have seen Wilkinson, as former governor and still commander of the army, as a source of power to create his own influence, independent from Lewis. Similarly, just as he had manipulated Burr, Wilkinson would have welcomed a man with Bates's vanities and ambitions as a bureaucratic spy to feed him intelligence on Lewis's actions, if not to maintain influence over his former office. Wilkinson may have lost his position as territorial governor, but he had not given up his plans to control the West.

The territory was primarily divided between families of original French immigrants and more recent settlers from the states to the east, particularly Tennesseans. Wilkinson had sided with the French faction when he served as governor, perhaps, in part, because the Spanish had also given them influence.[519] The French faction generally was anti-Republican, and Wilkinson used them to create his own sphere of power.[520] At least, that was the opinion of one of the judges who also found Wilkinson "vain and excessively fond of pageantry" with an "unbounded Love of Power" that made him "restless."[521]

Bates followed Wilkinson's example, if not his direction, to use the divisions to create his own power base. He turned to Wilkinson's supporters. Without consulting Lewis, Bates awarded appointments to three stalwarts of the French faction: Auguste Chouteau, Jr., as commander of the First Militia Regiment of the territory, his father, Auguste Chouteau, as a judge, and Manuel Lisa as Captain of the Militia.[522] Chouteau's family had helped found St. Louis, and he and Lisa had been given exclusive rights to trade with the Osage at various times.[523] Though Lewis had worked with Chouteau to stock supplies for the transcontinental expedition, the new French family officers could be expected to oppose Lewis's Republican policies and help undermine Lewis's influence. Bates could hold himself out as their voice in the territorial government.

After creating his own influence with expected Lewis opponents, Bates wrote to warn Lewis of the bitter factions he would face. He asserted that it would be necessary for the two of them and other officers to come to a "good understanding" to have any success in uniting the factions.[524] The language appeared friendly; however, given Bates's later opposition to Lewis, it should have been seen as a power play to force Lewis to negotiate and seek Bates's approval on decisions to win the support of the French faction. Bates protested in public letters that his political skills were no match for Lewis's, but privately, he bragged that he had skillfully brought harmony to the two St. Louis factions before Lewis's arrival.[525] However, the divisions Lewis found when he arrived would prove that Bates was blinded by his own ambition.

Bates was not the only crack in Lewis's hero pedestal. In the East, not everyone joined the chorus of praise. Future U.S. president John Quincy Adams spoke for the Federalist opposition in penning an anonymous poem mocking all the fuss. The poem offered false praise and suggested with ridicule that explorer Christopher Columbus be "degraded" as a hero, "Strike—Strike *Columbia* river out, And put in—River Lewis!"[526]

Then, when Lewis publicly objected to one of his expedition subordinates, Patrick Gass, publishing his own unauthorized account of the Lewis and Clark Expedition, Gass' angry editor sent Lewis an objection, dripping with sarcasm, in which he challenged Lewis's "rapid advancement in power and wealth" with Jefferson's help, while enjoying the "warbling of the Muses, who have been celebrating the '*Young Hero's name.*'"[527] The editor gave voice to the inevitable critics who thought Jefferson had given Lewis the position of Upper Louisiana Governor merely as a political plum.

Bates corresponded with Lewis for guidance on some decisions as governor before his arrival, but he also preemptively began collecting political ammunition that he could use against Lewis.[528] When Bates heard the hint of criticism of Lewis due to Gass' publications of journals, as well as a second proposed publication of a journal from expedition member Robert Frazer, Bates asked the St. Louis newspaper editor to help him obtain information about the controversy.[529] Lewis's former subordinates might provide less-than-flattering information that could be useful in undermining Lewis.

The cracks would only deepen, and Lewis's hero status would not last long enough to shield him from the political challenges he would face. A military structure had ordered his brief adult life. In St. Louis, he would jump into a bewildering cauldron of divided loyalties primed to burn a novice politician.

It would take little effort for an enemy such as Wilkinson to work through his former St. Louis minions and Bates to light and stoke the fire.

## CHAPTER 9

# STEPPING OFF THE PEDESTAL IN ST. LOUIS

> Alas! to hope for universal love is as vain as hope to build steps of sand to heaven.
>
> —*Missouri Gazette*, November 23, 1809
> To the memory of Governor Lewis

Lewis arrived in St. Louis on March 8, 1808, naively anticipating a bright future.[530] His hopes were still high four months later, as he wrote to his friend, Major William Preston. The letter between army mates differs from Lewis's usual formal writings and reveals his personality in private which attracted his nucleus of close friends. Lewis ribbed Preston for how his recent marriage had changed his priorities, "You have gained that which I have yet to obtain, a wife…," Yet he said that he still had so much passion for Miss Breckinridge that he could not bring himself to pursue her sister.[531]

The letter was like one Lewis wrote to a friend five months earlier, in which, after discussing financial transactions, he added, "So much for business, now for the *girls*." The letters reveal that, among friends, at least, Lewis had lost the stiffness his early school friend had observed. He went on to confide that he felt such a void in his heart as a bachelor that he "never felt less like a heroe than at the present moment." He was "determined, to *get a wife*."[532]

Instead, Lewis found himself married to his new position as governor—mainly as Jefferson's agent in the West—and his honeymoon period was short-lived. He seems not to have appreciated how quickly his hero status would fade as he became entangled in local political disputes to press for Jefferson's goals.

The French and Spanish laissez-faire culture did not meet Jefferson's needs for quick organization of the territory. Jefferson viewed the people in the Louisiana Territory, who had lived under undemocratic French and Spanish colonial governments, as inexperienced in self-government, like children who needed to be told what to do until they could gradually learn to manage their own affairs as citizens.[533] Despite his preference for limited government in the states, Jefferson had earlier approved giving Governor Claiborne of the Orleans Territory near-dictatorial authority over new citizens he considered similar to those in St. Louis. There is no reason to believe that Jefferson gave Lewis any different instructions for dealing with the citizens of his Upper Louisiana Territory as he pushed to extend western settlements.[534]

Militia Captain Manuel Lisa seemed to confirm Jefferson's opinion when he wrote to the secretary of war that the U.S. should not expect the inhabitants of the Upper Louisiana Territory to provide a disciplined fighting force.[535] Lewis's job of making the territory safe for settlement would have to be accomplished without a reliable militia.

The French community soon chafed under Lewis's orders. Bates would complain that Lewis acted too much as a military commander and that he refused to bend his will. He did not appreciate that Lewis's stern approach to governing fulfilled Jefferson's objectives, if not specific instructions. Bates would notice and take advantage of how Lewis's inflexibility caused him to lose popularity.[536]

As Lewis became aware of the actions taken in his absence, he did not fall for Bates's political tricks. He soon replaced officers from the French faction that Bates had appointed without his approval.[537] For reasons that would become obvious later, he also reversed Bates's decision to combine the Arkansas District along the Spanish Texas border with the middle New Madrid District. Bates reacted with fury, writing to his brother, "We differ in everything."[538]

Citizens who had staked claims to land under Spanish control also did not welcome Lewis's administration. The prior Spanish government had granted a floating right to exploit valuable mineral deposits without establishing fixed boundaries to those rights.[539] That system helped secure political support by keeping claim holders loyal to officials who could take away those rights.[540] However, it was antithetical to the U.S. recording system, which required fixed boundaries. The U.S. also questioned whether French or Spanish colonial officers ever had the authority to grant titles.[541]

The new territorial government established land boards to adjudicate contested claims. Their decisions as to who owned valuable mineral deposits could make or break fortunes. The governor's appointments to those land boards helped determine the outcomes of their decisions. As chief executive, then, part of Lewis's job would be to stand between dangerous, influential men and the people and resources they hoped to exploit to make quick fortunes.

Lewis's land board decisions and his goal of rooting out the Burrites earned him a particularly dangerous enemy in John Smith T, whose Upper Louisiana Territory mines yielded some some of the purest lead in America—at a time when lead for bullets was in high demand. The "T" in his name stood for his previous home of Tennessee. His business success contrasted with his fearsome reputation as a duelist; he was said to have shot and killed at least fifteen men. Often dressed in rough buckskin and polished boots, he was reputed to carry two pistols, two derringers, a long knife or dirk, and a rifle he called "Hark from the Tombs."[542]

Smith T epitomized a breed of ruthless, ambitious adventurers drawn to the frontier in search of quick fortune.[543] Years earlier, Wilkinson had attempted to wipe out Smith T's settlement at Smithland, Kentucky, when it served his purposes with his Spanish masters. But the two put their differences aside for mutual interests.[544] As governor, Wilkinson showed favoritism for Smith T's mining claims. He also allowed him to develop the private security forces for his mines into a small private military force, or junta, within the territory. Wilkinson, in fact, may have used Smith T and his junta to intimidate opponents, especially the judges. A territorial judge complained Wilkinson's administration had been punctuated with "open acts of violence, ... midnight riots, and above all... contempt of the Judicial authority."[545] When Smith T was indicted for attempting to supply ammunition to Aaron Burr for his rebellion, he threatened so much violence that local law enforcement officers refused to arrest him.[546]

Robert Frazer, one of the Corps of Discovery who had settled in the territory, was subpoenaed to testify as a witness in a trial in the East against Wilkinson's brother-in-law, Robert Wescott, one of Smith T's party of St. Louis Burrites.[547] In a chilling precursor to Lewis's fate, Frazer feared for his life as he took papers to Washington City in his trunks. Those papers apparently provided some corroboration for the testimony he would offer. He wrote:

> ... I was informed of a number of inquiries that some of the party (dispatched to overtake & wrest from me my papers) had been making relative to my business in Washington... I also learned... that Colo. John Smith (T) will not suffer himself to be taken by the civil authority; but has threatened and reviled me with the harshest and most bitter epithets. From this man's character as a desperado & from the servility of a vile and desperate junto of which he is the head, I really think I am in no small danger of assassination, or some other means of taking me off.[548]

Frazer reported that Smith T's small junta maintained its own arsenal and was fully capable of assassinating his enemies.[549] His report had spurred Lewis to appoint Clark as general of the territorial militia.[550]

Smith T went to work to hold meetings in St. Louis and in St. Genevieve to generate public support to petition Congress to separate his St. Genevieve fiefdom from the territory governed by Lewis. His supporters stopped short of attacking Lewis's integrity, even as they argued that the territorial government structure gave Lewis "colossal" powers as governor that negated their rights to act through their elected representatives.[551] Because of Smith T's family and political connections to Wilkinson, it should have been clear that Wilkinson wanted to undermine or remove Lewis as Upper Louisiana Governor.

To a military man with a mission to make the territory safe for settlement, local politics, as fractious and dangerous as they might be, were merely a nuisance compared to military threats. The more serious problem from Lewis's perspective was that he found the territory frontier "much extended and defenceless."[552] The U.S. lacked military forces even to explore the southwestern boundaries of the vast territory with its enemy, Spain, much less to defend against its patrols. On the northern boundary, the U.S. Army lacked forces to present a defense against the British military presence in Canada or to their tribal proxies. Before Lewis arrived in St. Louis, the territory had also lived in constant fear of being raided by tribal enemies. Amos Stoddard had experienced that the Osage attacked settlers at least once a year.[553] Soon after Lewis arrived in the territory, he sent out spies to determine what he could expect from the tribes, particularly those along the border with New Spain near Natchitoches.[554]

Making Lewis's work even more difficult, Spanish and British agents gave presents to the Osage in an effort to win their support—just as Jefferson's spies had attempted to shift the loyalty of southwestern tribes to the U.S.[555] Rodolphe Tillier, the federal factor or trade post operator, of Fort Bellefontaine just north of St. Louis, warned the secretary of war that white men were attempting to stir trouble among the tribes by spreading rumors that Spain, France, and Britain soon would regain control of the Louisiana from the United States.[556] Another warned that the British were encouraging the Sioux to attack St. Louis.[557]

Lewis correctly perceived that if the U.S. went to war with Britain, British traders would use their influence to turn tribes against the settlers.[558] The U.S. was not organized to match British bribes. British agents would tell tribal leaders that even though the Americans had taken their land, their "American Father is too poor to supply them with a blanket."[559] Spain appeared to be on the verge of regaining the loyalty of the Osage.[560] During Bates's temporary administration, he panicked and mustered the militia in anticipation of an attack.[561]

Lewis, as Governor, and Clark, as Indian agent, would spend four times more government funds on military defense than on developing the civil government.[562] As commander of a military post, Lewis set out to build forts at farther distances from St. Louis. Just before Lewis arrived in St. Louis, Clark had won the support of the Osage to build a fort in their nation by promising that the U.S. would protect them from their enemies. But forts alone would not provide safety. Tribes in the territory warred with each other even as they threatened established settlements. Clark said that the constant challenges of dealing with conflicting tribes kept him too busy to send regular reports to the secretary of war.[563]

As Lewis directed the construction of the new Fort Osage, the stated purpose was to create a meeting area for eight regional tribes.[564] The French community that benefited from trade with the Osage supported the effort when they thought Lewis planned to improve trade. Within a short time, however, they suspected the real purpose was to take tribal land. If so, Lewis fulfilled Jefferson's objectives at a further political cost.[565]

Lewis discovered that Wilkinson had issued licenses to unscrupulous traders who had charged the Osage exorbitant prices, making it impossible for the tribe to afford their necessities. Consequently, the Osage rebelled by taking the goods by force. Then, Wilkinson had failed to defend against the attacks, which Lewis said, produced an attitude among the Osage that "the white men are like dogs, the more you beat them or plunder them, the more goods they will bring you, and the cheaper they will sell them."[566] As Stoddard had warned, an Osage man attacked and killed a family on the Arkansas River.[567] Lacking a militia, Lewis responded by depriving the Osage of trade rather than by attacking them.[568]

In advising other territorial governors, Jefferson urged that they "press on the Indians, as steadily and strenuously as they can bear" to acquire land to open to settlement, and that the tribes "must see we have only to shut our hand to crush them, and that all our liberalities to them proceed from motives of pure humanity only."[569] Lewis assessed that the only tools to influence tribes were either their "love of merchandise" or "fear of punishment" and that without the power to provide one or threaten the other, a leader was like "Sampson with his locks shorn."[570] In essence, federal tribal policy was to offer the carrot with the threat of a stick. Lewis knew, however, that his unreliable militia was not a military stick he could wield.

Lewis followed the spirit of Jefferson's directives as he bluffed that he had resources to enforce them. The Osage chief White Hair told Lewis that he could not control unruly men in his tribe and that Lewis would have to do whatever he thought best.[571] When a few Osage men began stealing horses and taking traders prisoner, rather than engaging in protracted discussions with tribal leaders to bring gradual compliance with the laws, Lewis threatened to withdraw Clark's promise of protection of the tribe and allow them to be wiped out by their enemies.[572] It was a harsh threat. Lewis lost support from Chouteau and other French townspeople who traded with the Osage, but even those opposed to the policy admitted that horse stealing came to a stop.[573] Jefferson acknowledged his approval of Lewis's strategy.[574]

Lewis was equally stern with white traders, withdrawing their licenses to trade so that they would not constantly stir the tribes to war. By removing rogue traders and forcing tribes to trade only at government-run trading posts, Lewis hoped to reduce the influence of tribal leaders who could operate independently of the U.S. government and threaten war to enhance their leverage.[575] Trading posts would be established even at points where soldiers were not garrisoned. Though Lewis's actions helped calm the frontier, even his mild threats angered the secretary of war, who warned that the army could not devote more soldiers to putting down a war with the tribes when Britain threatened war from the North and East.[576]

Lewis soon grew frustrated that he was expected to bring harmony to much larger warring populations without the use of force or even the threat of it. He blamed Wilkinson for the conditions he found in St. Louis and wrote a newspaper article under the pseudonym "Clatsop" in which he criticized the prior Wilkinson administration.[577]

That public break with Wilkinson was pivotal—the wily general commanded most of the army in the Southwest. By that point, Lewis must also have suspected that Wilkinson influenced the territory's Spanish colonial neighbors. Yet, Lewis still talked frequently about his success on the expedition when he answered only to Jefferson. Given Lewis's continued personal connection to the president, he may have thought he could muster the political capital to bring even Wilkinson to heel in the West to accomplish Jefferson's mission.

Lewis's solution to harness the threat of the force of warring tribes was a creative way to play the weak hand he was dealt. But Fort Bellefontaine factor Tillier took note of Lewis's Osage policies to use later as ammunition against him.[578] Tillier, a once-wealthy Swiss immigrant who had lost his money in ventures in Philadelphia and in land speculation in the territory, was married to a sister-in-law of General Wilkinson.[579] His stepson, Clement Biddle Penrose, had been appointed to the Board of Land Claims.[580] Tillier certainly kept Wilkinson informed of Lewis's actions in St. Louis.

By 1809, Tillier was considered to have seen better days in his service and had become hot-tempered.[581] George Sibley, son of Jefferson's Natchitoches agent and spy Dr. John Sibley, had moved to St. Louis a couple of years earlier to work as Tillier's assistant.[582] Tillier and Sibley argued over bookkeeping practices and about Tillier's use of store goods for his family's personal benefit. When Tillier fired Sibley, Clark joined Bates and Fort Bellefontaine commander Captain James House in taking Sibley's side.[583] Sibley traveled to Washington to plead his case, no doubt drawing on his father's influence and his own willingness to collect intelligence for Jefferson.[584]

Jefferson's intervention does not appear in the records, but it was decided that the federal government would speed up plans to open several new posts and factories west of the Mississippi River and to close Tillier's factory at Fort Bellefontaine. George Sibley, then twenty-six, was appointed as factor of the government commissary to be established at the new Fort Osage at the Fire Prairie.[585] Tillier would not be awarded one of the new factories. It was a double insult when Sibley took goods for his new Osage factory from Tillier's closed store.[586] Jefferson's newly favored men had outmaneuvered the cranky, hot-tempered Tillier and his protector Wilkinson.

As it turned out, the real source of the fight between Sibley and Tillier may have been more than accounting differences. Besides operating a store, Sibley, like his father, would gain experience making diplomatic excursions into tribal nations, where he might also be expected to gather intelligence. Also like his father, George Sibley would take an interest in Santa Fe—after Lewis's death, George would board with spy Dr. Robinson, who would provide him a wealth of intelligence he had obtained in the West. Congress would eventually appoint George to survey a government road along the Santa Fe Trail.[587]

Lewis's conflicts with Wilkinson were mounting. Jefferson's replacement of Wilkinson with Lewis put the two at odds from the beginning for influence with the president over the course of the West.[588] Even if Lewis accepted Clark's favorable view of Wilkinson or Jefferson's transactional view of Wilkinson, Lewis's appointment weakened Wilkinson's influence as the force to be dealt with in the West.

Lewis's unexpected public criticism of Wilkinson confirmed that the general would not be able to control him. Wilkinson must have lacked the political dirt on Lewis that he usually used to manipulate other politicians. When that failed, such political operators often resorted to manufacturing it.

It may have been more than a coincidence, then, when General James Wilkinson's nephew, Benjamin ("Ben") Wilkinson, suddenly reached out to Lewis. Like Lewis, Ben had worked as a paymaster in the army, but he now operated a mercantile business with Captain Risdon H. Price directly across the street from a house rented by Clark for either his residence or store.[589] Price had formed a venture with the spy Dr. Robinson to supply hogs to Fort Osage—a contract that put them in regular contact with the outpost and provided opportunities to monitor Sibley's intelligence activities there.[590]

On a personal level, Ben was known in St. Louis for repeatedly assaulting a lawyer who defended a Wilkinson opponent, Seth Hunt, commandant of the St. Genevieve District. Hunt's only offence was his refusal to sign a statement declaring that General Wilkinson was performing an excellent job as governor—a statement Wilkinson drafted to lobby the government to renew his term.[591] The general suspected that Hunt refused to sign because he was acting as an agent for the general's local nemesis, Major Bruff.[592] A Wilkinson loyalist followed up on Ben's beating of the lawyer by catching Hunt on the streets, whipping him with cowhides, and kicking him.[593] The assault was so violent that Hunt charged General Wilkinson with attempting to assassinate him and using Ben as his designated assassin.[594]

A reputation for violence did not hinder business relationships on the western frontier. Lewis had transacted business with Ben at the end of the expedition, and he needed Ben's support.⁵⁹⁵ Banks had not yet been established in St. Louis. Most settlers traded skins or tangible goods instead of currency.⁵⁹⁶ One of Wilkinson & Price's stated lines of business was trading government bills of exchange, profiting in the trade of financial paper issued by government agents.⁵⁹⁷ When a government officer paid a debt with a bill of exchange drawn on the government, the officer pledged his personal credit that the government would stand behind the pledge by a certain date. The holder of the bill was unsure when, or even if, the government would pay the bill. The officer would be personally liable if the government did not honor the bill.

More than a decade earlier, the War Department had hired an accountant, William Simmons, to attempt to gain control over the budget at a time when the government was essentially bankrupt. Simmons met expectations by declining to pay bills of exchange from numerous officers. Ben Wilkinson's business could purchase a bill of exchange at a discount and take the risk of payment. When the bill was paid, the company made a profit on the difference between the bill and its discount. Ben's uncle was known to use his influence to control military contractors, and it is possible that he also aided his nephew's business by influencing the payment of those bills.⁵⁹⁸

Ben set out to convince Lewis that he was one of his closest friends. The general would have known from his army sources that Lewis frequently took advances against his salary and that his finances were stretched. Ben offered to honor Lewis's bills of exchange. Given the tactics that General Wilkinson used over his lifetime to manipulate and gain intelligence on people in power, it is conceivable that the general encouraged his nephew to gain Lewis's confidence to keep tabs on him—if not to influence his decisions and destroy him as a rival.

Rather than admitting defeat and loss of influence, General Wilkinson, Frederick Bates, and Rodolphe Tillier bided their time and waited for the right moment to strike back.

Aaron Burr

## CHAPTER 10

# HONOR AMONG SPIES

> I lament that in a free government like ours, we have so many detestable spies and secret informers, and it is the more to be lamented, when we see those basest of all human characters, encouraged, secreted, and protected by the public functionaries.
>
> —Ohio Senator John Smith, 1807[599]

Spies flourished where borders were fluid. The United States was only one of several competitors grappling to win control of the Mississippi Valley and the West. In that environment, ambitious men held multiple loyalties and frequently operated on multiple levels. Appearances were deceptive. Lewis should have looked behind everyone's words, and Ben Wilkinson's in particular, to question their true motives.

Compounding Lewis's challenges as governor of a young territory, Jefferson directed him to organize a new expedition. The president's promise to return Mandan chief Sheheke home remained unfulfilled.

Before Lewis arrived in St. Louis, the secretary of war had authorized a party of fourteen men under Clark's direction to return the chief.[600] Local trader Auguste Chouteau was tasked with leading the mission. As an incentive, Chouteau was authorized to engage in commercial trade with the tribes for personal profit once he was in tribal territory, though his half-brother, Pierre Chouteau, had been warned not to profit from his contact with the tribes.[601] But Chouteau failed to anticipate the risks from Sheheke's enemies. An angry rival Arikara tribe surprised Chouteau's party and overpowered them. Following a skirmish, Chouteau's party retreated to St. Louis with Sheheke.[602]

Only four months after Lewis arrived in St. Louis, Jefferson wrote to Lewis to scold him for failing to report on the status of Sheheke's return. He pressured Lewis to give the mission priority.[603] As events unfolded, Sheheke's return may have been the cover for a larger mission of greater concern to Jefferson. Whatever the true purpose, the response to Jefferson's scolding began Lewis's downfall.

Supposedly to correct the errors of the prior mission, Lewis publicly ordered the formation of a quasi-military corps of 140 U.S. volunteers to assure a force large enough to accomplish its mission.[604] Like Chouteau's operation, Lewis chose to subcontract the expedition to a private company rather than organizing it through the territorial government. Unlike the first mission, though, a new company would be formed to receive the government contract.

The company would be called "The St. Louis Missouri Fur Company."[605] Lewis would assign federal Osage Agent Pierre Chouteau to lead the portion of the expedition to the Mandan village at government expense.[606] After completing the government mission, the volunteers would travel deep into tribal territory to establish trading posts and forts for the private company.[607]

Ben Wilkinson took advantage of the expedition's combined military and commercial nature—perhaps even suggesting the idea of forming the new company at the direction of his uncle. Lewis turned to Ben to recruit the volunteers.[608] Ben would own a stake in the company, and more significantly, help direct its activities. Ben would also be expected to act as one of the factors or traders with the tribes to purchase their pelts.[609]

Partners would include Auguste Chouteau and Manuel Lisa, who had decades of experience trading and trapping. Clark and Clark's brother-in-law, Dennis Fitzhugh from Louisville, Kentucky, would also own shares.[610] In one of Lewis's reports on the earlier transcontinental expedition, he recognized, "We view this passage across the Continent as affording immence advantages to the fur trade..."[611] Lewis had counseled that if establishing a fur trade industry was essential to the nation, it should move quickly to build posts to trade fur pelts with tribes and secure the rivers to transport them to gain the advantage over British traders.[612] The new company could leverage the explorers' exclusive knowledge they had gained during the expedition.

Clark, who operated a store in St. Louis as a side business to earn additional income, would also benefit from his position as Indian agent to engage in trade with the tribes for personal profit. The fur company would be able to use government facilities under Clark's supervision to store company furs.[613] Lewis could be persuaded that men commonly sought public positions for private gain in the new republic, where ethical boundaries were less well-defined. After all, Chouteau had been given the right to engage in private trade in the prior mission.

Even as an inexperienced governor, Lewis had the political sense not to own shares in the private company at the same time as he would award it a lucrative contract. But he would not create the same standard for his brother, Reuben, who had joined Lewis in the territory. Reuben would own a share and take a major role in the administration of the business, which created the appearance that Reuben was Lewis's placeholder in the company. In fact, one of the men who volunteered for the Mandan Expedition repeated the public impression that Lewis owned an interest in the company.[614] In any case, there was no law to prevent Lewis from assuming Reuben's share once he was out of office.

In February 1809, the partners signed Articles of Agreement to form the company. Ben Wilkinson signed on behalf of Reuben, demonstrating his success in infiltrating Lewis's closest circle and likely his own role in advising Lewis to contract the mission to the company that Ben had helped direct. Three years earlier, General Wilkinson discovered that Lisa was attempting to create a trade with Santa Fe and asked Pike to stop him.[615] It is worth considering whether Ben was merely acting as an agent for his uncle to co-opt Lisa's plans through the new partnership or whether Ben used the expedition to further his uncle's plans to create a new country to rival U.S. control of the continent.

When Ben recruited Chouteau, Lisa, and others to join the expedition, he pledged to share its dangers by accompanying the party to western territory. He even promised not to return to St. Louis until Chouteau and Lisa had first returned. But Ben would either remain behind or return to St. Louis while the expedition was still in the West.[616]

As governor, Lewis then signed an exclusive agreement with the new company to return Sheheke to his home.[617] Lewis agreed to pay the company $1,500 on government credit, a healthy start for a new enterprise. More importantly, Lewis's agreement also gave the company a monopoly on trapping—no other fur company would be allowed to travel up the Missouri River beyond the Platte River. Beaver pelts were in high demand in Europe, where hunting had diminished. The expedition would have free rein to take as many pelts as possible.[618]

Even quasi-military expeditions into the West, so soon after the Burr Conspiracy panic, raised the specter that the real objective was to create a new country that would challenge the United States for territory. Lewis's attorney, William Carr, would assess that Lewis was an honest man, but an imprudent one.[619] Carr thought Lewis bore some responsibility for the troubles that would soon overwhelm him.

With Lewis's approval, Ben set out to Kentucky to recruit the 140 expedition volunteers described as "warriors, hunters, and trappers."[620] A few newspapers that had published breathtaking accounts of the Lewis and Clark Expedition now hinted that the Mandan Expedition would be a sequel worth following. Someone provided editors with information lauding the Kentucky settlers who would bravely venture into a hostile tribal frontier.[621]

A few newspapers reported that the number of volunteers was 140 "and upwards;" however, they apparently were not informed that an additional 200 French Canadians, Creoles, and private adventurers from St. Louis and other areas would comprise most of the party.[622] It is unclear whether their participation was to be made public.

The secretary of war approved $7,000 for the Mandan Expedition.[623] On March 7, 1809, Lewis paid the company with a bill of exchange for $1,500 and granted Pierre Chouteau authority to spend an additional $940 for supplies. The additional funds were to be used to buy gifts for other tribes the expedition party was expected to encounter. Lewis's personal credit was on the line until the government reimbursed him. He wrote to the secretary of war to seek payment.[624]

Lewis may not have known that Ben's or General Wilkinson's ambitions for the Mandan Expedition were likely set on prospects beyond returning the Mandan chief and northwestern fur trapping. Ben confided to tavern owner William Christy that he had sent a former Spanish territory surveyor, Ira P. Nash, to the "Spanish provinces" as part of a plan that, if successful, would make their fortunes.[625] The description of the mission to make a fortune from Santa Fe was similar to the one General Wilkinson had made to Seth Hunt for the Burr expedition into Texas.[626]

Nash, a small man known for wearing long hair and earrings, had the local reputation of being a brilliant crank. Born in Virginia, he had met with Jefferson two years earlier to help secure the release of men held in Tennessee on suspicion of being spies. Later in life, Nash admitted to having engaged in adventures in Spanish New Mexico and West Florida.[627] Nash reported to Ben that his efforts in the Spanish territory had been met with success.[628]

If Lewis had not already confided it to his new friend, Ben had probably learned that Lewis was invested in clandestine exploration of New

Spain under Jefferson's direction. A year earlier, Spanish colonial authorities led their prisoner Zebulon Pike back to Natchitoches from Santa Fe and released him.[629] General Wilkinson claimed to be relieved that Pike was safe but warned him, "you must be cautious, extremely cautious, how you breathe a word because the publicity may excite a spirit of adventure adverse to the interests of our government, or injurious to the plans which may hereafter be found necessary and justifiable by the government."[630] Publicity certainly would have been adverse to the interests of Spain and Wilkinson. The warning was ineffective. Rumors spread that Pike had discovered prospects of gold and silver mines near Santa Fe.[631]

Wilkinson instructed Pike to forward his intelligence and invited Pike to meet him for a debriefing in Washington. Pike stalled Wilkinson by claiming ill health and instead traveled to St. Louis to meet with Lewis.[632] Lewis personally reimbursed Pike, writing in his Memorandum Book that he paid Pike his expenses for hiring packhorse men "on his rout to Mexico in 1806."[633] Pike should have looked to the War Department for reimbursement if his mission was official, or to Wilkinson if, as he claimed, he had sent Pike into the Spanish provinces without Jefferson's authority. Lewis's payment for Pike's mission confirmed Lewis's role as Jefferson's agent in the Santa Fe and Texas objective and his attempt to wrest control of the mission from General Wilkinson. Ben would have known about Pike's presence in the small town of St. Louis and reported it to his uncle.

As the Mandan volunteers prepared to set out, interest in Santa Fe suddenly became more urgent as it appeared that Spain might not be able to hold its colonies in America. Spanish governor Folch had confided to Orleans Territory governor Claiborne and General Wilkinson in early 1809, that Spain could not hold off Napoleon's conquest in Europe.[634] Spain planned to cede the West Florida territory to the United States rather than to give it to France. Folch even offered the toast: "the Liberty of the new world; may it never be assailed with success by the old world."[635] As Spain revealed weakness in its ability to hold West Florida, adventurous men could assume that it also had lost the ability to defend Santa Fe. In New Orleans, Governor Claiborne noticed that his territory was filled with men who excited the public about the prospects of taking territory from Spain.[636]

The main Mandan Expedition set out from St. Louis in June 1809.[637] The St. Louis Missouri Fur Company and its successor company eventually would succeed in establishing a fur trade, but one expedition volunteer would later claim that much of the Mandan Expedition was a ruse. "We found ourselves taken in, cheated [,] chizzled, gulfed, and swindled...," he complained. The Kentucky volunteers, he said, were given no provisions or equipment for trapping. Instead, after Sheheke was returned to his home, the heralded Kentuckians were turned out to hostile tribal territory to fend for themselves without any firearms. Many of the Kentucky volunteers splintered off into companies and supposedly returned home as the French mercenaries and St. Louis adventurers, who had not been disclosed to the public, forged ahead westward.[638] Perhaps an exploratory mission toward New Spain had been Jefferson's overriding objective, masked by the trapping venture and the task to return Sheheke.

Even though Jefferson was out of office by the time the Mandan Expedition set out from St. Louis, the ex-president continued to press his goals through President Madison, urging, "we should have such an empire for liberty as she has never surveyed since the creation: & I am persuaded no constitution was ever before so well calculated as ours for extensive empire & self government."[639] From Jefferson's perspective, global dynamics had shifted, and it was no longer prudent to trust a weak Spanish colonial government to control the southwestern region of North America. The vast western territory was ripe for seizure by an enemy power, and if the U.S. failed to act quickly, the ability to extend the borders to the Rio Grande and to Santa Fe would be lost.

Adding to Lewis's challenges, if one purpose of the Mandan Expedition was to establish a Santa Fe trade route—or to position forces for a possible advance into Spanish Territory—it either rivaled, or more likely was supported by yet another expedition organized by Wilkinson's relative John Smith T. By summer 1809, Smith T's plans were already underway to send his brother Reuben Smith, Josiah T. McLanahan, and Tennessean James Patterson on a mission to Santa Fe, in part, to explore creation of a trade route that would eventually succeed as The Santa Fe Trail.[640]

Patterson's family lived in Maury County, Tennessee, where Lewis would meet his end.[641] Patterson's father, Nelson, would later serve as Secretary of the Texas Association from Tennessee, a group that pushed for Texas independence from Spain.[642] The Smith-McLanahan-Patterson party would depart St. Genevieve in November 1809, only to be captured by the Spanish and held prisoner for two years.[643]

Patterson was also friends with William P. Anderson, who had recruited mercenaries for Burr. Anderson and Jefferson spy Thomas Freeman were in the process of surveying land in Maury County, Tennessee, in late 1808, when Patterson and his father, Nelson, settled there. Anderson assisted Patterson's father by saving his land entry as Anderson made his own entry for vacant land in Maury County.[644] Patterson also had connections with Andrew Jackson protégé Captain John Brahan, who would help seek Patterson's release from the Spanish colonials. More significantly, by 1809, Patterson's connections Freeman, Anderson, and Brahan were all part of a land speculation cabal that included Andrew Jackson, and likely his silent land partner, Nashville judge John Overton. Anderson and Overton were already working on land deals with the future Fort Pickering commander, Gilbert C. Russell. Their immediate target was land in and near Tennessee, but like Senator Adair, Texas "glitter[ed]" in their eyes.

Through Ben's and, likely, the general's influence, Lewis was becoming entangled in extended missions involving men he would have suspected to be Burrites. If Lewis fully understood the extent of their connections, he would vie to seize the mission from Wilkinson.

Instead, several of Lewis's new entanglements would eventually help create the narrative that he committed suicide.

Frederick Bates

## CHAPTER 11

# HERO WEAKENED

British emissaries are bully in every quarter
—*Missouri Gazette*, September 6, 1809

In the hubris of his new appointment, Lewis boasted to his friend Major Preston that the St. Louis District offered more opportunity than any place in the United States. He encouraged Preston to move to the area "to purchase a princely fortune" before land prices rose, adding, "Were I to dwell on the advantages of this country I might fill a volume."[645]

Lewis did not hesitate to risk his personal credit to invest in his future in St. Louis. A territorial governor was required to own at least 1,000 acres of land in his territory.[646] Lewis purchased 5,700 acres in and around St. Louis, including a farm with a good spring and a house he intended as a home for his widowed mother. To finance the acquisition, he would need to sell some of the land in Charlottesville that he inherited from his father. Lewis paid $3,000 down for the land and signed an obligation to make two additional payments of $1,500—one in May 1809, and another in May 1810.[647] He also purchased cattle, possibly to provide beef for entertaining guests in his role as governor or to sell for profit.[648] St. Louis attorney William Carr correctly predicted that Lewis's land would make its owner a good return, but that owner would not be Lewis.[649] He stretched his limited finances too far and too quickly.

After Jefferson's difficulties in covering the expenses of his office as president, he and Lewis underestimated—or willingly ignored—the cash flow Lewis's new position would require.[650] The territorial government was unable to raise sufficient funds through taxes and other levies to cover its expenses. At best, it ran a deficit of over $2,000.[651] Public funds for the governor's office barely covered the cost of office rent and stationery. Lewis would be required to advance his own credit just to print a copy of the laws of the territory for public purposes.[652] Amos Stoddard had been shocked at the expenses he was expected to cover when he served as an essential predecessor to Lewis. One official dinner and ball cost him more than $600.[653] Frederick Bates was also surprised by the "considerable extra expenses" he incurred while serving as temporary governor in Lewis's absence. Bates was equally disappointed at the government's refusal to reimburse him.[654]

Lewis incurred one bill for eight barrels of whiskey—undoubtedly meant for entertaining—that amounted to more than one-tenth of his annual salary.[655] As he told Secretary of War Eustis, "The best proof I can give of my Integrity, as to the use or expenditure of public Monies, the Government will find at a future day, by the poverty to which they have now reduced me…"[656]

Lewis also found that some townspeople took advantage of his perceived wealth to overcharge him. When a doctor presented a bill amounting to more than two percent of the governor's annual salary to treat his servant, Peerny, Lewis vented that the bill was exorbitant, but "my situation in life comppels me to pay."[657]

He also overestimated the condition of the economy. An embargo Jefferson had placed against the British had thrown the country into severe recession. So many Tennesseans suddenly lacked the funds to pay their creditors that the Tennessee Legislature passed a law known to citizens as the "stay law," which gave debtors up to an additional year to pay their debts.[658]

Making matters worse, before Lewis left the East, War Department accountant Simmons informed him that the government had overpaid him for reimbursable expenses of the transcontinental expedition.[659] By May 1809, when former expedition member John Colter asked Lewis to pay him the $559 in service pay that the government had provided Lewis to pay Colter, Lewis no longer had the funds. Colter accepted Lewis's agreement to pay him at a later date.[660]

Lewis may have gambled that the expenses of public office would be worth the rewards of his stake in the fur trade. For the moment, he continued to take salary advances and borrow money from friends.[661] His servant, Peerny, claimed that Lewis had paid him little in wages since he began his service.[662]

Adding to Lewis's personal problems, the chasm between Bates and Lewis widened as the two fought over policies. Bates complained that Lewis had "been spoiled… and overwhelmed by so many flattering caresses of the *high & mighty*, that, like an overgrown baby, he began to think that everybody about the House must regulate their conduct by his caprices."[663] As the tone of Bates's writings suggests, he saw Lewis through his own lens of a jealous, persnickety bureaucrat. Bates eventually concluded that Lewis was accustomed to the military structure in which a commander expected orders to be followed without question.[664] He certainly did not appreciate that Jefferson had given Lewis military goals that required swift action. Unlike military enlisted men who were subject to lashes with a whip as punishment for insubordination, subordinate government officials had less incentive to follow their superiors' orders. Bates's vengeance was revealed when the contents of letters sent to Lewis as governor found their way into the public. Bates freely spread rumors about Lewis's problems and shortcomings.

Clark, who was known for his easy rapport with all types, thought that Lewis exaggerated Bates's untrustworthiness—until he had to work with the man after Lewis's death. It was not long until Clark began referring to Bates as "that little animale."⁶⁶⁵ Tillier's stepson later accused Bates of "barborous conduct" intended to drive Lewis insane to take his position as governor.⁶⁶⁶ Stung by the assessment, Bates would finally reflect—too late—that his own passions or ambitions blinded him.⁶⁶⁷

When Lewis concluded that he could not trust Bates, he delegated some of the territorial secretary's responsibilities to Clark.⁶⁶⁸ Bates reacted by refusing even to acknowledge Lewis in public. Relations between the two men once became so heated at a public event that Lewis challenged Bates to a duel, which only Clark's cooler head or bodyguard duties prevented.⁶⁶⁹

Lewis attempted to minimize the influence of Bates's opposition by creating his own base of support in St. Louis. One non-governmental benefit he could offer was the social prestige of membership in the Masons. Lewis established a Masonic lodge, St. Louis Lodge, No. 111, and advanced his own money to cover the expenses. The Masonic brothers chose to meet in a building that the local pool hall had formerly occupied. Ben Wilkinson and his business partner, Risdon Price, became members, as well as General Wilkinson's enemy James Bruff and spy Dr. Robinson.⁶⁷⁰

When other influential community leaders, such as Chouteau, were admitted as members, Bates also joined the lodge and challenged Lewis for leadership. Lodge members soon divided into factions.⁶⁷¹ Bates would act as lodge Master immediately after Lewis left St. Louis. As a further insult, it was Bates who would sign Clark's certificate to acknowledge his membership in the lodge.⁶⁷² Lodge records would disappear after Lewis's death.⁶⁷³

Lewis was not insensitive to public opinion. He asked Bates at least to give him the courtesy of speaking to him in public to present the appearance that the territorial government was functioning normally.⁶⁷⁴ Nevertheless, Lewis understood his mission in St. Louis as being primarily military rather than political. As an army man accustomed to taking orders and reporting missions accomplished, Lewis mainly concerned himself with whether he had the approval of the War Department, President Madison, and, more importantly, Jefferson, who, in his retirement, was still trying to control events in the West.

There were also more pressing military matters. As 1809 began, one of the most critical missions of an army post was to prepare for an impending war with Britain, the world's most powerful military force. The secretary of war ordered the militia to arm themselves and be ready for orders to defend the territory.[675] Jefferson warned Lewis to be careful in extending military obligations—as a former Virginia governor, he could recall watching the British attack Virginia cities because militia volunteers failed to muster.[676] The unreliable territorial militia put Lewis at a serious disadvantage. Detachments of the limited federal troops had marched toward the Fire Prairie and toward Des Moines, at times leaving only one company of artillerists at nearby Fort Bellefontaine in 1808.[677]

British invasion forces were still hundreds of miles and years away, but their threat loomed just over the horizon. There had long been rumors that tribal leaders were attempting to form confederations among the tribes to increase their power. As the British waited to complete a war with France before attacking the U.S., they worked to generate support among native tribes to join forces and act as their proxy soldiers to weaken the Americans. Reports came to Lewis that the British had approached the Sauk and Osage tribes. Though Clark had entered into a treaty with most of the Osage a few months earlier, some bands were not present for the signing, and the remainder now objected to it. The Osage were expected to reject British overtures, but the unknown created fear.

Further undermining Lewis's efforts, Bates gave a British agent, Robert Dickson, a license to trade with the tribes, naively accepting his vow to support the United States.[678] The license gave Dickson the right to travel among the tribes and reestablish non-American trading posts that had been closed when the U.S. took control of the territory.[679] Taking full advantage, Dickson then used his license to persuade the Sauk chief to support the British. Within five years, he would be able to deliver hundreds of tribal warriors to support the British side during the War of 1812.[680] More worrying for Lewis's missions was also the speculation that Dickson worked in league with the Spanish governor.[681] Spain's colonial government, like Wilkinson, certainly benefited from weakening Lewis's influence.

By early 1809, British merchants were said to have deposited between 10,000 to 12,000 pounds of black powder and bullets in the territory to arm regional tribes against Americans as British agents worked from Canada to encourage a coalition of northern tribes.[682] In April, rumors spread in St. Louis that parties of Sauk and Winnebago tribes threatened to attack the new Fort Belle Vue that Lewis built north of St. Louis. Townspeople were told that 300 tribal warriors were planning to enter the fort when the gates were open and kill all the soldiers with knives. One of the officers wrote that he had not slept in days, expecting an attack at any moment. Clark's spies in the territory confirmed the rumors.[683]

Lewis ordered Fort Bellefontaine commander Captain James House to send two companies of soldiers along with supplies to defend the fort.[684] He then called out volunteers and militia to muster in St. Louis and be ready to defend the territory in their absence.[685] Ben Wilkinson served as captain of the St. Louis Company.[686] But true to Lisa's prediction, most of the men in the territory refused to volunteer. Only three companies marched into St. Louis.[687] Volunteers then refused to march to defend Fort Belle Vue, and Lewis was forced to order the minutemen militia to march, leaving few soldiers to defend St. Louis.[688]

Rather than assuring the townspeople, the muster may have produced the opposite effect. Volunteer rank-and-file militia that generally elected their own commanders were known for each wanting to be the leader or to direct the leader. Troops with time on their hands milling around town added critics for every action Lewis took.

The overall effect was that the remainder of the St. Louis townspeople, vulnerable to attack by tribes on the edge of American settlement and situated hundreds of miles from any significant military force, panicked. A wealthy man who had spread the rumor of the Sauk attack further attempted to stir opposition to Lewis and his administration by claiming that Lewis had refused to meet with him. He implied that Lewis had little concern about protecting the people of St. Louis and that Lewis would be responsible for the slaughter that followed.[689]

Sauk chief Black Hawk later wrote that if his warriors had reached the new fort before it was fortified, they would have slaughtered all the soldiers by June 1809. But the immediate panic died down when it was discovered that the men spreading the rumors and sowing divisions were British subjects. More telling, they were members of a rival fur trading company.[690]

Jefferson may have counseled Lewis on the importance of having a newspaper to promote his administration's actions and counter its critics. As Lewis prepared to assume the governorship, he had encouraged Joseph Childress to move to St. Louis with a printing press.[691] Childress' *Missouri Gazette* called for calm as it revealed the identities of the original rumormongers and suggested that the laws honor the British agents with the title of "knights of the rope's end"—in other words, that they be hanged.[692] Lewis may have been imprudent in his land purchases and personal conflicts, but he demonstrated political skills in preventing a needless war with the tribes. And his newspaper dutifully, but rightly, gave him the praise for his prudence that his critics withheld.

Lewis's term as governor was set to expire in early 1810, unless President Madison chose to renew it.[693] For months, Lewis had planned to travel to Washington to ensure his position was secure in the new administration, and then to go to Philadelphia to meet with his publishers and prepare for the overdue publication of his expedition narrative.[694] The panic and its fallout forced Lewis to delay his trip east. The best he could do was to arrange for an unidentified "gentleman of respectability" to send a letter to the *National Intelligencer* newspaper in Washington praising his actions in putting down the British-influenced tribal threat.[695]

Though the rumored attacks from regional tribes never materialized, British agents nevertheless accomplished part of their mission. The settlers' lives and fortunes depended on their security from attack, and Lewis's reluctance to join in the panic, as well as his perceived failure to muster a credible military defense, raised doubts about his administration. Bates noticed that the public was left in a state of unease.[696] Bates's ambitious mind imagined that ninety percent of the territory would choose him over Lewis in an election. In his view, most people in the territory expected that Lewis would react to the growing opposition by leaving St. Louis permanently.[697] And that may have been a view he communicated to Wilkinson through their contacts.

Tillier and Wilkinson had waited for Lewis to lose his hero's invincibility. By March 1809, Jefferson was no longer in office to protect his protégé. When Wilkinson left from a stint in Washington and returned to the Southwest in mid-April 1809, he, Bates, and Tillier appear to have coordinated their political attack.

## CHAPTER 12

# SECRET SERVICE REVEALED

> [W]ill it not be proper to rebut... [the] charge of this government sending a spy to Santa fé by saying that this government has never employed a spy in any case
> —Thomas Jefferson to James Madison, August 30, 1807

The first of a series of letters charging Lewis with misconduct was addressed to the president and bore a signature purporting to be that of the former Fort Bellefontaine factor, Rodolphe Tillier. The letter first complained about Lewis's threats to the Osage and then complained that Lewis had ordered soldiers to march from St. Louis to defend Fort Belle Vue based on what it called "idle gossip." Neither charge appeared to be more than a typical grievance from a disgruntled former officer. But the letter then provided ammunition when it alleged that both Lewis and Clark would benefit personally from the expenditure of government funds for the Mandan Expedition due to their financial interest in the St. Louis Missouri Fur Company.

More significantly, the letter then derided Lewis's claim that hundreds of armed Mandan Expedition volunteers were merely marching west to hunt beaver, calling it an "absurdity." Some of the party, it claimed, operated under

"Hostile views about the Spaniards in Mexico." It suggested that after returning Sheheke to his home, expedition members planned to use the pretext of hunting beaver to attack foreign hunting camps, or worse, the interests of Spain.[698] At a minimum, it charged a violation of the Neutrality Act. But it also hinted that Lewis and Clark might be engaging in a Burrite takeover of western territory to establish a new country west of the Mississippi River.

Tillier was not the scribe for the letter written in plain English. The Swiss immigrant still wrote in French, and even in French, his syntax was difficult to decipher.[699] Assistants no doubt helped write his correspondence when he served as factor. The former factor no longer employed assistants, and if Tillier wrote the letter, someone certainly assisted.

The letter said that after "mature deliberation" Tillier decided to mail it to the Superintendent of Indian Trade and let him decide whether to forward the charges to the president or "bury them in oblivion." The superintendent was General John Mason, who had provided a home to Ben Wilkinson during his upper teenage years and who may have served as a mentor.[700] The effect was the same. Mason forwarded the letter to President Madison without any substantiation of the claims, though he pointed out that Tillier was a former factor at Fort Bellefontaine.[701]

Providing fodder for the Tillier claims if the few War Department clerks chose to investigate, newspapers across the country had reprinted the *Missouri Gazette's* touting of commercial enterprises progressing in the territory under the watchful leadership of Governor Meriwether Lewis. The editor cited a bullet factory built by John Smith T that could convert Missouri's rich lead deposits into enough bullets to corner the market on ammunition. Concerning to the War Department, the factory could supply an arsenal west of the Mississippi larger than the U.S. Army's in the East.[702]

The newspaper editor's praise of the Mandan Expedition could also be given a different interpretation in light of the Tillier allegations. The editor said that because of the St. Louis Missouri Fur Company's connection to Lewis, Clark, and the other men associated with the company, the expedition would become "a source of incalculable advantage." He bragged that the expedition force would be so strong that it would "bid defiance to any hostile band they may meet with" especially once they had constructed their fort in the West.[703]

On the surface, either project appeared to be an innocent commercial success that any governor would tout. In the bitterly divided political climate of the time, however, Lewis's enemies could portray the combination of a military expedition establishing an impenetrable fort near New Spain and the development of an ammunition production facility that would rival the one used by the U.S. Army as evidence of another separation movement.

Though the Mandan Expedition undoubtedly exceeded the numbers and possibly the limits approved by the War Department, and Ben Wilkinson's interest in the Spanish provinces made their activities questionable, accusations of Lewis's disloyalty should have been viewed with skepticism, given his service on the transcontinental expedition.

The timing suggests that Wilkinson persuaded Tillier to mail charges against Lewis. Tillier's April 27 letter coincided with Wilkinson's reappearance in the Southwest in April 1809. The general returned from Washington City, armed with bureaucratic intelligence and a new motivation to undermine Lewis. Wilkinson needed to prove his importance to the new administration and protect his influence in the West.

Near the time of Wilkinson's return, Tillier heard that he had lost his trading post because Clark had deceived his supervisor, General Mason. Perhaps the accusation came from information Wilkinson had obtained—or claimed to have received—from his sources in Washington City. Tillier was so infuriated by the allegation that he referenced it in his Last Will and Testament a year later.[704] In fact, Tillier's April 27 letter was just one of four that Tillier sent in rapid succession.

Near the same time as Tillier's barrage of letters, the secretary of war almost immediately received more serious charges that would prompt a strong rebuke—Governor Lewis was carrying on suspicious operations through Indian subagents outside the federal chain of command.[705] Those charges appear to have come from Wilkinson. Within days of Tillier's letter, Wilkinson sent the secretary of war a letter in cipher, making him aware that someone acting with apparent government authority was attempting to interfere in events in New Spain.[706] The secretary, through Wilkinson's charges or from a separate investigation, would conclude that Lewis was abusing the agency system to carry on work without the knowledge of Madison's War Department.

Tillier's charge that Lewis might be working to attack Spanish interests was lent credibility by Wilkinson's allegation that Lewis was engaged in secret operations because it was true. Lewis seems to have exploited the vagaries of Jefferson's new system of Indian agents and trading posts by appointing his own subagents to carry out his covert missions under the guise of tribal trade and regulation.[707]

Lewis may have discovered the idea when he delegated some of Bates's duties to Clark. It was a natural progression. The Indian agent's mission to win tribal loyalty inside U.S. territory matched the mission of Jefferson's spies to shift tribal loyalties beyond official borders. Lewis may also have discovered that other tribal agents used their positions to exercise government authority without direct supervision from Washington.[708] Secretary of War Eustis would later insist that his office was the only one with the authority to appoint subagents.[709] But Clark defended that Lewis obtained approval to appoint subagents, presumably with Jefferson's help and maybe at his encouragement, to facilitate missions off the record.[710]

Further adding fuel, Tillier's letter arrived in Washington near the same time as a letter from Clark reporting on the duties of Lewis's special agent, James McFarlane, and other subagents.[711] Clark sent his report in the normal course of his duties to receive reimbursement of expenses. Other than Lewis's brother Reuben, James McFarlane—whose uncle had been the rebel killed during the Whiskey Rebellion in Pennsylvania—was

Lewis's most-trusted subagent. Clark would refer to McFarlane as one of Lewis's "particular" or close friends.[712] He had moved west just prior to Lewis's arrival in St. Louis. McFarlane was the only subagent Clark listed as "special agent."[713]

Though Congress had approved St. Louis trapper and businessman Pierre Chouteau as the Osage agent, Lewis asserted authority as territorial governor to appoint McFarlane as Osage subagent and to hire McFarlane's brothers. Lewis explained his official appointment of McFarlane in December 1808, as an effort to correct irregularities in relations with the tribes.[714] His subagent appointments seemed to have escaped the attention of the War Department until Wilkinson's letter questioned Lewis's motives.

Like Jefferson's appointment of Dr. Sibley as Indian agent at Natchitoches, the title of "Special Agent in the St. Francis" gave McFarlane an official cover to carry out operations with the tribes.[715] Near the time Pike met with Lewis to discuss his Santa Fe mission, Lewis paid McFarlane over $700, nearly a third of his annual salary, to lead a party supposedly to search for saltpeter caves in the territory. Lewis was carrying documents related to that payment with him to Washington for reimbursement at the time of his death.[716] Lewis was also carrying sketches of the St. Francis River, where he had directed McFarlane to go.[717]

Under Lewis's orders, Clark had appointed Lewis's brother, Reuben, and Dr. John Hamilton Robinson, one of Pike's expedition spies, as tribal subagents.[718] Robinson was known to have worked on making maps, attempting to recruit adventurers, and acting as a diplomat to win support among groups friendly to liberating Texas from Spanish rule. The Madison administration eventually provided Robinson cover with another official title, and later, his work in the acquisition of Texas and Santa Fe would become public.[719]

Lewis's creative manipulation of the bureaucratic system in some ways mirrored Wilkinson's, but Lewis's choice of McFarlane as his special agent destroyed its cover. One of Bates's secret informants reported that

McFarlane was illiterate and rough, and noted that he bragged about having more authority than a subagent should have. When McFarlane's overconfidence drew the informant's attention to his actions, he found them "mysterious." And McFarlane was not as circumspect as Robinson. McFarlane eventually boasted to the informant that his real purpose as a special agent was to perform secret missions—presumably for Lewis.[720]

Lewis's novel use of subagents effectively circumvented the primary Osage Agent, Pierre Chouteau.[721] McFarlane would not be required to report his actions or the intelligence he acquired to anyone but Lewis or Clark. Perhaps Lewis delegated missions to McFarlane and Robinson as friends he thought he could trust, just as Jefferson delegated such missions to him—in effect, using subagents to Lewis in his role as Jefferson's principal agent for western missions.

The area where McFarlane's actions created the most conflict was the newly defined Arkansas District along the border with New Spain, which Lewis re-separated soon after arriving in St. Louis. Lewis's new law further prohibited white settlement in certain areas of the district, ostensibly to protect the bands of Osage, Cherokee, Chickasaw, and other tribes that lived there. However, prohibitions on settlement also gave Lewis's agents freer rein to move throughout the district along the border with Spain, unnoticed by settlers.[722] He sent McFarlane to the St. Francis and Arkansas rivers with the official mission to halt illegal traders.[723]

Lewis's subagents should have found support from federal soldiers manning a trading post that the federal government established on the Arkansas River in 1805. Like the federal garrison at Natchitoches, the Arkansas Post provided the military a justification for having a presence near the border with Spanish Texas.[724] The Arkansas District, supported by the Arkansas Post, should have given spies interested in Texas and Santa Fe a wide base of operations along the boundary with Spain.

But the Arkansas area had attracted groups of white men whose lives revolved solely around an abundance of hunting and whiskey.[725] Army officers reported that McFarlane became so anxious to remove the remaining white hunters from the district that he threatened to tie them to trees and whip them if they delayed.[726]

In a fashion more Federalist than Republican, Lewis may have attempted to keep the population of the territory closer together to make the citizens easier to regulate with a small number of enforcement officers. But it would not have escaped Wilkinson's attention that Lewis's orders extended his control over the district, preventing Wilkinson from amassing his own mercenary army along the border with Texas, as he would later. Maybe at Wilkinson's suggestion, Arkansas Post commander George Armistead argued that Lewis had no authority to prevent white settlers from entering the Arkansas District, and he refused to enforce the order.

Then, in late 1808, when McFarlane gave orders for federal troops to leave the Arkansas District to protect a band of Arkansas Osage as he led them to St. Louis, Armistead tried to stop him. Another officer even tried to persuade rival tribes to attack the Osage party. McFarlane could have been killed in the process. It is doubtful Armistead would have taken such a bold action without Wilkinson's approval.[727]

By summer 1809, McFarlane was forced to deal with a new Wilkinson loyalist, Captain Gilbert C. Russell, when Russell assumed command of the Arkansas Post in the Arkansas District. Russell, whose family lived near Dandridge in Jefferson County, Tennessee, also assumed command of Fort Pickering on the west bank of the Mississippi River in Tennessee.[728]

Significantly, McFarlane's "mysterious" actions in the Arkansas District took place at the same time as a burst of activity farther south near the Red River along the Texas border. A year earlier, Dr. Sibley had organized a new expedition up the Red River and recruited Natchez landowner Anthony Glass to lead it. The expedition represented a change in strategy because Glass was rumored to use a hardware store he owned at Walnut Hills on the Mississippi River to fence stolen property for the network of Natchez Trace and Mississippi River robbers. Glass carried a commission from the federal government in case he was challenged; however, Governor Claiborne knew nothing of any government involvement.[729]

Settlers noticed that the Glass Expedition was equipped with mining and assaying equipment. Rumors spread that Glass's party would search for the elusive Spanish silver mines. When Claiborne heard that the civilian Glass had been given the rank of "captain," he warned, "It has a squinting towards Burrism." Sibley denied the charges, but something in Sibley's denials made Claiborne suspicious.[730]

The Glass party lived among the tribes along the Red River for several months. In addition to engaging in trade with the tribes to win their support, Glass recorded intelligence about the Red River area that the War Department or Wilkinson could use. Then, his party discovered a mound of silver-colored metal that weighed more than a ton. Tribes in the area, he learned, made their spears from the metal.[731] Detachments of the Glass party returned to Natchitoches and Natchez in late 1808. Glass's discovery of "silver" was too exciting to keep a secret, and rumors flew.

The remainder of the Glass Expedition returned to Natchitoches in May 1809. Glass dutifully handed Dr. Sibley a journal in which he had documented his intelligence. He also turned over a chunk of the metal the party had extracted from the source. Dr. Sibley examined the metal specimen. He quickly concluded it was not silver; however, he speculated that it could be even more valuable, possibly platinum.[732] The discovery of the metal proved significant in testing the spies' motives and loyalty to the United States. When Sibley reported Glass's mission to the secretary of war, he forwarded the metal sample but withheld Glass's journal containing the intelligence. Instead, Sibley immediately sent out a follow-up expedition in June 1809, with funds to purchase the rare metal from tribes.

Time was of the essence. A member of the Glass party who returned to Natchez was able to organize excited adventurers into a private rival expedition.[733] Claiborne thought the party was more dangerous than an unaffiliated group of prospectors; he reported that a group of thirty men who were forming a party in Natchez had interests contrary to those of the United States.[734] He was unaware that "silver" had been found, because Sibley apparently also withheld the information from him.[735]

If Glass was connected to the Natchez Trace, Natchitoches, and Mississippi River network of robbers, as alleged, the discovery would have gained their attention as well. Any maps or journals showing the location of what the public considered a great silver lode would be easier for robbers to steal than the metal itself. Such documents could be almost as valuable.

A hidden lode of precious metal, closely guarded by the Spanish government, had the potential to upend all strategic calculations in the West. Eastern adventurers had long dreamed of finding the silver mines. Traitorous politicians had envisioned the mercenary armies they could raise with that wealth and create their own empires in the West. Once the public learned of the discovery, the small network of western spies sprang into action.

As McFarlane traveled through the Arkansas District, Major Amos Stoddard crossed over the Mississippi River from Fort Adams and traveled up the Red River toward Texas. If Stoddard met with Glass along the Red River, no record was made or survived. For public purposes, Stoddard had the cover of gathering information for a treatise on the Louisiana area, *Sketches, Historical, and Descriptive of Louisiana*, which he would publish three years later.[736] He was also attempting to find evidence of the establishment of a Welsh colony that predated Spain's claim to the continent, at least the portion west of the Mississippi River, which Spain claimed.[737] Stoddard recorded that he was in the Red River area in February 1809.[738] He certainly would have been in the area when Glass returned from his expedition with the intelligence he had gained and the chunk of supposed silver. Stoddard was known to have visited Natchitoches during that time and to have met with Dr. Sibley.[739]

143

The southwestern U.S. border with New Spain also drew men from Nashville, whose interest in wresting control of Texas from Spain would later become clear. One such man was Captain John Brahan, who was known to have traveled to Fort Adams in April 1809. He had led his company from Hiwassee Garrison in Tennessee to Fort Adams, where he relinquished command to serve simultaneously as receiver of public monies for Chickasaw land sales in Nashville. Brahan quartered at Wilkinson's Columbian Springs, where Wilkinson described him as "One of my Captains." Wilkinson gave Brahan a leave of absence due to his new position. With that freedom, Brahan remained in the Lower Mississippi for several weeks before returning to Nashville without his company.[740] Fort Adams was only a three-day journey by boat and horseback from Natchitoches. Brahan would have been in the Fort Adams-Natchitoches area at the same time as both Glass and Stoddard.

Before traveling to Fort Adams, Brahan had communicated with—and possibly met with—John Smith T at the Hiwassee Garrison, which was located near Smith T's Tennessee town Kingston. In February 1809, Smith T submitted a proposal to Brahan to sell large quantities of lead to U.S. forts, promising delivery to St. Genevieve on the Mississippi River in August 1809.[741] The timing and delivery location were reminiscent of Smith T's plans to supply Burr with lead and munitions on the Mississippi for his expedition in 1806.[742] Smith T's offer as an armament supplier more appropriately should have been sent to the military agent authorized to procure supplies for Mississippi River forts or directly to the War Department; Brahan had no authority to accept it. The unusual offer raises questions about Smith T and Brahan's relationship and whether they discussed upcoming expeditions to Santa Fe and Texas.[743]

In July 1809, another Nashvillian, Lieutenant Walter H. Overton, arrived in the Arkansas District to take command of the trading post and with orders to build a fort.[744] Overton was the nephew of Nashville lawyer, Judge John Overton, one of Andrew Jackson's partners in the Chickasaw Bluffs land where Fort Pickering was situated. In fact, Walter H. Overton's father was so close to Andrew Jackson that he had served as a second to Jackson in a duel. Walter would work in the Arkansas District, in contact with Andrew Jackson's protégé, Gilbert C. Russell, who had command of the federal trading post as well as a position as Fort Pickering commander.[745] Walter Overton had accepted his army appointment in Nashville at the same time Russell was recruiting soldiers for his own company there.[746] Just before leaving Tennessee, Walter helped Russell clear up a survey line on a lot Russell had purchased in Maury County, where Lewis would die a few months later.[747]

Wilkinson would have learned of the discoveries on the Red River when he returned to New Orleans from Washington, after a brief stop in Havana, Cuba.[748] He sent a letter to the secretary of war coded by cipher in May 1809, requesting permission to take action in New Spain.[749] Wilkinson followed up in early June with his letter, which apparently charged that Lewis was acting outside his authority.[750]

If Lewis or Wilkinson operated to keep their Red River activities secret, both lost control when explosive rumors leaked from Natchitoches and focused Madison's War Department's attention on the area. On May 1, 1809, First Lieutenant Francis Newman, who served in the artillery regiment with Major Amos Stoddard and Captain James House, wrote letters from Natchitoches to his wife's Spanish family back in New Orleans to warn that there was an active attempt to separate western territory from the Spanish. He claimed that the U.S. government and the Spanish Texas governor were in support of the plot. Newman urged his Spanish in-laws to leave the country to avoid the "horrible disaster" that he anticipated. [751]

Newman's letters were placed in the hands of New Orleans governor Claiborne, who forwarded copies to Wilkinson, demanding an explanation. Wilkinson professed that the letters were forgeries, but he waited until September 1809, to send copies of the letters to Secretary of War

William Eustis, after he had taken full advantage of them. News of the letters spread to Washington, nevertheless.[752] Newman denied writing the letters, but after Claiborne had him interrogated, he doubted the denial.[753] Claiborne also interrogated Aaron Burr's son to see whether Burr was involved in the plot. In fact, at that moment, Aaron Burr was in Europe seeking funding for such an expedition to pull Spanish territory and possibly western states into a new country.[754]

Wilkinson hedged his bets by alerting Spanish officials in Texas. Recognizing the threat as serious, from June through October 1809, Spanish colonials dispatched patrols from San Antonio to track down and stop American adventurers.[755] Claiborne understood that patrols arrested one group of men from New Orleans.[756] Presumably, like the earlier interaction with Nolan's party, the patrols also had the authority to kill American adventurers they encountered.

The spies' motives in 1809, the year of Lewis's death, would be revealed by the culmination of their coordination three years later. Whether the plot Newman reported or another finally proved successful, Spanish governor Salcedo would be deposed by American and Mexican adventurers at San Antonio in 1812 as part of a filibuster known as the "Gutierrez-Magee Expedition." The Tennesseans in the party would be shocked when their rogue Mexican conspirators chose to take the governor to the edge of town and assassinate him by cutting his throat.[757]

The leader, Lieutenant Augustus Magee, graduated from West Point in 1809 and went to New Orleans to serve under Wilkinson. By 1812, he joined with Mexican rebel Jose Bernardo Gutierrez, who, a year earlier, had traveled up the Natchez Trace to stay with Judge John Overton in Nashville before traveling to Washington to lobby for support.[758] Together, Magee and Gutierrez raised an army of adventurers from New Orleans along with highway bandits who had settled in the no man's land along the Sabine River on the temporary U.S. border with New Spain near Natchitoches.

The motley band they named "Republican Army of the North" was successful in driving Spanish officials from southeastern Texas for a brief period.[759] General Wilkinson's sons were major participants, as were John Smith T's brother Reuben Smith and his associates Patterson and McLanahan, whose release from captivity on their venture toward Santa Fe was supported in Nashville by Andrew Jackson and his protégé Brahan.[760] By 1812, Arkansas Post commander Walter H. Overton would command the U.S. fort at Natchitoches and offer assistance to the plot with army resources.[761] Lewis's subagent, Dr. Robinson, would play a duplicitous supportive role on behalf of the administration, and Jefferson's spy, Dr. Sibley, would coordinate support from area tribes.[762]

After Magee's forces suffered a setback and his agreement with Salcedo was rejected by his fellow adventurers, he became a liability to the mission. In a narrative similar to one later told about Lewis, it was reported that Magee suddenly became mentally deranged, walked into his tent alone around midnight, and killed himself.[763] His unexpected death created an opportunity for Gutierrez to command Magee's army briefly—until an exiled Cuban general arrived with reinforcements he had raised among Cuban immigrants in New Orleans to finish the mission.[764]

Additional evidence of Wilkinson's Cuban connections with the plot surfaced in 1809, when Newman reported that French mercenaries were waiting in Cuba for a signal to join the Texas separatists. In 1810, as Wilkinson traveled east to be tried for treason, his ship stopped in Cuba. According to a newspaper account, the ship's captain helped secure the release of French emigres who had been imprisoned on suspicion of being involved in the separate Miranda Expedition to South America.[765]

As the spies worked along the Arkansas District-Texas boundary in 1809 to fulfill Jefferson's mission to acquire Texas and Santa Fe, Lewis likely was aware of some of their activities and provided support. And, likely at Jefferson's prodding, he would have supported the view that the filibuster to take Texas was a continuation of the fight of republicanism versus monarchy that he had supported since the French Revolution. But like Dr. Sibley, the spies may not have made full disclosure to Lewis—Lewis did not know that Stoddard had left Fort Adams to travel up the Red River.[766]

The culmination of events in 1812, then, suggest that in the summer of 1809, Jefferson's and Lewis's spies were at work to take Texas and Santa Fe and that James McFarlane, Walter H. Overton, and Gilbert C. Russell not only would have been well-positioned in the southern Arkansas District to provide support to the effort, they would have been involved in the operation.

It is also clear that Wilkinson was working to remove or destroy Lewis as a rival for control over the mission. Wilkinson benefited from the fact that Lewis's attention during much of the period was distracted by the public panic from rumors of a tribal attack by the British or Spanish agents. If someone directed British agents to light a fire in the St. Louis tinderbox to limit Lewis's ability to control actions south along the border with New Spain or west, where the Mandan Expedition approached the New Spain border, it was an efficient move. For a political operator like Wilkinson, it would have been child's play.

Then, in a one-two punch, the succeeding damage caused by Tillier's and Wilkinson's charges to the War Department would consume Lewis's personal attention and threaten his power for the brief remainder of his time in St. Louis. The fallout from the charges would ensure that Wilkinson, rather than Lewis, would control the Texas invasion. On the eve of war with Britain, Lewis's Washington critics would hear rumors that parties in the West were again plotting to split the country, that Lewis had sent an expedition of hundreds of volunteer soldiers toward Spanish territory, and that Lewis had acted outside his authority by appointing his own agents to work with the tribes along the Texas border.

The political world that seemed to be Lewis's for the taking only a year earlier was about to come crashing down on him.

## CHAPTER 13

# HERO SHATTERED

> [D]id your Excellency never attend to the advice given to those who have glass houses?
> —David McKeehan to Meriwether Lewis, April 7, 1807[767]

Secretary of War William Eustis responded to letters from Tillier, Wilkinson, Clark, and Lewis by lobbing a political bomb from Washington in July 1809.[768] Eustis used ammunition from the letters to deny Lewis's request for reimbursement of a portion of the funds for the Mandan Expedition and other expenses totaling about $4,000—twice the amount of Lewis's annual salary. Eustis criticized Lewis for attempting to use government funds to benefit private commercial interests. He then warned that Pierre Chouteau would be fired as Osage agent due to Lewis's decision to take him from his post to lead the Mandan Expedition.[769]

For emphasis, Eustis topped off his insults to the man who seemed to have received unlimited favors from the government with the point that the president—now Madison—had been consulted and that he approved the harsh response. That statement shook the foundations of Lewis's new life in the West, built on holding a special trust from the president.[770]

Lewis had put everything in his life at risk to accomplish the president's goal to acquire and hold the territory that today is much of the Western United States. He seems not to have appreciated that the unique authority Jefferson delegated to him ended once Madison took office. Jefferson, too, may have overestimated his post-presidency influence over Madison as he still pushed Lewis to accomplish his goals. The secretary's stinging letter would have created an epiphany that the spying operations Lewis had engaged in through his subagents had lacked legal authority since Madison's inauguration in March. The letter would also have helped the normally prudent Lewis see his folly in taking a personal financial interest in the Mandan Expedition.

Worse, at a time when a man's reputation meant more to him than money or life, Lewis understood that the tenor of the letter amounted to the secretary of war's charge that the true purpose of the Mandan Expedition and Lewis's actions toward New Spain were to establish a rival nation. Eustis did not state that direct allegation, and Lewis must have interpreted Eustis's criticism based on Tillier's and Wilkinson's charges that he learned through his own informants. Lewis's response may also have revealed an already present worry that the Mandan Expedition and his spying activities toward Texas and Santa Fe could be perceived as skirting the boundaries of the law. Though Eustis's letter stopped short of accusing Lewis of anything more serious than acting outside his authority and self-dealing, Lewis heard "traitor." He heard "Burr."

Burr had been the focus of Lewis's anger when it appeared that he was the mastermind behind the conspiracy that threatened to undermine his mentor, Jefferson. If Lewis had not understood from Burr's trial in Richmond that Burr had merely been Wilkinson's fall guy, his experience fighting with Wilkinson and his Burrites in the West had made it more evident.

From the secretary of war's letter, Lewis believed that someone—likely Wilkinson—was working through the government to brand Meriwether Lewis as the new Aaron Burr. Wilkinson had just spent months in Washington with access to the secretary of war. Lewis may also have considered that Wilkinson could have entrapped him through the Mandan Expedition into providing the political dirt that he lacked. With that belief, Lewis could easily conclude that Wilkinson was setting him up as the new scapegoat for a new Wilkinson invasion of New Spain.

Lewis responded to the charges immediately. Expressing his Romanticism-Era sensibility in a rare display of emotion for his official correspondence, he admitted that Eustis's allegations had caused him pain. He denied that he had ever spent money on behalf of the government that was not for the public benefit or failed to account for it properly. As to Pierre Chouteau, Lewis defended his decision by asserting that, as militia commander of the territory, he had authority to order Chouteau to lead the Mandan Expedition; therefore, Chouteau had not abandoned his post.

Lewis admitted that the expedition would hunt and trade for commercial purposes once it returned the Mandan chief. But he denied that the expedition of armed volunteers near Spanish territory had a clandestine purpose like Aaron Burr's attempt to create a new country in the West. Lewis assured the secretary that the expedition party "have no intention with which I am acquainted, to enter the Dominions, or do injury to any foreign power."

By adding the conditional term "with which I am acquainted," he may have begun to suspect General Wilkinson's influence on his nephew, Ben. And by defending that the expedition would take no action to "do injury to any foreign power," perhaps he began to worry that his friends in the Mandan Expedition had exceeded their authority to involve him in legally "hostile actions" against Spain that violated the Neutrality Act. His real worry would have been the "hostile actions" he had coordinated for Texas and Santa Fe. At the least, Jefferson's critics could portray the actions as another Miranda Expedition that merited prosecution, and they could use the charges to hound Jefferson in his retirement.[771]

Lewis refused to be Wilkinson's fall guy. He protested, "Be assured Sir, that my Country can never make 'A Burr' of me—She may reduce me to Poverty; but she can never sever my Attachment from her."[772] "A Burr" was a description of how Aaron Burr signed his name. The bewildering implications of the charges would take time to process. Rather than cowering, Lewis's immediate instinct was to fight.

His reply would not reach Washington until September 8. In the meantime, Lewis feared that federal officials would believe the charges. If the president replaced him as governor before he had an opportunity to defend himself, his reputation would be ruined, and his mentor, Jefferson, could be vulnerable. Disappointing a patron was one result a protégé worked to avoid, but exposing the patron to harm was inexcusable.

The avalanche of crises triggered by Eustis's letter compelled Lewis to plan an urgent trip to Washington City, not only to straighten out his reimbursements. Lewis added that he would:

> therefore go on by the way of New Orleans to the City of Washington with all dispatch—… [25 August] I have appointed for my departure from St. Louis. I shall take with me my papers, which I trust when examined, will prove my firm and steady attachment to my Country, as well as the Exertions I have made to support and further it's interest in this Quarter.[773]

It was not uncommon at the time for letters to be opened by curious postmasters and mail riders. By stating the route he would take, Lewis notified any enemies who chose to monitor his mail where he could be found.[774] Maybe more critical for Lewis and his enemies, he revealed that he would take to Washington papers containing details of his activities in the West—and by implication, Wilkinson's.

The War Department's decision that Lewis would not be reimbursed for thousands of dollars due to impropriety leaked to the public—perhaps through Bates—and would have created a scandal in St. Louis. Pierre Chouteau was far away from the turmoil on the expedition, but his son wrote a letter to the War Department in his father's defense that revealed the seriousness of the charges. The son claimed that his father had been a victim. The younger Pierre revealed that Lewis had used McFarlane to carry out work with the Osage without consulting his father, the Osage agent.[775] Lewis's methods seemed to be intentional to keep Chouteau in the dark. To the extent Chouteau could be expected to be a Wilkinson informant, Lewis may have kept Chouteau in the dark to keep Wilkinson's informant, Frederick Bates, in the dark.

Chouteau's letter was written in clear English, but like Tillier, the younger Chouteau still wrote in French. According to one historian, the body of Chouteau's letter was in Frederick Bates's handwriting.[776] Bates would also write a letter under his own signature to the secretary of war to criticize Lewis's policies, no doubt to help assure Lewis would not return as governor.[777]

When the older Chouteau later returned, he also wrote to the secretary of war to defend his reputation. He stated that he had left his post as Osage agent only under Lewis's directives and that he had traveled only as far as the Mandan village to return the chief. He bragged that he had accomplished his official mission. He admitted that he had camped with fur trappers on his return as a convenience, implying not for military or commercial purposes. Like his son, he criticized Lewis for appointing subagents for work with the Osage, which had the effect of overriding his authority as Osage agent.[778]

Lewis said that the War Department's denial of his reimbursements sank his credit.[779] Creditors who held Lewis's notes rushed to be first to collect. Suddenly, he was insolvent though not bankrupt—he may have owned just enough property to pay off his debts, but not in time to satisfy his creditors who wanted immediate payment.[780] Lewis would confide that he was "excessively embarrassed" by his inability to pay his debts.[781] Men who could not pay their obligations could be sent to debtors' prison, where some languished until they died.

It would have seemed appropriate for Lewis to write to Jefferson to explain his predicament and to ask him to use his influence with President

Madison until Lewis had time to meet with him in person. Mail delivery had been unreliable, yet Lewis could have expected the postal riders to deliver a letter to Charlottesville sooner than he would arrive.[782] But Jefferson's latest letters had been brusque, demanding to know why Sheheke had not been returned. Lewis had not yet heard any news to report.[783]

Lewis also chose not to ask Jefferson for help in obtaining a loan. Instead, he found men in St. Louis who were willing to lend him money for his immediate crunch.[784] He offered to honor a bill of exchange he had given to Chouteau as a request for additional time to settle the payment.[785] To meet his debts, he would have no choice but to sell some of the land he had purchased in St. Louis and use the remaining cash as additional collateral to extend payment deadlines.[786] On August 19, he gave a power of attorney to Clark and William C. Carr to sell land on his behalf in his absence.[787] Carr took advantage of Lewis's predicament and agreed to purchase one of his tracts a few miles from St. Louis.[788]

Clark and Carr would sell the land Lewis had bought for his mother before Clark left St. Louis.[789] Lewis would hope to hold off creditors long enough to settle his affairs in Washington City. Not understanding the implications of the secretary's charges or Lewis's potential liabilities, the lawyer thought Lewis's reaction to the secretary of war's letter and the creditors' hounding was too rash. He criticized Lewis for leaving St. Louis with his "private affairs altogether deranged."[790]

On August 21, Lewis and Clark met to settle their accounts with each other. Clark could provide no help. He had made substantial advances for his own office, and he planned to sell one of his shares in the Fur Company to raise some cash.[791] When all obligations were tallied, Clark paid Lewis $53 in settlement of their debts.[792]

Though both men planned to travel to Washington, they chose to take different routes.[793] Clark selected a land route through Kentucky, and Lewis, as he said in his letter to the secretary of war, chose to travel by boat down the Mississippi to New Orleans, where he would board a ship to travel by sea.⁷⁹⁴ Carr expressed frustration that he did not know whether to tell people to direct mail to Lewis at Lexington, where Clark was headed, or to Washington City, suggesting that at first, he thought Lewis considered traveling with Clark.⁷⁹⁵

It is odd that the duo chose not to travel together when their circumstances were so dire. By that point, however, they were not just a duo. Clark had planned to travel with his wife, Julia, and eight-month-old son, Meriwether Lewis Clark, to visit family and friends in Kentucky and Virginia on his way east.⁷⁹⁶ Clark also may have been considering options for his future outside Lewis's shadow. Four months earlier, his supporters had lobbied for his appointment as governor of the Illinois Territory.⁷⁹⁷

Traveling by boat and ship, Lewis could expect to reach Washington City in one month, as opposed to the three it would take Clark by land, with lengthy stops for family. Lewis could also transport large trunks by boat that would be difficult to carry on horseback through the forests. Both routes presented dangers from pirates, whether by sea, river or land.⁷⁹⁸

The explorers could have divided the expedition journals they had each written to ensure that at least one version would return east for publication. But they apparently determined that the expedition papers would be safer with Lewis on the boat and ship. Nonetheless, if Lewis and Clark planned to take additional sensitive intelligence—either from the expedition or more recently regarding Texas or Santa Fe—then traveling separately increased the likelihood that at least one of them would reach their destination.⁷⁹⁹

On August 25, Lewis and Clark met again for what Clark thought would be the last time before they both set out east. Lewis confided the distress he felt from the press of creditors, as Clark described, "in Such terms as to Cause a Cempothy [sympathy] which is not yet off," adding, "if his mind had been at ease I Should have parted Cherefully…"

Though Clark worried about the stress on Lewis, he saw nothing so concerning as to insist that they travel together. Ever optimistic, Clark thought Lewis could show that all that he had done would "Come out to be much to his Credit" and that he would return to St. Louis "with flying Colours."[800] Lewis also thought he would return. Though he would carry some blankets and a few other personal items, he made no arrangements to have his furniture sent east.[801]

Bates wrote his brother that Lewis likely would not return.[802] To make sure, Bates had already begun spreading rumors that Lewis's time was limited. He had even sought out replacements. When Bates's close friend, John Coburn, visited St. Louis, Bates told him that Lewis's position would likely become vacant and pressed him to consider taking it.[803] By October, Bates followed up with a letter to a friend:

> [Lewis] has been too unfortunate to expect a second nomination—such, at least is the prevailing opinion: whether well founded or not a very general solicitude is felt, that some worthy man of talent and experience may be selected to succeed him in the Executive Office.[804]

Even Coburn apparently came to understand that Bates was attempting to destroy Lewis's governorship.[805] He may not have seen that Wilkinson was pulling Bates's strings. After Lewis's death, the signers to a petition requesting that Coburn be appointed to Lewis's vacant position included Bates and a who's who of Wilkinson's supporters in the territory.[806]

William Carr also thought Lewis would not return. He quickly shifted any remaining loyalty from Lewis and partnered with Bates to buy land on credit, including land from former members of the Corps of Discovery.[807]

Clark said that Lewis departed St. Louis for Washington City by August 25.[808] Carr said that he left earlier.[809] With only about 1,500 residents, St. Louis was small enough that both men should have known that he had left town, and it must be presumed that he did.[810] But if Lewis departed on August 25, he returned.

James McFarlane rode into St. Louis with delegations of Osage.[811] He somehow sent word to Lewis that the Arkansas band of Osage, who had not signed the treaty with Clark, was ready to hold a council with Lewis to give their consent. Lewis noted in his Memorandum Book that he intended to settle his debts with McFarlane when he saw him.[812]

Despite the urgency to meet with President Madison as soon as possible, Lewis prioritized his official duties over his personal needs.[813] Then, too, finalization of the treaty would be a success for Lewis's administration that he could present to the president as an argument to remain in office.

On August 27, as Lewis waited to meet with the Arkansas Osage, he focused on preparing his case for Washington. He dictated or wrote a rough draft for a four-page letter to the president to argue for reimbursement of his personal payment for printing the Laws of the Territory for the judge in a murder case in which a member of a local tribe was charged. Perhaps reflecting the effects of overwhelming distractions or the onset of illness, on the final version written by a scribe, Lewis signed the letter and personally penned the address to "Thomas Jefferson President. U'States," though Madison had been president for five months.[814]

Two days later, on August 31, according to the Osage Treaty, Lewis met with the Osage representatives and read to them the terms negotiated by Pierre Chouteau for Clark. The final tribal leaders consented and added their names to the treaty.[815] It would become Lewis's last significant official act. In Clark's estimation, the treaty was a major success for the United States, because the Osage ceded "200 miles square of the finest land in Louisiana."[816] Not only would the land provide additional buffers to encourage settlement near the Mississippi River, as Jefferson wanted, but the cession would open up settlement for much of the land that would become the states of Missouri and Arkansas. The *Missouri Gazette* reported that although a large number of Osage representatives appeared to accept American conditions, British agents muted their support before they returned to their villages.[817]

As Lewis waited to make another departure, business with McFarlane seems to have occupied much of his final days in St. Louis. Lewis would want to know about events in the Arkansas District where McFarlane had just left, including any news of expeditions along the Red River border with Texas. On September 1, Lewis took the opportunity to settle his accounts with McFarlane by asking him to extend credit. He wrote in his Memorandum Book, "Gave James McFarlane my note payable on demand for $718.45—which is in full of all our private transactions."[818]

On the same day in St. Louis, Ben Wilkinson sent Lewis a letter requesting that he sign a note to acknowledge the money that Ben or Wilkinson & Price had lent him. Ben said that he had been too "indisposed, to send the letter sooner." Ben closed the letter "yours affectionately," a closing used at the time among the upper-class to indicate loyalty through a personal friendship or brotherhood rather than merely a business association.[819]

Lewis met with McFarlane again two days later to reimburse his expenses for leading the Arkansas Osage band to St. Louis to finalize the treaty. He noted, "Gave James McFarlane my bond for $800... for vouchers for expenses on a trip to the St. Francis and the Osage Village of Arkansas. When bringing in the chiefs of that band to sign the treaty."[820]

Oddly, Lewis also made a note on the same page in his Memorandum Book to "deliver a receipt from Mr. McFarlane to Capt. Russell at Chickasaw Bluffs."[821] He apparently was unaware that Clark had hired James McFarlane to transport peltries for the St. Louis Missouri Fur Company down the Mississippi River, passing Chickasaw Bluffs to New Orleans. Since mid-August, Clark had advertised in the *Missouri Gazette* for a crew of boatmen to depart from St. Louis mid-September."[822] Like Lewis, McFarlane planned to travel to Washington City by boarding a ship for Baltimore once he arrived at New Orleans.[823] If Lewis considered McFarlane a close and reliable friend, as Clark claimed, it is curious that Lewis chose not to travel with McFarlane for additional safety, especially once Lewis's departure was delayed.[824]

It is also curious that McFarlane would have asked Lewis to deliver a receipt to Russell at Chickasaw Bluffs when McFarlane planned to pass the Chickasaw Bluffs about the same time as Lewis. The page preceding Lewis's notes on his meetings with McFarlane may have explained the receipt and the sensitive activities McFarlane was engaged in for Lewis—but at some point, that page was ripped from Lewis's Memorandum Book, leaving only a stub.[825]

Adding to Lewis's problems, on August 8, the secretary of war wrote separately to direct Clark to remove several of the Indian subagents and interpreters Lewis had appointed. In particular, Dr. Robinson was to be fired, and reimbursements would not be made for James McFarlane until the War Department received further explanation of his activities.[826] The War Department decided not to reimburse Clark for over $1,600 in payments he had made to the subagents at Lewis's direction.[827]

The political attack on Lewis would be sure to inflict pain on the network of his supporters and merchants who relied on them. Clark had noticed that salaries from the federal Department of Indian Affairs were one of the prime sources of income in the territory.[828] Wilkinson certainly would have been aware of that fact and used it to his advantage.

Clark did not receive the momentous letter by the time Lewis left on his trip downriver.[829] Within days of Lewis's departure from St. Louis, his subagents would lose control over ongoing operations in the West—if they remained loyal to Lewis. If Lewis never arrived in Washington to plead his case and reverse the course of events, Wilkinson would have no rival over the Texas and Santa Fe missions.

Lewis planned to carry five trunks, four of his own and one that he said belonged to Captain James House, the Fort Bellefontaine commander who was leaving his post at St. Louis. House had requested a furlough due to his poor health and exhaustion. He planned to travel overland to Baltimore, where he hoped he would be offered a new command.[830] The contents of Lewis's four trunks, in addition to clothing and other personal items, would be said to include the expedition journals and papers, Lewis's vouchers for reimbursement, and other important government papers. Lewis would show particular concern for who had access to his trunks.[831]

The actual date Lewis finally departed is uncertain. Frederick Bates reported to the secretary of war that Lewis left St. Louis on September 4, which was the day that the Arkansas Osage leaders were expected to return to their villages. In the meantime, Lewis directed Pierre Chouteau to provide presents to the Osage before they returned.[832] It was an opportunity to gain additional support from tribal leaders whose influence could be leveraged to control events along the border with Texas. Lewis's notes reflected meetings with McFarlane as he continued to sell land.

As Lewis waited to depart, seasonal late-summer sickness spread throughout the region.[833] Settlers often referred to summer in the Mississippi River Valley and lower Louisiana country as "the sickly months."[834] Fever and dysentery were so common in forts on the western frontier that some officers refused to command them.[835] New Orleans governor Claiborne said that river travel was particularly unhealthy in summer.[836]

But according to a physician's testimony to Congress, 1809 in the Lower Mississippi, "was much more sickly than any for many years."[837] One doctor testified that the inhabitants of the area said "that they had never before witnessed such a fatal season."[838] A travel guide published the prior year warned travelers that stories of the Mississippi River Valley's abundance of fish, fruit, and game:

> lead thousands into this country in search of a paradise, and they find a grave. The climate is horrid. On an average nine strangers die out of ten, shortly after their arrival in the city, and those who survive are of shattered constitution and debilitated frame.[839]

After a wet winter, the months of June and July 1809 had been unusually wet along the lower Mississippi River. The surgeon's mate at Fort Bellefontaine reported that by late spring 1809, several troops were sickened by "putrid fevers" that caused "great debility toward the end and have been Mortal in several cases." Sick reports doubled or tripled after heavy rains.[840] Swamps and standing water in low-lying areas were believed to be responsible for the disease, but the cause was unknown.[841]

A traveler in the area in 1807 described the sickness as "autumnal vomit and hoemorhage [with] intermittents, pleurasies, and a species of slow disease which consumes the body, ex-tinguishes the natural heat of the blood, [and] changes the complexion into a livid pale."[842] A Natchez physician described the 1809 fevers more particularly as a variation on severe disease they had experienced in 1807, as beginning with a chill, followed by an irritable stomach or vomiting, then fever "with excruciating pain of the head, back, and pit of the stomach" and "copious discharges of a dark color from the stomach and alimentary canal."[843] Not until decades later would it be understood that mosquitoes spread both malaria and a disease to be named "St. Louis encephalitis."

At Wilkinson's camp south of New Orleans, over 500 soldiers had been ill with fever since early spring.[844] The secretary of war had suggested that Wilkinson remove most of his troops from New Orleans during the summer and fall of 1809, to avoid disease from the heat.[845] So many men became ill that gunboats were approved to evacuate soldiers back north to Fort Adams and Fort Dearborn near Natchez.[846] Lewis had enough contact with the military that he would have heard about the outbreak. Though the causes of the illnesses in Wilkinson's camp were varied, and most were later determined to be related to poor drainage from latrines at the campsite, Lewis would only have known that there was an unusual widespread sickness in the Mississippi Valley. Concerns about that sickness would have influenced his decisions.

It was a time when political leaders and the wealthy across the country retreated to higher regions for the summer. In New Orleans, Governor Claiborne and his wife relocated to the countryside but were unable to abandon their post. By October, Claiborne felt the effects of severe fever, and his wife would die from the illness by December.[847]

George Sibley described St. Louis as a "sickly place" in general.[848] Lewis was not alone in worrying about the unknown causes of the illness and taking precautions. However, Clark may have been the one who later told Jefferson that Lewis's "hypochondria" had reached a level that began to worry his friends.[849] Lewis's mother's work in treating her neighbors certainly enhanced his awareness of early signs of illness and remedies. Lewis purchased $30 worth of medicine from local physician Dr. Anthony Saugrain the day before his first planned departure, paying with a note to come due in May 1810, after his planned return from the East.[850] It was not uncommon for military officers and gentlemen to carry their own well-stocked medicine chests containing medicines for various diseases when traveling. However, if Lewis purchased a medicine chest as the purchase price suggests, it was not listed among his personal effects after his death.

Or, perhaps, Lewis was already feeling the effects of illness. The day he purchased medicine was the same day he misaddressed a letter to the president, and he also failed to list the obligation to Dr. Saugrain in his Memorandum Book, as he had other debts. Despite the reports, Lewis booked passage south where sickness was expected to be at almost epidemic proportions and the cause unknown.

If Lewis was not already suffering the effects of whatever sickness infected the river valley, soon, he would. The national hero would be weakened at a time when he would expect to face Wilkinson's minions. Lewis could have used a friend's support on the upcoming perilous journey. His settling of accounts with James McFarlane and Ben Wilkinson indicates that neither man who held himself out as one of Lewis's close friends planned to travel with him to Washington City.

Yet, curiously, both men followed Lewis down the Mississippi River.[851]

## CHAPTER 14

# JOURNEY TO THE NEST OF HORNETS

> to brave the storms…—to be thus sped to an untimely grave!!
> —*Missouri Gazette,* on the Death of Meriwether Lewis[852]

Lewis boarded a boat with his servant Peerny to set out for a river voyage down the Mississippi. It was a time when generals traveled with bodyguards. Safeguarding five trunks would have been risky, even with the assistance of Peerny, whose duties as a household servant would not have required physical strength.

No one expressed concern that the governor would be traveling alone with valuable papers and money, nor did anyone mention that any other traveling companion accompanied Lewis. Clark had been careful to select trusted boatmen to transport valuable hides for the St. Louis Missouri Fur Company. It is not clear what security precautions, if any, Lewis took for his papers.

Boat crews were recruited from the toughest and meanest men in frontier towns. In addition to navigating the treacherous river passages, they might be called on to fight off river pirates to safeguard their cargo to its destination. Crews had reputations for "unruly tempers, and lawless conduct."[853] Like some of the people who lived along the riverbanks, they claimed to be part "horse, alligator, and snapping turtle."[854] One minister thought boatmen reflected "new features of atrocity."[855] Known also for their heavy whiskey drinking and fighting, boatmen were hardened. Their skin, leathered by years of sun on the water, was highlighted by the red flannel shirts they wore.[856]

There is no record that the local army commander, Daniel Bissell, supplied a boat for Lewis's voyage, nor that Lewis owned a boat or chartered a private boat.[857] His remaining option would have been to book passage on one of many riverboats that could be "procured at reasonable terms" for public travel on the Mississippi.[858]

Keelboats were generally sixty feet long and about ten or twelve feet wide. Box-like shelters were often built on top to protect passengers from the elements. Though separate passenger rooms were built on flatboats by 1812, it is doubtful that Lewis had the luxury of a private room in 1809.[859] Public boats generally offered only one main interior room, which could be used for shelter from the sun and rain, as well as for cooking at a makeshift brick fireplace.

Most boats on the Mississippi carried cargo as their primary source of income. Passengers were merely a sideline. Unless Lewis secured the use of a private military craft, he and other travelers likely shared space with hemp, apples, corn, and horses being hauled to market from upstream. At least farm animals or horses were usually tied outside the enclosed structure.[860] Still, passenger comfort and safety were not the main priorities.

September was known to be the time when the river was shallowest.[861] A trip from St. Louis to New Orleans, which typically took ten days, could stretch up to six weeks during periods of low water levels.[862] River travel presented unique dangers from unseen trees floating just below the surface. They could snag and sink a boat within minutes. Hidden river currents could crash a boat onto a sandbar or riverbank.

Because of the dangers, boats rarely navigated the Mississippi River at night. Instead, captains usually tied the boats at a sandbar along a riverbank. A crew member often brought along a fiddle to pass the evenings with dancing. Meals were usually limited to salt-preserved meat, potatoes, corn, and a type of hard cracker known as "hardtack."[863]

There is no record of Lewis's activities for significant points on his final journey. For the first fifteen miles south of St. Louis, boats floated past serene prairies dotted with grazing cattle and settlers' orchards.[864] Under normal circumstances, he or Peerny could have ventured into the towns at stops to purchase food and other supplies. But one of them, most likely Lewis, would have remained on the boat to protect the trunks. For the same reason, it is unlikely that he changed boats during the trip.

Boats descending the Mississippi often made regular stops at St. Genevieve, 109 miles by river south of St. Louis.[865] The town had maintained the language of its first French inhabitants, impressing one visitor that it exuded a "considerable degree of refinement."[866] Whitewashed mud brick buildings with thatched roofs complemented the European effect, though John James Audubon thought they looked dirty.

By 1809, St. Genevieve was a mining town that serviced the lead mines.[867] Even before becoming a U.S. territory, the area had attracted numerous speculators who hoped to make quick fortunes by obtaining title to land rich in lead deposits. The promise of quick riches from lead drew a rough crowd. Frederick Bates claimed that what defined the town more than its charming European-village effect were the numerous fights with guns, knives, and the gouging out of the eyes.[868]

Lewis may have considered that St Genevieve was located near the home of John Smith T, who, along with the town sheriff, Henry Dodge, belonged to the group of Burrites that Lewis had vowed to remove from power as traitors.[869] A few weeks earlier, at Smith T's urging, a group unhappy with Lewis's territorial administration had met in St. Genevieve to move forward with its petition to create a territorial sub-government separate from Lewis's in St. Louis.[870] They could argue that St. Genevieve had a population as large as St. Louis, as well as a larger number of buildings.[871] Like others in Lewis's orbit, Smith T was making plans to travel to Washington City. He wanted to deliver the petition to Congress in person.[872]

A wagon road had been built from St. Genevieve to St. Louis. At that point, the overland route was roughly equal in distance to the river route, but farther south, the river's sharp bends added miles compared to travel by land. Had it been necessary to send messages to Lewis, a rider could have met his boat at points along the river. Similarly, riders could have delivered messages to St. Louis from points where Lewis's boat was spotted or stopped, though there is no record that he sent or received any messages. Similarly, anyone who had an interest in Lewis's location could have followed the boat along the river at points where trails led to the river.[873]

South of St. Genevieve, boats passed a stark, 150-foot rock formation in the middle of the river known as "The Tower." Water swirled around its base, often catching boatmen by surprise. Lewis heard that a rite of passage for boatmen passing the formation the first time was the obligation to supply whiskey for the others on the boat or be dunked in the river.[874] He had previously passed The Tower en route to St. Louis in 1803.

South-bound boats also regularly stopped at Cape Girardeau, about 133 miles by river south of St. Louis. Members of tribes who had left their clans to find independence built camps along the riverbanks. Dunbar described them as "troublesome."[875] Stoddard called them "outlaws."[876] Shawnees and Delawares had just executed three of the tribesmen who tried to rouse the locals to revolution.[877] If Lewis was ill by that point, he could have found treatment from the town physician, a fellow Virginian who was also a Mason.[878] But Lewis thought much of the town was inhabited by hard-living, whiskey-drinking Tennesseans.

Thirty-eight miles south of Cape Girardeau, the boat would have passed the confluence of the Ohio River into the Mississippi. The abandoned Fort

Jefferson, where the Chickasaw had attacked American soldiers, could still be seen on the eastern bank. Boatmen would have worked to prevent the boat from spinning out of control from the powerful side currents of water from the Ohio River.[879]

Lewis's boat would have encountered other boats traveling in both directions on the Mississippi.[880] Peddlers built stores on boats and floated them from town to town. Somewhere during the trip, Lewis acquired silk for dresses for Clark's wife, Julia, and a lady's pocketbook, perhaps as a present for his mother.[881]

He would not have been able to put his troubles out of his mind to enjoy a slow-paced river voyage. Boatmen called the Mississippi a "wicked river."[882] Its muddy waters swirled to form whirlpools. At times, the water made a hissing sound that gave one traveler the impression that "the river always seems in wrath."[883]

Another traveler said that "of all the physical inconveniences of the country[,] exposure to the ague is undoubtedly the worst."[884] There were no floating hospitals, except for those specifically created for the movement of troops.[885] Boatmen who became sick on a voyage generally lay helpless in their bunks until they died. It was said to be common for two out of five boatmen to die on a Mississippi River voyage, and occasionally, disease would wipe out the entire crew before their boats reached New Orleans.[886] Swollen, dead bodies floating along with the current and the rotting remains of dead crews' wrecked boats were not uncommon sights.[887]

Names of boatmen who died on river voyages had been carved into trees along the banks as constant reminders of an invisible enemy.[888] If Lewis had begun to develop a fever, it would have been rational for him to consider the possibility that he would not survive the trip to New Orleans.

On September 11, likely somewhere between St. Louis and New Madrid—or perhaps at New Madrid—Lewis took out a sheet of paper and wrote his Last Will and Testament. His signature was witnessed by his servant, Jeau Peerny, and by a man named "F. S. Trinchard."[889] Trinchard was listed in the Missouri newspaper as "Mons Trinchard," likely for "Monsieur."[890] The fact that those men were the only two trusted witnesses Lewis could find seems to confirm that a bodyguard or close friend did not accompany him.

The text of the Last Will and Testament in Lewis's own handwriting was cogent, concise, and generally followed the norms. He also followed the standard of having two people sign the Will as witnesses. If Lewis was ill at that point on the journey, the Will did not hint that he had lost his ability to think or write. Lewis bequeathed all his property remaining after payment of his just debts to his mother, Lucy. Most of his debts were for funds he had spent as governor. In case his estate lacked assets to pay all his debts, he preferred that his private debts be paid before any claims for official obligations against his estate.

Lewis probably did not ask a lawyer to oversee his drafting of the Will because he did not name an executor to administer his estate. In the normal course of affairs, St. Louis attorney William Carr might have performed the work. Carr had short notice of Lewis's departure, and he wrote that he was rushed to draft Lewis's official papers to prepare for his absence.[891]

The document would be entered into probate after his death in Virginia, as Lewis's only Last Will and Testament. As evidence that Lewis had become so ill that he thought he might die, he noted that he had made a list of his debts in his "small minute book," most likely his Memorandum Book, and that he was depositing it with his servant "Pernia."[892]

There is no record dating Lewis's arrival at New Madrid. The town was located about 108 miles south of Cape Girardeau and 241 miles south of St. Louis by river or 180 miles by wagon road. It had been built at a prominent turn and was considered the most important landing and town for commerce on the Mississippi north of Natchez. A creek entering the Mississippi above the town provided a good harbor, allowing boats to float close to the riverbank where boatmen, passengers, and crew could easily disembark if they chose to visit the town.[893]

One traveler would describe New Madrid as a town of a few houses, a prison, and a church. Adding to the impression that the town would not prosper, the founder, George Morgan, did not appreciate the accretions and avulsions of the river and built some of the buildings so close to the bank that they collapsed into the river when the ground underneath subsided.[894]

Of the roughly 400 residents, a third were American settlers from the East, while the remainder were a mixture of French and German immigrants. A traveler in 1810 wrote that although she found several genteel families, "there is, however, a due proportion of the worthless and despicable part of society."[895] Another wrote that townspeople avoided work to drink and gamble and that their conversations were punctuated with frequent outbursts of rage.[896] Yet another noted, "A flow of tribes from the Ohio River Valley also created conflicts between the resident tribes and townspeople.[897] Worse, there was a regular influx of criminals from river traffic. Lewis had found it necessary to sign orders offering New Madrid military protection against robbers and counterfeiters who traveled the river.[898]

As in St. Genevieve, the inhabitants of New Madrid were unhappy that the United States had taken control over their government.[899] Lewis may have received another chilly reception, except for a probate judge who had written two years earlier to subscribe to the publication of his journals. The judge, who poured praise on the president's decision to appoint Lewis as governor, said that his neighbors also wanted to subscribe.[900] His flattery seems to have paid off with an appointment as a judge.

Worse than some other sites along the Mississippi, the poorly drained soil at New Madrid was believed to spread "putrid fevers and agues" from June to November.[901] As over a hundred yards of the town fell into the river, townspeople had moved their buildings back closer to the unhealthy swampland.[902]

Three weeks later, the *Missouri Gazette* reported that "his Excellency Governor Lewis was much indisposed at New Madrid," without stating the cause.[903] "Indisposition" was a term generally used at the time for sickness.[904] Despite being ill in a town filled with political opponents, Lewis could have found friends to help him. A sergeant in Lewis and Clark's expedition, John Ordway, lived on a farm on the riverbank nearby and may have served as a town constable. Expedition blacksmith William Bratton may have been Ordway's neighbor.[905]

Lewis wrote to Clark from New Madrid that he was considering changing his route to travel overland, but he had no way to transport his "papers."[906] Though Lewis did not mention a reason for his change of plans, his illness and fear of what diseases he would find on the Lower Mississippi must have weighed on his mind. In addition, the *Missouri Gazette* had just reported that the British government had refused to rescind its Orders of Council, which authorized its navy to intercept American ships, suggesting that war was still possible.[907] It also inaccurately reported that British ships had captured fifty American ships in the Caribbean.[908]

Weakened by illness, Lewis may also have wondered what threats he would face in New Orleans. Claiborne reported that one-fourth of the men in New Orleans were Burrites and that their loyalty was only to plunder. He had requested more military aid to protect the safety of his territory and its officers.[909] Lewis's papers and maps might be seen as a rich catch for their cause.

In addition to the Burrites, Claiborne worried about Cuban refugees who flooded into the city.[910] He knew nothing of their background, though most were French colonials, their slaves, and free men of color that Cuba expelled in April 1809. The emigres included men who had engaged in piracy against American ships in the Caribbean.[911]

Wilkinson described the emigres as "Thousands of French men, not of the best character, disgorged upon us by the government of Cuba" to argue that he needed to remain near New Orleans to protect the nation from them. He estimated their number to be 10,000, approximately equal to the number of citizens of New Orleans and more than five times the size of the U.S. Army in the area. The large number of European colonials could easily have overpowered the small New Orleans government. Ironically, the number of emigres was the same number Wilkinson warned Burr had recruited to invade New Spain four years earlier, though only a twelfth were estimated to be men of fighting age.[912] The risk was extraordinarily perilous, he said, due to an "impending crisis in the neighboring kingdom of Mexico."[913] That line gave away Wilkinson's plot.

Wilkinson first attempted to cast suspicion on his latest enemy, Daniel Clark, Jr. for "the influx of desperate & notorious brigands" and argued they would "expose N. Orleans to conflagration for the sake of pillage." Then, finally sending Newman's letters to Washington, he suggested that, through Clark, Jr.'s influence, the risk was not just to New Orleans. He said that a club of Frenchmen was attempting "to excite jealousies in the Spanish provinces" against the U.S. and Wilkinson.[914]

It suddenly became clear why Wilkinson waited three months to send the Newman letters to Washington. Clark, Jr. prepared to publish a book, *Proofs Of The Corruption Of Gen. James Wilkinson, And Of His Connexion With Aaron Burr*, with documentation proving that Wilkinson was a spy for Spain. Excerpts with copies of Wilkinson's letter to his Spanish paymasters would appear in newspapers by October 1809, and rumors of their contents may have leaked sooner. Wilkinson had needed time to put his plans in motion to invade New Spain, and when the time was right, he could use the letters simultaneously to divert blame for any military action in New Spain and destroy Clark, Jr., just before the publication of his book.[915] Even if the invasion failed, Wilkinson could expect enough chaos to give his supporters ammunition to defend him and attack Clark, Jr.

By late summer of 1809, Claiborne and Lewis may have known of Wilkinson's influence in Cuba and how easy it would be for Wilkinson to overwhelm New Orleans with mercenaries. Or Wilkinson could use the mercenaries as a pretext to declare a type of martial law in New Orleans to imprison his enemies as he had during the Burr Conspiracy. And it appears that he planned to do just that. In August 1809, Wilkinson informed the War Department that he might station 300 to 400 of his soldiers throughout the city to protect it from the French refugees.[916] In that environment, it would be easy for Wilkinson to create a diversion in which Lewis could be arrested, his papers stolen, and Lewis assassinated.

If any of Lewis's informants alerted him to the extraordinary developments in New Orleans, the similarities to Wilkinson's prior attempt to take New Spain in 1805 were striking: the 10,000 potential mercenary soldiers, the plan to use soldiers to impose a virtual martial law to take opponents prisoner, and John Smith T's offer to deliver lead for bullets to points along the Mississippi. The only element missing was Wilkinson's fall guy, Burr.

But Lewis had already come to believe that he was being set up as Wilkinson's next Burr. He had just not anticipated how far Wilkinson had implemented his plan. Wilkinson could have timed events to eliminate his rival Lewis as well as Clark, Jr. When Wilkinson returned to New Orleans from Washington, he had sent charges against Lewis that could have been designed to suggest that on returning, Wilkinson had confirmed slander he had whispered into the secretary of war's ear.

The secretary of war would be expected to send Lewis a response that would force him to travel to Washington to defend himself and to maintain his position. He had reacted just as Wilkinson could have anticipated and just in time for Wilkinson's invasion. Lewis would have every reason to suspect that his boat was traveling right into Wilkinson's trap.

Most recent Cuban emigres were unemployed. Desperate for money in a foreign land, more than a few would be expected to provide a ready supply of mercenary soldiers for an invasion—or assassins.

The slow pace of the river voyage gave Lewis time to think about Burr's expedition down the same river two years earlier. Because Lewis had focused so much attention on defeating Burr, he no had doubt studied every detail of Burr's actions in 1807. He would have learned that Wilkinson sent out assassins to target Burr and that he had offered a bounty for others to help capture him. And, like Burr, Lewis would have understood that his presence on an open river flowing through dense woodlands would make him an easy target for an assassin. His death could easily be blamed on illness.

Burr had saved his own life by halting his river trip toward Wilkinson-controlled New Orleans and seeking refuge on land. When Clark received Lewis's letter that he was considering leaving the river and traveling overland, Clark remarked that Lewis's most direct route from New Madrid would be to continue downriver to Chickasaw Bluffs and travel from there through Nashville. Lewis must have told Clark that he was considering an overland route for a reason other than that the British might capture his papers. Despite the actual reason that Lewis confided to Clark in the letter that has not been found, Clark still thought Lewis might persuade McFarlane or another trusted agent to take his papers to Washington by ship.[917]

Clark did not indicate that Lewis's letter gave him the impression that his illness had made him delirious, nor did he feel compelled to send help.[918] The *Missouri Gazette* later reported that Lewis recovered and departed New Madrid in good health.[919]

But in St. Louis, Frederick Bates spread rumors that Lewis "went insane" while he was at New Madrid.[920] His motives were clear. If Lewis survived the journey, his reputation would be too ruined to return. Pierre Chouteau appears to have believed Bates's rumors. He took the unusual step of recording Lewis's final requisition from him for goods for the Osage in the St. Louis Recorder's deed book to create a public record.[921] Perhaps he hoped to perfect a superior claim against Lewis's estate when he died.

Like Lewis's earlier letter to Madison, his letter to Clark could have been opened and read anywhere along the post road that led from New Madrid to St. Genevieve or the one from Cape Girardeau to Fort Massac.[922] By the time Lewis arrived at Chickasaw Bluffs farther south, events or people would conspire to make certain that he had no choice but to travel overland.

A few miles south of New Madrid, Lewis's boat would have passed Little Prairie, a small settlement surrounded by swamps, which a visitor described as "a wretched sickly place… attended by periodical, or rather perpetual attacks of sickness."[923] F. S. Trinchard, who witnessed Lewis's Will, owned a tract of land at Little Prairie.[924] He may have disembarked at that point if he had not already exited at New Madrid. Trinchard is not known to have written about his encounter with Lewis.

South of Little Prairie, few settlers lived along the riverbanks until the boat reached Fort Pickering at Chickasaw Bluffs. That leg of the journey was described as "a very lonesome stretch." The only diversion was watching the steersmen constantly taking action to avoid floating trees and other dangers that would sink a boat.[925] Thick forests formed a tunnel of trees. The few sounds were "the cry of wild beasts, the echo of thunder, or the crash of undermined trees, falling" into the river.[926] Even then, the float on the serpentine bends of the river was "long and dreary."[927] The current of the river ran only three and a half to four miles per hour.[928]

In normal times, if Lewis had not already traveled that far south on the Mississippi, the explorer might have been inclined to note his observations of the water course and soil, as well as the animal and plant life. His perspective would have contrasted his discoveries in the West, if not for his own or Jefferson's curiosity. No such notes have been found, though his Memorandum Book contains a penciled drawing of a lark near the water with trees in the background and with the words "upper crew" at the top of the page, just after the remains of another page that appears to have been ripped out.[929]

Farther south, the monotony would have been interrupted as steersmen jumped to action when the boat passed through two treacherous stretches known as the "Devil's Race Ground" and the "Devil's Elbow." In addition to keeping the boat in the channel, boatmen would have been on guard for river pirates hiding along the banks waiting to take advantage of the slow-passing craft.[930]

Lewis had already been delayed by a week. Boats traveled fifty miles a day on a slow day, an appropriate pace for Lewis to relax to the point of boredom—yet his reputation and political future depended on speed.[931] Perhaps due to low water levels or reports of fevers, late summer traffic on the river was lighter than usual. Only thirty flatboats landed at New Orleans from upstream in September 1809.[932]

It would later be reported that the intense heat on the river caused whatever sickness Lewis had contracted to recur.[933] As an army captain who had led an expedition, Lewis would have known the importance of keeping a supply of fresh drinking water in extreme heat.[934] Amos Stoddard hauled fresh water in barrels to fill cisterns for his troops on land when spring water was unavailable.[935] Seafaring ships also stocked supplies of fresh water, but boats on the Mississippi apparently did not at that time.[936] A stop at Cape Girardeau would have been Lewis's last opportunity to obtain water from springs.[937] From there, swampy communities at stops along the river would not have provided access to fresh water.[938]

Travelers noticed that water scooped from the Mississippi was clouded by mud and other impurities, which comprised about an eighth of any water stored for drinking. Most considered the hot, dingy river water undrinkable, unless it could be stored overnight in jars to cool and to allow the mud to sink to the bottom. A few hardy settlers even believed that if that process was followed, the water was not only drinkable, but that it could cure fevers.[939] Much depended on what materials flowed into the river at points upstream. Several soldiers, likely raw recruits, believed to have developed stomach ailments from drinking water from the Mississippi in 1809.[940] If Lewis had been vomiting, drinking river water could have made his condition worse. Seasoned military men knew that water in the Mississippi could cause sickness unless it was filtered with filtering stones.[941]

Boatmen were not so squeamish. They were known to drink a cup of river water, followed by a cup of whiskey—or more likely, drank the whiskey first.[942] They apparently believed from experience that strong alcohol would neutralize the impurities, even if they did not understand that those impurities could be bacteria.

Alcohol was also known to be a treatment for intestinal problems. When Lewis went into training for the transcontinental expedition, Dr. Benjamin Rush, one of the most respected physicians in the nation, had advised him, "When you feel the least indisposition… fasting and diluting drinks for a day or two will generally prevent an attack of fever."[943]

But British physician Thomas Trotter's recent 1804 book *An essay… on drunkeness*, warned:

> There can be no doubt that many person have to date their first propensity to drinking to the too frequent use of spiritous tinctures as medicines, rashly prescribed for hysterical and hypochondriacal complaint… There are certainly many well-meaning people who take frequent drams to relieve uneasiness of stomach, without at all suspecting that they are doing any thing wrong.[944]

Lewis carried his own liquor case. Boatmen may have encouraged Lewis to drink his own liquor or their higher proof drinks to counter any impurities he had consumed. He could even have decided that his liquor was the only liquid safe to drink. The effects of any alcohol on top of fasting, dehydration, fever, and exhaustion may have dulled his judgment and kept him from appreciating the new dangers he faced.

The *National Intelligencer* in Washington City later reported that while Lewis was on the boat, he became "deranged in his mind" and made attempts to take his own life. Several people, it claimed, "secured him and landed him at the Chickasaw Bluffs."[945] That story was likely supplied to the newspaper by Major Amos Stoddard, who claimed to have obtained the information secondhand.[946] In fact, Lewis had already planned to disembark at Chickasaw Bluffs to meet with fort commander Gilbert C. Russell.[947] Lewis did not record the purpose of the meeting, except to deliver a receipt from James McFarlane.[948]

Two or three miles north of Fort Pickering, Lewis's boat passed the commercial Chickasaw Bluffs boat landing, which was described as a poor landing.[949] With the support of the Spanish, Dutch immigrant Benjamin Fooy had built stores at that location to cater to river traffic on both banks.[950] Fooy had once served as a Spanish diplomat to the tribes, which likely placed him in contact with Wilkinson or his agents. By 1809, Fooy ran a commercial barge up and down the Mississippi River and transported lead to Fort Pickering.[951] Those activities would have placed Fooy in frequent contact with St. Louis area lead mine owner, John Smith T, or his rivals, and they certainly allowed him to convey information and people under the guise of transporting cargo. Wilkinson would have found his services invaluable.

Directly across from Fort Pickering on the western side of the Mississippi lay Lewis's new Upper Louisiana Territory Arkansas District. Five families surrounded Fooy's residence on the western Arkansas side at Hopefield, and another six had settled on the eastern side just below the Wolf River. Those buildings may have included two blockhouses moved across the river from the former Spanish Fort San Fernando De Las Barrancas when Spain abandoned it in 1797. Other families raised corn, chickens, and pigs that they sold to travelers on boats that stopped at the landing.[952] Fooy speculated that the forts would draw settlers to his town. In the meantime, his village had failed to prosper.

Lewis's Upper Louisiana territorial land board regularly traveled to Hopefield for district meetings as part of its circuit.[953] Fooy and his neighbors had accepted judges that Lewis commissioned for the settled areas of the district, particularly when Fooy was named as a judge. Still, it is unclear how Fooy reacted to McFarlane.[954]

Fort Pickering sat atop the southernmost of a series of four bluffs rising to the east of the river. Soldiers and travelers often referred to the fort simply as "Chickasaw Bluffs" or "The Bluffs." The Bluffs formed the western boundary of the Chickasaw Nation, and they had long served as a place where the Chickasaw interacted with river travelers for trade. That portion of their nation had been surveyed as part of the State of Tennessee fourteen years earlier. The surveyors were friends of Andrew Jackson, and immediately after the survey had been completed, they partnered with Jackson and John Overton to purchase the choicest land near the fourth bluff, "subject to the claim of the Chickasaw."[955]

Fort Pickering Surgeon's Mate W. C. Smith described Fort Pickering as "sequestered and sickly."[956] But its location had served as a significant point for Aaron Burr. And it remained an important part of the network for Wilkinson's control of the Southwest and plots to take Texas and Santa Fe.

If Lewis contemplated changing his route to travel overland to avoid Wilkinson's "nest of hornets" farther south, it was useless. As he would discover at Fort Pickering, Wilkinson's spies were everywhere.

## CHAPTER 15

# PERFECT STORM

> Some men are sordid, some vain, some ambitious... To detect the predominant passion, to lay hold of it, is the profound part of political science.
>
> —James Wilkinson[957]

As Lewis's boat floated through the Mississippi River Valley, the unusually hot and muggy September weather produced more than a slight chance of a hurricane. But by the time he landed at Fort Pickering, the brewing storms that should have been more of concern to him were political.

The first was a growing fight between Wilkinson and his rival General Wade Hampton. Forts that lined the riverbanks helped form the main U.S. defense of the West. To the outside, they projected American stability and power. Inside, army politics and divisions raged.

Federalists who remained in the army were anti-Jefferson, and they may have been anti-Lewis by association.[958] Except for elderly soldiers who fought in the Revolution and obtained their skills through their own experience, most soldiers were appointed based on political connections. Winfield Scott would describe most of the uneducated Republican soldiers newly enlisted by Jefferson as "swaggerers, dependents, decayed gentlemen, and others—'fit for nothing else.'"[959] It was an environment in which a scoundrel like Wilkinson could hide his actions with little accountability or oversight.[960]

Wilkinson had virtual free rein over what was then the U.S. Southwest from his headquarters at New Orleans, his staff at Columbian Springs, and his network of western forts, but he had never won the loyalty of the entire army. Officers who had been devoted to the late General Wayne coalesced their support around General Hampton. Hampton was one of the few men who posed a threat both to Wilkinson's control of the army and his position with Spain. As the owner of thousands of acres of South Carolina cotton plantations, he was one of the wealthiest men in the nation.[961] Because he did not need Wilkinson's favors, Wilkinson could not figure out how to manipulate him.

At the height of the Burr Conspiracy, Wilkinson used a potential war with Spain to propose that the federal government officially recognize the move of the U.S. Army headquarters to Fort Adams.[962] Jefferson wisely rejected Wilkinson's suggestion, but Wilkinson nonetheless concentrated his military power far from direct oversight. By 1808, the anticipated British attack along the Gulf Coast gave him justification.

By then, growing conflicts with Britain undermined Jefferson's plans to keep the number of regular army enlistments small. It became clear that Britain did not respect American sovereignty when it intercepted American ships on the high seas and forcibly impressed American seamen into service on British fleets. Britain may not have given up its quest to control its former American colonies, particularly when they could supply goods it needed. As Wilkinson had anticipated, New Orleans and the Mississippi River would be key to defending against a British invasion. It was said that Britain invading New Orleans would amount to "breaking the lock and opening the door to the Mississippi Valley."[963]

When Britain fired on a U.S. ship, Jefferson imposed an embargo, and Congress evaluated the capabilities of the army. Jefferson initially successfully reduced the size of the army to approximately 3,000 soldiers, in part, to rid it of opposing Federalist supporters.⁹⁶⁴ The total number was far too small to match European power, particularly when soldiers who served under short-term enlistments chose not to reenlist. Congressman John Randolph suggested that the army initiate a new program to recruit volunteers to prepare for war with Britain.⁹⁶⁵ Congress agreed and passed the Volunteer Act in 1807.

The following year, when the British navy began to intercept U.S. ships and it appeared that Britain might still consider invading its former colonies, the Secretary of War took advantage of the act and proposed increasing U.S. forces by 24,000 volunteers and 6,000 regular troops.⁹⁶⁶

By late 1808, when reports arrived in Washington that someone had spotted British ships entering the Caribbean, Wilkinson was still in Washington. The War Department perhaps could have reported accurately that the British had sent ships to capture an island totally unrelated to the United States. Instead, it allowed rumors to flourish that the British had sent the ships as a precursor to an invasion of the Gulf Coast.⁹⁶⁷ For the moment, the assessment produced the expected result—soldiers would be recruited to concentrate at New Orleans under Wilkinson's command.⁹⁶⁸

The directive originated from Jefferson and his secretary of war, but Wilkinson's critics might see his fingerprints all over it. At times, his small number of U.S. troops in the Southwest refused to reenlist, potentially embarrassing him as a powerless general with no one to command. Under the new plans, once captains in the Southwest met their recruitment numbers, they were to march their companies to Fort Adams or New Orleans and place themselves and their companies under Wilkinson's command. The threat of a British invasion from the Gulf was real, but it was still six years in the future. Once Wilkinson's hundreds of new recruits arrived, they had nothing to do but wait.⁹⁶⁹

Consequently, one effect of the plans in December 1808, was to increase Wilkinson's power by increasing the number of soldiers and future political leaders under his command by more than 2,000 at New Orleans—at the same time that his interests were focused on invading New Spain, and his loyalties were fluid.[970] Perhaps Wilkinson supported the plans solely to prepare a defense against Britain. But he would have been acutely aware that the new numbers under his command would strengthen his position in his fight with Lewis for influence with the president in the West.

By June 1809, the War Department would figure out that the immediate threat of a British attack was overblown and terminate additional recruitments. Until then, the ranks of Wilkinson's subordinates multiplied. The army lacked a large federal organization to find new recruits; therefore, ambitious men who saw an opportunity to use military service for future political leadership were encouraged to enlist with the rank of captain and recruit their own companies. Among those responding to the opportunity, future president Zachary Taylor opened a recruiting office in Kentucky, and Gilbert C. Russell began recruiting soldiers in Nashville.[971] Captain John Brahan left his post at Hiwassee Garrison in Tennessee to return to Staunton, Virginia, to recruit a new company to lead south to Fort Adams.[972] Captain William R. Boote, marched his company from the Creek Nation to Fort Dearborn just east of Natchez and joined Wilkinson as a loyal aide-de-camp in late 1808.[973] He arrived in time to participate in the events surrounding Lewis's death.

Wilkinson likely celebrated his political victory, but it was Pyrrhic. Congressman John Randolph understood the implications. The idea of placing Wilkinson in charge of such a large number of troops and equipment renewed questions about his role in the Burr Conspiracy and whether he could be trusted with the command of a larger army.

In May 1809, Randolph addressed the House of Representatives, suggesting that a large amount of funds would be better spent on a well-supplied militia controlled by state generals, and that the standing U.S. Army under Wilkinson should be dismantled. He railed that "the old army is rotten to the core; ... it is not the safe depository of the sword of this nation; [and] ... intrigue and corruption ha[s] cankered it to the very heart."[974]

Wilkinson's control over Washington politicians had begun to weaken. But no other general had posed a risk to Wilkinson's command because he was the only general with the rank of brigadier general. To make it easier to replace Wilkinson, Congress raised the ranks of two generals, one a Wilkinson loyalist and the other Wilkinson's rival, Wade Hampton.[975] Further threatening to Wilkinson, General Hampton would take over command of all the troops south of the Potomac, reserving only the Mississippi Territory and New Orleans in the southern command for Wilkinson.[976] Wilkinson would hang on by a thread, but that thread was a base from which he could still control the West, and by controlling New Orleans, he could influence the rest of the United States.

Like his intervention in the Burr trial, Jefferson may have used his influence to save Wilkinson again, thinking that he could still utilize him to take Texas and Santa Fe—and perhaps now fearing how Wilkinson would react if he had nothing to lose. Like a cornered animal, Wilkinson would become more dangerous. He would be forced to take action to avoid losing his base of power in the Southwest.

Randolph also revealed that as foreman of the Burr grand jury, he had seen proof that two army fort commanders had supported Burr's conspiracy. One, the commander of Fort Pickering (Jacob Jackson), had supplied Burr's rebels with arms from the public arsenal. The second was Captain Daniel Bissell, who commanded Fort Massac during Wilkinson and Burr's meetings and who supplied Burr with boats to travel to New Orleans to meet with co-conspirators.[977] Four days prior to Randolph charging Bissell with disloyalty on the House floor, Bissell arrived in St. Louis to assume command of Fort Bellefontaine, just north of the town, and to provide command of the small number of army troops on which Lewis would rely. Bissell would also act as superior to the commander of Fort Pickering.[978]

When Zachary Taylor reached his requisite number of recruits in Kentucky, he boarded them on boats to transport them to New Orleans to serve under Wilkinson. As he descended the Mississippi, he was ordered to stop short and take temporary command of Fort Pickering at the Chickasaw Bluffs in May and June 1809.[979] Taylor became so ill that he was forced to return home to Kentucky to recuperate.[980] He was replaced by a second temporary commander, Captain William Swan, who turned to Bissell for instructions.[981]

By March 1809, Gilbert C. Russell had met his quota and applied for funds to transport his recruits from Nashville to Fort Adams.[982] As Russell's boats approached Fort Pickering, Swan was preparing to lead his company south toward New Orleans.[983] Russell stopped at Fort Pickering on June 24, 1809, and assumed command of the fort from Swan. Russell's Nashville recruits replaced Swan's company to staff the fort.[984]

The second unraveling in Wilkinson's attempted invasion plans occurred on the ground. He had not given enough consideration to the fact that the U.S. lacked a fort and barracks to house troops south of Fort Adams. He sought land for a camp far enough away from the "licentious" town of New Orleans that it would not tempt his soldiers to break their discipline. Fortunately for the recent widower Wilkinson, the father of the woman he hoped to make his new bride was willing to lease land to the army southeast of New Orleans at "Terre aux Boeuf" near the English Turn in the Mississippi River. Wilkinson could justify a post at that spot because invading ships would be required to slow their advance at the turn, making them vulnerable to attack. Despite the strategic advantages of the site, the soil near sea level drained poorly, which would prove disastrous to the soldiers' health.[985]

When news arrived in Washington that most of the soldiers camped at Terre aux Boeuf had become deathly ill, the secretary of war ordered Wilkinson to withdraw the soldiers north until the sickly season was over.[986] If Wilkinson was plotting to use the idle troops to move on Texas, as his actions might suggest, shifting troops away from New Orleans and control of the Mississippi would spoil the timeline. He simply ignored the order and stalled.

But disease was a force Wilkinson had no power to manipulate. Over 900 soldiers, about a third of the old standing army, or a sixth, including new recruits, died from illness on the Lower Mississippi.[987] Politicians who believed that war with Britain was imminent were livid.

Critics who had long been leery of Wilkinson saw their opportunity. In September 1809, Wilkinson was ordered to relieve his southwestern command and to travel to Washington to face a rare and possibly illegal court-martial by Congress.[988] Newspaper editors salivated at the news. Wilkinson's comeuppance appeared finally at hand.

Some newspapers also began to attack Jefferson for his support of Wilkinson and questioned why Jefferson, as Randolph described it, hugged Wilkinson "to his bosom."[989] Jefferson should have worried. It would be rumored that Wilkinson said that if he "must fall he has it in his power to drag a *distinguished culprit* along with him.[990] When Wilkinson was threatened, he typically mounted both a full offense and a defense.

More satisfying for Wilkinson's enemies in the army, it was decided that his rival Hampton would take over the remainder of Wilkinson's command and become commanding general of the entire Southern Command.[991] But Wilkinson had not given up on Texas. He would simply need to find mercenary soldiers, and the Cuban refugees who flooded New Orleans could provide a source. He argued to the War Department that it was in the nation's interest for him to delay his departure until Hampton arrived at Fort Dearborn to relieve him of command. Simultaneously, he requested additional time to remain in New Orleans to prepare his defense for trial.[992] His primary defense tactic would be to determine which witnesses would testify against him and then gather enough dirt on them to undermine their credibility.

The careers of army officers at the forts in the Southwest hinged on the outcome of the generals' fight. As Wilkinson and officers who had done his bidding might have anticipated, once in command, Hampton would use his new authority to investigate Wilkinson's loyalists. He would quickly order that the Fort Adams commander be arrested and court-martialed, in part, for his role in building expensive housing for Wilkinson's officers at Columbian Springs and at Fort Dearborn.[993]

Though Wilkinson would profess his full support for Hampton, few believed it. Similar to Wayne's fate, Hampton would soon become deathly ill as Wilkinson remained behind in his camp. Newspapers would publish false reports that he had resigned his command or died, with pronouncements such as "Gen. Wade Hampton is no more."[994] The secretary of war would note facetiously that newspapers had "killed and buried" him.[995]

By the time of Lewis's death, the real division in the army was not between Federalists and Republicans but between officers who supported Wilkinson versus those who supported Hampton.[996] From the time of Wayne's appointment, they had divided themselves into "two distinct parties" within the organization.[997] The army had served as Lewis's extended family for most of his adult life. The generals' internal civil war and lingering allegations from the Burr Conspiracy would climax at a moment when Lewis relied on the army for survival as he descended the Mississippi.

Wilkinson would have heard that Lewis was traveling to Washington. Suspecting that Lewis had figured out his role in the War Department's accusations, Wilkinson could have anticipated that Lewis would fight him for his own influence and survival. At the least, Wilkinson certainly would have considered whether the trunks Lewis was transporting to Washington contained any evidence that could be used against him at his trial.

Lewis likely was even less aware of the second storm force—the fight between Wilkinson and Andrew Jackson, who also had an interest in Texas and Santa Fe, and who was still working to prove that Wilkinson was a spy for Spain.

Jackson's fight dated back almost a decade. As Wilkinson was overseeing construction of Jefferson's new military highway through Tennessee in 1801, Jackson persuaded Wilkinson's subordinate to move the road through Franklin, Tennessee, where his friends had invested.[998] Wilkinson objected to Jackson's interference in the project and threatened to court-martial the subordinate. Jackson asked Jefferson to intervene. Jefferson at first attempted to mollify Jackson, but Wilkinson eventually prevailed and court-martialed the subordinate in a trial that led to his death from yellow fever in New Orleans.[999]

Their fight intensified during the Burr Conspiracy, when Jackson became convinced that Wilkinson had used Burr as a puppet to destroy his reputation as a rival. Although Jackson had initially backed Jefferson and his Republican ideals of limited government, his attitude changed when Jefferson declined to appoint him governor of the Orleans Territory. Jefferson had been warned that Jackson was dangerous and unreliable, and he believed the allegations to be true. According to one Jackson biographer, this marked the point at which Jackson became increasingly anti-Jefferson.[1000]

Jackson served as patron to two ambitious young men: Gilbert C. Russell and John Brahan. Russell later wrote to Jefferson that he understood that Jefferson was Lewis's "patron."[1001] Russell's parallel meteoric rise suggests that he understood the concept of patronage, as he had his own powerful patron in Jackson.

Like Lewis, Russell had lived a remarkable life for a young man. Russell's family settled near Dandridge, Tennessee, about fifty miles east of Fort Southwest Point, and from an early age, he viewed military service as his means to success.[1002] Six years earlier, as President Jefferson worried that Spain would not recognize the transfer of the Louisiana Purchase, he directed the Tennessee governor to send 500 militia soldiers as federal volunteers down the Natchez Trace and the Mississippi River to Natchez to ensure an orderly transfer. Andrew Jackson, who was serving as major general of the Tennessee militia, assumed that he would be selected to lead the expedition. Jefferson's secretary of war appointed Russell's militia commander instead of Jackson.

Only eighteen years old, Russell raced his company to overtake the others and arrived in Natchez first, just in time to become the official U.S. representative for the transfer of power, an honor that should have been his commander's.[1003] While Russell was in Natchez, the notorious Natchez Trace bandit Little Harpe was arrested and convicted. Russell further burnished his reputation by using his company to assist the territorial government in overseeing Harpe's hanging.

Like Lewis, Russell enjoyed the militia experience, and he joined the U.S. Army with the rank of lieutenant. When Russell returned to Tennessee, he reached out to Jackson to lobby the secretary of war for an appointment as a captain.[1004] The daring teenager may have attracted Jackson's attention by outshining the experienced commander who had been awarded the position Jackson coveted. Russell soon received the appointment, and he should have felt indebted to his new patron.

Once in the army, Russell was assigned to Fort Adams, where he took the opportunity to befriend Jackson's nemesis, General Wilkinson. Wilkinson court-martialed him in 1807 for playing billiards in New Orleans.[1005] Russell resigned, but Wilkinson may have appealed to his ambition and convinced him that he would be useful or find success in the expected war with Britain.[1006] Two months later, Russell headed to Washington to lobby to be reinstated. He told the secretary of war that Wilkinson could plead his case for a new position.[1007] Similar to how Wilkinson had won Freeman's loyalty, he may have forced Russell's termination to indebt Russell to him when he was re-hired.

Russell claimed to have met Jefferson's son-in-law, T. M. Randolph.[1008] He would have passed through Virginia at the same time Lewis was preparing to travel to St. Louis, but there is no evidence that he attempted to meet with Lewis to seek his support. Russell spent over two months in Washington City lobbying for an appointment before finally receiving a renewal of his commission as captain.[1009] He reappeared in Nashville in late 1808 with money or credit to fund the recruitment of a company of soldiers.[1010]

Russell may also have known John Smith T, who built the settlement of Kingston, Tennessee, adjacent to Fort Southwest Point. Both men had served in the militia from that area at about the same time.[1011] If Russell referred to Dr. Sibley in a request to the secretary of war, Russell either demonstrated an ambitious willingness to overstate his influence or signaled a knowledge of Dr. Sibley's activities—likely from Wilkinson—that he could use as leverage for a favor from the War Department.

Andrew Jackson would call in his favors to Russell during the War of 1812. When Jackson decided to execute six of his own mutinous soldiers to halt a larger desertion, he tasked Russell with firing the shots.[1012] That action would become a major controversy during Jackson's presidential campaign. Given Jackson's efforts to obtain incriminating evidence on Wilkinson, it is not unreasonable to conclude that Jackson fostered Russell's army career to use Russell to spy on Wilkinson. But Russell's ambition was as large as Jackson's, and it appears that Russell served as protégé to both generals to further his own career in the army.[1013]

Jackson's second protégé, John Brahan, was a Virginian, sent to Fort Southwest Point to work as an army paymaster.[1014] While there, he would have met the future Fort Pickering commander, Gilbert C. Russell, and the future Chickasaw factor, David Hogg, if he had not already met them. When that camp was transferred to the nearby Hiwassee Garrison and Brahan became its commander, he contracted with Jackson to make improvements to the garrison.[1015] By November 1808, Brahan claimed friendship with Jackson associate William P. Anderson as he contacted Jackson about buying land from Judge Overton, and Brahan partnered with the judge's brother Thomas, whose son Walter would become commander of the Arkansas Post in 1809.[1016] Walter worked as a surveyor along with William P. Anderson in Tennessee.[1017] Brahan had also met Gilbert C. Russell. Before marching his company to Wilkinson's camp at Fort Adams in early 1809, Brahan traveled to Nashville in December 1808 to provide payment to Russell's company.[1018]

By 1809, a forty-two-year-old Jackson still contemplated his future. He had tried his hand at operating stores in Nashville and near Natchez and a boat-building business near Nashville, but they had proved unsuccessful. His Hermitage plantation did not produce enough income to provide the wealth he wanted. A new opportunity arose when Congress decided to sell recently ceded Chickasaw land in Madison County, in the upper Mississippi Territory, which would later become part of the State of Alabama.

When Brahan reached Wilkinson's camp in 1809, he sought a furlough to conduct the sales of the Chickasaw land as Receiver of Public Monies for the sales. In that position, he provided invaluable inside information to Jackson's business associates. Former congressman William Dickson, to whom Lewis had written to find a boat builder, was appointed Register of Property for the land sales.[1019] Jefferson's administration hired his spy, Thomas Freeman, to survey the land for the sales, and Freeman learned where the choicest land was located.

Due to a stagnant economy, land speculation in areas where new settlements created demand was one of the few ways investors could generate income on their assets. Rough forest land could be bought cheaply, cleared of trees, and then resold in parcels as farmland for several times the purchase price. Brahan encouraged poor squatters to move to the land with the promise that they would have the first chance to buy it at the public sale. In the meantime, the squatters would clear the land of timber and make other improvements to increase the value. Land sales were typically held near the tracts being sold, allowing the families who had settled and improved the land the opportunity to purchase it.

Taking advantage of Chickasaw complaints about settlers squatting on their remaining land, in July 1809, the army chose to enforce a law that prohibited settlers from living on the land they had been promised.[1020] Then, Freeman persuaded the federal government to move the sales to Nashville, arguing that sales there would bring higher prices.[1021] Sales were scheduled in Nashville for August 1809. Although Brahan was required to advertise the sale, no notice appears in any archived copies of the local Nashville *Democratic Clarion*.

The plan worked. Freeman made the largest single purchase. William P. Anderson and John Brahan also bought tracts.[1022] For perspective, Freeman and Brahan would eventually become wealthy men from purchasing the ceded Chickasaw land. Jackson would acquire most of his wealth from speculation in future sales, and Russell would also become a wealthy southern gentleman from his purchases.

The members of Jackson's land cabal were supportive of John Smith T's plan to send Patterson and others to Santa Fe and probably to take Texas. If for no other reason, Texas statehood moved the frontier so far west that their Tennessee and Madison County land would become safer and more valuable. Like Wilkinson, they would have had an interest in what maps and papers Lewis was carrying in his trunks to Washington. It was also not to their advantage to have too much attention focused on southern Tennessee and the Mississippi Territory area until the land sales had settled. A quick end to any discussion of Lewis's death in Tennessee would have served their interests. They should have been willing partners to spread a narrative that ended the discussion.

As Lewis traveled toward Washington, he was once again an explorer in a wild, uncharted landscape—this one political and commercial. The dangers from powerful and ambitious men whose interests were impossible to determine from appearances were just as great. More than a few could see Lewis as a threat to their interests. This time, Lewis did not have his team of fifty men, Clark's help, or Jefferson's backing.

He would encounter the unexpected storm alone.

I bequeath all my estate real and personal to my Mother Lucy Marks of the County of Albemarle and State of Virginia after my private debts are paid. of which a statement will be found in a small minute book deposited with Pernia my servant.—

September 11th 1809.

Meriwether Lewis.

in the presence of

A. S. Trinchard

Meriwether Lewis's Last Will and Testament

CHAPTER 16

# NECESSARY THAT HE BE STOPPED

[I determined it] necessary that he should be stop[p]ed.
—Capt. Gilbert C. Russell to Thomas Jefferson

Like whirlpools in the muddy Mississippi, Lewis's plans were already spiraling out of control by the time he neared Fort Pickering on the morning of September 15, 1809. He had traveled almost 400 miles by river from St. Louis in the muggy heat of late summer.

As the boat made its final approach, just above the broken bluffs covered in trees and shrubs, a watchtower atop the hill and wooden palisade walls would have come into view sixty feet above the water. Pyramids of shot were stacked on mounds beside cannons pointed toward the river. One visitor described the fort as a "small stoccado, commanding from its elevated situation not only the river, but also the surrounding country, which however is not yet sufficiently cleared of wood to make it tenable against an active enemy."[1023]

If fort commander Captain Gilbert C. Russell had advance notice of the governor's arrival, Lewis's boat should have been greeted with a salute by cannon fire as it approached. Those arriving by boat disembarked directly below the fort and climbed 120 log steps to reach the summit.

Young soldiers or boatmen would have been ordered to carry Lewis's trunks up the steep bluff.[1024] Lewis may not have been able to walk up the steps without assistance. Still feeling the effects of his illness, Lewis admitted that he was "much exhausted," but he passed off his condition as merely the effects of "the heat of the climate."[1025]

What made the ascent even more strenuous for a sick man was that the steps were likely drenched in blood. The startled visitor would eventually discover that the source of the blood was not human, but animals slaughtered for their fur. Nevertheless, the scent of death permeated the humid river air.[1026]

Once Lewis had climbed the six stories of steps in the morning sun, if he was able to endure a ceremony, he should have been received with honors by an assembly of the soldiers—at least those also well enough to stand at attention.[1027] Also from military customs, Russell should have given the governor an official welcome and formal assurances of hospitality. However, there is no record that Lewis was afforded any honors.

Russell, who would play a critical role in supporting the narrative that Lewis committed suicide, was only twenty-four years old, according to his own account, when the famed explorer arrived at Fort Pickering.[1028] He never claimed a prior friendship with Lewis in any letters that survive. Given Russell's young age and brief time on the Mississippi, it is unlikely that they had spent any significant time together.[1029] The prior month, as Lewis was tallying his debts, he noted what appeared to be an obligation to "Cap Russile" for $400.[1030] Perhaps that obligation related to some benefit McFarlane received as Lewis's subagent, and for which McFarlane asked Lewis to deliver a receipt. Russell would not attempt to collect that debt when he submitted his claim against Lewis's estate.[1031]

Russell later argued that Lewis was far sicker than he admitted upon his arrival. The illness, he claimed, had left Lewis "much depleted." Russell defended that an unnamed person—whether a fellow passenger or not is unknown—told him that Lewis had attempted to kill himself on the boat.

Russell said that based on the report, he concluded, "it was necessary he [Lewis] should be stop[p]ed."[1032] He implied that he stopped Lewis against his will. The young captain's justification for the astonishing arrest of the governor should have been substantiated by revealing the identity and credibility of the witnesses on whose word he relied, as well as the circumstances of Lewis's attempted suicide. Though it would have been to Russell's advantage to add those details in his defense, he chose to provide no further details.

Surgeon's Mate Smith complained that he had been "mortified" to see Russell and his Nashville company replace the former Commander Swan and his company three months earlier. Smith described Russell's rough recruits that now staffed the fort as "licentious creatures." Only one man besides Russell was an officer, and that officer was severely ill. With no one to challenge Russell's orders, Smith said that Russell was free to run the fort as a tyrant.[1033]

Russell insisted that Lewis not only be taken to his own fort commander's quarters to recover, but that he also be confined there under "strict" watch or guard.[1034] In effect, Lewis had become his prisoner. A month later, when Russell also ordered Surgeon's Mate Smith confined to quarters for an infraction, the secretary of war would conclude that Russell's order to confine the fort physician was simply evidence that Russell was an inexperienced commander. Dr. Smith was not so forgiving. He charged that confinement in the moldy, close quarters at Fort Pickering produced an illness he would not otherwise have suffered.[1035]

The army staffed a hospital with several physicians near Wilkinson's camp south of New Orleans.[1036] If Lewis was ill enough to be confined against his will and Wilkinson had not wanted to keep a public distance from the potential death of the governor, Russell took a significant risk in preventing Lewis from proceeding downriver to receive care. The Russell Statement claimed that he would have permitted Lewis to proceed downriver in the company of a friend who could guard his safety.[1037] It implied that Lewis had no such friend nearby who could help him.

Another effect of confinement to quarters was to shield Lewis from contact with outsiders. Otherwise, boatmen and traders could have offered their own evaluations of Lewis's health and offered to take him to New Orleans. One of those visitors should have been James McFarlane, who planned to travel down the river a few days behind Lewis, unless his boats were delayed.

Later, Clark questioned why Lewis failed to seek help from McFarlane, writing, "The Boats I sent down with the pelteres [peltries], under the derections of Mr. James McFarlane must have overtaken the Govr. Between new madrid and the Chickasaw Bluffs."[1038] If Clark's assessment of McFarlane is correct, he would have been concerned about his friend's condition and treatment. But there is no known evidence that McFarlane took any action.

Forts in the Southwest typically featured a house for the commander and his family, as well as guests, along with cabins or huts serving as barracks for lower-ranking soldiers. They also included a magazine for storing powder and outhouses for latrines.[1039] Cellars with heavy doors that locked and with iron bars across window openings could be used for storerooms. The only description of the details of the Fort Pickering commander's house is that a mantle tree had been placed over a fireplace where items could be hung.[1040]

An earlier visitor to Fort Pickering described the charming effect of the army offices and the two government stores, where the Chickasaw and Choctaw tribes traded. The traveler praised the extensive gardens and improvements.[1041] The fort was built to be a critical defense point, but once Spain relinquished control of the river, the U.S. spent its limited military resources elsewhere.[1042]

By 1809, Russell presented a completely opposite assessment. When Russell arrived to take command, he said that he found Fort Pickering in a "most wretched state."[1043] He discovered "[t]he pickets falling down [.] [t]he roof of the quarters intended for officers entirely decayed, ... the rafts totally rotten & not a chimney in the Fort."[1044] The conditions were so poor that he said that he would "have to repair the garrison which will require nearly as much labor and as many materials as to complete a fort of the same size from the beginning."[1045]

The leaky and moldering barracks took their toll on the soldiers quartered there. Surgeon's Mate Smith assessed that sickness prevailed at the fort as it did everywhere in the area. He suspected that the cause was the atmosphere.[1046] Swamps and ponds bordered the plain around the fort, and though local settlers did not consider the area particularly unhealthy, they suffered the usual fevers.[1047] Smith chose to take his quarters outside the fort, in part, to avoid what he suspected to be the cause of the fevers.[1048]

Russell had not made any repairs to the buildings. Exaggerating the number of his fellow officers, according to Smith, Russell stated, "out of forty eight officers & men I have sometimes had but eight or nine fit for duty."[1049] The manager of the Chickasaw trading post or "factory," factor David Hogg, had been sick with ague since the summer. His wife died from fever in September 1808, and the former Chickasaw agent had died at the agency from a "bilous complaint" that lasted six weeks.[1050] Hogg would resign due to sickness shortly after Lewis left the fort.[1051] As Dr. Smith had concluded in evaluating his own health, keeping Lewis confined at Fort Pickering did not provide an ideal environment for his recovery.

Whatever young Captain Russell's motives were for detaining Lewis, he knew that the governor's illness rendered him vulnerable. Russell's superior, Wilkinson, who had trained to become a physician earlier in life, once observed:

> A hardy, faithful, gallant, soldier, far removed from his natural friends and Connections, languishing on a sick bed under a parching fever has no where to look for Consolation for comfort or relief, but to his Officer and his surgeon, can a more interesting or affect-

ing Spectacle present to the human mind—surely none—and the man who under such Circumstances can with indifference turn from or treat with neglect, a comrade of honor and misfortune who looks up to him for Support, is ready to shed the last drop of blood in his defence and to die by his side in the field of battle, must be a monster in feeling and in principle.[1052]

But, of course, Wilkinson had proved himself to be the monster he described by providing enemies intelligence to kill U.S. soldiers who depended on him.

Russell would defend taking Lewis into his custody by claiming that the cause of Lewis's indisposition was simply "his free use of liquor." But rather than providing an opinion to that effect from Dr. Smith, as would have been common in military tribunals, Russell offered only his own assertion that Lewis promised him that he would never again overindulge in alcohol or snuff.[1053] Russell would be the only person who saw Lewis to write that he suffered from the effects of alcohol rather than from fever.[1054] Even Lewis's political enemies had never alleged that he abused alcohol, and if he did so privately, Lewis never acknowledged it in writing.[1055]

The *Missouri Gazette* published a story that Lewis was ill at Fort Pickering and under the care of Surgeon's Mate Smith.[1056] However, Russell claimed that he personally supervised Lewis's medical treatment. Russell said that he gave Lewis white wine and a little claret to drink, and suggested that he deprived him of stronger liquor and tobacco.[1057] Depriving Lewis of tobacco as well as alcohol suggests that Russell claimed to follow Dr. Benjamin Rush's 1785 pamphlet, *Effects of the Ardent Spirits*, or the later 1804 Trotter treatise, *An essay… on drunkenness*. The two of only a few sources on treatments for drunkenness both suggested a connection between tobacco and alcohol abuse.

Dr. Trotter also concurred in Dr. Rush's extreme warning, "I have classed death among the consequences of hard drinking. But it is not death from the immediate hand of the Deity, nor from any of the instruments of it which were created by him. It is death from suicide."[1058]

Dr. Trotter's book suggested treatments based on the belief that abuse of alcohol, tobacco, and opium resulted when the patient became "deranged"—the word Stoddard likely used to describe Lewis's illness on the boat and that The Neely letter used to describe Lewis's condition on the trip to Nashville. In addition, it warned that the condition could leave a patient's body "debilitated"—the word Russell chose to describe Lewis's body, ravaged from illness.

If Russell took charge of Lewis's treatment as he claimed, he may have misread Trotter's treatise. The physician recommended that patients be deprived of all addictive substances, cold turkey, and instead be given milk to drink to pass through a second healthy infancy.[1059] It was Dr. Rush who recommended wine as a healthy alternative to hard liquor.[1060]

If Russell treated Lewis's illness as he claimed, he breached protocol. Medical care was the job of the surgeon's mate.[1061] Surgeon's Mate Smith may have been one source for a news story from Nashville in November 1809, that Lewis had been deprived of the "necessities of life," similar to how Amos Stoddard referred to the daily allotment of bread for troops as "necessaries."[1062] The report suggested that Lewis was deprived of food. However, Lewis could have decided to fast based on Dr. Rush's advice to avoid eating as a treatment for general indisposition. Russell did not deny the allegation later when defending his care of Lewis. The newspaper report alleged that the mistreatment of Lewis eventually caused his fever to worsen to the point that it infected his brain.[1063]

Dr. Smith's allegations and the publication of the newspaper article would force Russell to defend his treatment of Lewis by writing a letter to Jefferson two and a half months after Lewis's death.[1064] In fact, Russell wrote his defense to Jefferson only two days after he compiled his defense of his arrest of Dr. Smith to send to the secretary of war.[1065] Allegations that Lewis was mistreated at Fort Pickering would be tamped down by

Madison's War Department and by Jefferson, who would thank Russell for Lewis's care.[1066]

But the allegations would not go away. Instead, the charges seem to have lingered still two years later when Russell was present in Fredericktown, Maryland, along with Wilkinson and Stoddard to testify at Wilkinson's trial for treason. Someone created a statement, The Russell Statement, purporting to detail Russell's recollection of Lewis's prior attempted suicide and mental derangement at the fort, Russell's treatment of Lewis, and Russell's later investigation of Lewis's death. Russell allegedly gave the statement to Wilkinson's extended relative, Jonathan Williams, and it contained a purported certification from Williams that Russell had signed the statement.[1067] Significantly, the only copy of the statement that has been found states that the original was signed by "Gilbert Russell," whom the statement claimed was "Major Gilbert Russell," though Gilbert C. Russell always signed his name with a distinctive "C." for his middle name. If the copy dated November 26, 1811, is an exact duplication of the original, someone forged Russell's signature on The Russell Statement original document. Williams' signature on the certification would also have been forged, because the signature contained only the first letter for his first name, and he regularly signed his first name as "Jon."[1068]

Perhaps it was only coincidental that Stoddard and Russell both used exact terms from Dr. Trotter's 1804 treatise to argue that Lewis exhibited signs of being a drunkard. In any event, their use of the terms could be expected to lead those familiar with the treatise to accept the later narrative that Lewis's drunken derangement caused his suicide.

Oddly, like other travelers on Lewis's boat, no soldier stationed at Fort Pickering, other than Russell or Smith, is known to have reported their contact with a supposedly drunken, delirious, and suicidal national hero. Russell would tell Jefferson that Lewis had perfectly recovered; Smith would tell his own family that the cause of Lewis's death was murder.[1069]

## Necessary That He Be Stopped

After learning herbal treatments from his mother and the most modern medical practices for the expedition directly from Dr. Rush, Lewis had no hesitation treating his own maladies. Whatever his illness, Lewis diagnosed himself and believed that some of the medicine he carried would cure him.[1070]

Russell suggested that Lewis agreed to follow the same treatment Dr. Rush recommended for alcohol abuse. Lewis also apparently did not use the natural bark and calomel that most settlers in the Mississippi Valley used to treat fever, as his mother might have recommended.[1071] He could have afforded the more modern cure-all, laudanum—an opiate not yet generally considered hazardous. One remedy Lewis noted in his Memorandum Book was to take one opium pill at bedtime each evening.[1072] Though Russell later claimed that it was necessary to confine Lewis and keep him under watch for six days, the day after arriving, Lewis wrote that he had taken medicine and already felt better.[1073] If Lewis followed Dr. Rush's expedition recommendations for fever and agreed to Russell's treatment for alcoholism, he may have fasted and taken opium pills at the same time he was given only claret and white wine to drink.

With Lewis confined to quarters, his trunks and their contents became a main focal point. Rather than placing the trunks in Lewis's quarters, Russell ordered that they be held in a locked storage room. Strangely, when the *Missouri Gazette* reported Lewis's illness at Fort Pickering, it also reported on the location of Lewis's trunks and made particular reference to Russell storing "the key" in his stores, or storeroom.[1074] By separating Lewis from his trunks, Russell would have had the opportunity to examine what papers Lewis was taking with him to Washington and send a report by express rider or boat to Wilkinson.

Unless Lewis had chartered private transportation, the boat he had taken to Fort Pickering proceeded downstream without him. Lewis's detainment even for a few days would breach the month-or-so timeline when the president would expect his arrival, increasing the likelihood that Madison would replace him as governor before he had a chance to defend himself. After declaring himself better the day after he arrived, Lewis likely would have pressed to proceed toward Washington City. If Lewis insisted on taking the next boat to New Orleans, someone may have emphasized the spurious reports that the British were seizing ships in the Caribbean. Lewis would use that reason as one justification for changing his route at Fort Pickering. Then, too, since his arrival in New Madrid, he had already contemplated the overland route.[1075]

News Lewis received at Fort Pickering about fever in New Orleans, the British threat, a sudden swelling of the numbers of French immigrants from Cuba, or suspicions that, as in the Burr Conspiracy, Wilkinson had hired assassins—whether true or false, confirmed his need to change course. Returning to St. Louis would only create further delays, fuel suspicions in Washington City, and jeopardize his reappointment. He could take a boat such as Fooy's back upriver to New Madrid, travel overland, and attempt to catch Clark, but Clark likely was too far ahead. The only option that remained was to proceed overland through the Chickasaw Nation to Nashville and then continue east.

Illness did not take Lewis's mind off the pressing need to defend his reputation to the president. On September 16, one day after arriving at Fort Pickering—when Russell would claim Lewis was so ill that he needed to be confined and The Russell Statement would claim that he was deranged and out of his senses—Lewis wrote a letter to President Madison to alert him that his health might delay his arrival. He had decided to change his route to travel overland through Tennessee, he wrote, for two reasons: he feared the heat of the Lower Mississippi (and illness by implication), and he feared that the original expedition papers might fall into the hands of the British. He may not have felt free to state his concerns about other confidential papers he may have carried.

Lewis mentioned that he was carrying vouchers to support his challenge to the War Department's refusal to reimburse his expenditures.[1076] Though he had previously assured the secretary of war that he would also bring papers proving that he had performed loyal services to the government, he did not mention papers related to those services in his letter to Madison.[1077] He might choose not to risk taking some of those papers overland.

The following day, on September 17, still supposedly so ill that he needed to be confined under watch, Lewis devoted time to straightening out his financial affairs. He had given his Memorandum Book to Peerny for safekeeping at New Madrid when he was so ill he did not think he would survive. Now, he felt well enough to regain possession of the book and noted, "There is enclosed my land warrant for 1600 acres to Bonley Robertson of New Orleans to be _____ for two dollars per acre or more if it can be obtained and the money deposited in the branch bank of New Orleans on the City of Washington subject to my order or that of William Meriwether for the benefit of my creditors." He signed it "M. Lewis" and dated the top of the page with the year 1809, unlike other pages, presumably to create an official authorization if something should happen to him. He went back to add the "for 1600 dollars" with a carrot for clarification.[1078]

Lewis showed no delusional effects from fever in his notes or letters at Fort Pickering other than possibly an increased number of corrections in his drafts. His business decisions were rational. Russell later confirmed that he complied with Lewis's instructions by sending the land warrant to the Secretary of the Treasury of the Orleans Territory. The secretary was asked to sell the warrant for a price above two dollars per acre and credit the funds to an account for Lewis.[1079]

Nevertheless, in his letter to President Madison, Lewis had again unwisely revealed his travel plans to anyone who opened his letter. Fort Pickering lay within the Chickasaw Nation, and mail from the fort was carried about ninety miles southeast to the U.S. post office located at McIntoshville, a settlement about eight miles north of the Chickasaw Agency house.[1080] Chickasaw horsemen were often hired to carry mail between the post office and the fort.[1081] Post riders for post offices on the Natchez Trace were required to ride fifty miles a day in 1809; however, mail riders between the Chickasaw Post Office and Fort Pickering were authorized to be express riders.[1082] With a change of horses, an express rider was expected to cover one hundred miles a day, about the distance between the Chickasaw Post Office and the fort.[1083]

The official postmaster in the Chickasaw Nation was the U.S. Agent to the Chickasaw Nation, Major James Neelly.[1084] The Neelly Letter said that Major Neelly arrived at Fort Pickering on September 18, two days after Lewis wrote his letter to Madison stating his change of route overland through the Chickasaw Nation. Neelly, a Tennessean who lived just south of Franklin, had just arrived in the Chickasaw Nation to take his position at the Chickasaw Agency in late August. The War Department had appointed him in July to fill the position of the agent who had died the previous year.[1085] Wilkinson was in Washington while the position was open, and when Fort Pickering factor David Hogg had applied for the position.[1086] Wilkinson would have been consulted to approve the appointment of Neelly before he left Washington for New Orleans.[1087]

In return, Wilkinson would have expected Neelly to be one of his government spies.

## CHAPTER 17

# STALLED

[Lewis had an] apprehension of being destroyed by enemies which had no existence but in his wild imagination.
—Alleged The Russell Statement, signed with a copy of Russell's forged signature

Major James Neelly had a good excuse to spend considerable time at the fort, where he could have won Lewis's confidence. The secretary of war had ordered him to distribute two years of annuities, consisting of annual payments of money for tribal leaders and blankets, cloth, lead, and other materials to the Chickasaw clans.[1088] As one of the two main places where the federal government conducted official business with the Chickasaw, it staffed interpreters and messengers at the fort.[1089]

Chickasaw made up a significant part of the population at Chickasaw Bluffs. Government trading posts and offices often attracted tribal members who benefited from trading with soldiers. A Chickasaw clan lived in a small village five miles east of the fort, and the army had cut a road through the forest to the village.[1090] Across the river in the Arkansas District, around a hundred Chickasaw men lived in a town where it was said they cultivated the soil.[1091] Chickasaw women typically performed farm work; therefore, the village likely contained scores of Chickasaw families.

The fort also contained a trading house or factory for the Chickasaw, as well as at least two stores for private contractors, one of which may have been operated by John Overton's agent. Much of the activity at the fort centered around trading pelts with the Chickasaw, preparing skins for shipping downriver, and packing them onto horses and mules to transport to market. A skin house, located adjacent to the store, provided space for workers to treat and flatten or "beat out" skins for transport.[1092] Chickasaw Bluffs was one of the most profitable factory trading houses operated by the government, and its use for the fur trade continued for several years after the army abandoned the post.[1093] One traveler would describe the rancid smell of skins drying in the sun at the Chickasaw Agency, and large numbers of skins near the skin house would likely have produced a similar odor at the fort.[1094]

Annuity items for the Chickasaw were normally transported by river from the East to Fort Pickering. There, Chickasaw leaders oversaw loading the goods onto wagons and transporting the annuities back to the tribal towns, as had been advised by the secretary of war. Similar to the prior delivery of annuities, a year later, a third to a half of the entire Chickasaw population, more than 1,500 Chickasaw men, women, and children, did not wait and appeared at the fort to receive their shares.[1095] If a comparable number traveled to Chickasaw Bluffs in 1809, Fort Pickering would have been a bustle of activity during the time of Lewis's confinement.

Any confusion created by deliveries of annuities hid tensions that simmered beneath the surface at Fort Pickering. A breakdown of discipline resulted in several courts-martial. Unknown to Russell, the trading post operator, David Hogg, had already secretly filed formal charges against him. Hogg was upset that Russell had not prosecuted a resident trader, Benjamin Allen, for privately trading with the Chickasaw, which was against the law, likely creating undue competition for the factor's purchase of peltries and other items.[1096] Surgeon's Mate Smith would soon bring charges against Russell for confining him to quarters. Russell would retaliate by bringing his own charges against Smith for staying overnight at the home of a young widow, spending three days away from the fort, and failing to provide adequate medical care.[1097] Smith would defend that the widow deserved additional support because her husband was part of the network of secret services operating out of Fort Adams and that he had died performing "confidential" services at the fort.

Neelly's own troubles were brewing. On September 20, while Neelly was at Fort Pickering, a blacksmith, George Lanehart, stole saddlebags at an inn on the Natchez Trace at McIntoshville. The theft created a diplomatic incident because the bags had been entrusted to Chickasaw inn owner James Colbert. The victim was Colonel Joseph VanMeter from Virginia, whose bags contained over $617 in silver.[1098]

Because Lanehart was a white man who had committed a crime in the Chickasaw Nation, he would be tried for his crime in the nearest federal court.[1099] It was Neelly's duty as Chickasaw agent to remove the prisoner from the Chickasaw Nation and take him to be tried. Neelly would choose Nashville as a venue because he already had plans to travel to Franklin, just south of the town.

On September 21, Chickasaw Bluffs factor Hogg wrote to the acting factor at the Arkansas Post to acknowledge that he was sending him a courier with a shipment of goods that had arrived at Fort Pickering, maybe along with the annuities. Hogg's letter raises the possibility that Lieutenant Walter Overton had been at the fort or was there at that time, possibly returning to the Arkansas Post along with the goods. After discussing business matters, Hogg interjected, "I refer you to Leiut. Overton for the news."[1100] He did not state the nature of the news that he chose not to put in writing. The most significant news would have been that Governor Lewis was confined at Fort Pickering and that he planned to travel overland to Nashville.[1101]

The following day, September 22, Lewis had recovered his health, according to the first letter Russell later sent to Jefferson to defend himself.[1102] Confirming that statement, on the same date, Lewis wrote to Major Amos Stoddard. Lewis felt well enough to begin thinking ahead and preparing for his return trip to St. Louis after meeting with the president and his publisher.

He needed funds. He asked Stoddard to send $200 that Stoddard had collected on his behalf, presumably when Stoddard served as attorney-in-fact under Lewis's Power of Attorney in St. Louis.[1103] Confirming that Lewis had not seen Stoddard since, Lewis admitted that Stoddard had reminded him several times that he was holding money for him, but Lewis had not replied.[1104]

Lewis thought Stoddard was still stationed south at Fort Adams on the east bank of the Mississippi, and he had planned to collect the funds from Stoddard when his boat made that stop. Russell informed him that Stoddard was on the west side, which would have been along the Spanish border at Natchitoches.[1105] Russell's knowledge that Stoddard was on the west side of the Mississippi raises questions of whether Russell also knew that Stoddard had traveled up the Red River toward Spanish Texas and how much information about those activities, if any, he provided Lewis.

Lewis again disclosed that he would be changing his route to travel overland through Tennessee, but this time, he blamed solely his "indisposition" or illness, rather than the safety of his papers or the threat of the British. Lewis instructed Stoddard to forward the payment to him to Washington City. Feeling relief from his illness, he was optimistic that his meeting with Madison would go well, and he planned to set out on his return to St. Louis by December. The amount of the funds Stoddard was holding roughly matched the amount Lewis would expect to take overland to Washington City. He could expect a similar amount to be enough to cover the expense of his return trip from Washington to St. Louis.

Lewis did not take the opportunity in his letters to Stoddard or Madison to complain about Russell's treatment of him. He may have considered the confinement helpful, as Russell claimed. Or, he may have considered that his letters could be opened, and he was at Russell's mercy. Two years earlier, Wilkinson had sent promises of bounties to government officers to capture Burr. Lewis had no way of knowing which of the military officers he met might have received similar bounties to capture him. It is also possible that he wrote additional letters that never went any farther than the mailbags for the Chickasaw Post Office.

Lewis addressed the letter to be mailed to Stoddard at Fort Adams, where Stoddard would have been expected to return after his trip on the west side of the river. Unknown to Lewis, by that time, Stoddard had completed his mission on the Red River and was already traveling up the Natchez Trace from Natchitoches and Fort Adams.[1106]

Russell suggested that Lewis pressed to leave.[1107] But Russell stalled him again. Like Lewis, Clark, and most army officers, Russell had been denied reimbursement from the War Department. Of the expenditures Russell had submitted for recruiting troops in Nashville, the War Department had protested his drafts in the amount of $1,798.[1108] He said that he had already sent Wilkinson a request to permit him to leave his post to go to Washington to straighten out his account. Russell offered to accompany Lewis to Washington City if Lewis could wait until Wilkinson sent his approval. Russell said that he persuaded Lewis to delay his departure for an additional six or eight days as they waited for a reply from Wilkinson.[1109] It would have been unusual for an ambitious fort commander to take a furlough so soon after starting a new command—his first—particularly when so few of his soldiers were fit for duty and when the only other officer at the fort was seriously ill.

Lewis should have doubted whether Russell made the request, but once Lewis altered his travel plans, he had little choice but to wait on Russell. Having set out aboard a riverboat for a voyage by ship, he had no reason to bring along the horses essential for an overland trip. In addition, according to Russell, after arranging to hold off his creditors in St. Louis, Lewis carried only about $120 in notes and specie to make the remainder of his journey.[1110] It would not be enough to purchase horses and provide for lodging until he reached Washington. Without Russell's help, he was stranded.

As Russell stalled Lewis, Neelly left Fort Pickering and returned to the Chickasaw Agency. He could have excused the trip on the need to make plans to transport the prisoner to Nashville or to oversee additional delivery of the annuities. While at the agency on September 24, Neelly issued a draft drawn on the War Department to the order of the Chickasaw factor Hogg for $100.[1111] Neelly would offer Lewis the use of horses from the Chickasaw Nation to transport Lewis's trunks to Nashville.[1112] Russell claimed that the horses Neelly provided were strays taken in from the Chickasaw Nation.[1113] Neelly may have taken horses from the agency area to offer to transport Lewis's trunks.

While at the Chickasaw Agency or in its vicinity, Neelly may have met with Amos Stoddard, who was traveling up the Natchez Trace toward Nashville. Stoddard later wrote that when he was in the Chickasaw Nation, he met a man coming directly from the Chickasaw Bluffs who told him that Meriwether Lewis had attempted suicide.[1114] Notably, Stoddard did not reveal the identity of the man who made such a consequential statement. James Neelly, who traveled from the Chickasaw Bluffs to the Chickasaw Agency about the time Stoddard passed the agency, fits the description of that man. The statement that a governor had attempted suicide was explosive, even if true. At a minimum, Stoddard was unlikely to chance repeating such a claim based on a statement from someone who was not working in an official capacity.

Lewis may have decided to write his letter to Stoddard on September 22, because he was aware that Neelly would be leaving the fort to return to the Chickasaw Agency and Chickasaw Post Office—Neelly was at the Chickasaw Agency two days after Lewis wrote the letter. If Neelly met with Stoddard near the agency or post office, he could have hand-delivered the letter to Stoddard. But Lewis's letter was marked as being received at the "Chickasaw" (Post Office) on September 25, then forwarded to Fort Adams. Someone crossed out "Fort Adams" under Stoddard's name and wrote "Washington City" where the letter should be forwarded. Stoddard had possession of the letter two months later in Washington.[1115]

Stoddard claimed that news of Lewis's condition gave him "much pain,"—but not so much that he took time from his trip to ride two days to Fort Pickering to check on Lewis's welfare.[1116] Instead, he continued up the Natchez Trace through Nashville and then on to Washington, spreading rumors along the way that he heard Lewis was acting deranged and that he had attempted suicide.[1117]

In 1809, such a public claim, whether true or not, could have prompted Lewis to challenge Stoddard to a duel—if Lewis survived. Perhaps Stoddard withheld Neelly's name as the source of his information because Neelly would be returning to Fort Pickering. If Lewis had found out, he would have challenged Neelly to a duel before he arrived in Nashville. Unless Stoddard acted uncharacteristically recklessly, those who knew Stoddard might draw the conclusion that he only took the risk of associating his own name with the rumor because he knew that he was beyond Lewis's immediate reach, and he already knew that Lewis would not survive to challenge him.

Russell said that he did not receive a reply from Wilkinson to his request to travel to Washington.[1118] Wilkinson reported his subordinates' requests for furloughs to the secretary of war and the register listing such requests during that period still exists—but the secretary's register does not mention Russell's request, and no other record has been located to verify that Russell ever made the request.[1119]

Whether or not Russell's motives were as innocent as he claimed, his extraordinary actions at Fort Pickering had the effect of stalling Lewis long enough to set up the course of events that would make Lewis's papers vulnerable and lead to the explorer's death.

Captain John Brahan

## CHAPTER 18

# FATEFUL DECISIONS

> Unfortunately for him this arrangement did not take place, or I hesitate not to say he would this day be living.
> —Gilbert C. Russell to Thomas Jefferson

More than 900 miles of trails and dirt roads through dense forests, canebrake thickets, and open plains lay between Fort Pickering and Washington City. Lewis armed himself with a pocket pistol, a long knife or dirk, a rifle, a tomahawk, and a pair of pistols that were probably long-barreled.[1120] Like the weapons John Smith T carried, they were standard outfitting for gentlemen on the frontier who could rely on no one else for defense.

If Lewis did not know that soldiers traveling from Chickasaw Bluffs overland to the East Coast normally began their trip on the Lower Chickasaw Trail, Russell or other men at the fort could have told him. The trail followed the top of a ridge southeastward across the northern Mississippi Territory. From Fort Pickering, the ride to McIntoshville also led to what a notorious highway robber called "the great road."[1121] That road was Jefferson's new Natchez Trace federal wagon highway that had been planned when Lewis acted as Jefferson's unofficial military advisor. Soldiers traveled the Natchez Trace frequently in both directions between Nashville and Fort Adams northwest of New Orleans or Fort Dearborn near Natchez.

From Nashville, travelers could follow one of several well-traveled roads running north or east.

Once Lewis decided he could wait no longer, he persuaded Russell to lend him money to purchase two horses along with additional travel funds.[1122] To keep a record for himself or to pass along to his executor if he did not survive the trip, on September 27, Lewis noted in his Memorandum Book, "I have borrowed of Capt. Gilbert C. Russell a check on the Branch Bank of New Orleans for this sum ($99.58 noted to the side with a bracket), for which I gave him my note. Ditto ($280) to the same for two horses."[1123]

Lewis had to decide what to do with the five trunks he carried. Wooden trunks designed to be packed or carried on horses were small and round. They could be easily tied on the sides of horses like a bedroll. The round sides would not injure the horses, and they could pass easily through narrow trails or roads.[1124] Trunks hauled by wagon or shipped by boat were more often rectangular in shape, with flat bottoms and square sides. It was still possible to tie such trunks to the sides of horses with blankets or hides acting as a buffer to prevent injury to the animal.[1125]

Lewis told Russell that one of the five trunks belonged to Captain James House. Unless Lewis explained why House could not transport his own trunk, he left the impression that he had offered to take the trunk because he would be traveling by boat, and House would travel by horseback to his new assignment in the East. Presumably, House would still have taken his own personal trunk, containing his clothing and other items he would have needed during his trip. If Lewis did not disclose the contents of the House trunk or Russell did not check, Russell may have wondered what additional items House would have been transporting east or whether the trunk even belonged to House.[1126] When House later wrote to Frederick Bates to pass along a rumor as to Lewis's condition and report on the safeguarding of Lewis's trunks, he did not mention that one of the trunks was his or express any concern for it.[1127]

Lewis chose to leave the House trunk in Russell's care at Fort Pickering with instructions to forward it on by boat to New Orleans:

> Capt. Russell will much oblige his friend Meriwether Lewis by forwarding to the care of William Brown Collector of the port of New Orleans, a Trunk belonging to Capt. James House addressed to McDonald and Ridgely Merchants in Baltimore. Mr. Brown will be requested to forward this trunk to its place of destination.[1128]

Lewis then noted in his Memorandum Book, "Left the trunk of Capt. House with Capt. Russell to be sent to the care of Mr. Brown as Orleans Collector to him forwarded to McDonald and Rigely of Baltimore as addressed."[1129]

Lewis decided to leave two of the remaining four trunks, a liquor case, and a package of blankets at Fort Pickering. He gave Russell a memorandum requesting that he safeguard those two trunks and other items until they could be turned over to attorney William Carr or wealthy St. Louis merchant Jean Cabanne, unless he heard otherwise from Lewis by letter from Nashville. He wrote instructions to Russell: "Capt. R. will also send two trunks, a package, and a case addressed to Mr. William C. Carr of St. Louis unless otherwise instructed by M. L. by letter from Nashville. ... a Mr. Cabboni of St. Louis may be expected to pass this place in the course of the next month, to him they may be confided."[1130] Lewis directed Russell to "be particular to whom he confides these trunks & ca."[1131]

Lewis then noted in his Memorandum Book, "Also left with Capt. Russell two trunks containing papers or a case for liquor and a package of blankets sheets and coverlets to be sent to Willim C. Carr of St. Louis for me—unless I shall otherwise direct.—." Like Lewis, Russell described the items as "two Trunks[,] a case)[,] and a bundle."[1132] Peerny later told Jefferson that the two trunks Lewis left at Fort Pickering contained only Lewis's "private property."[1133] But Lewis's written direction specifying who should have control of the two trunks demonstrated a concern more appropriate for the papers they contained than for any other personal items. Lewis's specific direction to Russell in the memorandum created a chain of custody for the contents of the trunks.

The remaining two trunks that Lewis planned to carry with him were later described as a long trunk and a square trunk.[1134] They contained Lewis's expedition papers, Morocco-bound expedition journals, and other government papers, as well as Clark's land warrant.[1135] Papers later generally described as relating to government and personal business would also be found in the trunks.[1136] Those papers may have included maps from spies' excursions into New Spain.[1137]

Lewis also carried a round portmanteau, likely an oblong leather bag tied with straps, where he would have packed clothing and a few other personal items. The portmanteau could be strapped behind the saddle when he was riding a horse or carried with a strap over the shoulder when he dismounted.

He could carry his notebook or Memorandum Book on his person if he chose, or continue to permit Peerny to carry it for safekeeping. His binder for papers or portfolio and pocketbook would need to be carried in one of the trunks or cases.[1138] He also may have carried a buffalo robe and bear skins, which would have been folded to be tied to the side of a horse.[1139]

Lewis could have hired a wagon driver to transport the two trunks. But wagons were expensive; they traveled much slower than horseback riders; and if they broke down in the wilderness, he would be stranded with the trunks while waiting for repairs. Russell implied that Lewis asked for his help in figuring out how to transport the trunks safely through the Chickasaw Nation to Nashville.[1140]

On the same day that Lewis made final travel plans at Fort Pickering, Major Amos Stoddard and Captain James House, whose trunk Lewis said he carried, met in Nashville, where they discussed Lewis.[1141] Stoddard had not been pressed for time to arrive in Washington as he traveled up the Natchez Trace; however, he may have been eager to arrive in Nashville to meet with House and Captain John Brahan. House's presence in Nashville seemed out of place. He was traveling from St. Louis to Baltimore.[1142] Nashville was at least a three-day ride out of House's way, unless he had first traveled from St. Louis south to the Lower Mississippi and then followed the Natchez Trace to Nashville, or unless he had traveled directly from St. Louis to Nashville to meet with Stoddard or Brahan.

Stoddard wrote a letter from Nashville to Captain Daniel Bissell in St. Louis, dated the same day, September 28 (though the *Missouri Gazette* would apparently misprint it as "September 8") to publish his claim that Lewis was extremely ill:

> I have some unhappy intelligence to give you. I saw a gentleman in the Chickasaw nation, directly from the Bluffs, who informed me that Governor Lewis was at that place much indisposed [.] that he was so for several days previous to his arrival. Capt. Russell received him into his quarters and stored his property. He was under the care of the surgeons mate Dr. Smith, but no alteration for the better had taken place when my informant left the bluffs. This affair has given me much pain, and I leave it with you to divulge it to the Governor's friends in such manner as you think proper.[1143]

If Stoddard also included the rumor that Lewis was suicidal, it may explain why the editor chose to print only a portion of the letter, leaving out those details.

The developing suicide narrative immediately suffered from contradictions as House also took a turn at spreading the rumors. On the same day that Stoddard wrote his letter from Nashville to Bissell, House wrote a letter from Nashville to Frederick Bates, who was acting as temporary governor of the Upper Louisiana Territory in St. Louis during Lewis's absence. The purpose of the letter was solely to pass along the rumor Stoddard claimed to have heard from a person coming from Chickasaw Bluffs that Lewis arrived there:

> in a state of mental derangement, that Lewis had made several attempts to put an end to his existence, which the person had prevented, and that Captain Russell, the commanding officer at the Bluffs had taken him into his own quarters where he was obliged to keep strict watch over him to prevent his committing violence on himself.

House's statement that the reason Russell kept watch over Lewis was to prevent him from violently injuring himself rather than to keep him from contact with alcohol, as Russell would tell Jefferson, was a significant detail that Russell never claimed. It would have been to Russell's advantage to use that fact in his later defense of taking Lewis into custody, if it had been true. Russell also never stated that another person prevented Lewis from taking his own life at Fort Pickering, or that Lewis had attempted to take his life more than two times.[1144]

House added that Russell had ordered Lewis's "boat to be unloaded and the key to be secured in his stores."[1145] House did not state whether "the key" that Russell secured was a key to a trunk, a key to a storeroom, or a key to ciphered messages, such as a book with the code designated. He presumed that Bates knew.

Though House concluded by stating that he did not think it improper that he communicate the rumor to Bates, House must have known that Bates was Lewis's political enemy—House would have written to Clark rather than Bates if his purpose was altruistic. House also likely knew that if the rumors were true, Bates would already have heard them from the network of military men and traders traveling on the river by the time his letter arrived from Nashville. House's purpose would not have been to ensure the continuity of the territorial government. On the contrary, House would have known at a minimum that the letter would undermine Lewis's reputation and make it more difficult for him to continue to serve as governor if he survived. Of course, like Stoddard, House also would have known that if Lewis survived, his claim that Lewis was mentally deranged and suicidal would have prompted Lewis to challenge him to a duel.

For emphasis, House added, "I am in hopes this account will prove exaggerated tho' I fear there is too much truth in it..." Whatever House's motives, the effect was to give Bates ammunition he could use to spread the rumor in St. Louis that Lewis had attempted suicide or to provide justification for the rumors that Bates had already spread.

Rather than keeping Stoddard's letter private until the facts could be verified, Bissell would see that an extract of Stoddard's letter was published in the *Missouri Gazette*.[1146] Interested parties would have been expected to have heard rumors of Lewis's illness, but they may not have known the location of "the key." By writing separate letters to both Bates and Bissell, House and Stoddard made it appear that the information, coming from more than one source, should be given credence.

Two days later, Stoddard met with Captain John Brahan in Nashville. Because Stoddard was traveling to Washington to meet with the secretary of war, Brahan handed Stoddard at least one letter to courier to the secretary to avoid sending it in the mail. In that letter, Brahan requested that he be permitted to retain his position as a captain in the U.S. Army if he had to choose between that position and his position as receiver, but he added that Stoddard could provide the secretary with additional details.[1147] Stoddard must have discussed his rumor that Lewis was at Fort Pickering after attempting suicide, and the source may have informed him that Lewis had discussed traveling overland to Nashville.

The secretary of war did not receive the letter Stoddard delivered for Brahan until November 10, about twenty days later than a letter mailed from Nashville near the same time. The delay raises questions of how long Stoddard remained in the Nashville area and where he was when Lewis died on October 11.[1148] As soon as he arrived in Washington City, Stoddard spread rumors that Lewis had attempted suicide by providing the Chickasaw Bluffs informant's rumor to *The National Intelligencer,* along with a copy of Lewis's September 22 private letter to him from Fort Pickering.[1149]

Neelly returned from the Chickasaw Agency to Fort Pickering. He said that he already planned to travel to Nashville, and he would be happy to have it in his power to escort Lewis.[1150] It would have seemed reasonable that the Chickasaw agent should escort the governor through the Chickasaw Nation, and the offer was accepted.[1151] Russell would later suggest that he did not trust Neelly.[1152] His language is ambiguous, but it seems that Russell may have arranged for a man he trusted to pack or transport Lewis's trunks by horseback "to the Nation," at least as far as the general Chickasaw Agency area. From there, Neelly would transport Lewis's trunks "from the Nation" to Nashville.[1153]

Trunks could be tied securely to the sides of horses with ropes and sticks; however, horses had their own minds, and even an unexpected noise could cause them to run away with their cargo. Army leaders often assigned several men the sole duty of keeping up with packhorses to make certain they did not stray. Lewis did not have that luxury.

By September 29, with funds and transportation secured, Lewis was ready to ride out of the confines of the fort into the forest. According to The Russell Statement, the traveling party consisted of Lewis, Neelly, the Chickasaw interpreter (likely Jeremiah K. Love), and some Chickasaw chiefs, who may have accompanied them in part to deliver annuities to their villages or simply to extend hospitality to the governor. The Russell Statement did not mention Lewis's servant Peerny or Neelly's servant or packman, though from circumstances it is known that they were part of the party. The statement said that Lewis's trunks were well-secured on the horses.

Though Russell later wrote Jefferson to defend that Lewis was "perfectly restored in every respect & able to travel" when he left Fort Pickering, The Neelly Letter claimed that Lewis had recovered his health only to some degree, and The Russell Statement related that Lewis suffered from "severe depletion during his illness [from which] he had been considerably reduced and debilitated, from which he had not entirely recovered when he set off."[1154]

Lewis would supposedly live another twelve days, but he never made another entry in his Memorandum Book. In effect, Lewis lost control of his biography on the day that Russell said he left Fort Pickering.

At a time when Congress was seeking evidence to court-martial Wilkinson, Wilkinson was building his defense and attempting to maintain control over events in the West, spies and mercenaries were plotting to invade Texas and Santa Fe, adventurers and robbers sought information about a silver lode along the Red River, Spanish patrols roamed the Southwest looking for intruders, and fortunes awaited in the new Northwest or along the Red River, several parties had a stake in the papers Lewis was carrying to Washington. The *Missouri Gazette* editor understood the significance when he highlighted the location of the papers in his article on Lewis's health.

Safeguarding those papers would be of such importance that Lewis wrote that he was changing his travel plans to protect them from confiscation by the British.

As it turned out, the British were the least of the threats Lewis faced.

Andrew Jackson

## CHAPTER 19

# RIDE INTO THE STORM

> I do not think mySelf Calculated to meet the Storms which might be expected…
>
> —William Clark, on his possible appointment as Lewis's replacement as governor[1155]

On the same day that Russell noted that Lewis left Fort Pickering, September 29, he said that Ben Wilkinson appeared at the fort or made his presence at Chickasaw Bluffs known.[1156] Ben met with Russell and no doubt discussed Lewis. It is not known whether Lewis had delivered McFarlane's "receipt" to Russell as he had promised or what information it contained. Russell did not disclose whether Ben traveled with James McFarlane on one of the peltry boats or whether McFarlane also appeared at the fort.

Ben Wilkinson must have read the *Missouri Gazette* reports of Lewis's illness or talked with people who had read them.[1157] Russell might have assured Ben that Lewis left the fort "perfectly restored in every respect" as he would later write to Jefferson. If Ben traveled to Fort Pickering out of concern for his friend, he could have caught up with Lewis on the Chickasaw Trail. Instead, Ben's primary concern was control of the House trunk. Russell turned the trunk over to Ben, presumably to follow Lewis's instructions to have it delivered to the New Orleans port collector, William Brown.[1158]

If Ben's uncle, General Wilkinson, wanted to examine the contents of the trunk, he could have been found on the Lower Mississippi, where he had been ordered to move his troops from New Orleans to Fort Adams or Natchez.[1159] Whether the general met with Ben or had access to the House trunk is unknown. General Wilkinson was said to have become so indisposed or sick that he took leave of his troops on September 22 and traveled to New Orleans to recover.[1160] But the general seems to have used much of his sick time preparing his defense for his upcoming trial. He obtained a statement from Captain William Tharp in New Orleans between September 25 and October 2 that he would use to undermine the credibility of Daniel Clark, Jr. in the trial. Tharp stated that he was a Wilkinson loyalist who was approached by Clark Jr.'s friends and offered a plantation and cattle to give testimony against Wilkinson.[1161]

Nor was General Wilkinson too sick to make the rounds to locations where Dr. Sibley's expedition party and the party from Natchez may have reported. The general was at Columbian Springs on October 18.[1162] He traveled to Natchitoches on October 20 and then back to Columbian Springs on October 24. General Wilkinson claimed that he posted bail in Natchez on October 25 for an arrest warrant issued for him on October 9 related to his arrest of a senator in New Orleans during the Burr Conspiracy.[1163] He sent letters from undisclosed locations on October 6 and October 9, but the known record does not account for his whereabouts during much of the period.[1164]

There is also no record of whether Ben met with the New Orleans port collector, William Brown, to deliver the House trunk as Lewis had instructed Russell. Brown's plantation at Chalmette lay about twelve miles northwest of Wilkinson's camp at Terre aux Boeuf, about halfway between the camp and New Orleans. On October 17, Brown notified the Treasury Department that his official accounts were short by over $130,000. He was then said to have withdrawn over $90,000 of government funds from the bank in the form of Spanish gold doubloons before absconding on a Spanish privateer's ship.[1165]

House would report that he received his trunk in Baltimore by December, as he fumed, "It fell into the hands of Ben Wilkinson at Orleans."[1166] But Ben disappeared. Frederick Bates reported that Ben died, which no one in St. Louis publicly contradicted. Someone spread the rumor that Ben boarded a ship that wrecked and that he was lost at sea.[1167] House heard that Ben boarded the sailing ship *Dart* for Baltimore and that he "died on his passage."[1168] He did not mention whether McFarlane was on the same voyage with Ben, but McFarlane would appear in Baltimore.[1169]

The *Dart* apparently did not sink, because General Wilkinson would travel on a ship named "*Dart*" to Baltimore in May 1810, en route to Washington for his trial for treason.[1170] The fact that the *Dart* would stop at Cuba to secure the release of French mercenaries during that voyage makes Ben's earlier voyage on the ship more intriguing. At the least, it should be presumed that Wilkinson would only have trusted travel on a ship captained by one of his loyalists, if not one of his agents.

The St. Louis building that had been occupied by Wilkinson & Price was already empty by the end of October 1809, indicating that Ben closed his mercantile business prior to traveling to Fort Pickering to take charge of the House trunk.[1171] No further public mention was made of Ben Wilkinson being alive. And no further direct location was given for "the key."

Leaving the House trunk and two additional trunks behind, the Lewis party and the retinue of Chickasaw leaders traveled the "usual route" of the Lower Chickasaw Trail through the Chickasaw Nation, according to The Russell Statement.[1172] Because Lewis was anxious to arrive in Washington City as soon as possible, Neelly could have led the party on a more direct upper Cherokee Trace, a trading path from Chickasaw Bluffs that intersected the Natchez Trace near Chickasaw Levi Colbert's inn.[1173] Either route was primarily a bridal path, but the lower trail intersected with paths leading south to Spanish settlements at Mobile on the Gulf Coast and east to Charleston on the Atlantic. The lower trail would have been the heavier traveled trail and more likely to be serviced by Chickasaw inns, such as the Love Inn located at a ferry crossing about halfway to the agency area.[1174] Chickasaw traders were known to sell pumpkins, squash, and beans to travelers along well-traveled routes.[1175]

By October 3, four days after leaving Fort Pickering, the Neely party had traveled as far southeast as the Chickasaw Agency area between the agency house at Old Houlka and the settlement of McIntoshville."[1176] McIntoshville had been a stop for travelers since 1771, when the British appointed founder John McIntosh as their agent to the Chickasaw and Choctaw tribes. Located about halfway between Nashville and Natchez, a post office was built there early on as a place for post riders, or mailmen, to swap mail bags. Also located at the crossroads of the north-south Natchez Trace and the southeast-northwest Lower Chickasaw Trail, the Agency House and Chickasaw Post Office attracted a small village of Chickasaw, traders, trappers, and others who hoped to benefit from trade and access to government business with the Chickasaw. By Lewis's time, it was described as a community of at least six farms with good springs and abundant peach and apple orchards.[1177]

Neelly had an additional incentive to follow the lower Chickasaw Trail to the Chickasaw Agency. He needed to take care of the repercussions from the Lanehart theft.[1178] Chickasaw leader James Colbert's inn on the Natchez Trace, where Lanehart had stolen money from a traveler, was located about a mile north of the Chickasaw Post Office.[1179] The Philadelphian Lanehart had performed odd jobs at Fort Pickering, and perhaps Colbert had hired him as a blacksmith to provide services that his guests needed to repair their wagons or shoe their horses.[1180] Apparently, there was concern that news of Lanehart's theft at the inn had spread and that travelers might avoid lodging there.

Neelly prepared a statement to vouch for James Colbert's honesty to people who would travel the road. James Colbert was educated by Spanish traders in St. Augustine, and he had been entertained by President Washington in Philadelphia.[1181] Neelly and interpreter Jeremiah K. Love signed the statement at the "Chickasaw Agency." Neelly evidently met with men employed by the agency and other respected men from the agency area who also signed the letter.[1182] The statement was evidence that the men were in the McIntoshville area during Lewis's visit, but no record has been found that any of the men mentioned seeing Lewis. Neelly likely placed copies of the statement in the mailbags for the postriders to deliver to Nashville and Natchez for publication in the newspapers.[1183]

McIntoshville resident James Allen's home was closer to the Tockshish post office building than Neelly's agency house, and the secretary of war said Neelly inappropriately delegated his ministerial duties as postmaster to Allen.[1184] Allen's family was said to be from Hillsboro, North Carolina, where Andrew Jackson was raised. Allen had practiced law in Nashville prior to moving to the Chickasaw Nation, and Jackson lodged with Allen when he traveled on the Natchez Trace.[1185] If Lewis talked with Allen, Allen could have supplied information about developments in the territory between the agency and Nashville. Allen may have been aware that Jackson's business associates Captain John Brahan and William P. Anderson were working with Jefferson's former spy, Thomas Freeman, to pursue a scheme to purchase thousands of acres of ceded Chickasaw land from the government for a fraction of its value.

Back at Fort Pickering, Russell stated that he received a "verbal message" from Lewis to continue holding the two trunks that Lewis had asked him to safeguard.[1186] If Russell had sent his own packman, he was likely the messenger returning to Chickasaw Bluffs after packing Lewis's trunks to the Chickasaw Agency.[1187] Russell later claimed that if his trusted packman had accompanied Lewis's party the entire journey to Nashville, Lewis would not have died.[1188]

After Russell's packhorse man—a potential witness—left to return to Fort Pickering, The Neelly Letter claimed that Neelly observed Lewis had become deranged and implied that it was necessary for the party to rest "in the Nation" (again, probably at McIntoshville) for two days. The Russell Statement would agree that Lewis's health deteriorated only after Russell's man left the party and emphasized that the deterioration did not begin until after Lewis began the final leg of the journey toward Nashville. Russell did not state that his informant provided any information about Lewis's condition that was concerning enough for Russell to send someone to assist Lewis.[1189]

The Chickasaw Agency complex consisted of a brick agency house, office, stables, and related buildings, where, among other activities, a weaver worked to teach Chickasaw women the art of weaving they had lost after becoming dependent on European goods.[1190] Lewis likely did not lodge with Neelly at the official Chickasaw Agency house, and it is doubtful that Neelly slept there. Just a month earlier, Neelly had described the condition of the agency house as uninhabitable and requested funding to build a new one. He said that the prior agent had begun reconstruction of the agency house to add a separate space as an inn for travelers. Even the prior agent boarded with his neighbor, who performed the construction, and then the agent died before the work was completed. Neelly complained that he would be required to board at a house near the post office several miles north.[1191]

Hardy Perry, who immigrated to the Chickasaw Nation years earlier to provide services to the Chickasaw Agency, operated an inn a mile north of James Colbert's.[1192] Perry had married a Chickasaw woman and had become a Chickasaw leader—his wife held the reputation of being the first woman in the Chickasaw Nation to wear a petticoat. A guest who stayed at Perry's two years later was pleased with the accommodations and their abundant dinner of venison, potatoes, and cornbread.[1193]

Perry claimed that Lewis stayed at his inn just prior to his death. The famed explorer impressed Perry with his tales from the expedition to the Pacific. Perry said that Lewis even gave him a copy of the prospectus for the publication of his forthcoming narrative and offered to send him one of his books when printed.[1194]

As Lewis waited for Neely to finish agency business, Lewis could have used his time at McIntoshville to gain information on Aaron Burr and Wilkinson. John McKee, who had entertained Burr at the Agency in 1805 and later received Burr's request for Chickasaw mercenaries to help invade Texas, likely still lived in the community. McKee, who had first collected intelligence on Wilkinson on Clark's boat, later presented himself to Wilkinson as one of his most loyal supporters, as he once flattered, "if it [my note to you] does not speak the language of a heart that loves you, I must have been very unfortunate in expressing myself."[1195] Through mail delivery and army traffic, news from the Lewis and Clark Expedition had reached McIntoshville as it had to other outposts. There, U.S. Soldiers traveling from post to post also spread rumors. During the explorers' absence, McKee heard that Lewis and Clark had been killed in the West— perhaps through contacts with an overly optimistic Wilkinson.[1196]

Lewis could also have attended to tribal matters for Upper Louisiana. Not only did a few Chickasaw families live in the Arkansas District, Chickasaw had begun to cross over the Mississippi to hunt in Osage territory. Osage Agent John Treat had suggested that the Chickasaw enter into a treaty to bring peace over its conflicting claims to hunting grounds.[1197] Within eighteen months, the Chickasaw would consider going to war with the Osage.[1198]

The party likely would have departed McIntoshville no later than October 6 or 7 if Lewis arrived at Grinder's Stand on October 10.[1199] Confirming that Russell's packhorse man left the Lewis party, The Neelly Letter states that Neelly supplied Lewis a horse to haul his trunks "through" the Chickasaw Nation "and a man to attend to them." Russell attempted to absolve himself from any liability for the safeguarding of Lewis's papers by defending that his man merely packed the trunks "to the Nation" and that Neelly's man transported the trunks from there.[1200]

It is possible that, as a military man who knew how packhorses should be controlled, Lewis would have insisted on hiring a trained packman to be responsible for the papers on which his future relied. If so, one man who regularly transported cargo by packhorse for the army on the Natchez Trace was John Kincaid.[1201] The Kincaid name would surface again in the rumors that swirled after Lewis's death.

Inn owner Perry said that he rode with Lewis for about a day as Lewis traveled toward Nashville. The Russell Statement would claim that Lewis's illness not only returned a week earlier, but that it grew progressively worse because he was drinking alcohol.[1202] However, Perry did not recollect that Lewis was ill or drunk or that he acted deranged. In fact, Lewis was well and alert enough to impress Perry as being "one of the greatest men in the world."[1203]

Perry also did not mention that Neelly was traveling with Lewis. If Neelly's man was placed in charge of the packhorses, Neelly could have separated for a time before rejoining the party.[1204] At some point, Neelly hired interpreter Jeremiah K. Love to escort the prisoner Lanehart in his stead.[1205] Control of the prisoner was a job that Neelly had no authority to delegate.[1206] However, by hiring Love, Neelly made it possible for Love and Lanehart to travel separately from Lewis's party, leaving Neelly and possibly the packman and two servants as Lewis's sole traveling companions. Even then, Neelly still might not have been able to prevent Chickasaw riders from attaching themselves to his party to show the governor the genuine hospitality for which Chickasaw were known.[1207]

If Perry parted with Lewis about a day's ride north of McIntoshville, the party would need to ride another 150 miles on the Natchez Trace to reach the safety of Nashville. There, Lewis could send arrangements for his trunks at Fort Pickering and perhaps board a stage with his trunks for Washington City.

Congress had given Jefferson's new wagon highway along the Natchez Trace the lofty name "Columbian Highway" in honor of explorer

Christopher Columbus. But the name never stuck. Travel was too dangerous. Travelers instead called it "The Devil's Backbone."

In Lewis's day, the name of the Devil was added to routes where one traveler claimed that danger was so great, safe passage was only possible through God's intervention.[1208]

The Natchez Trace

## CHAPTER 20

# CROSSING THE RIVER TO THE UNKNOWN

> The dangers on the road to Natchez are really serious…
> —Thomas Jefferson, 1803[1209]

Accustomed to hunting and exploring, Lewis would not have feared panthers that hid in cane breaks or bears that roamed the woods along the Natchez Trace. The greater danger was human. The road was notorious for bands of robbers who preyed on unsuspecting travelers. Jefferson had been alerted to the problem in 1801 and likely consulted Lewis for military advice before sending soldiers to patrol the route in 1803.

Lewis could have commiserated with the local military agent who grew frustrated with "the great length of this frontier, & the few troops in this quarter" that made it difficult to govern.[1210] Several Natchez Trace travelers carried gold and silver in the form of Spanish currency through sparsely populated areas with little law enforcement. Land pirates or highwaymen were drawn to victims they considered easy prey. Making the road even more dangerous, sensational newspaper accounts revealing the large amounts of gold and silver taken during Natchez Trace robberies had the effect of advertising to robbers from across the country. The highwaymen sometimes networked with pirates on the Mississippi River or made the circuit themselves.[1211]

Notorious bandits Thomas Hare, the Harpe brothers, and Samuel Mason had been eliminated by 1809, and soldier patrols had likely been withdrawn, but the dangers had not been eradicated. Two years after Lewis's death, the Tennessee governor would ask his legislature for funds to provide additional law enforcement on the Natchez Road in Tennessee due to numerous robberies.[1212] A Methodist circuit rider, recalling that travel on the Natchez Trace remained dangerous until after the War of 1812, said:

> Another consideration added greatly to the danger of traveling alone or in small companies along these horse-paths through the Indian Nations, which was that they were often infested by lawless white men, who not unfrequently robbed, and sometimes murdered, travelers for the sake of a small sum of money, or one of more horses, and then tried to make the impression that these crimes were perpetrated by the Indians.[1213]

Lewis's blue and white striped riding coat and other gentlemen's clothes would have made the governor an easy mark for robbers.[1214] Even more, trunks bobbing up and down on the packhorses as they tagged along with the party would have attracted attention. Lewis worried more about the papers in his trunks than his own safety. The Neelly Letter claimed that "Some days previous to the Governors death" Lewis told Neelly that if "any accident happened to him to send his trunks with the papers therein to the President."

The Neelly Letter said that Neelly was aware that Lewis carried "two trunks of papers," said to include his expedition journals.[1215] It stated that Lewis talked constantly about the government's refusal to reimburse his expenses. Lewis may have mentioned some of the papers he carried in his trunks when accepting Neelly's offer to use his packhorses to make certain they would be secure. Given Lewis's detail-oriented personality, he may have asked for specifics on how the packhorse would be tethered to the party and how the trunks would be secured at each stop. As a military man aware of the strategic and political interests in the Southwest, Neelly would have been aware of the various people who would have an interest in the papers. Some might even have been willing to pay a reward for them or expected access to them in return for a political favor.

Wilkinson was certainly one man who would have had an interest. A month prior to Lewis's death, Wilkinson reflected, "From the period of Gen'l Washington's administration, down through his successors, I have been taught to believe that it was my duty, to acquire every information topographical and political, which might inadvertently or eventually become interesting to our country."[1216] More accurately, he collected information that he could use for his own purposes, and as Lewis traveled up the Natchez Trace, Wilkinson was busy gathering information and plotting to discredit the reputations of witnesses who would testify against him.

The Lewis party would have passed several Chickasaw farms about a day's ride north of McIntoshville, but settlements were sporadic.[1217] Because the new highway was the main route taken by travelers between Nashville and Natchez, Lewis would have met other travelers over the course of a day.[1218] During dry weather periods such as late summer, they frequently navigated the eight-foot road in carriages and wagons.

Just prior to the construction of Jefferson's wagon highway, travelers referred to a trip through the Chickasaw and Choctaw nations as "'going through the wilderness' for the traveler saw little else than alternate forests and prairies, intersected by numerous bridgeless water courses, except the roving Indians and what few adventurers he might meet along the way."[1219] Those accustomed to town life often commented on their difficulty in adapting to the relatively solitary and quiet miles of the forest.

Travelers sometimes chose to sleep outdoors rather than risk sharing a room with strangers in an inn, though many stayed at trusted establishments.[1220] Accommodations varied widely; one Mexican traveler was surprised to find his Chickasaw hosts serving meals on fine chinaware and using steel forks and knives.[1221] While some inns, like Perry's, offered hearty meals for midday, evening meals were typically light and may have been little more than milk and cornbread, or corn mush.[1222]

Lewis's northbound party would have made at least one overnight stop between McIntoshville and the Tennessee River. The distance between the Chickasaw Agency and the Tennessee River was roughly ninety miles.[1223] Assuming that the party traveled up to fifty miles per day, Lewis could have lodged at Guntown, a settlement started by a Tory settler who had signed Neelly's affidavit to vouch for James Colbert, or at Brown's Bottom. Brown's Bottom was located at the intersection of Glover's Trace, which was the old Chickasaw hunting path, and Jefferson's new military highway. The old Chickasaw hunting trail ran due north through Kentucky toward Fort Massac. Neelly would later be instructed to negotiate with the Chickasaw to allow the federal government to develop that trail into a wagon highway like the Natchez Trace.[1224] For the time, soldiers traveling between Brown's Bottom and Fort Massac could follow the less improved path. It would have been one point where soldiers could have encountered Lewis's party or Wilkinson's couriers could have sent or delivered messages.

Three years later, Chickasaw leader James Brown, who operated an inn at Brown's Bottom, would file charges against Neelly and petition the War Department to have him replaced as Chickasaw agent. In addition to allegations of frequent drunkenness and self-dealing, Brown would allege that Neelly threatened such violence against him that he feared for his life.[1225]

Inn owners usually prepared a bill of charges to be settled when the traveler was ready to depart. Given charges posted for inns in that area at the time, Lewis might have spent about two dollars per day for lodging and meals for himself and Peerny and for fodder for the horses. A hired packman may have required a portion of his payment up front. Neelly claimed that he lent Lewis an unspecified amount of money, a claim that Captain Russell later disputed because he said that Neelly had no money.[1226] Neelly was the defendant in several lawsuits demanding payment, and, like Lewis, he was in financial straits.[1227] Notably, the payments Neelly made to Love and Hogg during the period were in the form of drafts drawn on the War Department rather than from Neelly's personal funds.[1228]

At the typical next northbound stop, fifty miles north of Guntown, George Colbert's inn sat on the south bank of the Tennessee River. One traveler said that the inn appeared "like a country palace with its abundance of glass in doors and windows."[1229] At some point, visitors were expected to lodge in cabins outside the main house because George's wife would not allow white people to stay in the main house.[1230]

George's brother Levi's house about seven miles south was even grander. Levi's house was said to have been several stories high, and both Colbert inns were known gathering places for military men.[1231] The Colberts and their servants could have provided a wealth of military gossip.

Lewis would have had much to discuss with the Colberts. George Colbert fought with General Wayne during the Battle of Fallen Timbers in 1794. He still used his army rank of major and still wore portions of his military uniform. Colbert prized the Jefferson peace medal that General Wilkinson gave him during the treaty negotiations for the Natchez Trace wagon road. Like his brother James, George had traveled to Philadelphia to meet with President Washington.[1232] As Chickasaw clan leaders, the Colberts also could have provided their views on conflicts with the Osage over hunting grounds on the west side of the Mississippi as well as relations with Spain.

George, at times with his brother Levi, operated a ferry across the Tennessee River, which was nearly a mile wide at that point and so rapid at the rocky shoals that it produced a deafening roar.[1233] Black slaves hauled wooden platforms across the swift current using chains. The Colberts charged travelers the unusually high price of one dollar per horse and fifty cents per man.[1234] Lewis would have paid another three or four dollars from his limited funds if the Colberts charged him.

Mail or post riders made the trek from Nashville to Natchez about three times per month in 1809.[1235] Post riders asked travelers for news from the locations they had passed and then shared that information at inns along the road. Doubling as post offices and community gathering spots, inns were places where travelers disseminated news. Inn owners and their communities would have received advance notice of the progression of the governor's and hero's trip.[1236]

Amos Stoddard, who had traveled the same route two or three weeks earlier, may have already alerted parties along the Natchez Trace that Governor Lewis was on his way to Nashville. If the Love party traveled in advance of Lewis's, they too could have spread word of his travel. Riders likely passed on news about the famed explorer and territorial governor who was traveling through their nation. Both fans of the American hero and highway robbers would have welcomed the news.

North of the river, travelers passed Chickasaw houses, as well as Young Factor's Stand, an inn which former and future Chickasaw agent James Robertson called "a fine house of entertainment."[1237] The inn would have provided appropriate accommodations for a governor and security for his trunks, but strangely, the party instead chose to camp outdoors, at least according to The Neelly Letter.[1238]

A traveling minister described his typical routine at an outdoor campsite on the Natchez Trace. He fed his horses with corn and tethered them to the grass. He made a campfire, then rolled himself in a blanket to sleep, his saddlebags serving as a pillow. Lewis may have carried bear or buffalo skins, though they would have been too heavy for sleeping if the weather was still warm. Even then, the minister said he was aware that he,

## Crossing the River to the Unknown

"unprotected... might become the prey of some carnivorous beast, or he might be murdered by the lurking savage or highway robber."[1239]

Hot, early October weather in the Tennessee River Valley would have caused wet-weather springs along the road to run dry. When Aaron Burr traveled the Natchez Trace four years earlier, he grew so desperate for water that he skimmed scum off mudpuddles in search of water to drink.[1240] If Neelly failed to disclose the location of safe spring water, Lewis may have had little choice but to drink whiskey or other liquor. Russell, who would accuse Neelly of being "extremely fond of liquor," later alleged that Neelly encouraged Lewis to drink, giving him the opportunity to harm himself.[1241] If true, Neelly's encouragement could have been the same as the earlier boatmen to use alcohol to kill impurities in the only water he could find. Neelly's urging Lewis to drink alcohol could have been by negligence, as Russell claimed, or it could have been intentional to dull Lewis's judgement and make him appear deranged.

When the secretary of war prepared to send a highly sensitive dispatch from Washington City to Natchez, he ordered his courier to secure an escort of a sergeant and six soldiers armed with rifles and pistols before setting foot on the Natchez Trace.[1242] Lewis had armed himself, but his failure to take similar precautions would become apparent at the encampment.

The Neelly Letter claimed that two of the horses were "lost" overnight. Brahan later said that Neelly told him that one of the horses belonged to Lewis and one was Neelly's packhorse.[1243] The Neelly Letter claimed that Neelly stayed behind to find the lost horses. Adding justification for Neelly to abandon Lewis on the notorious road, the letter claimed that the idea for Neelly to remain behind to search for the horses was Lewis's.

But The Russell Statement seemed to contradict The Neelly Letter. It reported, "one of his Horses and one of the Chickasaw agents with whom he was traveling strayed off from the camp and in the Morning could not be found."[1244] Consistent with what was later discovered about Neelly's whereabouts, it suggested either that Neelly disappeared without explanation or that a second agent traveling with the party remained behind to search for the lost horses.

The Russell Statement said that Chickasaw men—known horsemen—also stayed behind to assist. Chickasaw leader Levi Colbert may have been among them. On October 9, the day before Lewis arrived at Grinder's Stand, Colbert wrote a letter datelined "Tennessee" that focused on horse theft, recalling that Cherokee men had stolen horses from him the previous winter and appealing to the Cherokee agent for help.[1245] The letter certainly gave the impression that the topic of stolen horses motivated Colbert to write on the same day it would have been a focal point for Lewis and his party.

The only lost horse that would have justified Neelly leaving the governor in an area known for robbery and murder would have been a packhorse carrying Lewis's trunks with official and sensitive papers. Whether one packhorse or two, they would have been under the control of Neelly's man.[1246] If a packhorse man was part of the party, he also would have remained behind.

Brahan claimed Neelly told him that Lewis rode ahead with "a promise to wait for me [Neelly] at the first houses he came to that was inhabited by white people."[1247] Neelly would have known that Robert Grinder occupied the first house, about thirty feet north of the "Indian Line." That unofficial Chickasaw boundary was a significant landmark referenced in travelers' journals and likely appeared in the gazetteers that travelers often purchased for traveling on the Natchez Trace.[1248]

Grinder earlier had lived near Neelly's farm in the settlement just south of Franklin, Tennessee. Grinder opened an inn on the Natchez Trace near the same time that Neelly was appointed Chickasaw agent. Indian agents had a voice in the selection of inn operators, and it is likely Neelly recommended Grinder or at least supported his appointment. Nevertheless, the writer of The Neelly Letter chose not to disclose that Neelly and Grinder had any relationship.

Lewis's known traveling party had dwindled to three—Lewis, Peerny, and a third man whom Brahan called Neelly's "servant."[1249] Travelers on the Natchez Trace in Tennessee frequently banded together with larger parties for safety.[1250] Just six years earlier, the *Tennessee Gazette* warned that if a party on the Natchez Road numbered fewer than "two or three, [they] are almost sure to be killed or robbed." Three separate attacks occurred within a few weeks, about five miles from the spot where Grinder's Stand would be built. At least two separate robberies resulted in the victims' deaths.[1251]

Few travelers knew that caves in the Swan Creek area, where Grinder's Stand was located, provided shelter for robbers.[1252] In the early 1800s, the notorious Hare gang operated along the Natchez Trace, and after the Mason Gang robbed and killed travelers about five miles north of the future Grinder Stand location in 1804, the Tennessee governor complained, "The road leading through the Indian Country from Nashville to Natchez has for some time past been infested with a gang of Banditti."[1253] It was in response to that request following murders of travelers near the future Grinder's Stand that Jefferson agreed to establish inns and posts along the road for travelers' safety and ordered soldiers to be stationed at the Duck and Tennessee Rivers.[1254]

By 1809, Thomas Runions—rumored to be part Chickasaw and part French—was feared as a highwayman near the Indian Line.[1255] He lived near Grinder's Stand and was married to Robert Grinder's niece.[1256] The Neelly Letter did not state that Neelly warned Lewis about potential robbers, a courtesy that travelers were known to receive in Tennessee when traveling the road.[1257]

About three miles south of Grinder's Stand, as Lewis crossed the Buffalo River at a shallow rock ford, he would have seen the two-story inn operated by Chickasaw John McLish. Near the river, scores of black slaves dug iron ore from the ground and forged it into horseshoes and farm implements.[1258] If one of the horses needed shoeing, McLish's would have provided a good spot to find services. The inn offered lodging and a gathering place for travelers and settlers. It also served as a post office. A new road just cut for the postriders ran northeast toward the new Maury County seat, "Columbia," where Russell had bought a town lot. But Neelly had directed Lewis to Grinder's Stand, where he promised they would reunite, hopefully with the missing trunks and horses in tow.

Mile marker signs or carvings on trees along the Natchez Trace in Tennessee would have made Lewis aware that he was only a few miles from the Indian Line. Signs would also have stated distances to Nashville and possibly to Columbia and Franklin. Roads in Maury County, including the Natchez Trace, were also marked with posts at points to make settlers aware of the distances to towns along the road.[1259]

The terrain was reminiscent of Lewis's grandparents' Virginia farm, Cloverfields, where he had spent happier days hunting and exploring in the woods as a boy. Red, orange, and yellow forest leaves would have provided a feast for the eyes in early autumn. The early October traveler would have spotted deer and watched squirrels jumping from tree to tree, gathering nuts in preparation for winter. Aware that he was nearing the settlements in Maury County, perhaps Lewis began to let down his guard. By some accounts, he rode alone ahead of Peerny and Neelly's man. After the loss of horses at the encampment, unless one of the Chickasaw travelers supplied a horse, Peerny must have ridden with Neelly's servant for a portion of their journey to Grinder's.[1260]

Running north from McLish's inn, the Natchez Trace followed a ridge rising to hills that early mappers exaggerated as mountains.[1261] Their thousand-foot elevation made the spot one of the highest points within a 500,000-square-mile area in the Mississippi River Valley.[1262] As Lewis reached the crest of the ridge at Grinder's Stand, he should have seen a sign marking the Indian Line.[1263] Inns like Grinder's Stand also typically advertised their services with signs emblazoned with images such as eagles or bears for travelers who could not read.[1264]

The main building of Grinder's Stand sat diagonally at a clearing about 170 feet to the east. It should have provided a welcoming shelter from the road, particularly if Lewis was still ill or weakened by the earlier fever. But if Stoddard had spread rumors to innkeepers that Lewis was deranged and suicidal, as he would in Nashville, his warnings may have affected how Grinder's Stand innkeeper Priscilla Grinder received Lewis and interpreted his behavior. Hearsay accounts would later suggest that she was reluctant to take him in as a guest, looked for indications that he was deranged, and refused to sleep under the same roof with him.[1265]

Meriwether Lewis was one of the first to travel thousands of miles across the width of the North American continent; however, through Wilkinson's plotting and Russell's and Neelly's influence and direction, his life's journey on earth led him to this final destination as the sun began to set. If, as it would be reported, Lewis looked wistfully to the west and drank in the late afternoon peace in the autumn woods at Grinder's Stand, it was an illusion.[1266] He had not momentarily escaped the political storm of forces fighting for control of the continent—he had arrived at its vortex.

Meanwhile, English botanist John Bradbury was making his way from Charlottesville to St. Louis, carrying what would be Jefferson's final letter to Lewis. After relating some news of the day, Jefferson wrote that Lewis's friends in the Charlottesville area were anxious to see him, and Jefferson hoped that Lewis would give him a good portion of his time and attention at Monticello. Jefferson said that he had finally arrived at the time in his life when he could enjoy the luxury of his own personal happiness, implying that he looked forward to long talks with his protégé.

In his impatience to spur Lewis to complete his missions, Jefferson had become curt in his letters. Possibly due to routine delays in mail delivery, he thought Lewis had not written in reply.[1267] He may have wanted to make amends. At the age of sixty-six and with time now to reflect on his life, Jefferson may have realized that Lewis, who lost his father at an early age, had eagerly followed his direction without questioning. Lewis looked to him as a father figure as much as a political patron.

Perhaps Jefferson intended to spend time with Lewis at Monticello, giving him the kind of advice that fathers pass on to sons when reflecting on life towards its end. Jefferson's own son had died soon after birth more than three decades prior, and in politics, at least, Lewis had become to Jefferson a son to carry on his legacy. Three months later, Jefferson would name his newborn grandson "Meriwether Lewis Randolph."[1268]

Jefferson ended his letter with, "Present my friendly salutations to Genl. Clarke," and then added what was as close to anything he had written expressing a fatherly affection, "and be assured yourself of my constant & unalterable affections."[1269]

Lewis did not live to read the letter.

## CHAPTER 21

# LONG ROADS TO MONTICELLO

> pore fellow, what a number of Conjecturral reports we hear mostly unfavorable to him. I have to Contredict maney of them
>
> —Willam Clark, November 26, 1809[1270]

William Clark was also traveling toward Monticello to visit Jefferson.[1271] He had left St. Louis for Washington City on September 21, with his wife, Julia, and eight-month-old son, Meriwether Lewis Clark, whom he affectionately called his "man boy." Rather than taking the most direct course, he plotted his route to pass by homes of family members in Kentucky and Virginia.

Riding horseback with a wife and small child was out of the question. Clark chose to book stages, the most modern form of transportation, but hardly comfortable or private. Riders sat shoulder to shoulder on three or four wooden benches set into the wagon bed, crammed together with passengers from all walks of life. Small bags or trunks were stowed underneath the benches. Little room was left to move. A canopy overhead offered some protection against rain, but when lowered, riders sat in the dark for hours on end, viewing only the backs of the wagon drivers' heads.[1272]

Like many travelers of the time, Clark maintained a travelogue of his trip in a pocket journal, noting the number of miles he traversed each day and the places he stopped. He generally recorded the time he spent at each stop, as well as the people he met. He once even noted a recipe for sweetmeat that he enjoyed at one of the taverns.[1273]

Wheeled stages crept through the primitive woodland roads at about three miles per hour. When it rained, wheels mired down in the mud. Logs were sometimes laid across portions of the road, but their round surfaces jarred travelers to the bone.[1274] Clark had delayed traveling until fall, when cooler, drier weather left better road surfaces.

Terrified riders were sometimes asked to lean to the right or left to prevent the carriages from tipping over. Even then, stages frequently overturned on uneven surfaces, trapping passengers beneath them. Many travelers found it a harrowing experience.[1275] For Clark, placating a young mother and infant under such circumstances was a challenge different from keeping up the morale of soldiers on a cross-country expedition. The garrulous explorer's expedition stories could have kept other riders spellbound if he chose to talk about them as much as Lewis had.

After traveling a total of sixteen to twenty-four miles in a day, stages pulled up to primitive taverns for riders to spend the evening. Guests jostled for a place at the table to fight for their shares of dinner served family-style. Then, they were fortunate to find space in a bed with another traveler. That bed may have been one of eight in a room. Those who arrived too late had to sleep on the floor.[1276] The Kentucky tavern experience was similar to what Lewis may have encountered on the Natchez Trace, though some of the Kentucky taverns may have provided comforts that Natchez Trace travelers would not see for another five to ten years.

Clark booked travel on the lower Kentucky Road through Russellville, where his niece, Eleanor, and her husband, Jonathan Temple, lived.[1277] By the time the stage reached Louisville on October 12, Clark could look forward to relaxing at his brother Jonathan's home, Trough

Spring. He would plan to stay with Jonathan for two weeks to catch up on family affairs. Just a few years earlier, Trough Spring had been the scene of deliveries of specimens of skins, bones, and other artifacts that Clark sent from the expedition trail for Jonathan to forward to Jefferson. Trough Spring should have reminded Clark of his past victories with Lewis in the West and provided a relaxing homecoming with family.

But Clark's mail had been forwarded to Louisville, including the letter that claimed to be from Lewis at New Madrid, in which he said that he considered changing his route to travel overland. Clark noted that Jonathan saw Lewis's letter, and it is likely that he discussed Lewis's current financial and political predicaments.[1278]

Clark's infant son fell ill. The strain of a long, crowded carriage ride, the cries of a sick baby, and the weight of whatever Lewis had written in his letter left Clark so distracted that when he left Jonathan's home on October 26, he failed to pack the letters he had received or a small bag of money. He thought he had placed them in his trunk, which he had left open for Julia to pack her clothes, but he may have left them in a drawer.[1279] He later discovered that he had also misplaced an agreement with the St. Louis Missouri Fur Company that he had brought in hopes of raising some cash by selling a share.[1280] Clark resumed the carriage ride on the road to Frankfort, traveling about sixteen miles to spend the evening at Mr. Smith's, a tavern in Simpsonville.

Strikingly, troubles of the previous day suddenly seemed minor on October 28, and Clark's life changed forever. When the stage stopped briefly for lunch in Shelbyville, Clark picked up a newspaper, the Frankfort *Argus of Western America*. It reported that somewhere between the Chickasaw Bluffs and Nashville, Lewis had killed himself by cutting his own throat with a knife.[1281] Clark's journal did not record that he spent any money on lunch at Shelbyville. He lost his appetite.

Newspapers at that time frequently reported deaths prematurely—like Hampton, even Jefferson had read reports of his own passing.[1282] There was still hope that the Frankfort *Argus* had reprinted an erroneous report from another paper, but the news weighed on Clark's mind. After traveling another sixteen miles, the stage stopped for its customers to spend the evening at Mr. Shannon's tavern on Tick Creek near Graefenberg.[1283]

That night, Clark sat in the crowded common room with an assorted group of travelers and drunks and wrote to his brother Jonathan:

> I fear this report has too much truth, tho' hope it may have no foundation __ my reasons for thinking it possible is founded on the letter which I rec[ei]ved from him at your house, in that letter he Says he had Some inintion of going thro' by land... I fear O! I fear the waight of his mind has over come him, what will be the Consequence?[1284]

The portion of the letter that Clark said made him fear the truth of the account was that Lewis told Clark he was thinking of changing his route to travel overland.

Clark's next thought was what had become of the expedition papers. He decided to write to former Chickasaw Agent James Robertson or some friend in Nashville to ask for more details on Lewis and collect the papers.[1285]

The next day, on the road to Frankfort, a man Clark identified as "Mr. Fitzhugh" met up with the stage to tell him about Lewis's death. Fitzhugh was likely Clark's brother-in-law and St. Louis Missouri Fur Company partner Dennis Fitzhugh, who lived in Louisville. Fitzhugh might have provided additional information from his sources, but Clark did not include any further details. If he still had any hope that the story could be false, it ended when the stage crossed the Kentucky River by ferry. Someone he did not name added enough information that Clark thought he should note in his journal, "Heard about Gov. Lewis' death."

When the stage finally arrived in Frankfort, Clark went to the Wesinger House, the town's finest tavern, near the Capitol building. By that time, the town must have been abuzz with the news. Clark dined with the Kentucky governor and other town leaders. One man seemed to waste little time consoling Clark about the death of his friend—he lobbied Clark to be appointed as Lewis's replacement as governor. Clark took offense at the manners of the "green pompous new endlandr" as he described him.[1286] He stepped outside and was taken aback by a moment of reality when a beggar asked him for money. Clark handed the beggar twenty-five cents from his dwindling funds before boarding the stage for Lexington.

The next leg of the trip, midway between Frankfort and Lexington, took the Clark family through the flatter terrain of the future Kentucky horse country to arrive at Dailey's Tavern before nightfall. The complex, with its large stables, also served as the operational center for Dailey and Kennedy's stagecoach service between Frankfort and Lexington. At Dailey's, stagecoach customers often exited the carriages to gather at the well or cistern in the rear yard to wash off the dust from the road before entering the inn. Like other larger taverns, Dailey's also doubled as a community meeting center. It boasted a pull-up wall that turned two rooms into one for dances and events.[1287]

Clark searched for a space to write a letter and took on the task of locating the expedition journals and possibly other papers that Lewis was transporting to Washington. He tried to think of men who would be in a position to locate the trunks. Instead of writing to Robertson as he had considered, Clark reached out to Nashville Judge John Overton to inquire about Lewis's papers. Likely based on the newspaper reports he read, Clark wrote that he understood that the "Indian Agent" had gone to Nashville after Lewis's death, and he hoped the papers were in Overton's care.[1288] Clark did not name the agent, James Neelly, which suggests that he did not know him.[1289] It is not known whether Clark knew Overton; their families may have intermarried a few generations earlier.[1290] An address from Overton to students at Transylvania University was printed in the *Kentucky Gazette* on October 17, and perhaps

Clark saw a copy, determining that Judge Overton would be a known source in Nashville.[1291]

What Clark had planned as a relaxing trip through Kentucky and Virginia to visit family and friends had become stressful and endless. It was too late to save his friend. An action-oriented man would compensate for a feeling of helplessness by turning to things that he could still control. During the ride to Lexington the next day on October 30, Clark continued thinking about Lewis's papers. If they were lost, it would be difficult to recreate a narrative for publication. He was days away from anyone who had solid information about Lewis or who could help him locate the papers.

Once Clark arrived at the Kentucky Hotel across from the Lexington Court House—reportedly one of the grander establishments in the state—he made plans to act. To his brother Jonathan, he wrote, "I have herd of the Certainty of the death of Govr. Lewis which gives us much uneasiness." He asked Jonathan to forward the letter that Lewis had mailed him from New Madrid. Clark said that the letter would "be of great Service" to him. He also wrote to William P. Anderson, asking that he send Lewis's trunks to him if they were still in his area.[1292]

Clark worried about how he could pay to publish the expedition narrative now that Lewis was dead. Lewis had planned to fund the publication and then recoup the expenses from book sales. With that plan now lost, Clark would need money as well as a trusted editor to correct his grammar and creative spelling.[1293] He told Jonathan that he wanted to discuss Lewis's plans with him.[1294] Clark later wrote that Lewis's "neglecting to write our Journal has given me a great deel of trouble and expence __ and will give me Still more."[1295]

Jefferson had not heard about Lewis's death when he attended post-presidency dinners in his honor at the Eagle Tavern in Richmond, Virginia on October 21 and 22. He expressed his relief to the audience that his hardest public work was behind him, and he thanked the citizens for their hopes for "the tranquility and happiness of the remaining scenes" of his life.[1296] The following morning, Jefferson began his return trip to Monticello with a reasonable expectation that some of that happiness would come from his much-anticipated meeting with Lewis and his news of developments in the West.

In Kentucky, after Clark's stage left Lexington, it turned toward a new turnpike at Clinch Mountain to Bean's Station in northeast Tennessee. That road was the route people from the Nashville area traveled to the East. Lewis's servant, Peerny, was likely traveling a few days ahead on the same road to Monticello to hand-deliver The Neelly Letter with news of Lewis's death and to ask his former employer for money.

Clark was disappointed when he arrived at Bean's Station Tavern that no one there had learned any new information about Lewis. Living at one of the main stops on a well-traveled highway, the Bean family would have been a good source for news. The founding owner's grandson was one of the young men Philip Nolan had recruited to join him in his last foray into Spanish Texas, and the grandson was still held prisoner in Mexico.[1297] The Bean family hosts could have provided some information on New Spain, but Clark's focus was on Lewis.

Now that Clark had dealt with the initial shock of Lewis's death by doing what he could to locate the papers, he was left to face the emotional reality. He wrote to Jonathan:

> You have heard of that unfortunate end of Govr. Lewis, and probably more than I have heard. I was in hopes of hearing more particular[s] at this place, but have not... I am at a loss to know what to be at his death is a turble Stroke to me, in every respect. I wish I could talk a little with you just now.[1298]

On October 31, the secretary of war received a letter from Captain John Brahan that had been mailed from Nashville. Brahan wrote that Chickasaw Agent Neelly had informed him that Lewis had committed suicide at Grinder's house on the Natchez Trace in Tennessee by shooting himself. Brahan did not explain why he was sending the report rather than Neelly.[1299] The small federal bureaucracy was stunned. Acting Arkansas Indian Agent John B. Treat wrote to Frederick Bates from Washington:

> no one here undertakes to account for [the extraordinary death of Governor Lewis]…& certainly the short acquaintance I had with him at St. Louis in June last wholly precludes my having any reason to offer for his committing an act so very extraordinary & unexpected.[1300]

On November 21, Peerny arrived at Monticello several days ahead of Clark, riding one of the horses Lewis had bought at Fort Pickering. If he had not already heard the news, Jefferson would have been disappointed to see that his former servant was alone. The weather had turned cold and gray. Jefferson recorded that it was snowing.[1301] It was the kind of day that drew both traveler and the master of the house to the warmth of a fireplace or stove for an extended conversation.

Peerny delivered The Neelly Letter to Jefferson. Like the letter Brahan sent to the secretary of war, The Neelly Letter claimed that Lewis became "deranged in the mind" during Neelly's ride with Lewis from Fort Pickering to Grinder's Stand. It then added details that the innkeeper, Priscilla Grinder, told Neelly of how Lewis appeared deranged and killed himself. It said that Neelly had Lewis's body buried "as decently as I could in that area."[1302]

Forged letters were common at the time—the military agent in Tennessee received so many forgeries purporting to be from the prior Chickasaw agent that he routinely compared signatures to determine which letters were genuine.[1303] Jefferson seemingly had no prior letters from Neelly he could use to compare signatures. If he had, he could have recognized that U.S. Chickasaw Agent James Neelly's signature on The Neelly Letter was a forgery. The forger clearly wrote out each letter in "James," but all known correspondence from Neelly, even to the secretary of war, shows that Neelly consistently signed his first name as a "J" attached to the "N" in "Neelly, to appear as "JNeelly," and most often listed his title as U.S. Agent to the Chickasaws, with various spellings for "Chickasaws."[1304] It should also have caught Jefferson's attention at some point that the Neelly Letter claimed that Lewis committed suicide by shooting himself—twice.[1305] It made no mention of a cut throat or other wounds reported in the newspapers.

More than a week earlier, on November 13, the *National Intelligencer* in Washington City reported that Lewis had committed suicide. Then on November 15, it published news stories from the *Nashville Clarion* and the Frankfort *Argus of Western America* that were based on the same information as The Neelly Letter and added reports that Lewis's throat, arms, and legs had been cut.[1306] Jefferson maintained a subscription to the *Intelligencer*, but depending on the condition of the roads in the late fall, the stages may not yet have delivered those editions to Charlottesville, or Jefferson may not yet have picked them up from the post office.[1307]

It seems likely that someone who read the articles from one of the papers should have sent Jefferson a copy by the time that Peerny arrived. On the same day that Peerny delivered the letter to Jefferson, the *Virginia Argus* in Richmond published a reprint of an article from the Nashville *Democratic Clarion*. If Jefferson had received a copy of the *National Intelligencer* or if Peerny was still at Monticello when Jefferson read the article from the *Argus*, he certainly would have questioned Peerny about the contradictions. But Jefferson gave no indication in his letters that he had received news of Lewis's death prior to Peerny's visit.

Peerny told Jefferson that he had been paid to deliver The Neelly Letter and asked the former president for $240 in back wages he claimed that Lewis owed him.[1308] Jefferson declined to pay—such claims were typically filed against the deceased's estate, and Jefferson would make his own claim for funds he had lent Lewis.[1309] Nevertheless, Jefferson agreed to cover Peerny's travel expenses to Washington. Lewis family lore held that Peerny also attempted to meet with Lewis's mother, Lucy, and that she refused to see him because she believed him responsible for her son's death.[1310]

At that point, Lewis's Last Will and Testament had not yet been delivered. However, Jefferson assumed on November 26, that the administrator of Lewis's estate would be his half-brother, John Marks. Jefferson could only have known that Lewis did not appoint Clark or another executor if Peerny told him the contents of Lewis's Will.[1311]

Peerny continued on to Washington, where he sold Lewis's horse for partial payment for his wages. As evidence of both his and Lewis's strenuous trip through the frontier, the horse that Lewis bought for about $140 at Fort Pickering brought only $43.50.[1312]

Clark arrived at his wife Julia's hometown of Fincastle, Virginia, on November 22. William P. Anderson had mailed a letter to Clark at Fincastle, maybe in reply to Clark's letter to him, to report that Jenkins Whiteside, who was just appointed as U.S. Senator from Tennessee, would deliver Lewis's papers to Clark by stage on his way to Washington. That letter, which has not surfaced, would have been written some days prior to the inventory of Lewis's trunks in Nashville and the change of plans for Thomas Freeman to deliver one of Lewis's trunks. Clark relied on Anderson's letter and waited in vain for a week at Fincastle for Senator Whiteside to deliver the trunks.[1313]

As Clark was stalled waiting for Whiteside, he received delivery of The Suspicious Russell Letters, which must have borne signatures purported to be those of Captain Gilbert C. Russell.[1314] Clark presumed the letters to be genuine, though he was not known to have ever corresponded with Russell to recognize his signature. The letters have not surfaced, but Clark stated they claimed Lewis had attempted suicide on the boat before reaching Fort Pickering, that Lewis was mentally deranged for fifteen days at the fort, and that Lewis wrote a Last Will and Testament while he was there. Clark would understand from the letters that Lewis named him as co-executor of his estate, along with William Meriwether, and that Lewis bequeathed the expedition journals to him.[1315]

The statement in The Suspicious Russell Letters that Lewis's recovery at Fort Pickering took fifteen days, or until September 29, differed from other "Russell" accounts. When Russell later attempted to defend his confinement of Lewis to Jefferson, he assured him that Lewis's health was restored in six days, or by about September 22.[1316] If the timeline in The Suspicious Russell Letters was correct, Lewis purchased horses to leave the fort two days before he recovered, and he would not have recovered until the day he left the fort. More significantly, there would have been no reason for Lewis to wait for Russell to receive approval to accompany him if Lewis was not fit for travel until the day he left. Again, in separate letters, Russell would also assure Jefferson that Lewis's health was fully recovered when he left, but The Russell Statement said that Lewis had "not entirely recovered" at the Chickasaw Bluffs.[1317]

If Lewis had executed a Last Will and Testament at Fort Pickering, as The Suspicious Russell Letters alleged, he likely would have asked Russell to serve as a witness, assuming their relationship was as cordial as Russell claimed. Because Russell attempted to garner favor with Jefferson, he certainly would have used that fact to bolster his credibility. Russell claimed that he wrote to Jefferson to provide information about Lewis's property and other facts Jefferson should know; however, neither of Russell's letters to Jefferson mentions that Lewis executed a Will at Fort Pickering, and no such Will has ever surfaced.[1318]

The Suspicious Russell Letters also alleged that Peerny claimed Lewis had imagined hearing Clark coming up behind him at some point on the journey. According to Clark's recounting of the letters, Lewis told Peerny that Clark had learned of his condition and was coming to help him. The letter writer seemed to allege that Lewis suffered from a fever delirium or a psychological condition that would make it easier to accept the suicide narrative.[1319]

Although The Suspicious Russell Letters would conflict with statements Russell later gave to Jefferson, Clark did not yet have that reason to doubt them. For the moment, he gave them more weight than they merited.

On November 24, Jefferson received a letter in the mail from Captain John Brahan, which repeated essentially the same details of Lewis's death that Jefferson had read in The Neely Letter that supposedly had been signed by Neely. Brahan was particularly familiar with the details of The Neely Letter because the body of the forged letter was in Brahan's handwriting.[1320] In Brahan's letter to Jefferson under his own signature, he did not reveal that he had written The Neely Letter. In addition, by paying Peerny to hand-deliver The Neely Letter and by separately mailing the letter under his own signature, Brahan made it appear that the letters, both datelined from Nashville on October 18, 1809, had been sent independently. That false appearance gave the facts in both undue credibility.

Brahan claimed that he took the initiative to write Jefferson because Lewis "was a very particular friend of mine, being intimately acquainted, and one for whom I had the Greatest respect & Esteem."[1321] Lewis may have met Brahan more than a decade earlier when he served as a recruiter in Staunton, Virginia, but the assertion of a close friendship was dubious. Their paths had probably not crossed since that time, unless they had been in private communication about Texas and Santa Fe. Even then, their relationship was so distant that Brahan felt compelled to explain his role to Jefferson.

As he had in The Neely Letter, Brahan then turned to the important matter of Lewis's trunks, which he said were in Neely's possession. Brahan seemed to solicit Jefferson's approval to permit him to take charge of the trunks and to send them on to Jefferson.

In addition to the two letters that he sent to Jefferson and to the secretary of war, Brahan repeated essentially the same facts about Lewis's death in a fourth letter he wrote the same day to Major Amos Stoddard.[1322]

Back in Nashville on November 28, the prisoner George Lanehart's victim Joseph VanMeter, and three of the witnesses from McIntoshville who had signed Neelly's verification of the reputation of James Colbert, appeared and signed personal appearance bonds to remain in Nashville to give testimony.[1323] The federal grand jury met that day and returned an indictment against Lanehart.[1324] Two days later, the federal marshal escorted Lanehart into the courtroom for his trial before a jury that included Andrew Jackson's friend, John Harding. The jury quickly found Lanehart guilty. The judge ordered him to pay a two-dollar fine and sentenced him to two months in the debtor's room of the jail.[1325]

As Clark neared Charlottesville on December 3, he stopped first at Lewis's farm. Lewis's mother, Lucy, was not at home, but Clark met with Lewis's half-brother, John Marks. The family had heard the news. Marks said they were much distressed. Clark noted, "I shewed young Mr. Marks all the letters I had about his Brother's situation and I told him my opinion on that subject."[1326] Clark apparently spent three days at the Lewis home, mourning his friend and attempting to make some sense of his death.

On December 7, Clark finally arrived in Charlottesville, where he seems to have found Jefferson in town. Rather than discussing the matter in public, Jefferson invited Clark to visit him at Monticello and plan to spend the night. Jefferson had turned his east foyer into a private museum that he called his "Indian Hall." It was there he displayed some of the horns, skins, and minerals Lewis sent back from the expedition. Seeing those artifacts again would have reminded Clark of exciting days exploring the Far West with his friend and the Corps of Discovery.[1327] Those memories would have made the loss of Lewis more profound.

Jefferson could have shown Clark The Neelly Letter and the Brahan letter that seemed to confirm parts of the newspaper accounts reprinted from the *Nashville Clarion* that relied heavily on The Neely Letter. Clark could have told Jefferson about the report from the Frankfort *Argus of Western America* that apparently mentioned only the wounds from a cut throat. Jefferson and Clark may have read the fewer competing reprints from a Lexington, Kentucky, newspaper that claimed to have information from a witness who said that Lewis committed suicide by shooting himself three times and by cutting his own throat, arms, and legs.[1328] And Clark could have shown Jefferson The Suspicious Russell letters that had been timed for Clark to receive as he was waiting in Fincastle on his way to meet with Jefferson. The discrepancies in the accounts that appear obvious more than two centuries later may have been dulled by the immediate emotional impact of Lewis's sudden death.

The claim of suicide would have struck a familiar response from Jefferson. One of his favorite servants, James Hemmings, became an alcoholic and committed suicide. Jefferson's son-in-law, Thomas Mann Randolph, suffered from severe depression, which was feared of making him suicidal.[1329] The report of suicide could have been designed to manipulate Jefferson by playing on his emotions, creating guilt for not better guiding Lewis and placing him in the middle of conflicts he would not be able to control.

Jefferson also could relate the details of his conversations with Peerny. Jefferson never recorded or made public statements about what details, if any, Peerny revealed about Lewis's death. In the only written reference Peerny is known to have signed, he simply described Lewis's death as "Melancholy."[1330] The term seems to have been commonly used at the time as a synonym for "tragic."[1331]

It may have been the details of The Suspicious Russell Letters that later led Jefferson to thank Russell for how well he had cared for his protégé. Unless Peerny had also told Jefferson about Lewis's treatment at Fort Pickering, Jefferson would have relied solely upon Russell's self-serving statements and statements from letters that were likely forged. Clark would not be so generous. He later refused to pay Russell for Lewis's debt for the money and horses he provided to Lewis at Fort Pickering.[1332]

A common reaction to learning of the reported suicide of a friend, Jefferson and Clark attempted to recall any troubling signs in Lewis's behavior that should have warned them he was suicidal. Unlike Clark, who noted a recipe in his travel journal, Lewis noted remedies for illnesses in his. Clark may have thought Lewis carried concerns for his health too far, even though he had witnessed Lewis's successful doctoring of soldiers in their company.

Jefferson may have discussed the "sensible depressions" he had witnessed in Lewis, which he had always passed off as an attitude or a propensity that Lewis inherited from his family.[1333] Jefferson never saw anything that prompted him even to note the depressions or discuss them with Lewis. He certainly witnessed nothing that prevented him from selecting Lewis to lead the transcontinental expedition, one of the most important missions of his presidency, and then to appoint him as Upper Louisiana Governor, where Jefferson's legacy for purchasing the Louisiana Territory would rest in large part on Lewis's performance.

Clark could tell Jefferson how Lewis was overwhelmed by the attacks on his reputation and his sudden inability to pay his bills. Even then, to accept the idea that Lewis had taken his own life in an "act of desperation," Jefferson later speculated to Russell that Lewis's hypochondria was probably exacerbated from "the habit into which he had fallen & the painful reflections that would necessarily produce in a mind like his."[1334] Of course, that idea could have been based solely on Russell's and Brahan's claims, whether true or not. From whatever claims Jefferson believed from The Neelly Letter, the Brahan letter, the accounts that Clark and Peerny gave him in person, and newspaper reports, he referred to Lewis's death as "unfortunate" in letters to James Madison and to Lewis's publisher in November 1809.[1335]

Clark never wrote that he had witnessed Lewis suffering from any destructive habits, except maybe worrying too much about becoming ill or possibly overmedicating himself. His first reaction to news of Lewis's death had been to worry that the weight of Lewis's mind had overcome him, but in the space of a month, Clark said that he had begun to contradict many of the speculative reports he heard about Lewis.[1336] Unlike Jefferson, Clark never wrote that he believed Lewis committed suicide. The assumption that he accepted the suicide narrative has been based on Clark's apparently choosing not to contradict that claim or take any action to look further into the cause of Lewis's death.

Both Jefferson and Clark had the disadvantage of relying on unreliable hearsay and often contradictory accounts from Grinder's Stand and Fort Pickering. Though both would be expected to opine on how their friend died, neither was an eyewitness. Ultimately, their opinions as to how Lewis died would be only as conclusive as the unreliable information they read or were told.

If either held any suspicions that Lewis was murdered, there was little they could do. Both could call on influential contacts in high places, but investigations of deaths in the states fell under the legal jurisdiction of local counties. The Chickasaw agent's escorting of a governor through a tribal nation and Lewis's death on a military highway provided enough of a military connection that Jefferson or Clark could have asked Wilkinson to use a military pretext to send army officers to question witnesses in Tennessee. And perhaps Wilkinson did send officers for his own purposes to report information he thought necessary to satisfy the doubts of Lewis's friends.[1337]

Russell would write to Jefferson in late January 1810, to suggest that he had conducted a form of investigation to gather, as he said, "every thing I can learn."[1338] Jefferson and Clark may have accepted Russell's purported findings despite the numerous contradictions.

And circumstances had changed as General Hampton prepared to take over Wilkinson's command.[1339] The powerful army structure could be expected to be in a virtual civil war until Wilkinson or Hampton prevailed. Hampton's men, who had suffered under Wilkinson's persecutions, would not be expected to be friendly to Jefferson's interests.[1340]

Jefferson and Clark also had reason to avoid directing unnecessary attention to events in the West. Smith, Patterson, McLanahan, and possibly men from the Mandan Expedition were believed to be working their way toward Santa Fe from the north, while Dr. Sibley was launching an expedition from the south. Their parties risked provoking hostilities with Spain, which the U.S. could ill afford on the eve of war with Britain. Who knew what witnesses would reveal about Jefferson's and Lewis's actions in the West? Even if Madison secretly supported their goals, Federalist critics might seek revenge by suggesting prosecutions for Burr-like violations of the Neutrality Act, as they had for the conspirators in the Miranda Expedition and would later for adventurers attempting to take Texas.[1341] Stories of the prosecutions of Miranda's associates still sold newspapers through the summer of 1809.[1342]

Besides, the looming war with Britain or Spain was already the focus of the U.S. Army in the Southwest. Hampton had been advised to be cautious and maintain sufficient troops in the New Orleans area in the event of an attack.[1343] Any effort to divert resources for anything else would draw unnecessary attention.

Jefferson admitted to detesting any personal controversy about himself. His contemporaries claimed that he refused to face a crisis when in office.[1344] Now in retirement, he attempted to fade as a political target. A year after Lewis's death, Jefferson admitted, "my object too at present is peace and tranquility, neither doing nor saying any thing to be quoted, or to make me the subject of newspaper disquisitions."[1345]

Even if Jefferson suspected that Wilkinson had hired assassins, it was to his advantage to convince Clark otherwise. Wilkinson had successfully pretended to be a mentor to Clark in the army. Just as the magnanimous Clark was late to suspect Bates's conniving nature, he held Wilkinson in such high regard that he refused to see his treason. Clark viewed Wilkinson through his lens as a Revolutionary War hero.[1346]

And, too, Clark had reason to be distracted. He admitted feeling overwhelming pressure to see the expedition account published. Lewis could no longer supply the narrative. That subject could be helpful to divert attention to the immediate need Clark felt. Although Gass' account had already leaked, there would be an advantage to setting forth the fuller narrative of the expedition before critics were given their chance to distort its mission. One of the main achievements of their lives depended on it.

Clark had called Lewis's failure to complete the narrative "neglect." Ultimately, however, the missions that Lewis performed for Jefferson in the West rather than writing a narrative may have proved more consequential. For the moment, Clark felt the burden Lewis had shared as a weight cast solely on his shoulders, and he needed Jefferson's help.

Most revealing is that neither Jefferson nor Clark would be known to visit Lewis's grave, nor make any provision to mark his grave. Their inaction may have disclosed a knowledge that events in the Southwest were more volatile than their writings reveal, and they chose not to draw more attention to Lewis's sudden death.

Even if marking a grave was not a personal priority for either Jefferson or Clark, both knew that it had been important to Lewis. Lewis likely had told them that when he first volunteered for military service, he took the time to ensure that the grave of an Albermarle friend and fellow soldier who died from illness during the Whiskey Rebellion was properly marked with a stone.[1347] But rather than treat Lewis's death as the death of a friend, a surrogate son, or even as a soldier whose service merited a stone at his grave, Jefferson and Clark would treat Lewis's death more like the death of a spy on an unfinished clandestine mission.

In fact, as late as autumn 1835, it still could be said of Meriwether Lewis that, "No stone is raised to mark the spot where he sleeps, and no hand has written his epitaph." Only then would the son of a Natchez Trace inn owner mount a public campaign to mark Lewis's grave.[1348]

Perhaps it was purely coincidental that the first effort to mark Lewis's final resting place followed the Nashville newspaper publication of excited news stories declaring the "eve of a revolution" in Spanish Texas as Tennesseans again turned their attention to securing the remainder of Jefferson's Louisiana Purchase prize. The newspaper reported the groundswell of support as Tennesseans prepared to cross over the New Spain border, and Davy Crockett and others planned to join the effort.[1349] In the wave of the Texas excitement at the end of October 1835, a subscription to mark Lewis's grave circulated in Nashville.[1350] The announcement of public meetings to generate support for the marking would be made in early January 1836, just six weeks before the Battle of the Alamo and two months before the declaration of the independent Republic of Texas.[1351]

And perhaps it was also coincidental that during the debate to annex Texas to the U.S. in 1843, the Tennessee Legislature created a new "Lewis County" from the section of Maury County where Lewis was buried. And that the legislature finally approved funds to erect a monument worthy of a national hero at Lewis's grave two days after the signing of the treaty that ended the Mexican-American War in 1848—a treaty that fixed the southern boundary where Jefferson said it should be at the Rio Grande.[1352]

So, then, perhaps it also was coincidental, and fitting, that the leader of the sons of Andrew Jackson's friends who pushed to mark Lewis's grave was the son of the captain of General Andrew Jackson's U.S. Army Company of Spies.[1353] And by J. Nelson Patterson, whose grandfather served as Secretary of the Texas Association from Tennessee—and whose father, James, had served as John Smith T's spy to Santa Fe in 1809, before also serving in Andrew Jackson's Company of Spies.[1354]

Or perhaps it did not all happen by coincidence. The timing suggests that while other portions of the country highlighted Lewis's public role in securing the Northwest, Tennesseans memorialized the end of the Mexican-American War by honoring Meriwether Lewis's secret role in acquiring Texas— and the greater American West.

Perhaps army spies of Lewis's generation believed that his ultimate mission was Texas and Santa Fe all along and that he died while performing that mission. It could be possible that from their fathers, the men who eventually marked Lewis's grave with a hero's monument knew the kinds of "secrets" that could not be entrusted to paper, as George Washington had advised.

It would take time to process how Lewis's sudden death had changed everything. Clark gave the impression that he and Jefferson talked into the late hours at Monticello.[1355]

Unanswered questions about how Lewis died no doubt hung over their conversation and similar conversations for decades, like an aggrieved spirit that could find no rest until the truth be told.[1356]

Meriwether Lewis Grave and Monument at the Site of the Former Grinder's Stand in Tennessee.

# IMAGE CREDITS

xiv  George Washington by James House, Collection of the Maryland State Archives, George Washington (1732-1799), James House (1775-1835), after Gilbert Stuart (1755-1828) 1798, Oil on canvas 27¼ x 32¾" MSA SC 4680-10-0035.

xvi  From a portrait of Thomas Jefferson by Rembrandt Peale, Courtesy of the Library of Congress.

4  From a reproduction of a painting of Napoleon by Jean Baptiste Greuze.

18  From an engraving of William Clark, Courtesy of the Library of Congress.

30  From an engraving of General James Wilkinson by Charles Balthazar Julien Fevret de Saint-Mémin, Courtesy of the Library of Congress.

40  Photo of remains of a c. 1798 house at Fort Adams, Courtesy of the Library of Congress.

66  From a painting of Meriwether Lewis by Charles Balthazar Julien Fevret de Saint-Mémin, Courtesy of the Amon Carter Museum of American Art, Fort Worth, Texas, Gift of The Old Print Gallery, Inc.

92  From a portrait of Meriwether Lewis by Charles Willson Peale, Courtesy of the Library of Congress.

104  Illustration of flatboat and two keelboats on a river, Courtesy of the Missouri Historical Society.

116  From a portrait of Aaron Burr, Courtesy of the Library of Congress.

126  From a portrait of Frederick Bates, Courtesy of the Missouri Historical Society.

192  Meriwether Lewis Last Will and Testament, Courtesy of the Library of Virginia.

212  From a portrait of John Brahan, Courtesy of the Florence-Lauderdale Public Library.

222  From a print of Andrew Jackson, Courtesy of the Library of Congress.

232  The Natchez Trace.

265  Photo of Meriwether Lewis monument constructed at gravesite in 1848, Courtesy of the State of Tennessee Library and Archives. The photo was taken prior to the War Department modifications to the site in the 1920s.

# MAPS

Louisiana Purchase of 1803

267

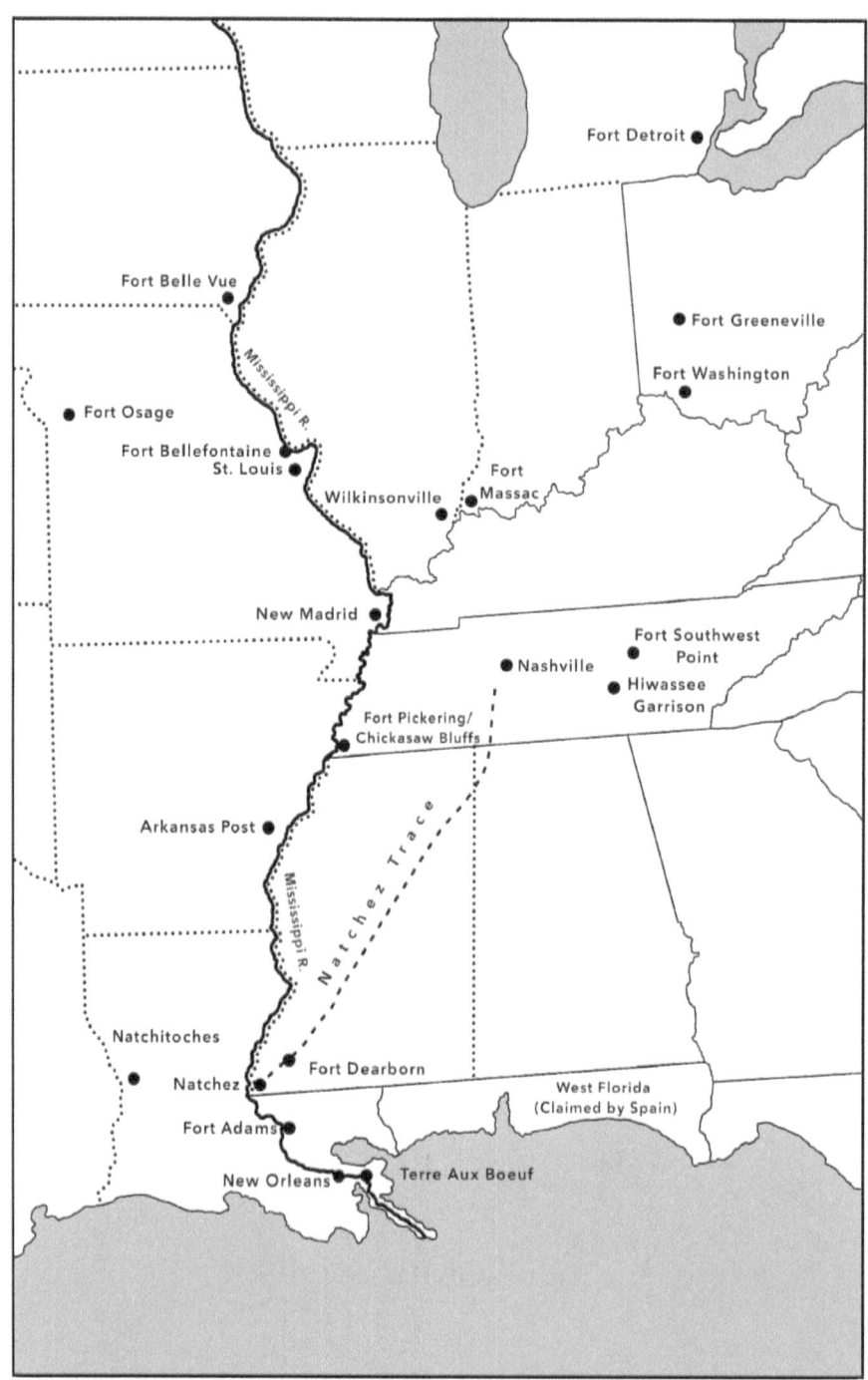

Selected Western Forts and Military Camps Referenced in the Text

# MAPS

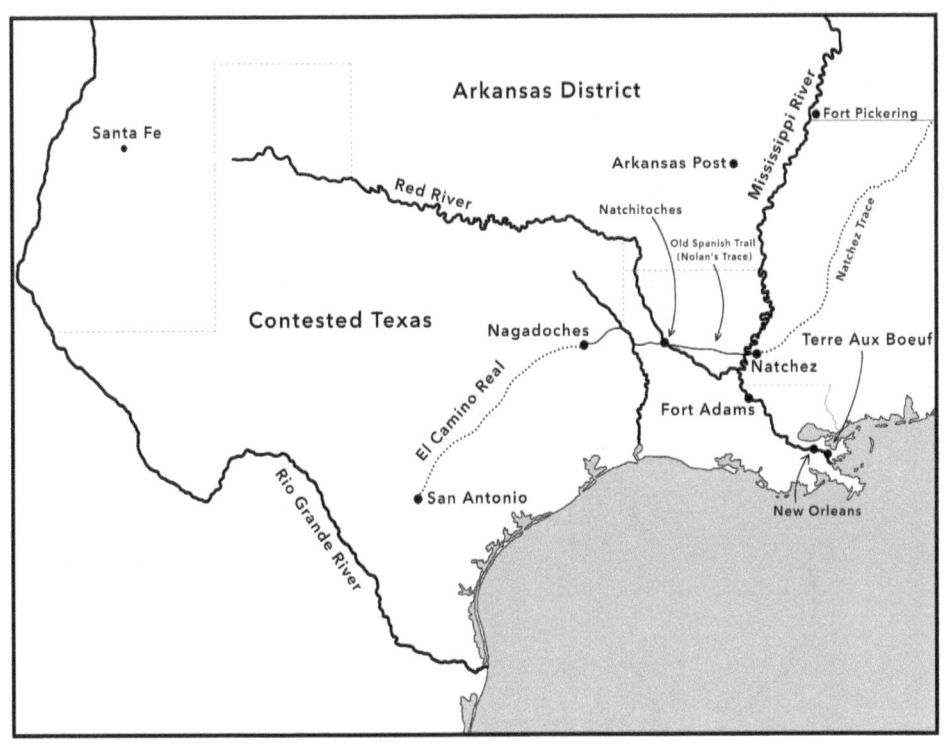

New Spain, 1809

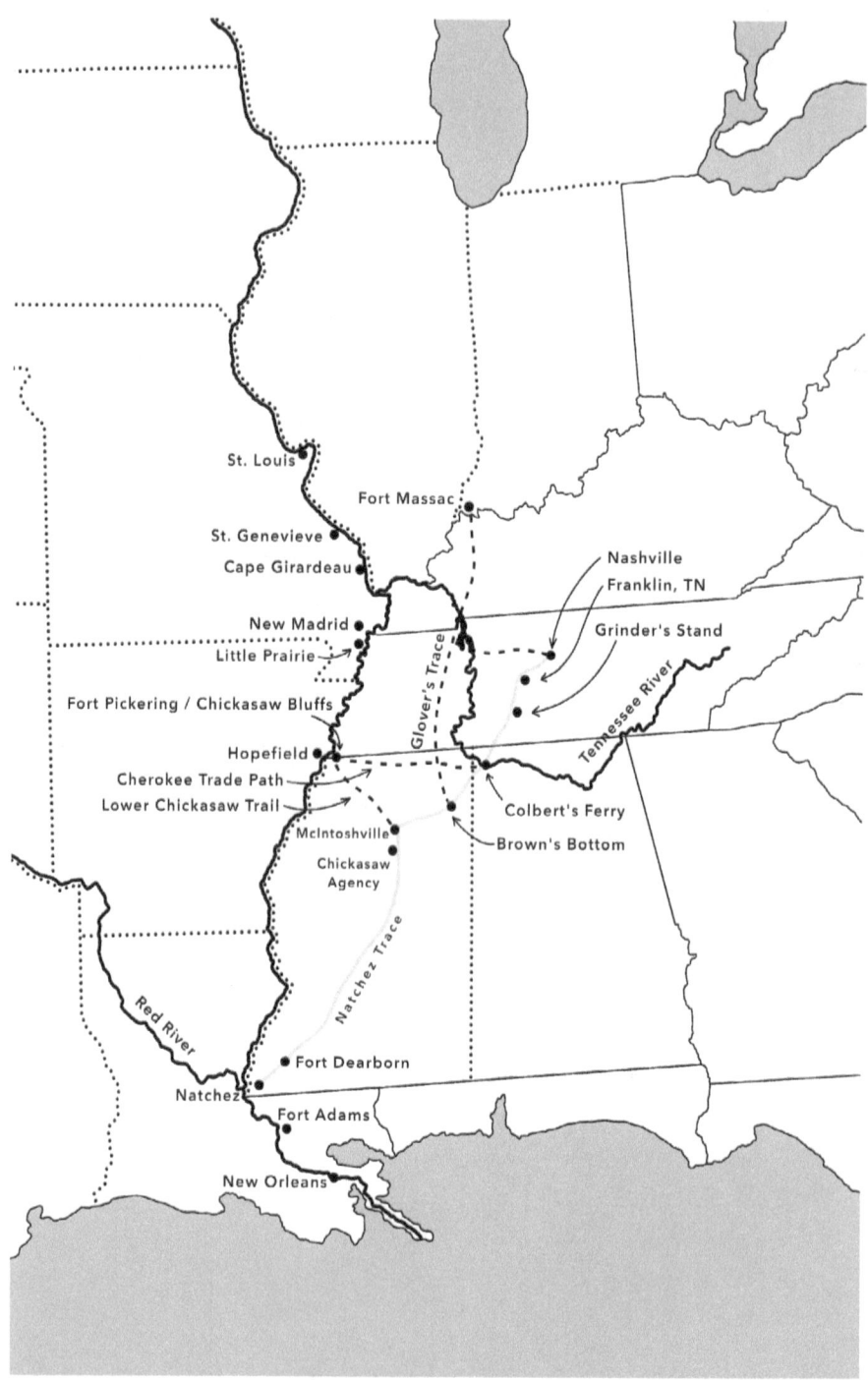

Levis's Final Journey

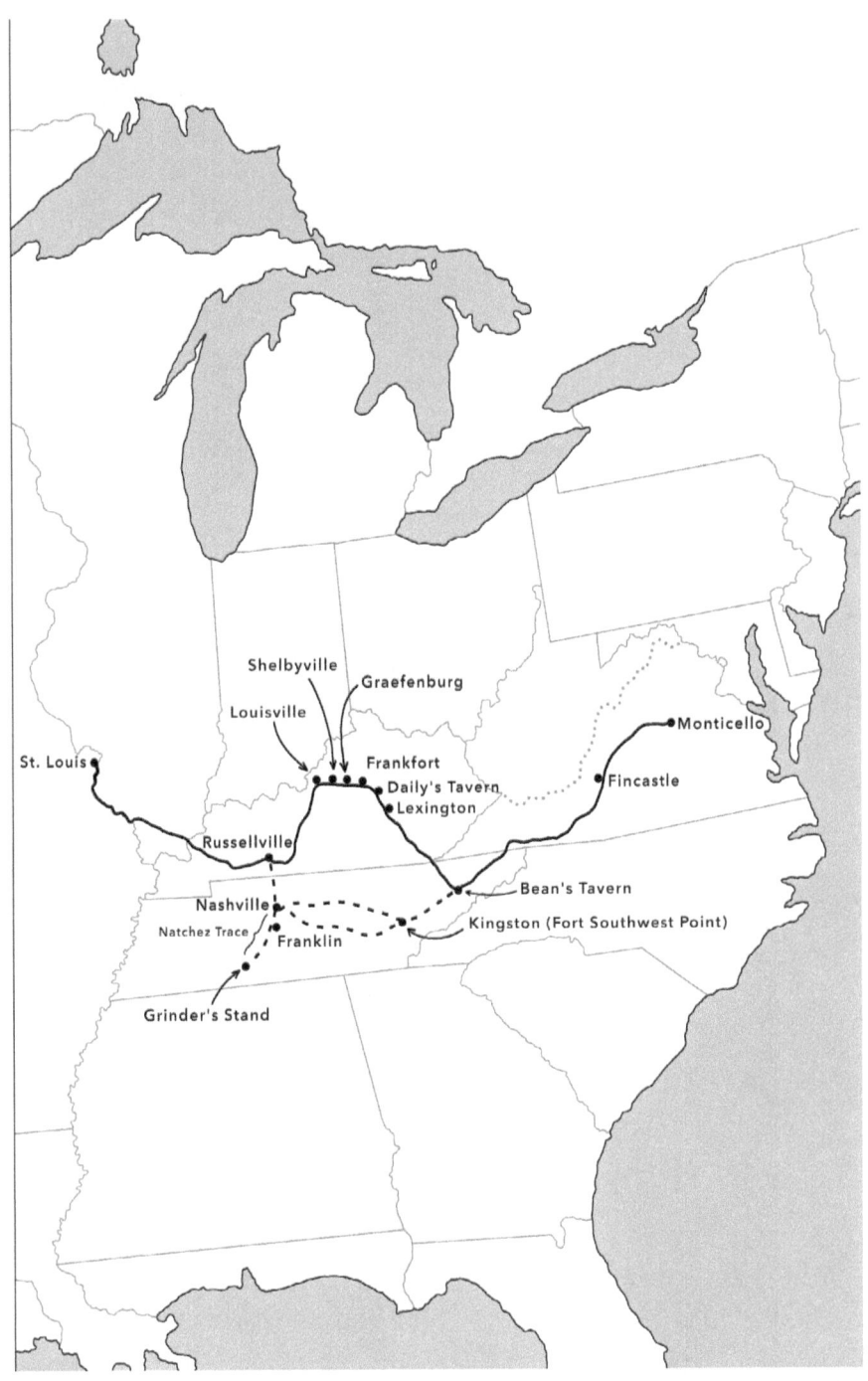

Roads to Monticello

# PREVIEW OF VOLUME TWO

## *Jefferson's Spy: The Mysterious Death of Meriwether Lewis*

Through Thomas Jefferson's planning, the Virginia farm boy Meriwether Lewis grew up to leave a public legacy of exploration and natural science. The full secret role Meriwether Lewis played in the eventual extension of the U.S. borders to the Rio Grande and to the Pacific were among the events of his life not memorialized in writing.

Most future generations of Americans would enjoy the benefits of his work in fulfilling Jefferson's goal to keep European powers from maintaining claims on North American land, from which they could constantly threaten war. As Jefferson anticipated, the large buffers of the Atlantic and the Pacific generally protected American homes from the kinds of wars that ravaged Europe.

However, Lewis also left a mystery that has endured for over 200 years. It would be alleged that while traveling on "The Devil's Backbone," Lewis took his own life by cutting his own throat, slicing his wrists to the bone, cutting his own hands and legs, and shooting himself two or three times—just before three of his expedition journals were discovered to be missing.

The details of that mystery will be explored in the second volume, *Jefferson's Spy: The Mysterious Death of Meriwether Lewis.*

For more information on the publication of the second volume and other books by the author, visit tonyturnbow.com.

# ACKNOWLEDGMENTS

I have received help from scores of people in the course of researching and writing this book over forty years. More than a few have provided information and expertise, and they have tolerated numerous questions without complaint. I did not keep a list to provide proper individual acknowledgments. I am certain that if I begin to list individuals, I will forget names and appear ungrateful. I could not have compiled the information in this book without their knowledge and the time they took to share it.

Like all other writers on history, I have built on the work of earlier writers, and I cite their works in the bibliography and notes. I have also credited Dr. Jessica Dunn, Dr. Chris Walker, and Dr. Nathan K. Moran in the notes for the time they recently took to provide their expertise. I also appreciate the recent generous assistance from archivists at the American Philosophical Society; Filson Historical Society; Jefferson County, Tennessee Archives; Indiana University Lilly Library; Lewis County, Tennessee Public Library; Library of Congress; Library of Virginia; Maury County Tennessee Archives; Memphis Public Library; Missouri Historical Society; National Archives; Tennessee State Library and Archives; University of Michigan, William L. Clements Library; University of North Alabama, Collier Library; University of North Carolina at Chapel Hill Collections; University of Southern Mississippi McClain Library & Archives; University of Tennessee, Andrew Jackson Papers; University of Virginia Archives; University of Virginia, James Madison Papers; and Williamson County, Tennessee Archives, as well as researchers and friends with the Chickasaw Nation; the Inkana Foundation, the National Park Service, and the Historic Natchez Foundation.

Friends with the Lewis and Clark Trust, Inc., the Lewis and Clark Trail Alliance, the Discovery Center of St. Charles, the Seventh U.S. Infantry Living History Association, Sevier Ranging Company, and the Natchez Trace Parkway Association provided invaluable insight from their research of the period as well as an understanding that comes only from experiencing the customs and routines of the period through their excellent living history programs.

I would be remiss if I did not acknowledge the late Kira Gale, who generously shared her own research and whose hundreds of emails pushed me to expand the limits of my own research. Kira and I did not always reach the same conclusions, but I always appreciated that she was motivated by a search for the truth. As it turns out, I think she anticipated several of the main conclusions that I have reached in this book a decade earlier than I did. In addition, the late Robert Thrower, Tribal Historic Preservation Officer for the Poarch Creek Band of Indians, engaged in hours of discussion on the tribal perspective of the period.

William Clark's descendant, Bud Clark, provided a great insight into Clark's perspective. Members of the Lewis family have also been supportive, and I want to give particular thanks to Lewis family member Howell Bowen, who, more than a decade ago, spent a day providing a personal tour of Lewis's grandparents' farm, Cloverfields, his boyhood home, Locust Hill, and other Charlottesville, Virginia area Lewis sites.

To all these, the hundreds of individuals within these groups, and others I am certain I am leaving out, I give my acknowledgment and heartfelt thanks.

# ABBREVIATIONS

| | |
|---|---|
| ASP | American State Papers |
| AW | Clark Hunter, ed. *The Life and Letters of Alexander Wilson* (Philadelphia: American Philosophical Society, 1983) |
| FB | Thomas Maitland Marshall, ed. *The Life and Papers of Frederick Bates* (St. Louis: Missouri Historical Society, 1926) |
| CA | U.S. Cherokee Indian Agency in Tennessee, 1801-1835, Correspondence and Misc. Records, NARA, M208 |
| GCR | Gilbert C. Russell |
| FO | Founders Online, National Archives |
| LC | Library of Congress |
| LR | Letters Received, Secretary of War, NARA |
| LS | Letters Sent, Secretary of War, NARA |
| JW | James Wilkinson |
| ML | Meriwether Lewis |
| MHS | Missouri Historical Society |
| NARA | National Archives, Washington, D.C. |
| PAJ | Papers of Andrew Jackson |
| SW | Secretary of War |
| TJ | Thomas Jefferon |
| TP | Carter, Clarence Edward, ed. *The Territorial Papers, of the United States,* Washington: U.S. Gov.t Printing Office, 1934-1962 |
| TSLA | Tennessee State Library and Archives, Nashville, Tenn. |
| WC | William Clark |

# SELECTED BIBLIOGRAPHY

Please note that the current URL links to online information are not provided, as links change frequently and e-book sources often disfavor outdated links. In addition, the increased availability of records with online search capabilities makes other details, such as National Archives record group numbers and microfilm reel numbers, unnecessary. Sufficient information is provided to locate the cited materials found online with a simple search. Archives referenced below have filed paper correspondence chronologically; therefore, box and file numbers are not needed to locate the documents.

## Books

Adams, Charles Francis. *The Works of John Adams.* New York: Little Brown and Company, 1856. 1.

Adams, Henry. *History of the United States of America During the Administration of Thomas Jefferson*, Reprinted, Library of America, 1986.

Alden, Rev. Timothy. "On the Fate of Seaman the Dog," *A Collection of Epitaphs and Inscriptions with Occasional Notes.* S. Marks Printer, 1814.

Allen, Paul. *History of the Expedition Under the Command of Captains Lewis and Clark to the Sources of the Missouri, Thence Across the Rocky Mountains and Down the River Columbia to the Pacific Ocean. Performed During the Years*

*1804-5-6. By the Order of the Government of the United States.* New York: Bradford and Inskeep, 1814. Vol. 1-2.

Ambrose, Stephen E. *Undaunted Courage: Meriwether Lewis, Thomas Jefferson, and the Opening of the West.* New York: Simon & Schuster, 1996.

Anderson, Sarah Travers and Lewis Scott. *Lewises, Meriwethers, and their Kin.* Richmond: 1938.

Atkinson, James R. *Splendid Land, Splendid People: The Chickasaw Indians to Removal.* Tuscaloosa: The University of Alabama Press, 2004.

Anton, May Sue. *New Madrid: A Mississippi River Town in History and Legend.* Cape Girardeau: Southeast Missouri State University Press, 2009.

Ashe, Thomas. *History of Missouri, Travels in America.* London: Printed for Richard Phillips, 1809) Vol. 2-4.

Bakeless, John. *Lewis and Clark: Partners in Discovery.* New York: William Morrow & Company, 1947.

Baldwin, Leland D. *The Keelboat Age on the Western Waters.* Pittsburgh: University of Pittsburgh Press, 1941.

———. *Whiskey Rebels: The Story of a Frontier Uprising.* Pittsburgh: University of Pittsburgh Press, 1939, reprinted 1967.

Barefield, Marilyn Davis, ed. *Old Huntsville Land Office Records & Military Warrants*, 1810-1854. Easely, SC: Southern Historical Press, Inc. 1985.

Bauer, K. Jack. *Zachary Taylor*, Baton Rouge: Louisiana State University, 1985.

Bean, Ellis P. *Memoir of Colonel Ellis P. Bean Written By Himself About the Year 1816.* Book Club of Texas, 1939.

Bernsen, James Aalan. *The Lost War for Texas: Mexican Rebels, American Burrites, and the Texas Revolution of 1811.* College Station: Texas A & M University, 2024.

Billion, Frederic L. *Annals of St. Louis In Its Territorial Days, 1804-1821.* St. Louis, 1888.

Brackenridge, Henry Marie Brackenridge. *Views of Louisiana: Together with a Journal of a Voyage up the Missouri River, in 1811.* Pittsburgh: Cramer, Spear and Eichbaum, 1814.

Breazeale, J. W. M. *Life As It Is.* Knoxville, 1842, Reproduced by Charles Elder.

Brown, Everett Somerville, ed. *William Plumer's memorandum of proceedings in the United States Senate, 1803-1807.* The MacMillan Company, 1923.

Brown, Samuel R. *Western Gazetteer; Or Emigrant's Directory.* Auburn, N.Y.: H. C. Southwick, 1817.

Brown, William Horace. *The Glory Seekers: The Romance of Would-be Founders of Empire in the Early Days of the Southwest.* Cambridge: The University Press: Cambridge, 1906.

Browman, David L. Browman. *Cantonment Belle Fontaine 1805-1825: The First U.S. Fort West of the Mississippi River.* St. Louis. Washington University in St. Louis, 2018.

Buckley, Jay H. *William Clark: Indian Diplomat.* Norman: University of Oklahoma Press, 2008.

Bush, Robert O. Bush, ed. *Pierre Clemaent de Laussat, Memoirs of My Life.* Baton Rouge: LSU Press, 1978.

Bynum, William F. Bulletin of the History of Medicine. The Johns Hopkins University Press. March-April 1968. Vol. 42, No. 2., 160-185.

Capers, Gerald M., Jr. *The Biography of a River Town, Memphis: Its Heroic Age.* Self-Published, 1966.

Carter, Clarence Edward, ed. *The Territorial Papers, of the United States.* Washington: U.S. Gov't Printing Office, 1934-1962. V. 10, 13, 14.

Chadwick, Bruce. *The First American Army.* Napierville, Illinois: Sourcebooks, Inc., 2005.

Cheatem, Mark R. *Andrew Jackson, Southerner.* Baton Rouge: Louisiana State University Press, 2013.

Christian, Shirley. *Before Lewis and Clark: The Story of the Chouteaus*, The French Dynasty That Ruled America's Frontier. Lincoln: University of Nebraska Press, 2004.

Claiborne, J. F. H. *Mississippi, as a province, territory, and state: with biographical notices of eminent citizens.* Jackson, Miss.: Power & Barksbale, 1880. Vol I.

Clark, Daniel. *Proofs of the Corruption of Gen. James Wilkinson and of His Connection With Aaron Burr: With a Full Refutation of His Slanderous Allegations in Relation to the Character of the Principal Witness Against Him.* Philadelphia: Wm. Hall, Jun. & Geo. W. Pierie, 1809.

Clarke, Charles G. *The Men of the Lewis and Clark Expedition.* Lincoln: University of Nebraska Press, 1970.

Clayton, W. W. *History of Davidson County, Tennessee, with illustrations and biographical sketches of its prominent men and pioneers.* Philadelphia: J. L. Lewis & co., 1880.

Clements, Paul, *Chronicles of the Cumberland Settlements.* Nashville: The Foundation of William and Jennifer Frist and Paul Clements, 2012.

Coale, Edward, *Trials of the Mail Robbers*. Baltimore: 1818.

Coates, Robert M. *The Outlaw Years: A History of the Land Pirates on the Natchez Trace*. New York: Maculay Company, 1930.

Coleman, J. Winston, Jr. *Stage-Coach Days In The Bluegrass*. Louisville: University Press of Kentucky, 1935.

Collot, Georges Henri Victor. *A Journey in North America*. Paris: Printed for Arthus Bertrand Bookseller, 1826. Vol. 2.

Colter-Frick, R. *Courageous Colter and Companions*. L. R. Colter-Frick, 1997.

Coues, Elliott ed. *The Expeditions of Zebulon Montgomery Pike*. New York: Francis P. Harper, 1895. Vol 1.

———. *The History of the Lewis and Clark Expedition*. New York: Frances R. Harper, 1895: 3.

Cox, Howard W. *American Traitor: General James Wilkinson's Betrayal and Escape From Justice*. Washington, D. C.: Georgetown University Press, 2023.

Cramer, Zadok. *The Navigator*. Pittsburgh: Cramer, Spear & Eichbaum, 1814 and 1821 editions.

———. *The Navigator* (Robert Ferguson & Co. Printers: Pittsburgh, 1814).

Crawford, Alan Pell. *Twilight at Monticello: The Final Years of Thomas Jefferson*. New York: Random House, 2008.

Crytzer, Brady J. *The Whiskey Rebellion: A Distilled History of an American Crisis*. Yardley, Penn.: Westholme Publishing, LLC 2023.

Cuming, F. *Sketches of a tour to the western country: through the states of Ohio and Kentucky, a voyage down the Ohio and Mississippi rivers, and a trip through the Mississippi territory, and part of West Florida, commenced at Philadelphia in the winter of 1807, and concluded in 1809*. Pittsburgh: Cramer, Spear & Eichbaum, 1810.

Cunningham, Noble E. Jr. *In Pursuit of Reason: The Life of Thomas Jefferson*. Baton Rouge: LSU Press: 1987.

Daniel, Susan G. *Rutherford County Tennessee Pioneers Born Before 1800*, Murfreesboro, Tenn.: Rutherford County Historical Society, 2003.

Danisi, Thomas C. and John C. Jackson. *Meriwether Lewis*, New York: Prometheus Books, 2009.

Danisi, Thomas C. *Uncovering the Truth About Meriwether Lewis*. New York: Prometheus Books, 2012.

Darby, John F. *Personal Recollections of Many Prominent People Whom I Have Known*. St. Louis: G. I. Jones and Col, 1880.

Daveiss, Joseph Hamilton. *View of the President's Conduct Concerning the Conspiracy of 1806*. Cincinnati: Abingdon Press, 1917, Reprint of 1007 edition.

Davidson, Donald. *The Tennessee. Volume One. The Old River: Frontier to Secession*. Nashville: J. S. Sanders & Co. 1991.

Davis, William C. *A Way Through the Wilderness: The Natchez Trace and the Civilization of the Southern Frontier*. Baton Rouge: Louisiana State University Press, 1995.

DeConde, Alexander. *This Affair Louisiana*. New York: Charles Scribner's Sons, 1976.

Denslow, Ray D. *Masonic Pioneers, Kessinger Publishing, an extract of Territorial Masonry: The Story of Freemasonry and the Louisiana Purchase*. 1925. Reprint. Whitefish, Mont.: Kessinger, 1997.

De Voto, Bernard. *The Course of Empire*. Boston: Houghton, Mifflin Company, 1962.

———. *The Journals of Lewis and Clark*. New York: Houghton Mifflin Company 1953.

Dickerson, Philip Jackson. *History of the Osage Nation: Its People, Resources, and Prospects*. Reprinted Alpha Editions, 2020.

Dillon, Richard. *Meriwether Lewis: A Biography*. New York: Coward-McCann, Inc., 1965.

Dupre, Daniel S. *Transforming the Cotton Frontier: Madison County, Alabama 1800-1840*. Baton Rouge: Louisiana State University Press, 1997.

Ellicott, Andrew. *The Journal of Andrew Ellicott*. Chicago: Quadrangle Books, 1962.

Ferling, John E. *Adams vs. Jefferson: The Tumultuous Election of 1800*. New York: Oxford University Press, 2004.

Ferling, Thomas. *The Intimate Lives of the Founding Fathers*. New York: Harper, 2009. Paperback version.

Fisher, Vardis. *Suicide or Murder? The Strange Death of Governor Meriwether Lewis*. Athens, Ohio: Ohio University Press, 1962.

Flint, Timothy. *Recollections of the Last Ten Years, Passed in Occasional Residences and Journeyings in the Valley of the Mississippi*. Boston: Cummings, Hilliard, 1826.

———. *The History and Geography of the Mississippi Valley*. Cincinnati: E. H. Flint and L. R. Lincoln, 1832. V 1.

Flores, Dan L., ed., *Journal of an Indian Trader: Anthony Glass and the Texas Trading Frontier, 1790-1810.* College Station: Texas A&M University Press, 1985.

———. *Southern Counterpart to Lewis & Clark: The Freeman & Custis Expedition of 1806.* Norman: University of Oklahoma Press, 1984.

Ford, Paul L., *The Works of Thomas Jefferson.* New York: G. P. Putnam's Sons, 1904-1905: 10.

Gale, Kira. *Fifty Documents Related to the Assassination of Meriwether Lewis.* Omaha: River Junction Press, 2018.

———. *Meriwether Lewis: The Assassination of an American Hero and the Silver Mines of Mexico.* Omaha: River Junction Press, 2015.

Gibson, Arrell M. *The Chickasaw.* Norman: University of Oklahoma Press, 1972.

Gillet, Mary C. *The Army Medical Department, 1775-1818.* Washington, D. C.: Center of Military History, 2004.

Gilpin, Alec R. *The War of 1812 in the Old Northeast.* East Lansing: Michigan State University Press, 1958.

Graham, James. *The life of General Daniel Morgan…* New York: Derby & Jackson, 1859.

Guice, John D. W. ed. *By His Own Hand?: The Mysterious Death of Meriwether Lewis.* Norman: Oklahoma University Press: 2006.

Guild, Josephus. *Old Times in Tennessee.* Nashville: Tavel, Eastman & Howell, 1878.

Hamilton, Holman. *Zachary Taylor: Soldier of the Republic.* New York: The Bobbs-Merrill Co., 1941.

Hamilton, Paul. *The Oxford Handbook of European Romanticism.* Oxford: Oxford University Press, 2016.

Hare, Joseph Thompson. *The Life and Dying Confessions of Joseph T. Hare, the noted robber who was executed at Baltimore in September last for robbing the mail.* Auburn, N.Y.: D. Rumsey 1818.

Harper's Magazine. "Dr. Mitchell's Letters from Washington." *Harper's Magazine v. 58 1878-1879 Dec-May.* New York: Brother and Brothers Publishers, 1879.

Hay, Thomas Robson and M. R. Werner. *The Admirable Trumpeter: A Biography of General James Wilkinson.* 1941. Reprinted, The Scholar's Bookshelf, 2006.

Haynes, Robert V. *The Natchez District and the American Revolution.* Jackson: University Press of Mississippi, 1976.

Haywood, John, *The Civil and Political History of the State of Tennessee.* Nashville: Publishing House of the Methodist, Episcopal Church, South, 1891. Reprinted, Knoxville: Tenase.

Heitman, Francis B., comp. *Historical Register and Dictionary of the United States Army, from Its Organization, September 29, 1789, to March 2, 1903.* 1903. Reprint, Urbana: University of Illinois Press, 1965.

Hogeland, William. *The Whiskey Rebellion.* New York: Simon & Shuster Paperbacks, 2006.

Holmberg, James J. *Dear Brother: Letters of William Clark to Jonathan Clark.* New Haven and London: Yale University Press, 2002.

Houck, Louis. *A History of Missouri from the Earliest Explorations and Settlements Until the Admission of the State Into the Union.* Chicago: R. R. Donnelley & sons Company, 1908. Vol 3.

———. *The Spanish regime in Missouri; a collection of papers and documents relating to upper Louisiana principally within the present limits of Missouri during the dominion of Spain, from the Archives of the Indies at Seville, etc., translated from the original Spanish into English, and including also some papers concerning the supposed grant to Col. George Morgan at the mouth of the Ohio, found in the Congressional library.* Chicago, Ill.: R. R. Donnelley & sons company, 1909. Vol. 2.

Hunter, Clark, ed., *The Life and Letters of Alexander Wilson.* Philadelphia: American Philosophical Society, 1983.

Jackson, Donald, ed. *Letters of the Lewis and Clark Expedition with Related Documents 1783-1854.* Urbana: University of Illinois Press, 1978.

James, Marquis. *The Life of Andrew Jackson. Indianapolis:* The Bobbs-Merrill Company, 1938: 1.

James, Gen. Thomas. *Three Years Among the Indians and Mexicans.* War Eagle: Waterloo: 1846. Republished 2017.

Johnson, Timothy D. *Winfield Scot: The Quest for Military Glory.* Lawrence, KS: University Press of Kansas, 1998.

Jones, John G. *A Complete History of Methodism.* Nashville: Publishing House of the M. E. Church South 1908: 1.

Kahn, David. *The Code Breakers: The Story of Secret Writing.* New York: McMillan Publishing Co., Inc., 1967.

Kincaid, Robert L. *The Wilderness Road.* Middlesboro, Kentucky: Mrs. Robert L. Kincaid, 1973.

Kline, Mary-Jo ed. *Political Correspondence and Public Papers of Aaron Burr.* Princeton: Princeton University Press, 1983.

Kohn, Richard H. *Eagle and Sword: The Beginnings of the Military Establishment in America.* New York: The Free Press, 1975.

Kukla, Jon A. *Wilderness So Immense: The Louisiana Purchase and the Destiny of America.* New York: Alfred A. Knoff, 2003.

Laussat, Pierre Clemaent de. *Memoirs of My Life.* Baton Rouge: LSU Press, 1978.

Leach, Josiah Granville. *History of the Penrose family of Philadelphia.* Philadelphia: Drexel, Biddle Publisher, 1903.

Leftwich, Nina. *Two Hundred Years at Muscle Shoals.* Birmingham: Multigraphic Advertising Co., 1935.

Lewis, William Terrell. *Genealogy of the Lewis Family in America.* Louisville: The Courier Journal Printing Co., 1893.

Link, Eugene P. *Democratic-Republican Societies, 1790-1800.* New York: Columbia University Press, 1942.

Linklater, Andro. *An Artist in Treason: The Extraordinary Double Life of General James Wilkinson.* New York: Walker, 2009.

Lomask, Milton. *Aaron Burr: The Conspiracy and Years of Exile, 1805-1836.* New York: Farar, Straus, Giroux, 1982.

Lynch, Louise Gillespie *Williamson County Tax Book 1.* Franklin, Tenn.: Louise Gillespie Lynch, 1977.

Malone, Dumas. *Jefferson The President: First Term 1801-1805.* Boston: Little Brown and Company, 1970.

———. *Jefferson the President: Second Term, 1805-1809.* New York: Little, Brown & Company, 1974.

Marhsall, Thomas Maitland, ed., *The Life and Papers of Frederick Bates.* St. Louis: Missouri Historical Society, 1926: 1-2.

Martini, Don. *Who Was Who Among the Southern Indians: A Genealogical Notebook, 1698-1907.* Falker, Miss: Don Martini, 1998.

Maury County Historical Society, Reprint of Century Review of Maury County, Tennessee, 1807-1907. Columbia: Board of Mayor and Aldermen, 1905.

McCallum, James. *Brief Sketch of the Settlement and Early History of Giles County, Tennessee.* Pulaski, Tenn.: The Pulaski Citizen, 1923.

McDonald, Robert M. S. *Thomas Jefferson's Military Academy: Founding West Point.* Charlottesville: University of Virginia Press, 2004.

McMurtrie, Henry *Sketches of Louisville and Its Environs.* Louisville: S. Penn, 1819.

Miranda, Francisco de. *The History of Don Francisco de Miranda's Attempt to Affect a Revolution in South America.* Boston: Oliver and Munroe, 1808.

Morris, Christopher. *Becoming Southern: The Evolution of a Way of Life, Warren County and Vicksburg, Mississippi, 1770-1860.* New York: Oxford University Press, 1995.

Morris, Larry E. *The Fate of The Corps: What Became of the Lewis and Clark Explorers After the Expedition.* New Haven: Yale University Press, 2004.

Moser, Harold D., Sharon Macpherson, and Charles F. Bryan, Jr., eds. *Papers of Andrew Jackson, 1804-1813.* Knoxville: The University of Tennessee Press, 1984. Vol. 2.

Moulton, Gary E., ed. *The Journals of the Lewis and Clark Expedition.* Lincoln: University of Nebraska Press, 1983-2001.

*Natchez Trace Parkway Survey.* Washington: United States Government Printing Office, 1941, Reprinted Pace Florida: Trent's Prints, 2002.

Onuf, Peter S. *Jefferson's Empire: The Language of American Nationhood.* Charlottesville, VA: University Press of Virginia, 2000.

Owsley, Frank Lawrence Jr. and Gene A. Smith. *Filibusters and Expansionists: Jeffersonian Manifest Destiny, 1800-1821.* Tuscaloosa: The University of Alabama Press, 1997.

Parton, James. *The Life and Times of Aaron Burr.* Boston: Osgood and Company, 1872: 1.

———. *Life of Andrew Jackson.* New York: Mason Brothers, 1863.

Peck, David J. and Marti E. Peck. *"So Hard to Die": A Physician and a Psychologist Explore the Mystery of Meriwether Lewis's Death.* The Marti and David Peck Family Trust of 1992: 2021.

Penick, James Lai Jr. *New Madrid Earthquakes Rev. Ed.* Columbia: Univ. of Missouri Press 1981.

Polk, Noel. *Natchez Before 1830.* Jackson: University Press of Mississippi, 1989.

Powell, William H. *List of Officers of the Army of the United States from 1779-1900.* New York: L. R. Hamersly & Co., 1900.

Putnam, A. W. *History of Middle Tennessee; or, Life and Times of Gen. James Robertson.* Nashville, Tenn.: A. W. Putnam, 1859, Reprint, Arno Press, 1971.

Remini, Robert V. *Andrew Jackson, and the Course of American Empire, 1767-1821.* New York: Harper and Row, 1977.

Rhodes, Richard. *John James Audubon.* New York: Alfred A. Knopf, 2004.

Rhonda, James P. *Lewis and Clark among the Indians.* Lincoln and London: University of Nebraska Press, 1984.

Ritten, Louis N. *Fort Adams, Wilkinson County, Mississippi.* Louis N. Ritten 2013.

Robert, Otto A. *The Outlaws of Cave Rock: historical accounts of the famous highwaymen and river pirates who operated in pioneer days upon the Ohio and Mississippi Rivers and over the old Natchez trace.* Cleveland: The Arthur H. Clark Company, 1924.

Ronda, James R. *Lewis and Clark Among the Indians.* Lincoln, NE: University of Nebraska Press, 1984.

Rowland, Dunbar. *Encyclopedia of Mississippi History: Comprising Sketches of Counties, Towns, Events, Institutions and Persons.* Madison, Wisc.: Sewelyn A. Brandt, 1907: 2.

Rowland, Dunbar, ed. *Official Letter Books of W. C. C. Claiborne, 1801-1816.* Jackson, MS: State Department of Archives and History, 1917. Vol. 1-4.

Rowland, Mrs. Dunbar. *Life, letters and papers of William Dunbar of Elgin, Morayshire, Scotland, and Natchez, Mississippi, pioneer scientist of the southern United States; compiled and prepared from the original documents for the National society of colonial dames in America.* Jackson, MS: Press of the Mississippi Historical Society, 1930.

Sandlin, Lee. *Wicked River: The Mississippi When it Ran Wild.* New York: Pantheon Books, 2010.

Schwartz, Ted. *Forgotten Battlefield of the Texas Revolution.* Fort Worth: Eakin Press, 1985.

Scott, Winfield. *Memoirs of General Winfield Scott.* New York: Sheldon and Company, 1864.

Seale, William. *The President's House.* White House Historical Ass'n, 1986.

Skeen, C. Edward. *Citizen Soldiers in the War of 1812.* Lexington: The University of Kentucky 1999.

Slaughter, Thomas P. *The Whiskey Rebellion: Frontier Epilogue to the American Revolution.* New York: Oxford University Press, 1986.

Smith, Frank Harrison. *Frank H. Smith's History of Maury County, Tennessee,* Reprinted, Maury County, Tennessee, 1969.

Smith, Samuel B. and Harriet Chappell Owsley, eds., *Papers of Andrew Jackson, 1770-1803.* Knoxville: The University of Tennessee Press, 1980, Second Printing, 1987: 1.

Speed, Thomas. *The Wilderness Road, a description of the routes of travel by which the pioneers and early settlers first came to Kentucky*. Louisville: The Filson Club, 1886.

Spence, W. Gerome D. and David L. Spence. *A History of Hickman County, Tennessee*. Nashville: Gospel Advocate Publishing Company, 1900.

Starrs, James E. and Kira Gale. *The Death of Meriwether Lewis: A Historic Crime Scene Investigation*. Second ed. Omaha: River Junction Press, 2012.

Stevens, Walter B. *Centennial History of Missouri*. St. Louis: The S. J. Clark Publishing Co. 1921. Vol. 2.

Steward, David O. *American Emperor: Aaron Burr's Challenge to Jefferson's America*. New York: Simon & Schuster Paperbacks, 2011.

Steward, Dick. *Frontier Swashbuckler: The Life and Legend of John Smith T.* Columbia: University of Missouri Press, 2000.

Stoddard, Amos, Major. *Sketches, Historical and Descriptive of Louisiana*. Philadelphia: Mathew Carey, 1812.

Stoddard, Robert A., ed. *The Autobiography Manuscript of Major Amos Stoddard*. San Diego: Robert Stoddard Publishing, 2016.

Switzer, W. F. *Switzler's History of Missouri, From 1541 to 1877*. St. Louis: C. R. Barnes, 1879.

Thwaites, Reuben G., ed. *Original Journals of the Lewis and Clark Expedition, 1804-1806*. New York: Dodd, Mead, 1904-1905.

Thwaites, Reuben Gold, William Faux, and Adlard Welby, eds. *Early western travels, 1748-1846* Cleveland, Ohio: The Arthur H. Clark Company, 1904-1907: 1, 4.

Trogdon, Jo Ann. *The Unknown Travels and Dubious Pursuits of William Clark*. Columbia: University of Missouri Press, 2015.

Trotter, Thomas, *An essay, medical, philosophical, and chemical, on drunkenness, and its effects on the human body* (London: T. N. Longman, and O. Rees, 1804).

Twain, Mark. *The Adventures of Huckleberry Finn*. A Glassbook Classic.

Van Doren, Mark. *Correspondence of Aaron Burr and His Daughter Theodosia*. New York: Covici-Friede, 1929.

Warren, Harris Gaylord. *The Sword Was Their Passport: A History of American Filibustering in the Mexican Revolution*. Port Washington, New York: Kennikat Press, 1943.

Watson, Thomas E. *The Life and Times of Andrew Jackson*. Thomason, Georgia: The Jeffersonian Pub. Co., 1912.

Weigley, Russell F. *History of the United States Army*. New York: MacMillan Publishing Co., Inc., 1967.

Wheelan, Joseph. *Jefferson's Vendetta: The Pursuit of Aaron Burr and the Judiciary*. New York: Carroll & Graf Pub. 2005.

White, R. H., ed. *Messages of the Governors of Tennessee, 1796-1831*. Nashville: Tennessee Historical Commission, 1952: 1.

Wilkinson, James. *Burr's Conspiracy Exposed and General Wilkinson Vindicated Against the Slander of his Enemies on that Important Occasion*. Washington City: James Wilkinson, 1811.

———. *Memoirs of My Own Times*. Philadelphia: Abraham Small, 1816. Vol. I-III 1-3.

Williams, Walter, ed. *History of Northeast Missouri*. Chicago: The Lewis Publishing Co., 1913: 1.

Winik, Jay. *The Great Upheaval: America and the Birth of the Modern World 1788-1800*. New York: Harper, 2007.

Wood, Gordon S. *Friends Divided: John Adams and Thomas Jefferson*. New York: Penguin Press, 2017.

Woodger, Elin Woodger and Brandon Toropov. *Encyclopedia of the Lewis and Clark Expedition*. Infobase Publishing, 2014.

Yates, W. C. *Tales of a Tennessee Yeoman*. Franklin, Tenn.: W. C. Yates, 1991.

Yoakum, Henderson K. *History of Texas: from its first settlement in 1685 to its annexation to the United States in 1846*. New York: Redfield, 1855: 1.

# Periodicals

Allen, John Logan. "'So Fine a Country': The Early Exploration of Louisiana Territory, 1540-1802." *We Proceeded On,* Vol. 49 No. 4 (November 2023): 4-39.

Allen, Milford F. Allen. "Thomas Jefferson and the Louisiana-Arkansas Frontier." *The Arkansas Historical Quarterly*, Vol. 20, No. 1 (Spring 1961): 39-64.

Andrews, Edward Deming. "The Shaker Mission to the Shawnee Indians." *Winterthur Portfolio*, Vol. 7 (1972): 113-128.

Arnold, Morris S. "The Soldiers of Spain in Colonial Arkansas." *Arkansas Historical Quarterly* Vol. 77, Issue 4 (Winter 2018): 305-354.

Balleck, Barry J. "When the Ends Justify the Means: Thomas Jefferson and the Louisiana Purchase." *Presidential Studies Quarterly*, Vol. 22, No. 4, America's Bill of Rights, Market Economies And Republican Governments (Fall 1992): 679-696.

Barksdale, Kevin T. "Our Rebellious Neighbors: Virginia's Border Counties during Pennsylvania's Whiskey Rebellion." *The Virginia Magazine of History and Biography*, Vol. 111, No. 1 (2003): 5-32.

Belko, William S. "The Origins of the Monroe Doctrine Revisited: The Madison Administration, the West Florida Revolt, and the No Transfer Policy." *The Florida Historical Quarterly* Vol. 90, No. 2 (Fall 2011): 157-192.

Bentley, James R., ed." Two Letters of Meriwether Lewis to Major William Preston." Assessed on FilsonHistorical.org.

Bolton, Herbert E. "Papers of Zebulon M. Pike, 1806-1807." *The American Historical Review*, Vol. 13, No. 4 (Jul. 1908): 798-827.

Brading, D. A. "Mexican Silver-Mining in the Eighteenth Century: The Revival of Zacatecas." *Hispanic American Historical Review* (1970): 665-681.

Brunot, William K. "The Building of the Barge: The Creation of the Lewis and Clark Flagship." *We Proceeded On*, Vol. 48 No. 1 (February 2022): 6-19.

Buckley, Jay H. "Exploring the Louisiana Purchase and Its Borderlands: The Lewis and Clark, Hunter and Dunbar, Zebulon Pike, and Freeman and Custis Expeditions in Perspective." *We Proceeded On*, Vol 46, No. 3 (August 2020): 10-21.

———. "William Clark, the Fur Trade, and Indian Affairs." *We Proceeded On*, Vol. 46, No. 4 (November 2020): 14-30.

Burns, Frank L. "Alexander Wilson: I. The Audubon Controversy." *The Wilson Bulletin* Vol. 20, No. 1 (Mar. 1908): 2-18.

Caldwell, Norman W. "Cantonment Wilkinsonville." *Mid-America, An Historical Review* Vol. 31, No. 1. (1949): 3-28.

———. "Fort Massac: The American Frontier Post: 1778-1805." *Journal of the Illinois State Historical Society (1908-1984)* Vol. 43, No. 4 (Winter 1950): 265-281.

Camp, Carl H. "Voyages from Montreal: Alexander Mackenzie reached the Pacific 10 years before the Corps of Discovery—an achievement that spurred Jefferson to action and influenced the planning of Lewis's 'darling project.'" *We Proceeded On*, Vol. 37, No. 2. (May 2011): 6-13.

Chinuard, Eldon. G. "The Actual Role of the Bird Woman: Purposeful Member of the Corps or Casual 'Tag Along'?" *Montana The Magazine of Western History* Vol. 26, No. 3 (Summer 1976): 18-29.

———. "The Masonic Apron of Meriwether Lewis." *We Proceeded On*, Vol. 15 No. 1 (Feb. 1989): 16-17.

Clifton, Frances. "John Overton as Andrew Jackson's Friend." *Tennessee Historical Quarterly*, Vol. 11, No. 1 (March 1952): 23-40.

Colter-Frick, L. Ruth. "Meriwether Lewis's Personal Finances." *We Proceeded On*, Vol. 28, No. 1 (Feb. 2002): 16-20.

Corrick, Michael E. Corrick. "Meriwether Lewis's Air Gun." *We Proceeded On*, Vol. 28, No. 4 (Nov. 2002): 15-21.

Cox, Isaac Joslin. "General Wilkinson and His Later Intrigues with the Spaniards." *American Historical Review*, Vol XIX, No. 4 (July 1914): 794-812.

———. "The Freeman Red River Expedition." *Proceedings of the American Philosophical Society* Vol. 92, No. 2 (May 5, 1948): 115-119.

———. "The Louisiana-Texas Frontier, II." *The Southwestern Historical Quarterly* Vol. 17, No. 1 (Jul. 1913): 1-42.

Crow, Jeffrey J. "The Whiskey Rebellion in North Carolina." *The North Carolina Historical Review* Vol. 66, No. 1 (Jan. 1989): 1-28.

Cutright, Paul Russell. "Rest, Rest, Perturbed Spirit." *We Proceeded On*, Vol. 12, No. 1 (Mar. 1986): 7-17.

Danisi, Thomas C., "The Real James Neelly: Meriwether Lewis's Caretaker." *We Proceeded On*, Vol. 40 No. 4 (November 2014), 9-26.

Davis, Jeffrey A. "Guarding the Republican Interest: The Western Pennsylvania Democratic Societies and the Excise Tax." *Pennsylvania History: A Journal of Mid-Atlantic Studies* Vol. 67, No. 1 (Winter 2000): 43-62.

DeJong, David H., "John M. Mason: Superintendent of Indian Trade (October 1807—April 1, 1816)" *Paternalism to Partnership: The Administration of Indian Affairs, 1786-2021*. University of Nebraska Press, 2021.

Dillon, Richard H. "Meriwether Lewis, Manuel Lisa, and the Tantalizing Santa Fe Trade." *Montana: The Magazine of Western History*, Vol. 17, No. 2 (Spring 1967): 46-52.

Din, Gilbert C. "Empires Too Far: The Demographic Limitations of Three Imperial Powers in the Eighteenth-Century Mississippi Valley." *Louisiana History: The Journal of the Louisiana Historical Association* Vol. 50, No. 3 (Summer 2009): 261-292.

DuBose, William Porcher and B. J. Ramage. "Wade Hampton." *The Sewanee Review* Vol. 10, No. 3 (Jul. 1902): 364-373.

Dugatkin, Lee Alan. "André Michaux's 'Almost Expedition' to the West in 1793." *We Proceeded On,* Vol. 47, No. 1 (Feb. 2021): 5-11.

Fleek, Sherman L. "The Army of Lewis and Clark." *We Proceeded On,* Vol 30 No 4 (Nov. 2004): 8-14.

Flick, Arend. "The Gilmer Daybook and the 'Constitutional Disposition' of William Lewis." *We Proceeded On,* Vol 47 No 2 (May 2021): 14-22.

———. "William Diven, the Jay Treaty, and the Court-Martial of Meriwether Lewis." *We Proceeded On,* Vol. 45 No. 4 (November 2019): 11-18.

Foley, Will E. "Lewis and Clark's American Travels: The View from Great Britain." *We Proceeded On,* Vol. 35, No. 2 (May 2009): 6-15.

Frick, Ruth L. Colter. "Meriwether Lewis's Personal Finances: The governor of Upper Louisiana was land rich but cash poor when he left on his last, fateful journey." *We Proceeded On,* Vol. 28 No. 1 (February 2002): 16-20.

Gallagher, Ruth A. "The Indian Agent in the United States Before 1850." *The Iowa Journal of History and Politics* 14 (1916): 3-55.

Garrett, Julia Kathryn. "John Sibley and the Louisiana-Texas Frontier, 1803-1814." *The Southwestern Historical Quarterly* Vol. 45, No. 3 (Jan. 1942): 286-301, Vol. 47, No. 1 (July 1943): 48-51.

Gilje, Paul A. "Commerce and Conquest in Early American Foreign Relations, 1750-1850." *Journal of the Early Republic* Vol. 37, No. 4 (Winter 2017): 735-770.

Govanm, Thomas P. "The Death of Joseph Dennie: A Memoir by Nicholas Biddle." *The Pennsylvania Magazine of History and Biography* Vol. 75, No. 1 (Jan. 1951): 36-46.

Greg, Kate L. "Building of the First American Fort West of the Mississippi." *Missouri Historical Review,* Volume 30 Issue 4 (July 1936): 345-364.

Greifenstein, Charles. "Benjamin Rush: Man of Many Parts." *We Proceeded On,* Vol 28, No. 2 (May 2002): 26-30.

Gronet, Richard W. "United States and the Invasion of Texas, 1810-1814." *The Americas* Vol. 25, No. 3 (Jan. 1969): 281-306.

Harvey, Charles M. "The Story of the Santa Fe Trail." *The Atlantic* (December 1909). Atlantic Magazine Archive.

Hendrix, James P. Jr. and Guy M. Benson. "Did Meriwether Lewis Ever Live in Georgia?" *We Proceeded On,* Vol. 44, No. 3 (Aug. 2018): 12-14.

Henley, Jane and Guy Benson. "Clark & Lewis Homeplaces Featured at Annual Meeting." *We Proceeded On,* Vol. 21 No. 2 (May 1995): 1-12.

Hickey, Don. "America's Response to the Slave Revolt in Haiti, 1791-1806. *Journal of the Early Republic*, Vol 2, No 4 (Winter 1982): 361-379.

Hoagland, H. E. "Early Transportation on the Mississippi." *Journal of Political Economy, The University of Chicago Press* Vol. 19, No. 2 (Feb. 1911): 111-123.

Hollon, W. Eugene. "Zebulon Montgomery Pike and the Wilkinson-Burr Conspiracy." *Proceedings of the American Philosophical Society* Vol. 91, No. 5 (Dec. 3, 1947): 447-456.

Holmberg, James J. "'Fairly launched on my voyage of discovery: Meriwether Lewis's Expedition Letter to James Findlay." *We Proceeded On,* Vol. 35 No. 3 (August 2009): 20-28.

Isenberg, Andrew C. "The Market Revolution in the Borderlands: George Champlin Sibley in Missouri and New Mexico, 1808-1826." *Journal of the Early Republic* Vol. 21, No. 3 (Autumn 2001): 445-465.

Jackson, Donald. "On the Death of Meriwether Lewis's Servant." *The William and Mary Quarterly* Vol. 21, No. 3 (Jul. 1964): 445-448.

Jackson, John C. "Reuben Lewis: Fur Trader, Subagent, and Meriwether's Younger Brother." *We Proceeded On*. Vol 38, No. 4 (Nov. 2012): 8-17.

Jandebeur, Thomas Schroeder. "Thomas Freeman in Madison County: Mississippi Territory, 1807-1810." *Huntsville Historical Review* Vol. 5, No. 2, Article 3 (Fall-Winter 2020).

Jenkinson, Clay S. *The Character of Meriwether Lewis: Explorer in the Wilderness.* Washburn, North Dakota: The Dakota Institute Press of the Fort Mandan Foundation, 2011.

Jennings, Jesse D. "Nutt's Trip to the Chickasaw Country." *Journal of Mississippi History*, Vol. 9, No. 1 (Jan. 1947): 34-61.

Kent, Charles A. "The Treaty of Greeneville, August 3, 1795." *Journal of the Illinois State Historical Society (1908-1984)* Vol. 10, No. 4 (Jan. 1918), 568-584.

Kent, Stephen F. "America Was Founded on Secrets and Lies." *Foreign Policy.* Accessed Online.

Lachance, Paul F. "The 1809 Immigration of Saint-Domingue Refugees to New Orleans: Reception, Integration and Impact." *Louisiana History: The Journal of the Louisiana Historical Association* Vol. 29, No. 2 (Spring 1988): 109-141.

Lerche, Charles O. Jr. "Jefferson and the Election of 1800: A Case Study in the Political Smear." *The William and Mary Quarterly*, Vol. 5, No. 4 (Oct. 1948): 467-491.

M'Caleb, Walter Flavius. "The First Period of the Gutierrez-Magee Expedition." *The Quarterly of the Texas State Historical Association* Vol. 4, No. 3 (Jan. 1901): 218-229.

Moore, J. H. "The Death of Meriwether Lewis." *The American Historical Magazine*, 9 (July 1904): 218-230.

Moore, Robert J. Jr. "Lewis and Clark, Remaking the American West, 1808-1838." *We Proceeded On*, Vol 33, No. 2 (May 2007): 6-15.

Moulton, Gary E. Moulton. "The Missing Journals of Meriwether Lewis." *The Magazine of Western History* Volume 35 (Summer 1985): 28-39.

Murphy, William J. Jr. "John Adams: The Politics of the Additional Army, 1798-1800." *The New England Quarterly* Vol. 52, No. 2 (June 1979): 234-249.

Narrett, David E. "Geopolitics and Intrigue: James Wilkinson, the Spanish Borderlands, and Mexican Independence." *The William and Mary Quarterly* Vol. 69, No. 1 (January 2012): 101-146.

———. "Liberation and Conquest: John Hamilton Robinson and U.S. Adventurism toward Mexico, 1806-1819." *Western Historical Quarterly* Vol. 40, No. 1 (Spring, 2009): 23-50.

Nazor, Mary Louise Graham. "The Indian Trading House on the Chickasaw Bluffs, 1803-1810." *The Tennessee Genealogical Magazine* Vol 47, No. 4 (Winter 2000): 11-15.

Nicandri, David L. "The Rhyme of the Great Navigator." *We Proceeded On*, Vol. 42, No. 2 (May 2016): 17-23, and Vol. 42, No. 3 (August 2018): 24-27.

Norton, Paul. "One Hundred Years of American Trunk Innovation." *The Journal of Antiques and Collectibles*, online.

Phelps, Dawson A. and John T. Willett, "Iron Works on the Natchez Trace." *Tennessee Historical Quarterly*, Vol. 12, No. 4 (December 1953), 309-322.

Phelps, Dawson A. "Stands and Travel Accommodations on the Natchez Trace." *The Journal of Mississippi History*. 9: 1 (Jan. 1949): 1-54.

———. "The Tragic Death of Meriwether Lewis." *The William and Mary Quarterly* Vol. 13 (July 1956): 305-318.

———. "Tockshish." *Journal of Mississippi History* Vol. 78: No. 1, Article 6 (2016): 69-78.

Plaisance, Reverend Aloysius. "The Chickasaw Bluffs Factory and Its Removal to the Arkansas River, 1818-1822." *Tennessee Historical Quarterly* Vol. 11, No. 1 (March 1952): 41-56.

"Point-5 Acquisition: A Piece of American History." *American Archaeology* Vol. 18, No. 4. Winter 2014-15: 47.

Ravenholt, R. T. "The Death of Sergeant Charles Floyd: Was it the Water or the Cure?" *We Proceeded On,* Vol. 39 No. 1 (Feb. 2013): 27-31.

Rees, Mike. "Ocean in View?: A Scientific Analysis of the view from Pillar Rock on November 7, 1805" *We Proceeded On,* Vol. 35, No. 2 (May 2009): 22-31.

James E. Roper. "Benjamin Fooy and the Spanish Forts of San Fernando and Campo de la Esperanza." *West Tennessee Historical Society Papers* (Oct. 1982): 41-64.

Sanchez, Joseph P. "Old Heat and New Light on Spanish Diplomacy Regarding the Louisiana Purchase and the Defense of New Mexico, 1762-1819." *Louisiana History: The Journal of the Louisiana Historical Association* Vol. 64, No. 1 (Winter 2023): 5-44.

Schakenbach, Lindsay. "Schemers, Dreamers, and a Revolutionary Foreign Policy: New York City in the Era of Second Independence, 1805-1815." *New York History* Vol. 94, No. 3-4 (Summer/Fall 2013): 267-282.

Schoenbachler, Matthew. "Republicanism in the Age of Democratic Revolution: The Democratic-Republican Societies of the 1790s." *Journal of the Early Republic* Vol. 18, No. 2 (Summer 1998): 237-261.

Schofield, Merry Ellen. "The Fatigues of His Table: The Politics of Presidential Dining during the Jefferson Administration." *Journal of the Early Republic* Vol. 26, No. 3 (Fall 2006): 449-469.

Sibley, John and Penny S. Brandt. "A Letter of Dr. John Sibley, Indian Agent." *Louisiana History: The Journal of the Louisiana Historical Association* Vol. 29, No. 4 (Autumn 1988): 365-387.

Sioli, Marco M. "The Democratic Republican Societies at the End of the Eighteenth Century: The Western Pennsylvania Experience." *Pennsylvania History: A Journal of Mid-Atlantic Studies* Vol. 60, No. 3 (July 1993): 288-304.

Smith, Ralph A. Smith. "Account of the Journey of Bénard de la Harpe Discovery Made by Him of Several Nations Situated in the West." *The Southwestern Historical Quarterly* Vol. 62, No. 1 (July 1958): 75-86; Vol. 62, No. 2 (Oct. 1958): 246-259; Vol. 62, No. 3 (Jan. 1959): 371-385.

Stagg, J. C. A. "James Madison and George Mathews: The East Florida Revolution of 1812 Reconsidered." *Diplomatic History* Vol. 30, No. 1 (Jan. 2006): 23-55.

———. "George Mathews and John McKee: Revolutionizing East Florida, Mobile, and Pensacola in 1812." *The Florida Historical Quarterly* Vol. 85, No. 3 (Winter 2007): 269-296.

Sturdevant, Dan and Jay H. Buckley. "Spanish Attempts to Apprehend Lewis and Clark." *We Proceeded On,* Vol. 45 No. 1 (Feb. 2019): 18-25.

Tachau, Mary K. Bonsteel. "The Whiskey Rebellion in Kentucky: A Forgotten Episode of Civil Disobedience." *Journal of the Early Republic* Vol. 2, No. 3 (Autumn 1982): 239-259.

Thompson, Edmund R. "George Washington: A Master at Deception." *American Intelligence Journal* Vol. 12, No. 1 (Winter 1991): 7-10.

———. "George Washington: Master Intelligence Officer." *American Intelligence Journal* Vol. 19, No. 1/2 (Spring 1999): 79-83.

Walcheck, Kenneth C. "Exit, Pursued by a Bear." *We Proceeded On,* Vol. 43 No. 3 (Aug. 2017): 24-28.

———. "Portable Soup: Ration of Last Resort." *We Proceeded On,* Vol. 29, No. 3 (Aug. 2003): 24-27.

Wallace, Anthony F. C. and Timothy B. Powell. "How to Buy a Continent: The Protocol of Indian Treaties as Developed by Benjamin Franklin and Other Members of the American Philosophical Society." *Proceedings of the American Philosophical Society* Vol. 159, No. 3 (Sept. 2015): 251-281.

Way, Royal B. "The United States Factory System for Trading with the Indians, 1796-1822." *The Mississippi Valley Historical Review* VI, No. 2. (June 1919): 220-235.

Weber, David J. "Spanish Fur Trade from New Mexico, 1540-1821." *The Americas,* Vol. 24, No. 2 (Oct. 1967): 122-136.

Weir, Stuart. "Guns of Lewis and Clark." *We Proceeded On,* Vol. 32, No. 2 (May 2006): 10-19.

West, Elizabeth Howard. "Diary of José Bernardo Gutiérrez de Lara, 1811-1812." *The American Historical Review* Vol. 34, No. 1 (Oct. 1928): 55-77.

William and Mary Quarterly. "Hamilton on the Louisiana Purchase: A Newly Identified Editorial from the New-York Evening Post." *The William and Mary Quarterly*, Vol. 12, No. 2 (Apr. 1955): 268-281.

Williams, Samuel C. "Tennessee's First Military Expedition." *Tennessee Historical Magazine* Vol. 8, No. 3 (Oct. 1924): 171-190.

Woodard, Ralph Lee, Jr. "Spanish Commercial Policy in Louisiana, 1763-1803." *Louisiana History: The Journal of the Louisiana Historical Association* Vol. 44, No. 2 (Spring 2003): 133-164.

Worcester, Donald E. "The Significance of the Spanish Borderlands to the United States." *Western Historical Quarterly* Vol. 7, No. 1 (Jan. 1976): 4-18.

## Primary Sources and Collections

12 U.S. Army Order Book, October 1809-April 1810, LSU, as transcribed in the William S. Hamilton Papers, George M. Lester Collection. Louisiana State University.

American State Papers, 1789-1838, "ASP." Library of Congress. 38 Volumes.

Becthel, Henry to Lyman Draper. Draper Collection at the Wisconsin Historical Society at MS. 1 O 81 (4-5).

Boote, William R. Boote Company Book, NARA.

Burbeck, Henry. Henry Burbeck Papers. William L. Clements Library. University of Michigan.

Butler, Thomas S. Thomas S. Butler Regimental Order Book, Andrew Jackson Papers, LOC.

Carr, William. Carr Papers. Missouri Historical Society.

Chickasaw Bluffs Factory Ledger, 1806-1808, University of Memphis Library. Digital Commons.

Clark, William. William Clark, and Meriwether Lewis Memorandum Book, 1809. C1076. The State Historical Society of Missouri, Columbia, MO.

Cooper, Robert M. to Dr. L. C. Draper, 20 April 1873, Wisconsin Historical Society, Thomas Sumter Papers, 4 VV, Pgs. 22-23.

Cooper, Duncan Papers. TSLA.

Cushing, Thomas. *Trial of Col. Thomas H. Cushing before a General court martial... by Brig. Gen. Wade Hampton, Reported by the late judge advocate*. Philadelphia: Moses Thomas, 1812.

Dickinson, John McGavock Papers, Box 15, No. 9, TSLA.

Fisher, Vardis, Papers, Beinecke Library, Yale University.

Hamilton, Alexander. *The Papers of Alexander Hamilton Digital Edition*, ed. Harold C. Syrett. Charlottesville: University of Virginia Press, Rotunda, 2011.

Jackson, Andrew, Papers of Andrew Jackson. LOC.
Jefferson, Thomas. *The Papers of Thomas Jefferson*, Retirement Series, 1809, Vol 1. Princeton University Press, 2004.
Lewis, Meriwether. Meriwether Lewis Memorandum Book, Meriwether Lewis Collection, MHS.
Lewis, Meriwether. Meriwether Lewis Last Will and Testament, Sept. 11, 1809, Virginia State Library.
Madison, James. *The Papers of James Madison Digital Edition*, J. C. A. Stagg, editor. Charlottesville: University of Virginia Press, Rotunda, 2010.
Marks, Lewis. Papers (including letters and Meriwether Lewis estate records). University of Virginia Archives.
McClean, Papers Concerning Robertson's Colony in Texas, 1: 76-83. Accessed online, Texas Historical Association
McKee, John. Diary, Jan. 31, 1804-Oct. 11, 1805, Folder 1: Papers, 1793-1829, Scans 107-110, University of North Carolina Special Collections.
Monroe, James. *The Papers of James Monroe Digital Edition*, Daniel Preston and Robert Karachuk, editors. Charlottesville: University of Virginia Press, Rotunda, 2021-.
Natchez Trace Research Collection, McCain Library and Archives, University of Southern Mississippi.
Overton, John Papers. Murdock Collection of John Overton Papers, TSLA.
Wilkinson, James. James Wilkinson Papers, Chicago Historical Museum Research Center Online.

## Monographs and Reports

Anderson, Sally. "Brief Biography of Meriwether Lewis." 1886, University of Virginia Archives Accession Number 9041.
Avery, Marty. "Tragedy at Grinder's Stand: The Death of Meriwether Lewis." Middle Tennessee State University Library Special Collections, Murfreesboro, Tennessee.
Hagan, Olaf T. "Grinder's Stand." 19 Oct. 1933, NPS Loose Files, Natchez Trace Parkway Headquarters, Tupelo, Miss.
Jones, Charles T. Jr. "George Champlin Sibley: The Prairie Puritan (1782-1863)" Dissertation 1969. Online Digital Commons.

LaLa, Betty Horner. Robert Evans & Pricilla Knight Grinder of Hickman County, Tennessee.

McDonald, William Lindsey. "George Colbert and His Tennessee River Ferry." University of North Alabama Archives, Florence, Alabama.

Museum of Geoscience, prepared for U.S. Army Corps of Engineers, Cultural Resources Survey of Fort Adams Reach Revetment, Mile 312.2 to 306.0-L, Mississippi River, Wilkinson County, Mississippi, Louisiana State University Baton Rouge, Aug. 1993, 39-40, accessed online.

Tillier, Rodolphe. "Translation of a memorial of Rodolphe Tillier's justification on the administration of Castorland, county of Oneida, state of New York." Rome: Thomas Walker, 1800.

## Local Archives

Deed Book D, page 70-71, Maury County Register of Deeds, archives in Maury County Archives, Columbia, Tennessee.

Lewis County, Tennessee Court Minutes, Vol. 1, Lewis County Public Library, Hohenwald, Tenn.

Masterson v. Neelly, Williamson County, Tennessee Archives, Franklin, Tenn.

Maury County, Tennessee County Court Minutes, Minute Book 1, Maury County Archives, Columbia, Tennessee.

Williamson County Minute Book, Vol. 1, 1800-1812, 392, Williamson County, Tennessee Archives, Franklin, Tennessee.

*State of Tennessee v. John Campbell*, October 18, 1813, Circuit Court of Maury County, loose files, Maury County Archives, Columbia, Tenn.

*John Colter vs. Edward Hempstead, Admin*, 1810, Saint Louis, Court of Common Pleas Case Number 38 Folder 009, Missouri Digital Heritage.

Last Will and Testament of Rodolphe Tillier, File No., 0597, St. Louis Probate Court, St. Louis, Missouri.

*Falconer Comegys vs. Edward Hempstead*, Circuit Court Records Collection, identifier no. ccr1811.01067.004, Washington University at St. Louis.

*Peter Chouteau v. Edward Hempstead*, Circuit Court Records, Washington University of St. Louis, identifier no. ccr1811.01072.014.

Diary of John McKee, July 4-July 27, 1805, Williams Special Collections, University of North Carolina.

SELECTED BIBLIOGRAPHY

Papers of Original Claimants, 1777-1851; First Board of Land Commissioners; U.S. Recorder of Land Titles, Record Group 951; Missouri State Archives, Jefferson City.

# Newspapers

*Alexandria Gazette*, July 10, 1809; Feb. 10, 1837 / *American Republic*, Oct. 25, 1806; Dec 22, 1809/*Aurora General Advertiser*, April, 27 1810 / *The Buffalo Commercial*, Feb. 13, 1845 / *Chattanooga News*, Oct. 10, 1903 / *Democratic Clarion and Tennessee Gazette*, June 10, 1812 / *Enquirer*, March 2, 1810 / *Evening Post*, May 29, 1809; Dec. 14, 1809 / *Exeter Flying Post or, Trewman's Plymouth and Cornish Advertiser*, Jan. 14, 1808 / *Impartial Review*, Jan. 10, 1807 / *Kentucky Gazette*, October 17, 1809; May 22, 1810 / *Louisiana Gazette*, Dec. 28, 1809; January 4, 1810; April 10, 1810; March 14, 1810 / *Louisiana State Gazette* June 14, 1811/ Madison Democrat, Aug. 15, 1905 in Wisconsin Historical Collections / *Missouri Gazette and Public Advertiser*, March 8, 1809; June 28, 1809; Aug. 9, 1809; Aug. 16, 1809; Sept. 6, 1809; Sept. 13, 1809; Oct. 4, 1809; Oct. 12, 1809; Oct 19, 1809; Jan. 25, 1810; Apr 25, 1810; Aug. 16, 1810 / *Nashville Democratic Clarion*, 8 Sept. 1809 / *Nashville Gazette*, Nov 18, 1820 / *Nashville Republican*, Oct 31, 1835, Jan. 9, 1836 / *Natchez Weekly Democrat*, Jan. 1, 1810 / *National Intelligencer*, June 5, 1809, August 11, 1809, Nov 13, 1809 Nov. 15, 1809, Nov. 27, 1809 / *National and Washington Advertiser*, Oct 27, 1806 / *Palladium*, Dec 16 1809/ *Republican Argus*, May 24, 1809 / *Republican Banner*, Oct. 2, 1835 / *Richmond Enquirer*, May 9, 1809; June 9, 1809 / *The Rutland County Herald*, Aug. 26, 1809 / *Tennessee Gazette*, May 18, 1803; Aug. 24, 1803; Sept. 27, 1806; May 18, 1803; June 9, 1803; Aug. 24, 1803 / *Times*, January 17, 1807 / *United States Gazette*, June 1, 1809; July 19, 1810 / *Vermont Gazette*, November 27, 1809 / *Vermont Phoenix*, May 19, 1843 / *Virginia Argus*, Nov 17, 1807; Jan. 30, 1810; Feb.

6, 1810 / *Washingtonian*, Nov. 29, 1809 / Weekly Raleigh Register, Jan. 11, 1810 / *Weekly Wanderer* Jan. 26 1807 / *Weekly Raleigh Register*, Sept. 7, 1809; Jan. 11, 1810.

## Selected Federal Records at NARA

Annals of Congress, 8th Cong., 1st Sess. (1805), 1124-26.
Letter Book of the Natchitoches-Sulphur Fork Factory, 1809-1821.
Letters Received by the Secretary of War, LR.
Letters Sent by the Secretary of War Related to Military Affairs, LS.
Minute Books of the U.S. Circuit Court for West Tennessee, 1797-1893, and of the U.S. District Court for the Middle Dist. Of Tennessee, 1839-65.
Registers of Letters Received by the Office of the Secretary of War, 1800-1870.
Registers of Letters Sent by the Office of the Office of the Secretary of War.
Special Files of the Office of Indian Affairs, 1807-1904, US, Cherokee Indian Agency (Tenn.), 1801-1835.
*United States v. George Leanheart*, November 30, 1809, Minutes of the Court of Pleas at Nashville.

## Other

Conversation with Sarah Cannon, descendant of Robert and Pricilla Grinder neighbors, c. 1987.
Conversation with Susan Travis, W. C. Smith family descendant, c. 2010.
Conversations with Dr. Jessica Dunn, 2025.
Conversation with Cecil Whiteside, descendant of Samuel Whiteside, c. 2009.
Conversation with Dr. Chris Walker, c. 2010 and 2025.

# NOTES

1. George Washington to Patrick Henry, Feb. 24, 1777, LC.
2. WC to Jonathan Clark, Aug. 26, 1809, James J. Holmberg, *Dear Brother: Letters of William Clark to Jonathan Clark* (New Haven: Yale University Press, 2002), 209-214.
3. See, e.g., *The Times*, January 17, 1807, 3. For a contrary view from British critics, see, William E. Foley: "Lewis and Clark's American Travels: The View from Great Britain," *We Proceeded On*, Vol. 35, No. 2 (May 2009): 6-15.
4. Independent American, Nov 16, 1809, 3 (Washington, D. C.).
5. Sally T. Anderson, "Brief Biography of Meriwether Lewis," 1886, University of Virginia Library Accession Number 9041.
6. This was the opinion of historian James J. Holmberg in James J. Holmberg, *Dear Brother*, 198-199, n. 4.
7. Bernard De Voto, ed., *The Journals of Lewis and Clark* (Boston: Houghton Mifflin Co, 1955), lviii. Astor began a major push to expand his fur business months after Lewis's death. *The Buffalo Commercial*, Feb. 13, 1845, 2.
8. Lewis held no shares in the company, but his brother Reuben did, giving the impression that Lewis had an interest in the company.
9. TJ to ML, Feb. 23, 1801, Donald Jackson, ed. *Letters of the Lewis and Clark Expedition with Related Documents 1783-1854* (Urbana: University of Illinois Press 1978), 2-3. (Abbreviated hereafter as "Donald Jackson, *Letters*"), TJ to ML, March 31, 1801, FO. Carpenters partitioned two smaller rooms in the southern portion of the White House East Room for Lewis to use one as his bedroom and one as his office. The remainder of the East Room was used for storage. Jefferson's office was down the hall in what is now the State Dining Room. Adams' personal secretary had used what is now the adjoining "Green Room" as his bedroom. Jefferson used that room as a private dining room to entertain most of

his guests. William Seale, *The President's House* (Washington and New York: White House Historical Ass'n, 1986), 91, 93-94. See also Dumas Malone, *Jefferson The President: First Term, 1801-1805* (Boston: Little Brown and Company, 1970), 43-44.

10. See, excerpt from TJ to William A. Burrell, in Donald Jackson, *Letters*, 3, n. 1. Though Jefferson promised that he would write most of his own letters, there are several Jefferson administrative letters in Meriwether Lewis's handwriting. See, e. g., "To the Speaker of the House of Representatives and the President of the Senate," December 8, 1801, FO.

11. Dumas Malone, *Jefferson the President: First Term*, 206-211.

12. ML to TJ, March 10, 1801, Donald Jackson, *Letters*, 3-4.

13. TJ, "Biographical Sketch of Meriwether Lewis," Donald Jackson, *Letters*, 593-594. On the frontier, children often did not wear shoes until they were twelve years old. Jo C. Guild, *Old Times in Tennessee* (Tavel, Eastman & Howell: 1878), 42. Western Virginia may have followed similar customs. See also Sally T. Anderson, "Brief Biography of Meriwether Lewis." Letters of Lewis and Clark editor Donald Jackson, noted that the handwriting of the Lewis Biography he supplied to Allen was not Jefferson's, but Jefferson acknowledged the information by accepting it and writing Lewis's name as a heading for the notes.

14. Sally T. Anderson, "Brief Biography of Meriwether Lewis."

15. Ibid.

16. TJ, "Biographical Sketch of Meriwether Lewis," Donald Jackson, *Letters*, 593-594.

17. The town center consisted only of a courthouse, tavern, and about a dozen houses. John Bakeless, *Lewis and Clark: Partners in Discovery* (New York: William Morrow & Company, 1947), 11.

18. Jefferson's sister Lucy married into the Lewis family. William Terrell Lewis, *Genealogy of the Lewis Family in America: From the Middle of the Seventeenth Century Down to the Present Time* (Courier-Journal Job Printing Company, 1893), 1: 41.

19. *Alexandria Gazette*, Feb. 10, 1837, 3.

20. James P. Hedrix, Jr. and Guy M. Benson, "Did Meriwether Lewis Ever Live in Georgia?" *We Proceeded On*, Vol. 44, No. 3 (Aug. 2018): 12-14. Lewis's mother and siblings filed a claim for his father William Lewis's services as a Lieutenant in Cap't Nicholas Lewis's Company of Infantry

in the Virginia Continental Line during the Revolutionary War; however, the claim was denied when no official record of his services could be found. June 9, 1835, Power of Attorney, signed by Lucy Marks, et. al, and letters in response, Lewis Marks Papers, University of Virginia Archives.

21. TJ, Biographical Sketch of Lewis, Donald Jackson, *Letters*, 593-594.
22. John Bakeless, *Lewis and Clark*, 13.
23. Jane Henley and Guy Benson, "Clark & Lewis Homeplaces Featured at Annual Meeting," *We Proceeded On*, Vol. 21, No. 2 (May 1995): 1-12, 10, and with thanks to Howell Bowen for tours of Cloverfields and Locust Hill.
24. John Bakeless, *Lewis and Clark*, 18. Arend Flick, "The Gilmer Daybook and the 'Constitutional Disposition' of William Lewis, *We Proceeded On*, Vol. 47 No 2 (May 2021): 14-16.
25. John Ferling, *Adams vs. Jefferson: The Tumultuous Election of 1800* (Oxford University Press 2004), 21.
26. ML to Lucy Marks, May 22, 1795, MHS. TJ to Paul Allen, Aug. 18, 1813, Donald Jackson, *Letters*, 586-593.
27. Biographical Sketch of Lewis, 18 Aug. 1813, Donald Jackson, *Letters*, 593-594. TJ to the Rev. Matthew Maury, Jan. 8, 1790, FO. Lewis studied under Maury hoped to study under Maury for another year, but William Meriwether thought he had learned enough and that he could then study under other local schoolmasters Dr. Charles Everitt and Rev. James Waddell. John Bakeless, *Lewis and Clark*, 19-2. ML to Reuben Lewis, March 7, 1791, MHS.
28. He commented that William Meriwether decided that he could study geography at home. ML to Reuben Lewis, Mar. 7, 1791, MHS. Jefferson suggested that Lewis ended his formal education at age 15, TJ to Paul Allen, Jackson, Donald Jackson, *Letters*, Aug. 18, 1813, 586-593.
29. John Bakeless, *Lewis and Clark*, 20.
30. Biographical Sketch of Lewis, Donald Jackson, *Letters*, 593-594.
31. Jefferson said that Lewis made the offer during the time he was stationed as an army recruiter in Charlottesville. TJ to Paul Allen, Aug. 18, 1813, Donald Jackson, *Letters*, 586-593. Lewis recollected that he had wanted to lead the expedition about 1795, about three years earlier. ML, Journals of Lewis and Clark, entry April 7, 1805, *Journals of the Lewis and Clark Expedition*, University of Nebraska, Accessed Online.

32. Mark Cheatam discusses how gentlemen of the era used the system in Mark R. Cheatem, *Andrew Jackson, Southerner* (Baton Rouge: Louisiana State University Press, 2013).
33. Historians have sometimes referred to Jefferson's Anti-Federalist party as the "Democratic-Republican Party" to distinguish it from the party of Lincoln's time and later. The early political societies that ultimately provided supporters for Jefferson's Republican Party were called the "Democratic Republican" societies. Some called party members "Democrats" (James Parton, *The Life and Times of Aaron Burr* (Osgood and Company, Boston 1872) Vol 1. 223). But in Jefferson's day, they were frequently referred to as "Republican" (John Ferling, *Adams vs. Jefferson*, 147-149), and that name is used for the party in this book.
34. WC to ML, after March 15, 1807, Donald Jackson, *Letters*, 387-388.
35. Winfield Scott, *Memoirs of Winfield Scott* (New York: Sheldon and Company, 1864) Reprint, 27.
36. Discussed in Noble E. Cunningham, Jr., *In Pursuit of Reason: The Life of Thomas Jefferson* (Baton Rouge: LSU Press, 1987).
37. ML to Lucy Marks, May 22, 1795, MHS, Gordon S. Wood, *Friends Divided: John Adams and Thomas Jefferson* (New York: Penguin Press, 2017), 274.
38. Paul Hamilton, *The Oxford Handbook of European Romanticism* (Oxford: Oxford University Press, 2016), 53, 170, 621. David L. Nicandri made reference to the influence of the budding Romantic Movement on Lewis's writings in "The Rhyme of the Great Navigator," *We Proceeded On*, Vol. 42, No. 2 (May 2016): 17-23, 19 and Vol, 42, No. 3 (August 2018): 24-27 in which he discusses Lewis's birthday passage quoted in part in the next chapter. Though the Romantic Movement is considered to have taken root by the U.S. in the 1820s, people in the U.S. who followed European trends, such as Jefferson and young fans of the French Revolution, would have been influenced by it sooner.
39. Thomas Fleming, *The Intimate Lives of the Founding Fathers* (New York: Harper Collins, 2009), 262-263, 276-277.
40. ML to TJ, March 10, 1801, Donald Jackson, *Letters*, 3-4.
41. TJ to Paul Allen, Aug. 18, 1813, Donald Jackson, *Letters*, 586-593. With credit to Dr. Chis Walker for first mentioning the influence of the Romanticism Movement on the youths of ML's age.
42. ML to Dr. John Thornton Gilmer, June 18, 1801, MHS.

43. Jefferson closed his letters to Lewis with phrasing similar to "Accept my affectionate salutations" (see, e.g. April 30, 1803; May 16, 1803; July 15, 1803), which has little difference to the closings in letters to Charles Willson Peale "Accept affectionate salutations" (Oct. 9, 1805) or William D. Meriwether "Your's affectionately." The exceptions may have been in his letters of Oct. 26, 1806, and Aug. 16, 1809, as discussed later. Letters in Donald Jackson, *Letters*, 44-45, 49, 108-110, 263.
44. Jefferson said that Lewis joined the militia as a private, though he seems to have mixed up the timing of Lewis's ranks, "Biographical Sketch of Lewis, Donald Jackson, *Letters*, 593-594 and TJ to Paul Allen, Aug 18, 1803, Donald Jackson, *Letters*, 586-593. Sally T. Anderson in her "Brief Biography of Meriwether Lewis" quotes from Jefferson and noted that Lewis's decision to participate in the militia during the Whiskey Rebellion was a seminal event in his life.
45. The federal government had also imposed a customs tax, but most citizens did not pay that tax directly.
46. James Parton, *The Life and Times of Aaron Burr*, 1: 212. TJ to David Howell, December 15, 1810, FO. Peter S. Onuf, *Jefferson's Empire: The Language of American Nationhood* (Charlottesville, Virginia: University Press of Virginia, 2000), 41-42.
47. John Ferling, *Adams vs. Jefferson*, 62-63.
48. Jay H. Buckley, *William Clark: Indian Diplomat* (Norman: University of Oklahoma Press, 2008), 63. For discussion of Jefferson's views on the British, see Gordon S. Wood, *Friends Divided*, 273-274.
49. Farmers generally produced crops for food for their families, but they relied on extra "cash crops" to sell to raise money for additional items they needed. Hamilton's tax was used to collect funds to pay off the debts of states for the Revolutionary War, part of a bargain reached by Jefferson and Hamilton over dinner. Hamilton wanted to give the federal government more control over the states and agreed that it would assume the debt; Jefferson wanted the federal capitol to be located on the Potomac and agreed to the tax as a compromise. How the debt would be paid was apparently not part of the bargain, Leland D. Baldwin, *Whiskey Rebels: The Story of a Frontier Uprising* (University of Pittsburgh Press: Pittsburgh 1939), 61.
50. William Hogeland. *The Whiskey Rebellion* (New York: Simon & Shuster Paperbacks, 2006), 102.

51. *U.S. Constitution*, preamble and Article 10.
52. William Hogeland, *The Whiskey Rebellion*, 51-57, 105-106, 110.
53. George Washington to Bryan Fairfax, July 20, 1774, FO.
54. Brady J. Crytzer, *The Whiskey Rebellion: A Distilled History of an American Crisis* (Yardley, Penn: Westholme Publishing, LLC 2023), 174.
55. Jay Winik, *The Great Upheaval: America and the Birth of the Modern World 1788-1800* (New York: Harper, 2007), 487. John Ferling, *Adams vs. Jefferson*, 64.
56. Jay Winik, *The Great Upheaval*, 485.
57. James Graham, *The life of General Daniel Morgan, of the Virginia line of the army of the United States, with portions of his correspondence* (New York: Derby & Jackson, 1859), 418. William Hogeland, *The Whiskey Rebellion,* 104-105.
58. James Parton, *The Life and Times of Aaron Burr*, 220-221.
59. Richard H. Kohn, Eagle and Sword: *The Beginnings of the Military Establishment in America* (New York: The Free Press, 1975), 202-203.
60. Jay Winik, *The Great Upheaval,* 483-495. Jefferson did not contemplate extending those ideals to enslaved people or non-property owners during his time. The right of self-determination was linked to the ownership of property and the duty to participate in the defense.
61. Russell F. Weigley, *History of the United States Army* (New York: MacMillan Publishing Co., Inc., 1967), 102.
62. George Washington to Maj. Gen. Morgan, Oct. 8, 1794, as quoted in James Graham, *The life of General Daniel Morgan*, 428.
63. William Hogeland, *The Whiskey Rebellion*, 187-189.
64. Thomas Jefferson's Explanations of the Three Volumes Bound in Marbled Paper (the so-called "Anas"), 4 February 1818," FO, National Archives, Original source: *The Papers of Thomas Jefferson, Retirement Series*, vol. 12, *1 September 1817 to 21 April 1818*, ed. J. Jefferson Looney (Princeton: Princeton University Press, 2014), 417-429.
65. Kevin T. Barksdale, "Our Rebellious Neighbors: Virginia's Border Counties during Pennsylvania's Whiskey Rebellion," *The Virginia Magazine of History and Biography*, Vol. 111, No. 1 (2003): 5-32, 25, n 48.
66. William Hogeland, *The Whiskey Rebellion,* 276. Governor Morris also concluded that Hamilton was willing to force the country into a civil war to create a dominant federal government, Russell F. Weigley, *History of the*

*United States Army*, 102. Washington concluded that the resulting dominance of the federal government was "fortunate," Thomas P. Slaughter, *The Whiskey Rebellion: Frontier Epilogue to the American Revolution* (New York: Oxford University Press, 1986), 220.

67. Brady J. Crytzer, *The Whiskey Rebellion*, 159-164. William Hogeland, *The Whiskey Rebellion*, 225-227.
68. TJ to Volney, Dec. 9, 1795, FO.
69. TJ to George Washington, May 23, 1792, FO. John Ferling, *Adams vs. Jefferson*, 63. Jefferson would later work to repeal the tax as president.
70. Russell F. Weigley, *History of the United States Army*, 104-105. Winfield Scott, *Memoirs of Winfield Scott*, 27.
71. C. Edward Skeen, *Citizen Soldiers in the War of 1812* (Lexington: The University of Kentucky, 1999), 8, 43.
72. Jay Winik, *The Great Upheaval*. 490. Kevin T. Barksdale, "Our Rebellious Neighbors, 22-25. Morgan shared family with one of the main tax collectors, General Neville. (Morgan left his camp briefly to run for office as a Federalist, James Graham, *The life of General Daniel Morgan*, 438), Lewis's detachment was left under the co-command of Major Armstead who may be the same Armstead who would refuse to follow Lewis's orders as governor in 1808. Bakeless said that Washington marched with the militia for a portion of their trip. John Bakeless, *Lewis and Clark*, 57. John Ferling, *Adams vs. Jefferson*, 64. Morgan was known during the Revolutionary War for leading riflemen or sharpshooters, and Lewis may have received some training in sharpshooting from Morgan, but there is no record of it. (Leland D. Baldwin, *Whiskey Rebels: The Story of a Frontier Uprising* (University of Pittsburgh Press: Pittsburgh 1939), 15.
73. John Bakeless, *Lewis and Clark*, 59-60. Lewis's letters to his mother were generally ambiguous as to his own feelings of supporting the cause of attacking the "Whiskey Boys."
74. TJ to Paul Allen, Aug. 18, 1813, Donald Jackson, *Letters*, 586-593. As to the troops in general, James Graham, *The life of General Daniel Morgan*, 441.
75. ML to Lucy Marks, April 6, 1795, MHS. James Graham, *The life of General Daniel Morgan*, 433-434.
76. Thomas P. Slaughter, *The Whiskey Rebellion*, 220.
77. Slaughter put the number of troops that remained behind at 1,500. Ibid. C. Edward Skeen, *Citizen Soldiers in the War of 1812*, 7.

78. Marco M. Sioli, "The Democratic Republican Societies at the End of the Eighteenth Century: The Western Pennsylvania Experience," *Pennsylvania History: A Journal of Mid-Atlantic Studies*, Vol. 60, No. 3 (July 1993): 288-304, 297.
79. James Graham, *The life of General Daniel Morgan*, 434.
80. James Graham, *The life of General Daniel Morgan*, 436.
81. Lewis wrote a letter to his mother datelined "McFarlin's Farm, Nov. 24, 1794, and "Garrison, McFarlins," April 6, 1795, MHS. Lewis mentioned that Andrew McFarlane asked him to supply a letter in support of his time on the McFarlane Farm as part of McFarlane's claim for damages. Lewis confirmed that he was there from Fall 1794 to Spring 1795 (*Journals of the Lewis and Clark Expedition*, Dec. 19-20, 1803). Clark described James McFarlane as one of Lewis's close friends by the time of his death, WC to Jonathan Clark, Oct. 28, 1809, James J. Holmberg, *Dear Brother*, 216-223. Also, Holmberg concludes that Lewis's friend was the Monongahela River ferry operator's son, ibid. at n. 10. The Pennsylvania McFarlane's brothers' names matched those of the agent that Governor Lewis appointed in the Upper Louisiana Territory. The McFarlane brothers' parents met and lived for a time in Staunton, Virginia before moving the short distance north to Pennsylvania. Their mother was a Lewis family member, though it does not appear that she was a close relative to Meriwether.
82. John Bakeless, *Lewis and Clark*, 58.
83. Ricard H. Kohn, *Eagle and Sword*, 239, 262, but Kohn argues that Hamilton did not use the Whiskey Rebellion to push for a standing army. He states that the Quasi War became a better vehicle to use the army to reduce the power of the militia and the states, 278.
84. Richard H. Kohn, *Eagle and Sword*, 175.
85. Dumas Malone, *Jefferson and the Ordeal of Liberty* (Little, Brown and Company, Boston: 1962), 189, citing TJ to James Monroe, May 26, 1795, FO. Lewis wrote in May that because he had joined the army, he could not leave "this Country" until the end of the summer campaign. ML to Lucky Marks, May 22, 1795, MHS. Whether he meant Pennsylvania or the East is ambiguous, but it is possible that he was in contact with Jefferson through letters or mutual contacts.
86. Richard H. Kohn, *Eagle and Sword*, 262-268. Russell F. Weigley, *History of the United States Army*, 103.

87. Eugene P. Link, *Democratic-Republican Societies*, 1790-1800 (Octagon Books 1965), 206. Jeffrey J. Crow, "The Whiskey Rebellion in North Carolina," *The North Carolina Historical Review* Vol. 66, No. 1 (Jan. 1989): 1-28. Mary K. Bonsteel Tachau, "The Whiskey Rebellion in Kentucky: A Forgotten Episode of Civil Disobedience," *Journal of the Early Republic*, Vol. 2, No. 3 (Autumn, 1982): 239-259, John Ferling, *Adams vs. Jefferson*, 65. The controversy was soon followed by a fight over the ratification of the Jay Treaty that divided Federalists and Republicans as well as easterners and westerners. Matthew Schoenbachler, "Republicanism in the Age of Democratic Revolution: The Democratic-Republican Societies of the 1790s," *Journal of the Early Republic*, Vol. 18, No. 2 (Summer, 1998): 237-261, 239.
88. Richard H. Kohn, *Eagle and Sword*, 262-268. Fleek, Sherman L., "The Army of Lewis and Clark," *We Proceeded On*, Vol. 30 No. 4 (November 2004): 8-14, 5. Crytzer, *The Whiskey Rebellion*, 174-175. Russell F. Weigley, *History of the United States Army*, 103.
89. Lewis's militia service ended around April 1795. He entered the army on May 1, 1795 (John Bakeless, *Lewis and Clark*, 60). On May 26, Jefferson had assessed that there had never been an insurrection. Lewis did not return home before enlisting with the army. It is possible that he returned home before traveling to the Ohio frontier and that he communicated with Jefferson through acquaintances traveling between Virginia and Western Pennsylvania.
90. George Washington to Major General Thomas Mifflin, April 10, 1777, FO.
91. John Bakeless, *Lewis and Clark*, 59. Unlike Lewis's formal writing in official government documents, Lewis's letter to his army friend Major William Preston a year before his death reflected the relaxed friendship he found among his army friends, ML to Maj. William Preston, July 25, 1808, James R. Bently, Ed., "Two Letters of Meriwether Lewis to Major William Preston," Assessed on FilsonHistorical.org) Lewis took time to see that a young soldier's body was properly buried and that his grave was marked. He wrote to the boy's father to let him know that he had made certain that his son's remains received proper respect.
92. ML to Lucy Marks, Oct. 4, 1794, MHS, Identifier: A0897-00004. Richard Dillon, *Meriwether Lewis: A Biography* (Coward-McCann, Inc: New York 1965), 19-20.

93. Mary Newton Lewis, "Meriwether Lewis: Devoted Son," *We Proceeded On*, Vol. 16 No. 2 (May 1990): *n*, 14-20, 15. The letter was written after Lewis joined the regular Army.
94. James Graham, *The life of General Daniel Morgan*, 431.
95. John Bakeless, *Lewis and Clark*, 60. Jefferson said that Lewis' entered the army as a lieutenant, but he was not promoted to lieutenant until 1799. Biographical Sketch of Lewis, Donald Jackson, *Letters*, 593-594. The recruitment of Lewis's company into the army is discussed in James Graham, *The life of General Daniel Morgan*, 441. The rank of ensign, the lowest officer rank, eventually became the rank of lieutenant, which is what Jefferson may have meant; however, War Department records show later promotions from ensign to lieutenant.
96. Edward Deming Andrews, "The Shaker Mission to the Shawnee Indians," *Winterthur Portfolio*, Vol. 7 (1972): 113-128, 118. Spellings "Greenville" and "Greene Ville" are also used. This book uses the spelling on the treaty.
97. "Point-5 Acquisition: A Piece of American History," *American Archaeology*, V. 18, No. 4 (Winter 2014-15): 47. Thomas Robson Hay and M. R. Werner, *The Admirable Trumpeter: A Biography of General James Wilkinson*. 1941 reprinted The Scholar's Bookshelf 2006, 110-111.
98. Charles A. Kent, "The Treaty of Greeneville. August 3, 1795," *Journal of the Illinois State Historical Society (1908-1984)*, Vol. 10, No. 4 (Jan. 1918): 568-584. Anthony F. C. Wallace and Timothy B. Powell, "How to Buy a Continent: The Protocol of Indian Treaties as Developed by Benjamin Franklin and Other Members of the American Philosophical Society," *Proceedings of the American Philosophical Society*, Vol. 159, No. 3 (Sept. 2015): 251-281. The authors argue that the Treaty of Fort Greeneville became the standard by which later treaties were written. Clark initiated the 1808 Osage Treaty. Lewis met with Osage bands that had not approved the treaty to finalize it in 1809.
99. John Bakeless, *Lewis and Clark*, 60.
100. Sally T. Anderson "Brief Biography of Meriwether Lewis."
101. John Bakeless, *Lewis and Clark*, 37. Bakeless noted that Lewis was fair haired and that he was put in Clark's unit because soldiers were assigned to units based on hair color to add to uniformity of appearance. Jim Hardee, "The Influence of the Red-Headed Chief: William Clark's

Post-Expedition Interaction with Indian Nations," *We Proceeded On*, Vol. 40 No. 2 (May 2014): 8-80, 8.

102. WC to Fanny Clark, June 1, 1795, James J. Holmberg, *Dear Brother*, 273-276.
103. ML to WC, June 19, 1803, Donald Jackson, *Letters*, 57-60.
104. Mark Twain, *The Adventures of Huckleberry Finn* (A Glassbook Classic), 149.
105. Eventually, both Lewis and Clark would join a small number of men on the army payroll such as Zebulon Pike, Thomas Freeman, Peter Custis, James Wilkinson (the General's son) and Richard Sparks, and men such as Philip Nolan off the army payroll. Wilkinson would use as spies to gain military intelligence. Jefferson told the Osage of his plans for two expeditions, one to the headwaters of the Red River and one to the head rivers of the Kansas, Jefferson to the Osage, July 16, 1804, Donald Jackson, *Letters*, 200-203. Wilkinson sent his son James, Jr. and Zebulon Pike west into Spanish Territory to Santa Fe in 1807. He sent Thomas Freeman to the Red River area to obtain intelligence about the southern boundary of the Louisiana Purchase.
106. Washington approved funds for secret service, Orders to Nathaniel Sackett, Feb. 4, 1777.
107. Stephen F. Kent, "America Was Founded on Secrets and Lies," *Foreign Policy*, Accessed Online. A word search for "secret service" in FO reveals numerous examples.
108. Jon Kukla, *A Wilderness So Immense: The Louisiana Purchase and the Destiny of America* (Alfred A. Knopf, New York 2003), 19.
109. Peter S. Onuf, *Jefferson's Empire*, 70-71.
110. TJ to Archibald Stewart, Jan. 25, 1786, FO.
111. Frank Lawrence Owsley, Jr. and Gene A. Smith, *Filibusters and Expansionists: Jeffersonian Manifest Destiny, 1800-1821* (The University of Alabama Press, Tuscaloosa: 1997), 16, 26-27.
112. Jefferson's spelling. TJ to Archibald Stewart, Jan. 25, 1786, FO.
113. For descriptions of expeditions led by Hunter and Dunbar, Zebulon Pike, and Freeman and Custis, in addition to ML and WC, see, Jay H. Buckley, "Exploring the Louisiana Purchase and Its Borderlands: The Lewis and Clark, Hunter and Dunbar, Zebulon Pike, and Freeman and Custis Expeditions in Perspective," *We Proceeded On*, Vol 46, No. 3 (August 2020): 10-21.

114. TJ to William Dunbar, May 25, 1805, Donald Jackson, *Letters*, 244-246.
115. Jefferson, Madison, and Monroe's goal of acquiring territory without war is discussed in Frank Lawrence Owsley, Jr. and Gene A. Smith, *Filibusters and Expansionists*, 7-14.
116. Jay H. Buckley, *William Clark: Indian Diplomat*, 37. Jo Ann Trogdan, *The Unknown Travels and Dubious Pursuits of William Clark*, 45-47.
117. Governor Gayoso to Governor Carondelet, July 25, 1793, Paul Clements, *Chronicles of the Cumberland Settlements* (The Foundation of William and Jennifer Frist and Paul Clements, 2012), 401.
118. The Treaty of San Lorenzo. Milton Lomas, *Aaron Burr: The Conspiracy and Years of Exile, 1805-1836*. New York: Farar, Straus, Giroux, 1982), 19.
119. Jo Ann Trogden, *The Unknown Travels and Dubious Pursuits*, 54.
120. Howard W. Cox, *American Traitor: General James Wilkinson's Betrayal and Escape From Justice* (Washington, D. C.: Georgetown University Press, 2023), 95. The supervisor was Isaac Guion. Future Secretary of War John Armstrong made the allegation. Guion led a company to Fort Pickering in 1797, which led some writers to suspect that the Capt. Lewis at Fort Pickering in 1797 was Meriwether, but Meriwether Lewis was not a captain at the time and a Capt. Thomas Lewis soon traveled from Fort Pickering to Fort Adams. See note 129.
121. John Bakeless, *Lewis and Clark*, 5, 62-66.
122. Ibid., 70.
123. Kira Gale, *Meriwether Lewis: The Assassination of an American Hero and the Silver Mines of Mexico* (Omaha: River Junction Press, 2015), 84, noting that Grace Miller said that he may also have carried a separate set of Wilkinson documents.
124. Isaac Craig to Samuel Hogden, Nov. 21, 1796, Document No. 1796112180101, Papers of the War Department, 1784-1800.
125. Alexander Hamilton to Rufus King, Aug. 22, 1798, FO. National Archives. (Original source: *The Papers of Alexander Hamilton*, vol. 22, *July 1798—March 1799*, ed. Harold C. Syrett (New York: Columbia University Press, 1975), 154-155.)
126. General James Wilkinson, *Memoirs of My Own Times* (Philadelphia: Abraham Small, 1816), 1: vii.
127. Joseph Wheelan, *Jefferson's Vendetta: The Pursuit of Aaron Burr and the Judiciary* (New York: Carroll & Graf Publishers, 2005), 110, Milton

Lomask, *Aaron Burr, The Conspiracy and Years of Exile, 1805-1836* (New York: Farrar, Straus, Giroux, 1982), 180. French commissioner Pierre Clemaent de Laussat described him as [h]eavy, squat. Robert O. Bush, Ed., *Pierre Clemaent de Laussat, Memoirs of My Life* (Baton Rouge: LSU Press, 1978), 73-74.

128. James J. Holmberg, *Dear Brother*, 164-165, n. 8. Mary Newton Lewis, "Meriwether Lewis: Devoted Son," *We Proceeded On*, Vol. 16 No. 2 (May 1990): 14-20, 14-15. Lewis noted to be on furlough, SW to James McHenry, July 7, 1799, *The Papers of Alexander Hamilton* Digital Edition, Harold C. Syrett, ed. (Charlottesville: University of Virginia Press, Rotunda, 2011).

129. ML to Lucy Marks, May 2, 1797 and July 24, 1797, MHS. John Bakeless, *Lewis and Clark*, 70. The family-owned property on Brush Creek in Kentucky that Lewis purchased on April 4, 1799 (Lewis Marks Papers, University of Virginia Library). ML to Col. Nathaniel Massie, Feb. 18, 1801, Box 1, Folder 7, MHS. Bakeless also said that Lewis briefly commanded Fort Pickering in 1797 (a fort erected a few miles north of the fort Lewis would visit in 1809, John Bakeless, *Lewis and Clark*, 70. The Captain Lewis who appeared at Chickasaw Bluffs at the time was most likely Capt. Thomas Lewis and not Meriwether, who was still an ensign. Thomas Lewis was identified as the captain who subsequently took troops from Fort Pickering to Fort Adams. For more information on Thomas Lewis, a friend of William Clark's, see Arend Flick, "Did Meriwether Lewis's Cousin Introduce Him to William Clark?" *We Proceeded On*, Vol. 44, No. 3 (August 2018): 15-18.

130. TJ to ML, Feb. 23, 1801, Donald Jackson, *Letters*, 2-3.

131. Clark also had become discouraged with the prospects for advancement within the army. Private enterprise could use his unique skills, and he certainly had an opportunity to make more money. Jay H. Buckley, *William Clark: Indian Diplomat*, 38-39.

132. Years earlier, he said that he had considered creating a business on the Mississippi River. Jo Ann Trogden, *The Unknown Travels and Dubious Pursuits*, 3.

133. Jo Ann Trogden, *The Unknown Travels and Dubious Pursuits*, 27-28. Jay H. Buckley, *William Clark: Indian Diplomat*, 39-40. James J. Holmberg states that Clark traveled pursuing business interests among other things during the 1797 to 1802 period, James J. Holmberg, "The Man Behind

the Icon: The Personal World of William Clark, *We Proceeded On*, Vol 46, No. 4 (Nov. 2020): 5-13, 7.

134. John R. Williams to Maj. Amos Holton, May 20, 1845, Elliott Coues, ed., *The Expeditions of Zebulon Montgomery Pike* (New York: Francis P. Harper, 1895) I: xxvi. Williams said that Lewis was an officer in the camp in 1800. The War Department directed letters to Lewis at Charlottesville and at Staunton from 1797-1800; however, they at least once lost track of his location, See War Department Papers, 1784-1800.

135. Jefferson actually couched the mission in opposite terms to the way it was presented to the public. The educational value would be secondary to the military mission. Some writers suggest that Jefferson was being coy because he had no authority under the constitution to organize a mission that would be primarily educational in its purpose. More likely, even as much as Jefferson wanted to know every scientific detail the expedition gleaned, it was more important to him to find a way for the U.S. government to prevent European governments from dominating the continent.

136. As stated earlier, Jefferson said that Lewis made the offer during the time he was stationed in Charlottesville. TJ to Paul Allen, Aug. 19, 1813, Donald Jackson, *Letters*, 586-593. In the same letter, Jefferson said that Lewis renewed his request to lead the expedition two years after he began work as private secretary.

137. Lewis's superior Isaac Guion led his company to Fort Pickering and Natchez in 1797, but no documentation has surfaced to confirm that Lewis traveled to the southwestern frontier. Amos Stoddard, *Sketches*, 98.

138. TJ to Benjamin Smith Barton, Feb. 27, 1803, Donald Jackson, *Letters*, 16-17.

139. Jefferson also sent a separate message directly to Lewis though Tarleton Bates, an officer Lewis must have discussed with Jefferson as one of his close friends. TJ to Tareleton Bates, Feb. 1801, FO.

140. John Bakeless, *Lewis and Clark*, 69. Bakeless suggested that Lewis was promoted to the rank of lieutenant because the rank of ensign was abolished on the same date of his promotion, but officers who held the rank of ensign in 1809 were later promoted to lieutenant, SW to A. Y. Nicoll, July 1, 1809, LS.

141. Lewis traveled to Washington to work with Jefferson before he took charge of the company that bore his name.

142. TJ to ML, Feb. 23, 1801, Donald Jackson, *Letters*, 2-3.
143. John Bakeless, *Lewis and Clark*, 71. Richard Dillon, *Meriwether Lewis*, 25.
144. For a description of Jefferson's dinners, see, Merry Ellen Scofield, "The Fatigues of His Table: The Politics of Presidential Dining during the Jefferson Administration," *Journal of the Early Republic*, Vol. 26, No. 3 (Fall, 2006): 449-469. In 1802, Lewis at least once shared the table with future Secretary of War William Eustis, whose letter would send Lewis's life spinning out of control in 1809, "Dr. Mitchell's Letters from Washington," 10 Jan. 1802, *Harper's Magazine* v. 58 1878-1879 Dec-May (New York: Brother and Brothers Publishers 1879), 744.
145. Noble E. Cunningham, Jr., *In Pursuit of Reason*, 255. Everett Somerville Brown, ed., *William Plumer's memorandum of proceedings in the United States Senate, 1803-1807* (The MacMillan Company: 1923), 212. The dinner he referenced was served in 1804 after Lewis was no longer at the White House, but Jefferson had even more reason to serve it prior to authorization for the expedition to the Northwest. The writer said that the water was "exposed" in bottles along with some of the mammoth cheese, but the implication was that guests were invited to taste.
146. The "hush money was paid to a journalist James Thomas Callendar. For a discussion of the event, see, Dumas Malone, *Jefferson the President: First Term,* 206-211. Jefferson penned the bulk of his own letters; however, for Lewis's work as a scribe, see, e. g., Enclosure: Outline of Government Offices, December 27, 1801. FO. A recent search on FO shows several Jefferson's letters in Lewis's handwriting. Earlier historians concluded that Lewis did not serve as a scribe for Jefferson. Thomas Callender was prosecuted by the Federalists under the Alien and Sedition Act. John Bakeless, *Lewis and Clark*, 76-77. TJ to James Monroe, May 29, 1801, and James Monroe to TJ, June 1, 1801, FO.
147. William Seale said that Lewis and Jefferson created their plans in Jefferson's office, William Seale, *The President's House* (New York: White House Historical Association, 1986), 95-96. Bakeless suggested that Jefferson converted a portion of the basement to a workroom to lay out maps and scientific instruments. John Bakeless, *Lewis and Clark*, 74.
148. Dan L. Flores concluded that Lewis seemed to have been groomed for the Northwest Passage expedition at least after arriving in Washington to serve as Jefferson's personal secretary. Dan L., Flores, ed., *Southern Coun-*

terpart to Lewis & Clark: The Freeman & Custis Expedition of 1806 (Norman: University of Oklahoma Press, 1984), 7.
149. Wilkinson to Manuel Gayoso de Lemos, Feb. 6, 1767, as published in Daniel Clark, *Proofs of the Corruption*, 42.
150. Joseph Wheelan, *Jefferson's Vendetta*, 110.
151. Howard Cox noted Jefferson's notes of concerns of Wilkinson's "unapprovable points," Howard W. Cox, *American Traitor*, 87.
152. Divisions in the ranks even led to duels among supporters of each general, Richard H. Kohn, *Eagle and Sword*, 180.
153. Per U.S. Army Corps of Engineers.
154. TJ to Archibald Stewart, Jan. 25, 1786, FO.
155. Gilbert C. Din, "Empires Too Far: The Demographic Limitations of Three Imperial Powers in the Eighteenth-Century Mississippi Valley," *Louisiana History: The Journal of the Louisiana Historical Association*, Vol. 50, No. 3 (Summer 2009): 261-292, 276-277.
156. Ralph Lee Woodward, Jr, "Spanish Commercial Policy in Louisiana, 1763-1803," *Louisiana History: The Journal of the Louisiana Historical Association*, Vol. 44, No. 2 (Spring, 2003): 133-164, 151, 153.
157. Hay and Werner, *The Admirable Trumpeter*, 56-58. Andro Linklater, *An Artist in Treason*, 72.
158. Milton Lomask, *Aaron Burr, 1805-1836*, 17-18. Hay and Werner, *The Admirable Trumpeter*, 83-95. Jon Kukla, *A Wilderness So Immense*, 128-129. The Spanish paid Wilkinson for his services but did not grant him a commission.
159. David E. Narrett, "Geopolitics and Intrigue: James Wilkinson, the Spanish Borderlands, and Mexican Independence," *The William and Mary Quarterly*, Vol. 69, No. 1 (January 2012): 101-146, 108. Jon Kukla, *A Wilderness So Immense*, 127.
160. The 1794 treaty known as "Jay's Treaty," supported by Federalists, assured shipping to Atlantic markets while agreeing to delay American's rights to ship on the Mississippi River.
161. John Haywood, *The Civil and Political History of the State of Tennessee...* (Tenase Company, Reprint 1969), 250-254.
162. Milton Lomask, *Aaron Burr, 1805-1836*, 18. Colton Storm, Ed., "Up the Tennessee in 1790: The Report of Major John Doughty to the Secretary of War," *The East Tennessee Historical Society's Publications*, 17: 119-132.

163. Wilkinson made the suggestion for defenses in his paper Reflections that he sent to the Spanish governor, Howard W. Cox, *American Traitor*, 91.
164. Jon Kukla, *A Wilderness So Immense*, 132-133.
165. D. A. Brading, "Mexican Silver-Mining in the Eighteenth Century: The Revival of Zacatecas," *Hispanic American Historical Review* (1970) 50 (4): 665-681.
166. Jon Kukla, *A Wilderness So Immense*, 33.
167. *Annals of Congress*, 8th Cong., 1st Sess. (1805), 1125-1126. LeRoy R. Hafen, "The Old Spanish Trail, Santa Fe to Los Angeles," *Huntington Library Quarterly*, Vol. 11, No. 2 (Feb. 1948): 149-150.
168. Major Amos Stoddard, *Sketches, Historical and Descriptive of Louisiana* (Philadelphia: Mathew Carey, 1812), 3.
169. Alexander DeConde, *This Affair Louisiana* (New York: Charles Scribner's Sons, 1976), 68.
170. Ibid., 103.
171. Ibid., 68.
172. Andro Linklater, *An Artist in Treason: The Extraordinary Double Life of General James Wilkinson* (New York: Walker Publishing Company, 2009), 159.
173. Arend Flick, "William Diven, the Jay Treaty, and the Court-Martial of Meriwether Lewis." *We Proceeded On,* Vol. 45 No. 4 (November 2019): 11-18.
174. Richard Dillon, *Meriwether Lewis*, 20-21.
175. Howard W. Cox, *American Traitor*, 94.
176. Howard W. Cox, *American Traitor*, 93-95. John Bakeless, *Lewis and Clark*, 46-47.
177. John Bakeless, *Lewis and Clark*, 46-47.
178. Jo Ann Trogden, *The Unknown Travels and Dubious Pursuits*, 37. John Bakeless, *Lewis and Clark*, 39.
179. John Bakeless, *Lewis and Clark*, 38.
180. Ibid., 56.
181. Ibid., 55.
182. Hay and Werner, *The Admirable Trumpeter*, 154.
183. Howard W. Cox, *American Traitor*, 98, 108.
184. JW to John Adams, December 20, 1797. FO, National Archives.
185. AJ to Henry Dearborn, March 17, 1807, PAJ 2: 155-159.

186. Howard W. Cox, *American Traitor*, 109.
187. Andro Linklater, *An Artist in Treason*, 2. Joseph Wheelan, *Jefferson's Vendetta*, 110.
188. Ted Schwartz, *Forgotten Battlefield of the First Texas Revolution* (Fort Worth: Eakin Press, 1985), 4.
189. Daniel Clark, *Proofs of the Corruption*, 27.
190. Jo Ann Trogden discovered these facts in Clark's journal and detailed them, Jo Ann Trogden, *The Unknown Travels and Dubious Pursuits*, 155-159. WC to Jonathan Clark, Oct. 4, 1798, James J. Holmberg, *Dear Brother*, 28-30 and n. 3.
191. Jo Ann Trogden also describes McKee's activities in *The Unknown Travels and Dubious Pursuits*, 193-197, 239.
192. An example of subjective standards for reimbursement of advancement for secret services, TJ to James Madison, June 15, 1804, LC.
193. A discussion of the early U.S. Army can be found in Sherman L. Fleek, "The Army of Lewis and Clark, *We Proceeded On*, Vol 30, No. 4 (November 2004): 8-14.
194. Reuben Gold Thwaite, ed., *Early Western Travels 1748-1846*, IV (The Arthur H. Clark Co: Cleveland 1904), 328-329. Museum of Geoscience, prepared for U.S. Army Corps of Engineers, Cultural Resources Survey of Fort Adams Reach Revetment, Mile 312.2 to 306.0-L, Mississippi River, Wilkinson County, Mississippi, Louisiana State University Baton Rouge, August 1993, 39-40. *Trial of Col. Thomas H. Cushing* (Moses Thomas, Philadelphia: 1812). Cushing's house was 60' x 30' and he refused to share it with other officers. Hampton also charged him with building excessively expensive buildings at Fort Dearborn in Washington, Mississippi Territory.
195. Amos Stoddard to Henry Burbeck, March 4, 1810, Henry Burbeck Papers, William L. Clements Library. The reference was most likely to Lt. Constant Freeman. The phrase most often was used to reference a sniper's nest, but the only military action in the area at the time of the statement was a small West Florida separation movement and it would have been unusual for a soldier to celebrate a friend's lack of a chance to earn honors in battle.
196. Howard Cox details the failures of the War Department to hold Wilkinson accountable in Howard W. Cox, *American Traitor*.

197. Wilkinson to Manuel Gayoso de Lemos, Feb. 6, 1767, as published in Daniel Clark, *Proofs of the Corruption*, 42.
198. Dan L. Flores, *Southern Counterpart*, 25.
199. Robert V. Haynes, *The Natchez District and the American Revolution* (Jackson: University Press of Mississippi, 1976), 21, 91.
200. Dan L. Flores, *Southern Counterpart*, 32-33. See also Noel Polk, ed., *Natchez Before 1830* (Jackson: University Press of Mississippi, 1989), 96-100.
201. Dan L. Flores, *Southern Counterpart*, 32-33. Wilkinson made reference to one of Nolan's maps to the Secretary of War, July 27, 1805, Clarence Edwin Carter (comp, and ed.). *The Territorial Papers of the United States*. Volume XIII: The Territory of Louisiana-Missouri. 1803-1806 (Washington. D.C.: G. P. O., 1948), 164-172.
202. Daniel Clark to Thomas Jefferson, November 12, 1799, FO, National Archives, Original source: *The Papers of Thomas Jefferson*, vol. 31, *1 February 1799—31 May 1800*, ed. Barbara B. Oberg (Princeton: Princeton University Press, 2004), 236-238.
203. Dan L. Flores, *Southern Counterpart*, 32.
204. Daniel Clark, *Proofs of the Corruption*, 9.
205. TJ to William C. C. Claiborne, July 13, 1801, *FO,* National Archives, Original source: *The Papers of Thomas Jefferson*, vol. 34, *1 May—31 July 1801*, ed. Barbara B. Oberg (Princeton: Princeton University Press, 2007), 560-562.
206. Dan L. Flores, *Southern Counterpart*, 29. James Aalan Bernsen, *The Lost War for Texas: Mexican Rebels, American Burrites, and the Texas Revolution of 1811* (College Station: Texas A & M University, 2024), 18.
207. David E. Narrett, "Geopolitics and Intrigue," 115-116. The Columbian Springs cantonment was the site of the surviving Brandon family cemetery. According to early maps for Wilkinson County, Cummings' descriptions for travel to the cantonment match early maps that show the site as just northeast of Clark, Jr.'s property on the road to Fort Adams, with credit to Smokye Joe Franks for the information.
208. Amos Stoddard, *Sketches*, 188.
209. The entire New Orleans and western Mississippi Territory area attracted fugitives from justice, John G. Jones, *Methodism in Mississippi* (Nashville: Publishing House of the M. E. Church South 1908), V. 1, 22.

210. James Aalan Bernsen, *The Lost War for Texas*, 38. Of the 4,000, about 1,000 were soldiers.
211. Dan L. Flores, *Southern Counterpart*, 304-305. New Orleans governor Claiborne mentioned Sibley's activities to James Madison, who apparently then made Jefferson aware of them. Charles T. Jones, Jr., "George Champlin Sibley: The Prairie Puritan (1782-1863)" (Dissertation 1969, Online Digital Commons), 26t65b, citing C. C. Claiborne to James Madison, September 1, 1804, *Letter Books of W. C. C. Claiborne*, 2: 315, One of Nolan's maps was reproduced in Dan L. Flores, ed., *Journal of an Indian Trader*, 7, and described on pages 12-13.
212. Dan L. Flores, *Journal of an Indian Trader*, 18-20. Dan L. Flores, Southern Counterpart, 31.
213. See, Andrew Ellicott, *The Journal of Andrew Ellicott*, 29-30, 43-46. Nolan discusses the intelligence he received from confidential sources.
214. William H. Cox, *American Traitor*, 112-114, citing Deposition of Andrew Ellicott, May 22, 1808, ASP, Misc. IV 2: 89-91.
215. TJ to Albert Gallatin, Jan. 13, 1803, FO.
216. J. F. H. Claiborne, *Mississippi, as a province, territory, and state* (Jackson, Miss: Power and Barkdale, 1880), 1: 198.
217. Dan L. Flores, *Southern Counterpart*, 50-51.
218. Lewis had time to travel southwest from Kentucky or Georgia, though there is no known record that he did.
219. David E. Narrett, "Geopolitics and Intrigue," 101-146, 113.
220. Milton Lomask, *Aaron Burr, 1805-1836*, 20. Gilbert C. Din, "Empires Too Far," 287. The plan was to use Britain to help take the territory away from Spain. Cf, Hay and Werner, *The Admirable Trumpeter*, 173-174, who speculated that Blount wanted Wilkinson's participation but who found no evidence of Wilkinson's or Jefferson's participation.
221. Dan L. Flores, *Southern Counterpart*, 5.
222. William H. Cox, *American Traitor*, 125.
223. TJ to Philip Nolan, June 24, 1798, FO. As a young man, Jefferson had also been known as an athletic horseman, John Ferling, *Adams vs. Jefferson*, 23.
224. Daniel Clark to TJ, Nov. 12, 1799, FO, and May 29, 1800, LC.
225. Daniel Clark to TJ, Nov. 12, 1799, FO.
226. TJ to Daniel Clark, June 23, 1799, *Founders Online*, National Archives, Original source: *The Papers of Thomas Jefferson*, vol. 31, *1 February 1799*

—*31 May 1800*, ed. Barbara B. Oberg (Princeton: Princeton University Press, 2004), 135-136.
227. TJ to William Dunbar, June 24, 1799, *Founders Online,* National Archives, Original source: *The Papers of Thomas Jefferson,* vol. 31, *1 February 1799—31 May 1800,* 137-139. William Dunbar to TJ, October 1799, *Founders Online,* National Archives, Original source: *The Papers of Thomas Jefferson,* vol. 31, *1 February 1799—31 May 1800,* 203.
228. See, e.g. TJ to William Dunbar, Jan. 16, 1800. *Founders Online,* National Archives, Original source: *The Papers of Thomas Jefferson,* vol. 31, *1 February 1799—31 May 1800,* 311.
229. Dan L. Flores, *Southern Counterpart,* 33, n.
230. Henderson K. Yoakum, *History of Texas from Its First Settlement, 1:*111-114, Ellis Bean, *Memoir of Colonel Ellis P. Bean Written By Himself About the Year 1816,* 6.
231. Dan L. Flores, *Southern Counterpart,* 32-33. Andrew Ellicott, *The Journal of Andrew Ellicott,* 29, n. Pike spoke with some of Nolan's associates, Elliott Coues, *The Expeditions of Zebulon Montgomery Pike* (New York: Francis P. Harper, 1895), 1: lii-liv.
232. Dan L. Flores, ed., *Journal of an Indian Trader,* 20, 35-35.
233. JW to TJ, Nov. 29, 1800, NARA, Original source: *The Papers of Thomas Jefferson,* vol. 32, *1 June 1800—16 February 1801,* ed. Barbara B. Oberg (Princeton: Princeton University Press, 2005), 262.
234. Hay and Werner, *The Admirable Trumpeter,* 187.
235. Andrew Ellicott, to TJ, March 20, 1801, FO.
236. Andrew Ellicott to James Wilkinson, Jan. 21, 1808, as published in Daniel Clark, *Proofs of the Corruption,* 69-72.
237. Dan L. Flores, *Southern Counterpart,* 15.
238. Isaac Joslin Cox, "The Freeman Red River Expedition," *Proceedings of the American Philosophical Society,* Vol. 92, No. 2, *Studies of Historical Documents in the Library of the American Philosophical Society* (May 5, 1948), 115-119.
239. Fears of a large standing army were a factor leading to the constitutional convention. James Madison claimed that every member of the convention was indignant over the idea of a large standing army. Russell F. Weigley, *History of the United States Army,* 85-86. States wary of giving up power to a federal government were eventually persuaded that it

would be used only for limited purposes of mutual interest as stated in the preamble to the U.S. Constitution: "to form a more perfect Union, establish Justice, insure domestic Tranquility, provide for the common defense, promote the general Welfare, and secure the Blessings of Liberty to ourselves and our Posterity."

240. Russell F. Weigley, *History of the United States Army*, 101. William J. Murphy, Jr., "John Adams: The Politics of the Additional Army, 1798-1800," *The New England Quarterly*, Vol. 52, No. 2 (Jun. 1979): 234-249. Charles Francis Adams, *The Works of John Adams* (Little Brown and Company, New York: 1856), 1: 526-527.

241. An example is the Federalist's attempted imprisonment of Republican Congressman Matthew Lyon for criticizing actions of the Federalist administration under the Alien and Sedition Act. By the time of Lewis's death, Lyon had moved to Kentucky and had been awarded the contract for the delivery of mail on the Natchez Trace. *Natchez Trace Parkway Survey*, 88.

242. Howard W. Cox, *American Traitor*, 119.

243. Robert, M. S. McDonald, *Jefferson's Military Academy: Founding West Point* (Charlottesville: University of Virginia Press, 2004), 6.

244. Andro Linklater, *An Artist in Treason*, 194.

245. TJ to ML, Feb. 23, 1801, Donald Jackson, *Letters*, 2-3.

246. Meriwether Lewis's Classification of Army Officers, [after 24 July 1801], FO. Russell F. Russell F. Weigley, *History of the United States Army*, 102.

247. Meriwether Lewis's Classification of Army Officers, FO. Andro Linklater, *An Artist in Treason*, 192.

248. *Lancaster Intelligencer*, March 21, 1801, 7. Frances Peyton to TJ, March 13, 1801, FO. Original source: Barbara B. Oberg., ed, *The Papers of Thomas Jefferson*, vol. 33, *17 February—30 April 1801*, 271.

249. Wilkinson knew that Jefferson was adamant about extending the borders of the country. Though Washington and Hamilton had supported a build-up of troops on the western frontier, they opposed extending the borders too quickly because the small military did not have the resources to fight too many native tribes at one time. The Adams administration had passed a bill to acquire land from the Southeastern tribes, but it had not followed through. Most of their Federalist supporters who lived along the East Coast were not clamoring for expansion.

250. Jefferson's Message to Congress, Jan. 18, 1803, Donald Jackson, *Letters*, 10-13. That letter would become known as the request for funds to send Lewis and Clark to the Northwest; however, the letter equally emphasized the need to secure Chickasaw land to exert control over the Mississippi River in the Southwest. Henry Adams wrote that Jefferson's cabinet was not assembled until July 1801, which raised questions as to the advisors who were present. Henry Adams, *History of the United States, 1801-1809*, Library of America, 148-149.

251. TJ, May 17, 1801 Cabinet Meeting Notes, The Thomas Jefferson Papers at the Library of Congress: Series 1: General Correspondence. 1651 to 1827 (Reference date listed as May 15, 1801). Congress had appropriated funds in May 1800 to negotiate for Cherokee land, but the Adams administration took no action on it. In February 1801, Tennessee senators Joseph Anderson and William Cocke wrote Jefferson to suggest that he move forward on the process of purchasing Cherokee land between settlements in East and West (now Middle) Tennessee, and if land could not be obtained, building stations along the road between the settlements in Tennessee. Joseph Anderson and William Cocke to TJ, Feb. 26, 1801, FO. Original source: *The Papers of Thomas Jefferson*, vol. 33, *17 February—30 April 1801*, ed. Barbara B. Oberg (Princeton: Princeton University Press, 2006), 69-70. TJ to the Senate, Dec. 23, 1801, *ASP, Indian Affairs*, IV 1: 648-50. For Jefferson's motivations to secure the river, see, Memorandum for Henry Dearborn on Indian Policy, 20 October 1804," FO. Original source: *The Papers of Thomas Jefferson*, vol. 44, *1 July to 10 November 1804*, ed. James P. McClure. (Princeton: Princeton University Press, 2019), 570-572.

252. TJ to Horatio Gates, July 11, 1803, FO.

253. Dan L. Flores, *Southern Counterpart to Lewis & Clark*, xii.

254. Matthew Lyons to TJ, Aug. 12, 1801, FO.

255. Daniel Clark, Jr. provided evidence of Jefferson's knowledge in his book. Daniel Clark, *Proofs of the Corruption*, 144-150. See also Andro Linklater, *An Artist in Treason*, 193.

256. The Spanish governor had warned that the earlier construction of Fort Massac a few miles from where Wilkinsonville would be constructed would enable the U.S. to use the river to take over Chickasaw land at Chickasaw Bluffs and Muscle Shoals. Governor Carondelet to Governor

Gayoso, Aug. 20, 1794, Paul Clements, *Chronicles of the Cumberland Settlements*, 432. Wilkinson was advising the Spanish at the time.

257. Norman W. Caldwell, "Cantonment Wilkinsonville," *Mid-America*, Vol. 31, no. 1 (Jan. 1949), 3-28; and "Fort Massac: The American Frontier Post: 1778-1805," *Journal of the Illinois State Historical Society (1908-1984)*, Vol. 43, No. 4 (Winter, 1950): 265-281.

258. Thomas S. Butler Regimental Order Book, Aug. 9, 1801—Aug 25, 1801, Andrew Jackson Papers, LC.

259. *Natchez Trace Parkway Survey* (United States Senate 1941, reprinted Trent's Prints, Pace. Florida 2002), 37. Work began south of the boundary in winter 1801. The treaty was not ratified until spring, 1802. The Choctaw Treaty had not even been signed.

260. Quoted in *Natchez Trace Parkway Survey*, 81. The map, sometimes called the "Butler Map" is on record in the National Archives. A copy can be found at the Tennessee State Library and Archives, Map #486. For early construction of the road north of the Chickasaw Nation, see SW to Brig. Gen. Wilkinson, June 11, 1801, Military Book "A", 83-84, Natchez Trace Research Collection, McCain Library and Archives, MSU.

261. Andro Linklater, *An Artist in Treason*, 320-322, quote at 321. See also Howard W. Cox, *American Traitor*, 156.

262. TJ to ML, July 4, 1803, Donald Jackson, *Letters,* 105-106.

263. Flores says that Jefferson made four attempts to organize an expedition, Flores, *Southern Counterpart*, 6. H. Carl Camp, "Voyages from Montreal," *We Proceeded On*, Vol. 37, No. 2 (May 2011): 6. Lee Alan Dugatkin, "André Michaux's 'Almost Expedition' to the West in 1793," *We Proceeded On*, Vol. 47, No. 1 (Feb. 2021): 5-11.

264. Carlos Martinez de Yrujo to Pedro Cevallos, Dec. 2, 1802, Donald Jackson, *Letters*, 4-7 and Carlos Martinez de Yrujo, Jan. 31, 1803, Donald Jackson, *Letters*, 14-15.

265. *Transcript of the Louisiana Purchase Treaty Between the United States of America and the French Republic*, April 30, 1803, National Archives Online. For the negotiators' instructions that anticipate the ambiguities, see Henry Adams, *History of the United States, 1801-1809* (Reprinted, The Library of America 1986), 306-310. Milton Lomask, *Aaron Burr, 1805-1836*, 92.

266. Dan L. Flores, *Southern Counterpart*, 24-26.

267. "Hamilton on the Louisiana Purchase: A Newly Identified Editorial from the New-York Evening Post," *The William and Mary Quarterly*, Vol. 12, No. 2, "Alexander Hamilton: 1755-1804" (Apr. 1955): 268-281.
268. Jon Kukla, *A Wilderness So Immense*, 291.
269. Ibid., 289.
270. Frank Lawrence Owsley, Jr. and Gene A. Smith, *Filibusters and Expansionists*, 27-29. Peter S. Onuf, *Jefferson's Empire*, 72.
271. Milton Lomask, *Aaron Burr, 1805-1836*, 80. Evidence of Major James Bruff, ASP, X, 1: 571-577.
272. Jon Kukla, *A Wilderness So Immense*, 292. Dan L. Flores, *Southern Counterpart*, 3, citing *Columbian Centinel*, Aug. 24, 1803. Barry J. Balleck, "When the Ends Justify the Means: Thomas Jefferson and the Louisiana Purchase," *Presidential Studies Quarterly*, Vol. 22, No. 4, America's Bill of Rights, Market Economies And Republican Governments (Fall, 1992): 679-696.
273. Peter S. Onuf, *Jefferson's Empire*, 53.
274. Jefferson's Instructions to Lewis, June 20, 1803, Donald Jackson, *Letters*, 61-66. The written instructions were the formality of authorization of plans already discussed. Lewis had already invited Clark to become his co-captain the day prior, ML to WC, June 19, 1803, Donald Jackson, *Letters*, 57-60.
275. Numbers 13.
276. Jefferson's Instructions to Lewis, June 20, 1803, Donald Jackson, *Letters*, 61-66.
277. ML to TJ, April 7, 1805, Donald Jackson, *Letters*, 231-242. Lewis sent information to the SW because Lewis thought it was important the secretary have it before the Corps' return.
278. Compare the authority Lewis was given to the confines the commanders of the lunar missions worked under. Leaders of other Jefferson expeditions similarly submitted reports to the president, but Wilkinson loomed as a larger influence and constraint.
279. Charles Greifenstein, "Benjamin Rush: Man of Many Parts," *We Proceeded On*, Vol 28, No. 2 (May 2002): 28-30. See also e.g. Robert Patterson to TJ, March 15, 1803, Donald Jackson, *Letters*, 28-31, TJ to Benjamin Smith Barton, Feb. 27, 1803, Donald Jackson, *Letters*, 16-17.

280. Dr. Rush to Capt. Lewis for preserving health. June 11, 1803, Donald Jackson, *Letters*, 54-55.
281. Receipt from Francois Baillet, Donald Jackson, *Letters*, 78, 81-82, between pages 106 and 107. Kenneth C. Walcheck, "Ration of Last Resort," *We Proceeded On*, Vol. 29, No. 3 (Aug. 2003): 24-27.
282. Stuart Weir, "The Guns of Lewis and Clark," *We Proceeded On*, Vol. 32, No. 2 (May 2006): 10-19. See also Michael E. Corrick, "Meriwether Lewis's Air Gun," *We Proceeded On*, Vol. 28, No. 4 (Nov. 2002): 15-21.
283. ML to TJ, July 22, 1803, Donald Jackson, *Letters*, 111-112. Lewis declined to take his own long knife.
284. ML to TJ, April 20, 1803, Donald Jackson, *Letters*, 37-41. William K. Brunot, "The Building of the Barge: The Creation of the Lewis and Clark Flagship," *We Proceeded On*, Vol. 48, No. 1 (February 2022): 6-19, 12.
285. SW to AJ, December 6, 1803, PAJ 1: 406, Tennessee's First Military Expedition," *Tennessee Historical Magazine*, Vol. 8, No. 3 (Oct. 1924): 171-190. Jefferson ordered the Tennessee governor to supply Tennessee militia as volunteers to travel to Natchez to assure Spain's recognition of the Louisiana Purchase. As discussed later, Gilbert C. Russell would take over the virtual lead of that expedition. Jackson subcontracted the project to a company owned by associates.
286. John Bakeless, *Lewis and Clark*, 69.
287. ML to WC, June 19, 1803, Donald Jackson, *Letters*, 57-60. Original located at MHS, Identifier, A0289-21435If Clark was unable or unwilling to undertake the entire expedition, Lewis invited Clark to join him for as much of the trip up the Missouri that Clark was willing to make.
288. WC to ML, July 18, 1803, Donald Jackson, *Letters*, 110-111. When Clark's response was delayed and Lewis needed to make a selection, Lewis asked an able commander Moses Hooks to consider the position if he did not hear from Clark in time.
289. ML to WC, May 6, 1804, Donald Jackson, *Letters*, 179-180.
290. William K. Brunot, "The Building of the Barge," 6-19. Elin Woodger and Brandon Toropov, *Encyclopedia of the Lewis and Clark Expedition* (Infobase Publishing, 2014), 196. Lewis included some specifications in his letter to William Dickson, who never responded. Clark added the side panels as the Corps waited to launch at Camp Dubois. According

to *The Navigator*, boats were specially designed based upon the hazards they were expected to encounter.
291. Jefferson's Message to Congress, Jan. 18, 1803, Donald Jackson, *Letters*, 10-14.
292. Charles G. Clarke, *The Men of the Lewis and Clark Expedition* (University of Nebraska Press: Lincoln 1970), 15.
293. WC to ML, Aug. 21, 1803, Donald Jackson, *Letters*, 117-118.
294. James J. Holmberg, "'Fairly launched on my voyage of discovery:' Meriwether Lewis's expedition letter to James Findlay," *We Proceeded On*, Vol. 35, No. 3 (August 2009): 20-28.
295. William K. Brunot, "The Building of the Barge," 16, citing Dwight L. Smith and Ray Swick, eds., *A Journey Through the West: Thomas Rodney's 1803 Journal from Delaware to the Mississippi Territory* (Athens: Ohio University Press, 1997), 50-53.
296. Charles G. Clarke, *The Men of the Lewis and Clark Expedition*, 37.
297. TJ to ML, June 20, 1803, Donald Jackson, *Letters*, 61-66.
298. David Kahn, *The Code Breakers: The Story of Secret Writing* (McMillan Publishing Co., Inc., New York: 1967), 194-195, 513.
299. Ibid. Kahn noted that Jefferson's cylinder produced a code more difficult to break and it would be re-invented independently and used by the military into the early 1900's.
300. Cipher for Correspondence with Jefferson, Donald Jackson, *Letters*, 9-10.
301. It is possible the explorers wrote the notes directly in the leather journals but the orderliness of the writing suggests that notes were transferred to the journals. For a discussion, see Gary E. Moulton, "The Missing Journals of Meriwether Lewis." From the University of Nebraska "Journals of Lewis and Clark Expedition" website, Article originally appeared in *Montana: The Magazine of Western History*, Vol. 35, Summer 1985, 28-39.
302. Charles G. Clarke, *The Men of the Lewis and Clark Expedition*, 17-22.
303. James J. Holmberg, "Into the Wilderness, from Pittsburgh," *We Proceeded On*, Vol. 45 No. 3 (Aug. 2019): 10-15, 11, citing ML to TJ, Sept. 8, 1803, Donald Jackson, *Letters*, 121-123.
304. TJ to Benjamin Rush, June 24, 1803, Donald Jackson, *Letters*, 68.
305. Jay H. Buckley, "Exploring the Louisiana Purchase and Its Borderlands," *We Proceeded On*, Vol. 46, No. 3 (August 2020): 10-21, 17, citing ML to

TJ, Oct. 3, 1803, Donald Jackson, *Letters*, 126-132, and Dan L. Flores, "Red River Expedition," Texas Handbook Online.

306. It is possible that Lewis proposed the hundred-mile excursions simply to provide reports on the new territory the U.S. had acquired, as he said, and an excursion toward Santa Fe expedition could be justified politically to help confirm the southern Red River boundaries with Spain. Albert Gallatin had suggested exploration of the territory south of the Missouri to locate Spanish forts and the waters of the Missouri, Albert Gallatin to TJ, April 13, 1803, Donald Jackson, *Letters*, 32-34. But Lewis's abandonment of the "main" object of the expedition just prior to launch is comparable to Neil Armstrong proposing to take a three-month sailboat excursion off the coast of Cape Canaveral just prior to the moon launch. Too much preparation had gone into the mission to lose focus and the risks that a critical crew member would be injured or lost too great. Taking Lewis's statements at face value it must be assumed that Lewis did not understand the risks of Spanish patrols and the need to provide the training to his new company that Clark provided during that period. The letter presumes that Lewis had Jefferson's approval for the excursions, and it seems more likely that Lewis chose not to put his true purpose into writing.

307. Gary E. Moulton, "The Missing Journals of Meriwether Lewis." From the University of Nebraska website, Article originally appeared in *Montana: The Magazine of Western History*, Volume 35 (Summer 1985): 28-39.

308. Jay H. Buckley, "William Clark, the Fur Trade, and Indian Affairs," *We Proceeded On*, Vol. 46, No. 4 (November 2020): 14-30, 16-17, citing ML to TJ, Oct. 3, 1803, Donald Jackson, *Letters*, 126-132 and TJ to ML Nov. 16, 1803, Donald Jackson, *Letters*, 136-140. Jefferson noted that he was planning a second expedition to the Southwest, ibid., Dan L. Flores, *Southern Counterpart*, 8.

309. ML to WC, June 19, 1803, Donald Jackson, *Letters*, 57-60. TJ to ML, June 20, 1803, Donald Jackson, *Letters*, 61-66. TJ to ML, Nov. 16, 1803, Donald Jackson, *Letters*, 136-140. cf. Dumas Malone was of the opinion that Jefferson's objectives were three-fold—commercial, scientific, and military—and that Jefferson masked his true commercial purpose of the expedition with the other two. Dumas Malone, *Jefferson the President: First Term*, 275-276. Certainly, Jefferson used broader objectives to achieve support for funding.

310. JW to The Officers of the Territory, Aug. 22, 1805, TP 13: 188-189.
311. John Bakeless, *Lewis and Clark*, 103-104. Charles G. Clarke, *The Men of the Lewis and Clark Expedition*, 18, 20.
312. SW to JW, TP, 9: 3-6, JW to Amos Stoddard, Jan. 24, 1804, TP, 9: 170-171.
313. Upper Louisiana Transfer Document, March 9, 1804, Louisiana Purchase Transfer Collection, 1783-1953, MHS.
314. John Bakeless, *Lewis and Clark*, 108. TP 13: 3-5. Stoddard and Daniel Bissell were among the group ordered to establish a garrison at St. Louis. Stoddard's duties at first was both civil and military, until Bruff was appointed military commandant.
315. ML to Amos Stoddard, May 16, 1804, Donald Jackson, *Letters*, 189-192. It has often been suggested that Lewis and Stoddard were old friends (John Bakeless, *Lewis and Clark*, 108), but Stoddard's descendant could find no evidence that Lewis and Stoddard had met prior to or after Lewis's brief encampment at Camp Dubois (Robert A. Stoddard, ed., *The Autobiography Manuscript of Major Amos Stoddard* (Robert Stoddard Publishing 2016), 70.) Though Lewis previously mentioned Stoddard's troops as possible recruits, I have found no evidence indicating a friendship other than from the winter of 1803-04. Stoddard sent Lewis a letter to inform him of his appointment as military commandant in St. Louis, *Journals of Lewis and Clark*, Jan. 2, 1804, University of Nebraska, but it is unclear whether the letter was for business purposes or as a letter from a friend. Among other encounters during their brief time together, Lewis and Clark dined and attended a ball with Stoddard on April 7, 1804, WC Entr, *Journals of Lewis and Clark*, University of Nebraska online. Stoddard left St. Louis in 1805 to accompany tribal leaders to Washington and when he returned to the Southwest, he spent time in the lower Louisiana area around Fort Adams and Wilkinson's Columbian Springs writing a book about the Louisiana Territory and exploring the Red River. Note JW forwarded Stoddard's observations about the natural science and suitability for military purposes of the area, JW to TJ, Nov. 6, 1805, TP 13: 265-267.
316. James R. Ronda, *Lewis and Clark Among the Indians* (University of Nebraska Press: Lincoln, 1984), 10-14.
317. Charles G. Clarke, *The Men of the Lewis and Clark Expedition*, 20-24.
318. Lewis's Estimate of Expenses, Donald Jackson, *Letters*, 8-9. Final Summation of Lewis's Account, Donald Jackson, *Letters*, 424-430.

319. Colter-Frick calculated that of the $16,778.54 bills of exchange charged to Lewis, approximately $11,393.78 were paid to the Chouteau family, L. R. Colter-Frick, *Courageous Colter and Companions*, 307. Financial Records of the Expedition, Aug. 5, 1807, Donald Jackson, *Letters*, 419-431.
320. Shirley Christian, *Before Lewis and Clark*, 21, ML to TJ, May 18, 1804, Donald Jackson, *Letters*, 192-195.
321. Amos Stoddard to Henry Dearborn, June 3, 1804, Donald Jackson, *Letters*, 196-198. WC, Entry of May 21, 1804, *Lewis and Clark Journals*, University of Nebraska Online.
322. Various entries, *The Journals of Lewis and Clark*, Entry May 16, 1804, University of Nebraska, Online.
323. ML to Lucy Marks, March 31, 1805, MHS.
324. John Logan Allen, "'So Fine a Country': The Early Exploration of Louisiana Territory, 1540-1802," *We Proceeded On*, Vol. 49 No. 4 (November 2023): 4-39, 28-33. Shirley Christian believes the Chouteaus traveled as far north as present-day Council Bluffs, Shirley Christian, *Before Lewis and Clark: The Story of the Chouteaus, the French Dynasty That Rules America's Frontier* (Lincoln: University of Nebraska Press, 2004), 10.
325. ML, Journal Entry April 7. 1805, *Lewis and Clark Journals*, accessed online from *Journals of the Lewis and Clark Expedition*, University of Nebraska.
326. E. G. Chuinard, "The Actual Role of the Bird Woman: Purposeful Member of the Corps or Casual 'Tag Along'?" *Montana The Magazine of Western History*, Vol. 26, No. 3 (Summer, 1976): 18-29.
327. Kenneth C. Walcheck, "Exit, Pursued by a Bear," *We Proceeded On*, Vol. 43 No. 3 (August 2017): 24-28; R. T. Ravenholt, "The Death of Sergeant Charles Floyd: Was it the Water or the Cure?" *We Proceeded On*, Vol. 39 No. 1 (February 2013): 27-3, Kenneth C. Walcheck, "Portable Soup: Ration of Last Resort," *We Proceeded On*, Vol. 29 No. 3 (August 2003): 24-27.
328. WC, Journal Entry, July 4, 1804 and ML, Journal Entry of April 27, 1805, *Journals of the Lewis and Clark Expedition*, University of Nebraska, Online.
329. Bernard De Voto, *The Course of Empire* (Boston: Houghton, Mifflin Company, 1962), 432. Jefferson had asked Spain to provide the explorers a passport through their territory. He assured that the mission would be solely scientific in nature. Spain refused. Carlos Martinez de Yrujo to Pedro Cevallos, Dec. 2, 1802, Donald Jackson, *Letters*, 4-7. Wilkinson

had sent his intelligence about the Lewis and Clark Expedition to the Spanish two months before the Corps of Discovery set out from St. Louis.

330. Andro Linklater, *An Artist in Treason*, 219. Linklater connects the timing of the disclosure and other information to Spanish Governor Folch but suggests that the information on Lewis and Clark and other information about the West made the information worth $12,000 to the Spanish.

331. Marques de Casa Calvo to Pedro Cevallos, March 30, 1804, Donald Jackson, *Letters*, 173-175.

332. Nemesio Salcedo to Pedro Cevallos, May 8, 1804, Donald Jackson, *Letters*, 183-189, 185. Dan Sturdevant and Jay H. Buckley, "Spanish Attempts to Apprehend Lewis and Clark," *We Proceeded On*, Vol. 45 No. 1 (Feb. 2019): 18-25.

333. Ibid.

334. William Clark Entry, Nov. 7, 1805, *The Journals of Lewis and Clark*, University of Nebraska. Mike Rees, "Ocean in View?: A Scientific Analysis of the view from Pillar Rock on November 7, 1805," *We Proceeded On*, Vol. 35, No. 2 (May 2009): 22-31.

335. Dan L. Flores, *Southern Counterpart*, 24, citing To the Special Commissioner on the Spanish Boundary, July 15, 1803, Paul L. Ford, ed., *The Works of Thomas Jefferson* (New York: G. P. Putnam's Sons, 1904-1905), 10: 16-19.

336. Dan L. Flores, *Southern Counterpart*, 52. See also Thomas Freeman to TJ, July 13, 1805, LOC.

337. Dan L. Flores, *Southern Counterpart*, 53.

338. Ibid., 54.

339. Ibid., and n. 76. For McKee's meeting with Burr, see John McKee, *Diary*, Jan. 31, 1804—Oct. 11, 1805, Folder 1: Papers, 1793-1829, Scans 107-110, University of North Carolina Special Collections.

340. Dan L. Flores, *Southern Counterpart*, 54.

341. W. C. C. Claiborne to Secretary of State, May 14, 1809, *State Department Territorial Papers*, Orleans, 1764-1823, NARA.

342. J. C. A. Stagg, "James Madison and George Mathews: The East Florida Revolution of 1812 Reconsidered," *Diplomatic History*, Vol. 30, No. 1 (January 2006): 23-55. J. C. A. Stagg, "George Mathews and John McKee: Revolutionizing East Florida, Mobile, and Pensacola in 1812," *The Florida Historical Quarterly*, Vol. 85, No. 3 (Winter, 2007): 269-296.

343. Alexander Wilson to Joshua Sullivan, Feb. 21, 1806, AW 251-252.
344. Alexander Wilson to TJ, Feb. 6, 1806, AW, 249-251. Dan L. Flores, *Southern Counterpart*, 57-58.
345. Flores explains participants and historians' confusion as to which expedition Wilson applied to join. Dan L. Flores, *Southern Counterpart*, 58. See, e.g., Isaac Joslin Cox, "The Freeman Red River Expedition," *Proceedings of the American Philosophical Society*, Vol. 92, No. 2 (May 5, 1948): 115-119.
346. Alexander Wilson to TJ, March 18, 1805 (232-233), TJ to Alexander Wilson, April 4, 1807 (236-238) and TJ to Alexander Wilson, October 9, 1807 (266), AW.
347. Freeman's team included Peter Custis and Richard Sparks. Jay H. Buckley, "Exploring the Louisiana Purchase and Its Borderlands," Part One, 17. Jefferson moved forward with the Santa Fe expedition soon after receiving Lewis's letter, sending Dunbar on a short expedition up the Ouachita River to Hot Springs in 1804 as he planned the longer "Grand Expedition." Dan L. Flores, *Southern Counterpart*, 39-46.
348. Jay H. Buckley, "Exploring the Louisiana Purchase and Its Borderlands," Part One, 18.
349. Jay H. Buckley, "Exploring the Louisiana Purchase and Its Borderlands," Part One, 19-20.
350. Elliott Coues, ed., *The Expeditions of Zebulon Montgomery Pike* (New York: Francis P. Harper, 1895). V. I, Z. M. Pike's Preface to Original Edition, 1: ii. See also Lt. Zebulon Pike's *Notebook of Maps, Traverse Tables, and Meteorological Observations, 1805-1807*, RG 94, NARA.
351. JW to Zebulon Pike, July 30, 1805, TP 13: 185-186.
352. Andro Linklater, *An Artist in Treason*, 157.
353. Zebulon Pike to JW, Oct. 2, 1806, quoted in Joseph Wheelan, *Jefferson's Vendetta*, 138. Pike denied that Wilkinson was involved in a nefarious plot, Elliott Coues, *The Expeditions of Zebulon Montgomery Pike*, 1: ii-iii. Herbert E. Bolton, "Papers of Zebulon M. Pike, 1806-1807," *The American Historical Review*, Vol. 13, No. 4 (Jul. 1908): 798-827.
354. David E. Narrett, "Liberation and Conquest: John Hamilton Robinson and U.S. Adventurism toward Mexico, 1806-1819," *Western Historical Quarterly*, Vol. 40, No. 1 (Spring, 2009), 23-50, 27. Salcedo to James Wilkinson, April 8, 1807, Elliott Coues, *The Expeditions of Zebulon Montgomery Pike*, 2: 815-817.

355. Statement and Affidavit of Timothy Kirby, July 6, 1807, TP 13: 133-136.
356. Dan L. Flores, *Southern Counterpart*, 290-291.
357. Thomas Jefferson to James Madison, Aug. 30, 1807, FO.
358. Milton Lomask, *Aaron Burr, 1805-1836*, 82-83. Flores points out that Wilkinson understood that the mountain range was minor, but it was actually the Rockies, Dan L. Flores, *Southern Counterpart*, 17.
359. TJ to Congress, December 2, 1806, Message to Congress, Library of Congress.
360. Jay H. Buckley, "Exploring the Louisiana Purchase and Its Borderlands," Part One, 19-20.
361. William Clark, Entry of Sept. 17, 1806, *The Journals of the Lewis and Clark Expedition*, University of Nebraska, online.
362. *The Evening Post*, Dec. 14, 1809, 3. He appears to be the "McCleland" referred to in the article.
363. John McKee to JW, Feb. 26, 1807, ASP, Misc, 594, The rumor was repeated by McClallen, John Bakeless, *Lewis and Clark*, 371 (who spelled the name "M'Clelan").
364. TJ to ML, Oct. 26, 1806, Donald Jackson, *Letters*, 350-351.
365. *The National Intelligencer and Washington Advertiser*, Nov 14, 1806, 2.
366. *The National Intelligencer and Washington Advertiser*, Oct. 27, 1806, 3.
367. TJ to Henry Dearborn, July 14, 1805, Donald Jackson, *Letters*, 252.
368. WC to William D. Meriwether, Jan. 26, 1808, Donald Jackson, *Letters*, 490-491.
369. See also James J. Holmberg, "'Fairly launched on my voyage of discovery:' Meriwether Lewis's expedition letter to James Findlay," *We Proceeded On*, Vol. 35 No. 3 (August 2009): 20-27, on Lewis's method of sending letters back to family and friends that he intended to be published in newspapers.
370. Gary Moulton, editor of the *Journals of the Lewis and Clark Expedition*, stated that the safe view is that the explorers often wrote their observations directly in the red leather journals on the expedition and then carefully sealed the journals in waterproof containers to carry back home, because field notes have not been located for many entries. He notes, however, that one of the early publishers of the journals, Eliott Coues, thought the writings in the journals were too uniform and clean to have been written at different times under sometimes extreme circumstances. Gary E. Moulton, "The Missing Journals of Meriwether Lewis," from the University of

Nebraska website. Article originally appeared in *Montana: The Magazine of Western History,* Volume 35 (Summer 1985), 28-39.

371. ML, *The Journals of the Lewis and Clark Expedition,* Entry of June 14, 1805, University of Nebraska, online.

372. ML, *The Journals of the Lewis and Clark Expedition,* Entry of Aug. 18, 1805, University of Nebraska, online. Compare to Jefferson's succinct midlife epiphany, "I am burning the candle of life without present pleasure or future object," quoted in Thomas Fleming, *The Intimate Lives of the Founding Fathers,* 297.

373. Cf. David L. Nicandri, "The Rhyme of the Great Navigator: The Literature of Captain Cook and Its Influence on the Journals of Lewis and Clark (Part 1: A Canoe's Teeth)," *We Proceeded On,* Vol. 42 No. 1 (Feb. 2016): 22-28, and in two subsequent articles posits that Lewis used language from the expedition of Captain James Cook as well as from poetry studied by young gentlemen of the enlightenment period.

374. Winfield Scott, *Memoirs of General Winfield Scott,* 17.

375. Milton Lomask, *Aaron Burr, 1756-1805,* 13.

376. Dumas Malone, *Jefferson the President: First Term, 1810-1805* (Little Brown & Company: Boston 1970), 123.

377. Milton Lomask, *Aaron Burr, 1805-1836,* 43. Joseph Wheelan argues that Jefferson prevailed over Burr because Jefferson reached an accommodation with the Federalists, Joseph Wheelan, *Jefferson's Vendetta,* 2-3, 60-61.

378. Milton Lomask, *Aaron Burr, 1805-1836,* 28. Joseph Wheelan, *Jefferson's Vendetta,* 88-91.

379. Milton Lomask, *Aaron Burr, 1805-1836,* 24-25.

380. Joseph Wheelan, *Jefferson's Vendetta,* 122-123. Milton Lomask, *Aaron Burr, 1805-1836,* 30-35, 49-52.

381. Hay and Werner, *The Admirable Trumpeter,* 49. Milton Lomask, *Aaron Burr, 1805-1836,* 45.

382. Wilkinson to Burr March 26, 1804, Dan L. Flores, *Southern Counterpart,* 78 n. 121. David O. Stewart, *American Emperor: Aaron Burr's Challenge to Jefferson's America* (New York: Simon & Schuster Paperbacks, 2011), 73. Also described in Milton Lomask, *Aaron Burr, 1805-1836,* 45.

383. Milton Lomask, *Aaron Burr, 1805-1836,* 45. James Aalan Bernsen, *The Lost War for Texas,* 21-22.

384. Milton Lomask, *Aaron Burr, 1805-1836*, 112. Milton Lomask states that Burr's maps found after his death, included Latin America.
385. David O. Stewart, *American Emperor*, 84. Milton Lomask, *Aaron Burr, 1805-1836*, 44-45. Joseph Wheelan, *Jefferson's Vendetta*, 74-75. Jefferson previously offered the position to the Marquis de Lafayette, who declined, TJ to Lafayette, Nov. 4, 1803, FO NARA, Original source: *The Papers of Thomas Jefferson*, vol. 41, *11 July—15 November 1803*, ed. Barbara B. Oberg (Princeton: Princeton University Press, 2014), 665-666.
386. Milton Lomask, *Aaron Burr, 1805-1836*, 44. Burr's brother-in-law was Dr. Joseph Browne.
387. As Howard Cox points out, other territorial governors also served as generals, Howard W. Cox, *American Traitor*, 149.
388. General Orders, March 19, 1805, General Orders and Circulars of the War Department and Headquarters of the Army, 1809-1860, NARA.
389. David O. Stewart, *American Emperor*, 84, Milton Lomask, *Aaron Burr, 1805-1836*, 71-72. Dan L. Flores, *Southern Counterpart*, 29.
390. Aaron Burr to AJ, June 2, 1805, Harold D. Moser and Sharon Macpherson, and Charles F. Bryan, Jr., eds. PAJ, 2: 59.
391. Andrew Jackson to James Winchester, Oct. 4, 1806, PAJ 2: 110-111.
392. AJ to George Washington Campbell, April 28, 1804, Harold D. Moser, Sharon Macpherson, and Charles F. Bryan, Jr., *Papers of Andrew Jackson*, 2: 18-19.
393. Jackson accepted Jefferson's second proposal to build boats a few months later. He had a greater interest in participating in some way with the expedition to Natchez, and the contract for the larger number of boats was more lucrative.
394. Joseph Wheelan, *Jefferson's Vendetta*, 37.
395. James Parton, *Life of Andrew Jackson* (New York: Mason Brothers, 1863), 97.
396. Parton 1: 310. Joseph Wheelan, *Jefferson's Vendetta*, 125-127.
397. Milton Lomask, *Aaron Burr, 1805-1836*, 69.
398. Ibid., 78-80. Joseph Wheelan, *Jefferson's Vendetta*, 250-251. ASP, Misc. 1: 572.
399. Evidence of Major James Bruff, ASP, Misc 1: 572-577.
400. Joseph Wheelan, *Jefferson's Vendetta*, 120. Evidence of Major James Bruff, ASP, Misc 1: 572-577.
401. Milton Lomask, *Aaron Burr, 1805-1836*, 78.

402. Hay and Werner, *The Admirable Trumpeter*, 247.
403. Lindsay Schakenbach, "Schemers, Dreamers, and a Revolutionary Foreign Policy: New York City in the Era of Second Independence, 1805-1815," *New York History*, Vol. 94, No. 3-4 (Summer/Fall 2013): 267-282. Hay and Werner, *The Admirable Trumpeter*, 247.
404. Entry for July 27, 1807, Diary of John McKee, Jan. 31, 1804-Oct. 11, 1805, Folder 1: Papers, 1793-1829, Scans 107-110, University of North Carolina Special Collections.
405. Andro Lanklater, *An Artist in Treason*, 230.
406. Henry Adams, *History of the United States of America During the Administration of Thomas Jefferson*, Reprinted, Library of America, 1986, 759. Joseph Wheelan, *Jefferson's Vendetta*, 127-128.
407. Dick Steward, *Frontier Swashbuckler* (Columbia, Missouri: University of Missouri Press, 2000), 6.
408. Milton Lomask, *Aaron Burr, 1805-1836*, 75-78. Joseph Wheelan, *Jefferson's Vendetta*, 128.
409. Milton Lomask, *Aaron Burr, 1805-1836*, 83-88.
410. Andro Lanklater, *An Artist in Treason*, 232.
411. Joseph Wheelan, *Jefferson's Vendetta*, 128-129.
412. Commission of Governor Wilkinson, Jan. 30, 1806, TP 13: 421-422.
413. Certificate of Joseph Dorr, Nov. 5, 1805, TP 13: 252. SW to Amos Stoddard, May 16, 1804, LS. Stoddard held both civil and military authority until the territorial government was organized. Stoddard then retained civil authority and Bruff assumed military authority.
414. SW to JW, May 6, 1806, LS. Joseph Wheelan, *Jefferson's Vendetta*, 136.
415. JW to SW, June 17, 1806, and JW to Samuel Smith, TP 13: 521-522.
416. Aaron Burr to Andrew Jackson, March 24, 1806, PAJ 2: 91-92.
417. Milton Lomask, *Aaron Burr, 1805-1836*, 117.
418. David O. Stewart, American Emperor, 122-123. Milton Lomask, *Aaron Burr, 1805-1836*, 97-100. See also Francisco de Miranda, *The History of Don Francisco de Miranda's Attempt to Affect a Revolution in South America* (Boston: Oliver and Munroe 1808).
419. Jackson was one, even referencing the Miranda quote. AJ to Daniel Smith, Nov. 12, 1806, PAJ 2: 117-120.
420. James Parton, *Life of Andrew Jackson* (New York: Mason Brothers, 1860), 1: 316.

421. Ibid. Milton Lomask, *Aaron Burr, 1805-1836*, 134-136.
422. Ibid.
423. Robert V. Remini, *Andrew Jackson, and the Course of American Empire*, 1767-1821, 147-148. See also Andrew Jackson to [William Preston Anderson], September 25, 1806, PAJ 2: 110, and Thomas E. Watson, *The Life and Times of Andrew Jackson* (Thomason Georgia: The Jeffersonian Pub. Co., 1912), 124.
424. Account with Aaron Burr, Harold D. Moser and Sharon Macpherson, and Charles F. Bryan, Jr., eds. PAJ 2: 113.
425. Order to Brigadier Generals of the 2$^{nd}$ Division, Oct. 4, 1806, PAJ 2: 111-112.
426. Andrew Jackson to TJ, Nov. 5, 1806, PAJ 2: 114-115.
427. David O. Stewart, *American Emperor*, 147, quoting Joseph Hamilton Daveiss, *View of the President's Conduct Concerning the Conspiracy of 1806* (Cincinnati: Abingdon Press, 1917, original in 1807), 85-87.
428. Howard Cox, *American Traitor*, 153-154. Parton, *Life of Andrew Jackson*, 99-100.
429. Milton Lomask, *Aaron Burr, 1805-1836*, 170-174.
430. Ibid., 179.
431. Hay and Werner, *The Admirable Trumpeter*, 257.
432. James Parton, *Life of Andrew Jackson*, 100. PAJ 2: 115, n, AJ to George Washington Campbell, Jan. 15, 1807, ibid., 147-150. J Marquis James, *The Life of Andrew Jackson* (Indianapolis: The Bobbs-Merrill Company, 193,), 128-129, fn. 30, 388-389. Silas Dinsmoor recounted the rumor in disbelief, Milton Lomask, *Aaron Burr, 1805-1836*, 218-219.
433. Milton Lomask, *Aaron Burr, 1805-1836*, 180-181. Joseph Wheelan speculates that Jefferson also may have feared that Burr's supporters might join with Federalists to become the dominant political party. Joseph Wheelan, *Jefferson's Vendetta*, 19.
434. PAJ 2: 124-125, n. Milton Lomask, *Aaron Burr, 1805-1836*, 180-181.
435. *Impartial Review*, January 3, 1807, 3.
436. PAJ 2: 124-125. To the Adams County Superior Court from John Coffee and AJ, March 25, 1813, ibid., 398-400. A. W. Putnam, *History of Middle Tennessee; or, Life and Times of Gen. James Robertson* (A. W. Putnam, Nashville, Tenn, 1859, Reprint Ed., Arno Press 1971), 579.

437. James Parton, The Life of Andrew Jackson, 102. Robert V. Remini, *Andrew Jackson and the Course of American Empire, 1767-1821* (New York: Harper & Row Publishers 1977), 153. John Overton, August 15, 1828, John Overton Papers, TSLA.
438. Account with Aaron Burr, PAJ 2: 113. The editors speculated that the payment related to a draft Anderson held; however, if the seventy-five men who accompanied Burr from Nashville were paid in advance with funds Burr had deposited with Jackson, that payment is the most-likely source.
439. Parton drew the conclusion that W. P. Anderson's brother Patton "was all in activity in raising a company of young men to accompany Burr down the river," James Parton, Life of Andrew Jackson, 99-100, but payments were made to W. P. ("Preston") Anderson. W. P. Anderson may have used his brother to recruit the soldiers. cf. Patricia Givens Johnson, "William P. Anderson and the 'May' Letters," *The Filson Club Historical Quarterly*, Vol 47 (April 1973), 171-178, 174. Ms. Johnson states that Patton Anderson accepted money from Burr. Payments were made to his brother William Preston Anderson.
440. "Journal of the Road Between Natchez and Nashville, By Sto. D. Hayes, June 20, 1807," Andrew Jackson Papers, LC. When Anderson's first wife died just prior to Lewis's death, he married the sister of Burr conspirator, General Adair, James Barnette Adair, *Adair History and Genealogy* (Los Angeles, 1924), 107. His home at the time of Lewis's death was in Jefferson, Rutherford County, TN and was called "Federal Bottom."
441. PAJ 2: 164-166, n, and cited by Wilkinson in James Wilkinson, *Burr's Conspiracy Exposed and General Wilkinson Vindicated*, 37.
442. David O. Stewart, *American Emperor*, 147.
443. Milton Lomask, *Aaron Burr, 1805-1836*, 195-196.
444. May Sue Anton, *New Madrid: A Mississippi River Town in History and Legend* (Southeast Missouri State University Press: 2009), 69. Milton Lomask, *Aaron Burr, 1805-1836*, 196.
445. John McKee to James Wilkinson, Jan. 25, 1807, John McKee Testimony, ASP, Misc., 593-595. McKee was interested in pursuing adventures in Spanish Territory, but he soundly rejected Burr's plot.
446. Ibid. Note that McKee said that a French Indian countryman was to have called on him to receive the letter for Wilkinson. McKee denied that he

was a Burrite, *Beginnings of West Tennessee: In the Land of the Chickasaw 1541-1841* (The Watauga Press, Johnson City, TN 1930), 71-73.
447. Evidence of Lt. Jackson, ASP, Misc. 1: 610-611, David O. Stewart, *American Emperor*, 185.
448. Dick Steward, *Frontier Swashbuckler*, 76.
449. Ibid., 77, citing Darby, John F., *Personal Recollections of Many Prominent People Whom I Have Known* (G. I. Jones and Col, St Louis: 1880), 87-89.
450. Wilkinson wrote to Jefferson that martial law should be imposed, Milton Lomask, *Aaron Burr: 1805-1836*, 172-173, and members of the New Orleans business community later wrote a memorial declaring Wilkinson's actions illegal, Hay and Werner, *The Admirable Trumpeter*, 258-265. Andrew Jackson accused Wilkinson of making "civil authority subservient to the military" in connection with his activities in New Orleans, Andrew Jackson to Henry Dearborn, March 17, 1807, PAJ 2: 155-159. It was virtual martial law, because it does not appear that the legislature gave his consent to make it official. It appeared to make no difference to Wilkinson whether it was official. He imposed military law. Joseph Wheelan, *Jefferson's Vendetta*, 164.
451. Hay and Werner, *The Admirable Trumpeter*, 262-266. Joseph Wheelan, *Jefferson's Vendetta*, 7-8.
452. James Wilkinson to TJ, July 16, 1808, FO.
453. David O. Stewart, *American Emperor*, 199, citing, James Wilkinson Testimony ASP, Misc., 545-46, John McKee *Testimony*, ASP, Misc, 593-594.
454. Milton Lomask, *Aaron Burr, 1805-1836*, 215.
455. James Wilkinson to Thomas Jefferson, July 16, 1808, FO.
456. John Graham Testimony, ASP, Misc, 528-532. Milton Lomask, *Aaron Burr, 1805-1836*, 219. Lomask mentions rumors in Natchez that Wilkinson had ordered gunboats be sent to capture Burr. Ibid. at 215.
457. Everett Somerville Brown, ed., *William Plumer's memorandum of proceedings in the United States Senate, 1803-1807* (The MacMillan Company: 1923), 616.
458. Milton Lomask, *Aaron Burr, 1805-1836*, 214.
459. Ibid., 220.
460. The agent was Nicholas Perkins. Joseph Wheelan, *Jefferson's Vendetta*, 3-5. Milton Lomask, *Aaron Burr, 1805-1836*, 220-224.
461. Winfield Scott, *Memoirs of Winfield Scott*, 16.

462. Joseph Wheelan, *Jefferson's Vendetta*, 254.
463. William Preston Anderson to Andrew Jackson, May 10, 1807, PAJ 2: 166-167. Anderson could not attend the trial.
464. Testimony before the Grand Jury in the Case of Aaron Burr, June 25, 1807, 2: 168-169. See also PAJ 2: 164-166, n.
465. Joseph Wheelan, *Jefferson's Vendetta*, 182, Marquis James, *Life of Andrew Jackson*, 138-139.
466. Henry Adams, *History of the United States of America During the First Term of Thomas Jefferson, 1801-1805* (The Library of America 1986), 918.
467. *The Franklin Repository*, Jan. 19, 1808, 3.
468. Series of letters printed in Freeman's *Journal and Daily Commercial Advertiser*, Feb, 18, 1808, 4.
469. Randolph to Nicholson, cited in Joseph Wheelan, *Jefferson's Vendetta*, 169, Timothy D. Johnson, *Winfield Scott: The Quest for Military Glory* (University of Kansas 1989), 10.
470. Milton Lomask, *Aaron Burr, 1805-1836*, 289.
471. ML to WC, March 13, 1807, MHS.
472. See, e.g., AJ to William Preston Anderson, June 16, 1807, PAJ 2: 167-168, AJ to Daniel Smith, Nov. 28, 1807, ibid., 174-177. William Oliver Allen to AJ, Jan. 10, 1810, ibid., 228-229.
473. The Wilmington Gazette, Jan. 27, 1807, 2.
474. *The National Intelligencer and Washington Advertiser*, Nov 14, 1806, 2.
475. *The Impartial Review and Cumberland Repository*, Feb 14, 1806, 2.
476. Shirley Christian, *Before Lewis and Clark*, 148. Everett Somerville Brown, ed., William Plumer's memorandum of proceedings in the United States Senate, 1803-1807 (The MacMillan Company: 1923), 554.
477. L. R. Colter-Frick, *Courageous Colter and Companions*, 220-221. Thomas James, *Three Years Among the Indians and Mexicans* (War Eagle: Waterloo: 1846, Republished 2017), 2.
478. Jefferson's Annual Message to Congress, Dec. 2, 1806, Donald Jackson, *Letters*, 352-353.
479. The Act Compensating Lewis and Clark, March 3, 1807, and Petition to the Senate and House, and "Messrs. Lewis & Clarke's Donation Lands," Donald Jackson, *Letters*, 377-378, 378-380, and 380-382, respectively. Lewis had requested that he and Clark receive equal grants of land because he considered Clark equal in rank as co-captain of the expedi-

tion though he held a lower rank. H. Dearborn to Willis Alston, Jan. 14, 1807, Donald Jackson, *Letters*, 363-364.
480. ML to Mahlon Dickerson, Nov. 3, 1807, Donald Jackson, *Letters*, 2: 719-720. The girl did not find the same attraction for Lewis and left town rather than to meet with him, ibid. 2: 721 n 2. Lewis discusses his passion for her in ML to William Preston, July 25, 1808, University of Virginia, Accession No. 9041. John Bakeless, *Lewis and Clark*, 384-385.
481. See, e.g., *Weekly Wanderer*, Jan 26, 1807, 2.
482. Donald Jackson, *Letters*, 554, n. 3, 5.
483. *The Evening Post*, Jan. 19, 1809, 3.
484. Richard Dillon, *Meriwether Lewis*, 283-284.
485. Elliott Coues, *The Expeditions of Zebulon Montgomery Pike*, I: cxiii. Coues's reference may have occurred later. Independence Hall was restored as part of the fiftieth-year celebration of the Declaration of Independence.
486. Charles Willson Peale to TJ, Jan. 29, 1808, Donald Jackson, *Letters*, 439-440.
487. For examples of Wilson's artistic prose, see, AW to David Brodie, Nov. 10, 1789, and AW to William Batram, March 31, 1804, AW, 128-130, and 209-212, respectively. The only record of the contact between Lewis and Wilson was Wilson's; however, Wilson obtained access to birds and sketched them for his book.
488. AW, 100.
489. An Act for the Government of Louisiana Territory, TP 13: 92. Frick, Ruth L. Colter, "Meriwether Lewis's Personal Finances: The governor of Upper Louisiana was land rich but cash poor when he left on his last, fateful journey," *We Proceeded On*, Vol. 28 No. 1 (February 2002): 16-20. For Lewis's appointment, see "Commission of Meriwether Lewis as Governor," TP 14: 107.
490. John Pernier or Peerny to TJ, Feb. 10, 1810, FO.
491. TJ to Samuel Smith, May 4, 1806, FO. Jefferson made the statement in defense of Wilkinson holding a civil position as governor while also serving as general. Jefferson noted that Congress had just approved Harrison holding both positions in the Indiana Territory, and that it had initially approved making the first office that of a commandant to blend military and civil authority.
492. The qualifications the War Department looked for in the first appointment of a commandant was a man of "military character of respectable standing," SW to Samuel Hammond, May 30, 1804, LS.

493. Frederick Bates to Richard Bates, May 31, 1807, FB 1: 135-138. Based on the description of Smith T's small junta, Bates is likely referring to groups of armed men rather than individual owners.
494. Example of an invitation. "Dr. Mitchell's Letters from Washington," Jan. 7, 1807, *Harper's Magazine* v. 58 1878-1879 Dec-May (New York: Brother and Brothers Publishers 1879), 750. Lewis noted a number of actions he took related to publication of his narrative from May to July 1807, Lewis Memorandum Book, MHS.
495. ML to TJ, June 27, 1807, Donald Jackson, *Letters*, 418.
496. Meriwether Lewis Personal Memorandum Book, notation of May 20, 1808, MHS.
497. Burr's first trial opened on August 3rd and the second concluded in mid-October. Joseph Wheelan, *Jefferson's Vendetta*, 190-247.
498. Clark apparently asked Wirt to look over his journals and make corrections, William D. Meriwether to WC, Jan. 22, 1810, Donald Jackson, *Letters*, 489-490.
499. Personal Memorandum Book of Meriwether Lewis. Entry of Oct. 8, 1807. The debt was owed to the estate of Thomas Bell, who was identified as a Justice of the Peace in Albermarle County, Virginia in 1797, Lewis Marks Papers, University of Virginia, Archives.
500. Given Lewis's understanding of his new job to root out Burrism in the West, the most logical reason Lewis would have attended Burr's trial is to determine what influence Burr had on people in power in the West.
501. Scott's list included participants in the trial. He also did not mention Washington Irving or Andrew Jackson, who was not yet a national celebrity, but who made his presence known in Richmond. Winfield Scott, *Memoirs of Winfield Scott*, 17.
502. The timing would have worked for Lewis to be in Richmond. Lewis did not note additional expenses related to publication of the book after July 1807. Burr's trial began on August 3rd. The first trial ended on Sept. 1, 1807, and the second on October 10. Lewis was back in Charlottesville by late October. He arrived in St. Louis on March 8, 1808. Allowing for travel time on winter roads and his stops in Kentucky in mid-February noted in his Memorandum Book, if Lewis was in Richmond for Burr's trial, his time is unaccounted for from November 1807 to mid-January 1808, some of which could have been weather-related. He could even

have used the time to transfer edits of his field notes to the formal red leather-bound journals. An alternate theory has been argued that Lewis simply was dilatory in taking charge of his western administration and negligent in publishing his book. There are no known letters from Jefferson expressing frustration in Lewis's failure to travel west sooner, and as stated later in the text, Lewis's letter to Clark stated his understanding that the Burr matters were paramount.

503. Robert J. Moore, Jr., "Lewis and Clark, Remaking the American West, 1808-1838," *We Proceeded On,* Vol 33, No. 2 (May 2007): 6-15.
504. William C. Carr to the Attorney General, Nov. 13, 1805, TP 13: 270-273.
505. Ibid.
506. Rufus Easton to the President, Dec. 1, 1806, TP 14: 43-47.
507. Joseph Brown to James Madison, Aug. 26, 1806, *The Territorial Papers of the United States,* compiled and edited by TP 14: 4-5. Wilkinson would face similar problems in New Orleans. W. C. C. Claiborne to Henry Dearborn Jan. 10, 1809, *Letter books of W. C. C. Claiborne,* 4: 288-289.
508. Frederick Bates to Augustus B. Wood, Feb. 23, 1808, FB, 1: 301-303.
509. ML to WC, March 13, 1807, MHS. Cf. Robert Frazer had been sent to Missouri to take out the Burrites in 1807 and had felt too threatened to take action. Robert Frazer to TJ, April 16, 1807, Donald Jackson, *Letters,* 2: 409-411.
510. William Clark's Commission as Indian Agent, March 7, 1807, *The Territorial Papers of the United States,* compiled and edited by TP 14: 109-110. Jefferson first recommended Clark's appointment of Lt. Col., but the Senate rejected the nomination because Clark would have been promoted over men with greater seniority. Donald Jackson, *Letters,* 376, n.
511. ML to WC, March 13, 1807, MHS. ML to WC, March 15, 1807, Donald Jackson, *Letters,* 387.
512. WC to ML, March 15, 1807, Donald Jackson, *Letters,* 387-388.
513. Jay Buckley in *William Clark: Indian Diplomat,* states that Lewis quickly moved to take quarters with the Chouteau family, 69.
514. Historians have often used one of Jefferson's spellings, "John Pernier," for the servant's name. Peerny spelled his own name "Jeau Peerny" on the two writings that have been found bearing his signature: Lewis's Last Will and Testament and Peerny's letter to TJ requesting money for his services to Lewis (John Pernier to TJ, Feb. 10, 1810, FO, NARA. Original source:

*The Papers of Thomas Jefferson*, Retirement Series, vol. 2, *16 November 1809 to 11 August 1810*, ed. J. Jefferson Looney (Princeton: Princeton University Press, 2005), 208-209. The signatures on both documents match. The letter to TJ purports to be signed by Peerny, and Peerny was known to have accompanied Lewis on the trip when he signed his Last Will and Testament, and Peerny's name was signed as a witness. Unless a mysterious third person was present to sign Peerny's name to both Lewis's Will on the Mississippi and Peerny's letter later in Baltimore, the signature was Peerny's. Lewis generally spelled the name "John" "Perna," "Pernia," or "Pearny." Lewis's original Last Will and Testament is stored in the Virginia State Library (See copy on page 192). A transcribed copy from the Albermarle Court sent to the Missouri Historical Society years ago interpreted the handwriting of Peerny's name as "Geau Peaeny" and that is spelling most historians have cited as one of the two witnesses to Lewis's Will. Transcribed Copy of Meriwether Lewis Last Will and Testament, Meriwether Lewis Collection, MHS. With thanks to Dr. Jessica Dunn for research and insight into the fact of differences in how children in France and children in other parts of the world were taught to draw the same letters.

515. Commission of Frederick Bates as Secretary, Feb. 4, 1807, *The Territorial Papers of the United States*, compiled and edited by TP 14: 117-118.

516. Frederick Bates's father had wanted one of his sons to become Jefferson's personal secretary, the position that Lewis was given. L. R. Colter-Frick, *Courageous Colter and Companions,* 360.

517. L. R. Colter-Frick, *Courageous Colter and Companions*, 360-361, quoting Bates's letter that Jefferson's policies would relegate them to live as farmers.

518. L. R. Colter-Frick, *Courageous Colter and Companions,* 377. Further evidence of Bates's ambition is that he successfully ran for Missouri governor in 1824.

519. Dick Steward, *Frontier Swashbuckler*, 33. For comparison, the new Illinois territorial governor in 1809 also found his territory "divided." Governor Edwards to James Gilbreath, June 28, 1809, *The Territorial Papers of the United States*, compiled and edited by TP 16: 47-48. Some divisions in St. Louis were certainly from local politics, but there were distinct factions based upon culture. For an analysis of the chasm, see, "Enclosure: Confidential Communication on Louisiana District, 17 January 1805," *Founders Online*, National Archives, Original source: *The Papers of Thomas Jef-*

*ferson*, vol. 45, *11 November 1804 to 8 March 1805*, ed. James P. McClure et al. (Princeton: Princeton University Press, 2021), 348-353.
520. Dick Steward, *Frontier Swashbuckler*, 33.
521. Judge Lucas to the Secretary of the Treasury, Nov. 19, 1805, TP aTP 13: 286-289.
522. L. R. Colter-Frick, *Courageous Colter and Companions*, 362, 390. Commission of Auguste Chouteau, Jr., FB, 1: 157-158. Frederick Bates to Auguste Chouteau, Aug. 20, 1807, FB 1: 174.
523. Shirley Christian, *Before Lewis and Clark*, 103.
524. Frederick Bates to ML, April 5, 1807, FB, 98-100. For a different view, the editor of *The Life and Papers of Frederick Bates* accepted Bates's evaluation of his own popularity and suggested that a suspicious Lewis was to blame for their conflicts, FB, 1: 30.
525. Frederick Bates to Augustus B. Wood, Feb. 23, 1808, FB 1: 301-303.
526. Richard Dillon, *Meriwether Lewis*, 276.
527. [David McKeehan] to ML, April 7, 1807, Donald Jackson, *Letters*, 399-407. The editor also warned that Lewis would be able to take commercial advantage of his political position with land warrants Congress awarded him. The warning should have made Lewis cautious about taking greater risks with the Mandan Expedition.
528. See, e.g., Frederick Bates to ML, April 5, 1807. FB 1: 98-11, 1: 100-102, April 28, 1807, 1: 102-109, May 15, 1807, 1: 114-119, Nov. 7, 1807, 1: 228-233, Jan. 16, 1808, 1: 264-266.
529. Frederick Bates to Joseph Charless, Mar. 12, 1808, Donald Jackson, *Letters*, 440-441. FB 1: 309-310.
530. Frederick Bates to Robert Dickson, March 9. 1808 and March 20, 1808, FB 1: 307-308, 312-314.
531. Meriwether Lewis to Majr. William Preston, July 25, 1808, Transcribed copy in Accession No. 9041, University of Virginia Library.
532. ML to Mahlon Dickerson, Nov. 3, 1807, Donald Jackson, *Letters* (Chicago: University of Illinois Press, 1978), 2: 719-720.
533. Jon Kukla, *A Wilderness So Immense*, 310.
534. Ibid., 310-313, citing TJ to De Witt Clinton, Dec. 2, 1803, FO. National Archives. Original source: *The Papers of Thomas Jefferson*, vol. 42, *16 November 1803—10 March 1804*, ed. James P. McClure (Princeton: Princeton University Press, 2016), 70-71.

535. Frederick Bates to SW, May 30, 1807, FB 1: 132-123, and transcribed in L. R. Colter-Frick, *Courageous Colter and Companions*, 362.
536. Frederick Bates to Richard Bates, 15 April 1809, and FB 2: 67-73. L. R. Colter-Frick, *Courageous Colter and Companions*, 366.
537. Frederick Bates to James Madison, April 1, 1808, FB 1: 319-333.
538. Extract of a Letter to Richard Bates, April 15, 1809, FB 2: 64, L. R. Colter-Frick, *Courageous Colter and Companions*, 365-366.
539. Dick Steward, *Frontier Swashbuckler*, 33-34. For explanations, see *Bissell v. Penrose*, 49 U.S. 317 (1850) and *Stoddard v. Chambers*, 43 U.S. 284 (1844).
540. The Spanish government governed citizens through decisions from local governors based upon principles of equity rather than the complex Spanish legal code, which the new American government saw as a government of men rather than law." Stuart Banner, "Written Law and Unwritten Norms in Colonial St. Louis," *Law and History Review*, Vol. 14, No. 1 (Spring, 1996): 33-80.
541. Shirley Christian, *Before Lewis and Clark*, 122-123. See, e.g., *Bissell v. Penrose*, 49 U.S. 317 (1850).
542. Dick Steward, *Frontier Swashbuckler*, 68-69.
543. Ibid. They were a hardy breed that valued their independence. More than a few were running from debts or prosecution back home. That segment in the territory was willing to gamble on dangerous risks, even if violence would be required to improve their chances. Joseph Browne to Secretary of State, Aug. 26, 1806, TP 14: 3-5.
544. Dick Steward, *Frontier Swashbuckler*, 6. It mattered little to Wilkinson when he tried to destroy Smith T's settlement, Smithland, a few years earlier, but by 1808, the two put their differences aside for their mutual interests.
545. Rufus Easton to the President, Dec. 1, 1806, TP 14: 43-47. Dick Steward, *Frontier Swashbuckler*, 6-7. Smith T.'s grandfather married a Wilkinson named "Lucy." Smith T's grandmother was his grandfather's second wife. For more information on conflicts arising from Smith T's claims and Seth Hunt, see JW to SW, Sept. 8, 1806, LR, and enclosures, TP 13: 196-204. See also Dick Steward, *Frontier Swashbuckler*, 33, regarding General Wilkinson's relationship with Smith T in St. Louis.
546. John F. Darby, *Personal Recollections of John F. Darby*, 88.
547. ML to WC, March 15, 1807, Donald Jackson, *Letters*, 387, n 1.

548. Robert Frazer to TJ, April 16, 1807, Donald Jackson, *Letters*, 409-410.
549. Ibid. Frazer was to provide testimony against Robert Wescott.
550. ML to WC, March 15, 1807, Donald Jackson, *Letters*, 387. Wilkinson had even appointed Smith T to the St. Genevieve Court of Common Pleas. List of Appointments and Removals, April 1, 1807-March 31, 1808, FB 1: I320-333.
551. See Editorial in the *Missouri Gazette*, March 1, 1809, 1-2. TP 14: 252-256. Representation to Congress by Committee of Inhabitants, Oct. 10, 1809, Carter, *Territorial Papers*, 14: 323-327.
552. Meriwether Lewis under the name "Clatsop," "Observations and reflections on the subject of governing and maintaining a state of friendly intercourse with the Indians of the Territory of Louisiana No. 1," *Missouri Gazette and Public Advertiser*, Aug. 2, 1808, 2-3.
553. Dick Steward, *Frontier Swashbuckler*, 35.
554. ML to SW, July 1, 1808, TP 13: 196-203, and SW to ML, July 8, 1808, TP 14: 204.
555. Richard Dillon, *Meriwether Lewis*, 293.
556. Rudolph Tillier to the Secretary of State, Jan. 12, 1807, TP 14: 78. Sometimes spelled "Fort Belle Fontaine," but "Bellefontaine" is common in the early writings. Tillier was appointed May 24, 1805, SW to R. Tillier, May 24, 1805, TP 13: 132.
557. Richard Dillon, *Meriwether Lewis*, 291.
558. ML to SW, Aug. 20, 1809, TP 14: 212-219.
559. Nicholas Boilvin to WC, 21 April 1808, TP 14: 272-273. Charles T. Jones, Jr., 103, citing Frederick Bates to Henry Dearborn, Oct. 22, 1807, FB 1: 221-223.
560. Richard Dillon, *Meriwether Lewis*, 306.
561. Ibid., 294.
562. SW to WC, Aug. 7, 1809, TP 14: 289-290. The Secretary of War criticized Clark for hiring subagents and denied some of his requests for reimbursements.
563. William Clark to Secretary of War, Aug. 18, 1808, TP 14: 207-210.
564. Secretary of War Dearborn ordered the building a fort for the Osage, which Clark built as Fort Osage. L. R. Colter-Frick, *Courageous Colter and Companions*, 415-417.
565. Pierre Chouteau, Jr. to SW, Sept. 1, 1809, TP 14: 312-319.

566. Editorial signed by ML as "Clatsop," *Missouri Gazette and Public Advertiser*, Aug 2, 1808, 3.
567. Deveney Reber and Jay H. Buckley, "Forgotten Brother Reuben Lewis: Missouri River Fur Trader and Indian Agent for the Arkansas Cherokee," *We Proceeded On*, Vol. 49 No. 1 (February 2023): 20-50, 25.
568. *Missouri Gazette and Public Advertiser*, Aug 2, 1808, 2. ML to SW, July 1, 1808, TP 13: 196-203.
569. Jon Kukla, *A Wilderness So Immense*, 302.
570. ML to SW, Aug. 20, 1808, TP 14: 212-226.
571. ML to SW, July 1, 1808, TP 13: 196-203.
572. WC to SW, Feb. 20, 1810, transcribed in L. R. Colter-Frick, *Courageous Colter and Companions*, 433-438.
573. Pierre Chouteau, Jr. to SW, Sept. 1, 1809, Carter, 14: 312-319.
574. The President to Governor Lewis, Aug. 24, 1808, TP 14: 219-221.
575. Richard Dillon, *Meriwether Lewis*, 306, 316.
576. SW to ML, July 2, 1808, TP 14: 204. WAR. Richard Dillon, *Lewis and Clark*, 311. Dillon suggested that Jefferson also wanted Lewis to take a less aggressive approach, but he drew that conclusion from Jefferson's approach to another situation.
577. *Missouri Gazette and Public Advertiser*, Aug 2, 1808, 2-3. "Clatsop" was the name of the Corps of Discovery's winter fort at the Pacific Ocean.
578. Rodolph Tillier to James Madison, April 27, 1809, enclosed in a letter from Rodolphe Tillier to John Mason, June 9, 1809, The Papers of James Madison Digital Edition, J. C. A. Stagg, editor (Charlottesville: University of Virginia Press, Rotunda, 2010.)
579. Josiah Granville Leach, *History of the Penrose family of Philadelphia, 1842-1922* (Philadelphia: Drexel, Biddle Publisher, 1903), 50; Wilkinson's wife Anne Biddle was sister to Sarah Biddle who married Rodolphe Tillier as her third husband, TJ to Francis Hopkinson, May 8, 1788, n, FO, National Archives. Original source: *The Papers of Thomas Jefferson*, vol. 13, *March—7 October 1788*, ed. Julian P. Boyd (Princeton: Princeton University Press, 1956), 144-146. Tillier also worked as the administrator for a failed speculative village for emigres from the French Revolution. Alexander Hamilton had represented him as an attorney in the venture. Rodolphe Tillier, *Rodolphe Tillier, Translation of a memo-*

rial of Rodolphe Tillier's justification on the administration of Castorland, county of Oneida, state of New York (Rome: Thomas Walker, 1800).

580. Josiah Granville Leach, *History of the Penrose family of Philadelphia, 1842-1922* (Philadelphia: Drexel, Biddle Publisher, 1903), 66-68.

581. John Mason to ML, May 17, 1809, TP 14: 274-276. For Sibley's appointment as assistant factor, see, SW to George Sibley, Aug. 17, 1805, TP 13: 187-188. For Tillier's appointment, see SW to Rudolph Tillier, May 25, 1805, TP 13: 131-132.

582. Charles T. Jones, Jr., "George Champlin Sibley: The Prairie Puritan," 33-36.

583. James House to Frederick Bates, Oct. 1807, FB 1: 224-225.

584. Charles T. Jones, Jr., "George Champlin Sibley: The Prairie Puritan," 37-42.

585. John Mason to Rudolph Tillier, May 27, 1809, TP 13: 185.

586. John Mason to WC, Dec. 31, 1808, TP 14: 247-248.

587. Charles T. Jones, Jr., "George Champlin Sibley: The Prairie Puritan," 65, 128.

588. Richard Dillon surmised that Wilkinson voluntarily left the post in 1806 because he grew frustrated with the impossibility of governing the opposing factions, Richard Dillon, *Lewis and Clark*, 288-289. The Secretary of War had ordered Wilkinson to his post at Fort Adams in July 1807. Wilkinson did not leave St. Louis until August. Though Dr. Browne assumed the role of Acting Secretary in his absence, Wilkinson received the salary as governor until March 2, 1806, the day of Lewis's appointment. TP 14: 3-5, 107, n. Wilkinson's appointment was a recess appointment. His term began on July 3, 1805, and he was to serve until the next session of the Senate.

589. Cornelius Burns Taylor Advertisement, *Missouri Gazette*, Nov. 2, 1809, 3.

590. Charles T. Jones, Jr., "George Champlin Sibley: The Prairie Puritan," 74.

591. John B. Lucas to Secretary of the Treasury, Feb. 13, 1806, *Territorial Papers*, 13: 444-447. Edward Hempstead later would serve as the administrator of Lewis's decedent estate in St. Louis.

592. JW to Samuel Smith, TP 13: 521-522.

593. J. Rankin to Seth Hunt, Dec. 14, 1803, printed in *The American Republic*, Oct. 25, 1806, 3.

594. Secretary of War Dearborn stated he that considered Hunt an honest but imprudent man. SW to JW, Oct. 16, 1805, TP 13: 240-241.
595. See, e.g., Bill of Exchange dated Oct. 1806, enclosed in letter from ML to Henry Dearborn, Oct. 12, 1806, Donald Jackson, *Letters*, 348-350, n. 14.
596. James Cox, *Old and New in St. Louis* (St. Louis: Central Biographical Publishing Co. 1901), 12.
597. Frederic L. Billion, *Annals of St. Louis In Its Territorial Days, 1804-1821* (St. Louis 1888) accessed through MHM online, 109. Another business was selling dry goods, some of which were supplied to federal factories or stores. L. R. Colter-Frick, *Courageous Colter and Companions*, 430.
598. Howard W. Cox, *American Traitor*, 89, 94, 96. Russell F. Weigley, *History of the United States Army*, 113.
599. Quoted in letter from Matthew Nimmo to TJ, Jan. 23, 1807, FO. Smith had been accused of supporting Burr.
600. Nathanial Pryor to WC, Oct. 16, 1807, Donald Jackson, *Letters*, 432-438. SW to WC, March 9, 1807, TP 14: 108-109, and WC to SW, May 18, 1807, TP 14: 122-125.
601. Cf. Shirley Christian states that the idea to allow a private company to support the mission was Secretary of War Dearborn's. Shirley Christian, *Before Lewis and Clark*, 145.
602. Secretary of War Dearborn directed Clark to prepare to return the Mandan chief to his village as soon as he arrived in St. Louis in 1807, Henry Dearborn to WC, March 9, 1807, Donald Jackson, *Letters*, 382-383. The first attempt was unsuccessful when the party was attacked due to conflicts among the tribes, Nathaniel Pryor to WC, Oct. 16, 1807, Donald Jackson, *Letters*, 432-438.
603. TJ to ML, July 17, 1808, Donald Jackson, *Letters*, 444-445. Mail service to St. Louis was frequently interrupted. The town did not receive mail service for nine weeks in winter 1808, and at times in 1809, the post rider lost the mail entirely, *Missouri Gazette and Public Advertiser*, Sept. 13, 1809, 3.
604. Thomas James provided an account, Gen. Thomas James, *Three Years Among the Indians and Mexicans* (Waterloo, Ill.: War Eagle 1846), Also described in L. R. Colter-Fricke, Courageous Colter and Companions, 220-225. Jefferson biographer Dumas Malone discussed the "embarrass-

ing cost" Lewis paid in following Jefferson's directions to return Sheheke in Dumas Malone, *Jefferson the President: Second Term,* 1805-1809 (Boston: Little, Brown and Company 1974), 210-211.
605. Jay Buckley gave Lisa credit for organizing the company, Jay H. Buckley, "William Clark, the Fur Trade, and Indian Affairs," *We Proceeded On,* Vol. 46, No. 4 (November 2020): 14-30, 18.
606. Shirley Christian, *Before Lewis and Clark,* 164-165.
607. Jay H. Buckley, "William Clark, the Fur Trade, and Indian Affairs," 18.
608. Ben, for example, traveled to Kentucky to recruit volunteers, *The Natchez Weekly Democrat,* Jun. 10, 1809, 2.
609. Shirley Christian, *Before Lewis and Clark,* 165.
610. Cf. James J. Holmberg casts doubt on whether Fitzhugh owned a share based upon Clark's letter dated May 28, 1809, James J. Holmberg, 198, n. 4.
611. ML to TJ, Sept. 23, 1806, Donald Jackson, *Letters,* 319-325.
612. Ibid. Discussed in Richard Dillon, *Lewis and Clark,* 260-261.
613. Jay H. Buckley, *William Clark: Indian Diplomat,* 79-80.
614. L. R. Colter-Frick, *Courageous Colter and Companions,* 220-221, Thomas James, *Three Years Among the Indians and Mexicans,* 3.
615. Richard H. Dillon, "Meriwether Lewis, Manuel Lisa, and the Tantalizing Santa Fe Trade," *Montana The Magazine of Western History,* Vol. 17, No. 2 (Spring, 1967): 46-52, 50.
616. Chouteau returned to St. Louis on May 10, 1810, *Missouri Gazette and Public Advertiser,* May 10, 1810, 3. Ben wrote Lewis from St. Louis on Sept. 1, 1809, Ben Wilkinson to ML, Sept. 1, 1809, Identifier: A0289-01392MHS.
617. Agreement for Return of the Mandan Chief, February 24, 1809, Donald Jackson, *Letters,* 446-450. Secretary of War Dearborn directed Clark to prepare to return the Mandan chief to his village as soon as he arrived in St. Louis in 1807, Henry Dearborn to WC, March 9, 1807, Donald Jackson, *Letters,* 382-383. The official articles for the company were signed on March 3, 1809, after the authorization of funds. John C. Jackson, "Reuben Lewis: Fur Trader, Subagent, and Meriwether's Younger Brother," *We Proceeded On,* Vol. 38 No. 4 (November 2012): 8-17, 9.
618. Jay H. Buckley, "William Clark, the Fur Trade, and Indian Affairs," 14-30, 18.

619. William Carr to Charles Carr, Aug. 25, 1809, MHS, transcribed in L. R. Colter-Frick, *Courageous Colter and Companions*, 320-323. Carr did not specify how Lewis was imprudent, but the following line related to his expenditures that the War Department refused to reimburse. Carr attempted to interest his brother in purchasing land that Lewis had purchased. He noted that the land would be a good investment, and he must have acknowledged Lewis's savvy in selecting the land. It is possible that he thought Lewis had overextended himself in purchasing the land in reliance on government reimbursements, but the most apparent scandal at the time seemed to be Lewis's agreement with The St. Louis Missouri Fur Company for the Mandan Expedition.

620. *National Intelligencer*, May 3, 1809, 3.

621. See e.g. *The United States Gazette*, June 1, 1809, 1; *Virginia Argus*, May 9, 1809, 3; *Weekly Raleigh Register*, Sept. 7, 1809, 3.

622. *The Democratic Clarion*, Sept. 8, 1809, 2, reported "140 and upwards." Thomas James, said that the numbers were roughly equal between Americans and others (Thomas James, *Three Years Among the Indians and Mexicans*, 20), but if the newspaper accounts were correct, there would have been more participants who were not from Kentucky.

623. Secretary of War to ML, July 15, 1809, TP 14: 285-286.

624. ML to Henry Dearborn, March 7, 1807, Donald Jackson, *Letters*, 450-451. ML to William Eustis, May 13, 1809, Donald Jackson, *Letters*, 451.

625. Wm. Christy deposition, March 9, 1811, transcribed in L. R. Colter-Frick, *Courageous Colter and Companions*, 382. Governor Lewis appointed Christy to command the "Louisiana Spies," *Edenton Gazette*, June 2, 1809, 1. He also purchased furniture that Christy made for the troops in the sum of $1,488.76, Meriwether Lewis Memorandum Book.

626. Evidence of Major James Bruff, ASP, Misc 1: 572-577.

627. Ira Nash to TJ, Oct. 3, 1807, FO. Ira P. Nash to TJ, Oct. 7, 1807, and November 8, 1807, University of Virginia, Founders Early Access Online, Walter Williams, ed., *History of Northeast Missouri*, Vol 1 (Chicago: The Lewis Publishing Co. 1913), 262-265. Nash, later a Deputy U.S. Surveyor, was a founder of the settlement of Nashville on the Missouri, Switzer's *History of Missouri, From 1541 to 1877* (St. Louis: C. R. Barnes, 1879), 177.

628. Wm. Christy deposition, March 9, 1811, transcribed in L. R. Colter-Frick, *Courageous Colter and Companions*, 382. Jeffrey Einboden, in "On Thomas

Jefferson and the Little-Known Presence of Enslaved Muslims in the U.S.," July 15, 2020, *Literary Hub*, states that the people held as spies were Africans who wrote in Arabic and who were being held as runaway slaves.

629. Zebulon Pike to SW, July 15, 1807, printed in Elliott Coues, *The Expeditions of Zebulon Montgomery Pike* 1: 1-11. Hay and Werner, *Admirable Trumpeter*, 226.

630. John Sibley, Penny S. Brandt, "A Letter of Dr. John Sibley, Indian Agent," *Louisiana History: The Journal of the Louisiana Historical Association*, Vol. 29, No. 4 (Autumn, 1988): 365-387, 385, n 29.

631. Pike's story confirmed an 1808 account of silver mines Jefferson received from an Anthony Bettay. Jay H. Buckley, "Exploring the Louisiana Purchase and Its Borderlands," Part One, 19.

632. Pike was in St. Louis in August 1808. Zebulon Pike to SW, Aug. 18, 1808, Elliott Coues, *Memoirs of Zebulon Pike*, lxii. John Sibley, Penny S. Brandt, "A Letter of Dr. John Sibley, Indian Agent," 365-387, 385, n 29.

633. Lewis Personal Memorandum Book, June 1808, MHS, also noted by Colter-Frick in L. R. Frick, *Courageous Colter*, 319. See also Z. M. Pike at Fort Bellefontaine to SW, Aug. 18, 1808, ibid. The secretary of war authorized the payment of horses Pike and Wilkinson's son purchased from the Osage in 1807, SW to Peter Chouteau, Aug. 18, 1807, LS.

634. W. C. C. Claiborne to Robert Smith, March 19, 1809, *Letter books of W. C. C. Claiborne*, 4: 332-334. Wilkinson received the same intelligence.

635. W. C. C. Claiborne to Robert Smith, April 21, 1809, *Letter books of W. C. C. Claiborne*, 4: 342-344. Wilkinson received the same intelligence, William S. Belko, "The Origins of the Monroe Doctrine Revisited: The Madison Administration, the West Florida Revolt, and the No Transfer Policy," *The Florida Historical Quarterly*, Vol. 90, No. 2 (Fall 2011), 157-192, 159.

636. W. C. C. Claiborne to Robert Smith, Nov. 5, 1809, Dunbar Rowland, *Letter Books of W. C. C. Claiborne*, 4: 419-423.

637. Shirley Christian, *Before Lewis and Clark*, 166. Reuben had still not heard about his brother's death in April 1810, when he wrote a letter to him to provide an update on the progress of the fur hunters. Reuben Lewis to ML, April 21, 1820, MHS, Identifier: D02485.

638. L. R. Colter-Frick, *Courageous Colter and Companions*, 225-228. Thomas James, *Three Years Among the Indians and Mexicans*, 6, 17-18, 65-66. James did not blame "Capt. Lewis," Reuben Lewis, for his treatment.

James eventually would join an expedition to Santa Fe in 1821. George Sibley wrote that 40 men had deserted by July, Charles T. Jones, Jr., "George Champlin Sibley: The Prairie Puritan," 83.

639. TJ to James Madison, April 27, 1809, FO.
640. Charles M. Harvey, "The Story of the Santa Fe Trail" *The Atlantic,* December 1909, Atlantic Magazine Archive. The author claims that Smith, Patterson, and McLanahan were the first party that attempted to create the trade route. I credit the late Kira Gale with first suggesting to me that the Smith, Patterson, and McLanahan expedition would have been one of the significant events in play at the time of Lewis's death and for her translations of letters included in Wilkinson's letter to the Secretary of War. In her book, *Fifty Documents Related to the Assassination of Meriwether Lewis,* Kira suggested that keeping the expedition secret was a motive for someone to assassinate Lewis.
641. The portion of Maury County where the Patteson or Patterson (see note below) family lived was later sectioned off as Giles County. James and his father Nelson Patterson became involved in the Texas Association that pushed for Texas independence (McClean, *Papers Concerning Robertson's Colony in Texas,* 1: xliii). Nelson served as Secretary. For more on Nelson Patteson, see Nelson Patteson to TJ, 30 May 1820," *Founders Online,* National Archives, Original source: *The Papers of Thomas Jefferson,* Retirement Series, vol. 15, *1 September 1819 to 31 May 1820,* ed. J. Jefferson Looney (Princeton: Princeton University Press, 2018), pp. 619-621. McClean, *Papers Concerning Robertson's Colony in Texas,* 1: xxxix, 1: xliii, 1: 76-83, Texas Historical Association, James later served in John Gordon's Company of Spies under Andrew Jackson in the War of 1812. In addition, a McLanahan family lived nearer Grinder's Stand in Maury County, but I did not find a family connection.
642. Ibid., Nelson Patteson to TJ, May 30, 1820, n, FO. Like the distinction between the spellings of "Grinder" and "Griner" for the innkeepers, the "Patterson" name was said to be "Patteson," but even the Nashville newspapers published the same advertisement with different spellings, The *Clarion* and *Tennessee Gazette,* Apr 20, 1813, 6, and *National Banner* and *Nashville Whig,* Apr 28, 1813, 4. The family eventually seemed to have agreed on "Patterson" but the cemetery memorial stone for James spells the name "Patteson."

643. See James Monroe to Gov. Howard, Sept. 3, 1812, *Papers Relating to the Foreign Relations of the United States, Transmitted to Congress with the Annual Message of the President*, December 2, 1872, Part 2, Vol. 1. James Patterson apparently related his story to James M'Callum, "Brief Sketch of the Settlement and Early History of Giles County, Tennessee," *The American Historical Magazine*, Vol. 2, No. 4 (Oct. 1897), 303-323. When the party was released, they joined the Gutierrez-Magee Expedition against their former captor Spanish governor Salcedo. See Harris Gaylord Warren, *The Sword Was Their Passport: A History of American Filibustering in the Mexican Revolution* (Port Washington, New York: Kennikat Press, 1943), 24-25. O. P. Patterson (James Patterson's great-grandson) to unnamed newspaper, March 3, 1938, in looseleaf "Patterson" file with Giles County Historical Society, Pulaski, Tennessee. Patterson claimed that he went to Missouri in early 1809 to search out the lead mines. He later moved back to Giles County (formerly the Maury County portion) Tennessee and opened a hotel.
644. James McCallum, *Brief Sketch of the Settlement and Early History of Giles County, Tennessee* (Pulaski, Tenn.: The Pulaski Citizen, 1923), 24-26. Giles County split off from Maury County in November 1809. Nelson Patterson, later applied to be a suttler for General Andrew Jackson (Nelson Patteson to Thomas Jefferson, May 30, 1820, n. FO. National Archives. Original source: *The Papers of Thomas Jefferson, Retirement Series*, vol. 15, *1 September 1819 to 31 May 1820*, ed. J. Jefferson Looney (Princeton: Princeton University Press, 2018), 619-621.
645. ML to Major William Preston, July 24, 1808, James R. Bentley, ed., "Two Letters of Meriwether Lewis to Major William Preston," *The Filson Club Historical Quarterly*, V. 44, 170-175, 173.
646. L. R. Colter-Frick pointed this fact out at page 307, *Courageous Colter and Companions*. See also Section 3, of the 1787 Northwest Ordinance. NARA.
647. ML to Lucy Marks, Dec. 1, 1808, MHS. L. R. Colter-Frick, *Courageous Colter and Companions*, 309-314. ML to William Preston July 25, 1808, University of Virginia Archives, Accession No. 9041.
648. *Missouri Gazette and Public Advertiser*, Aug. 16, 1810, 3. Lewis's Missouri estate administrator sold 20 head of cattle after his death.
649. Will C. Carr to Charles Carr, Aug. 25, 1809, MHS.

650. Jefferson ended his presidency with about $10,000 in personal debt. Dumas Malone, *Jefferson the President, Second Term 1805-1809* (New York: Little, Brown & Company, 1974), 666.
651. Editorial in the *Missouri Gazette*, March 1, 1809, 1-2. TP 14: 252-256.
652. Frederick Bates to Albert Gallatin, July 16, 1809, FB 2: 73-74.
653. Capt. Amos Stoddard to Mrs. Beham, June 16, 1804, Robert A. Stoddard, *The Autobiography Manuscript of Major Amos Stoddard*, 58-59, original at Missouri Historical Museum. His experience was consistent with the experience of New Orleans Territorial Governor Claiborne who found that expenses for alcohol and cigars for entertainment during the transfer from Spain in 1803 put him in debt, Governor Claiborne to the Secretary of State, June 21, 1809, TP 9: 846-848. Shirley Christian wrote that the bill was for the dinner celebrating the transfer of the Upper St. Louis territory to the U.S., Shirley Christian, *Before Lewis and Clark*, 17.
654. Frederick Bates to Gabriel Duval, Aug. 13, 1808, FB 2: 11.
655. David J. Peck and Marti E. Peck, *"So Hard to Die": A Physician and a Psychologist Explore the Mystery of Meriwether Lewis's Death* (The Marti and David Peck Family Trust of 1992: 2021), 115-116. Drs. Peck surmised that Lewis could have used a portion of his large purchase of alcohol for his personal consumption.
656. ML to William Eustis, Aug. 18, 1809, Donald Jackson, *Letters*, 459-461.
657. ML entry of Nov. 9, 1808, Meriwether Lewis Memorandum Book, MHS.
658. J. W. M. Breazeale, *Life As It Is* (Knoxville, 1842, Reproduced by Charles Elder), 240.
659. William Simmons to ML, April 15, 1807, Donald Jackson, *Letters*, 408-409. Howard W. Cox suggests that one reason Lewis remained in the East through 1807 was to attempt to settle his reimbursements with Simmons, Howard W. Cox, *American Traitor*, 207.
660. *John Colter v. Estate of Meriwether Lewis, Ded'd*, as transcribed in L. L. R. Colter-Frick, Courageous Colter and Companions, 69-71. See also John Colter's Receipt to Edward Hempstead, Donald Jackson, *Letters*, 567, n. It was common for the War Department to send payment for a company of troops to their captain to see to payment of troops under the captain's command. Lewis paid Clark $6,896.34 to distribute the Corps' salaries except for Colter and John Ordway. Clark, in return, was to obtain receipts from the men and forward to Lewis or to the War Department

(Clark's Receipt to Lewis, March 10, 1807, Donald Jackson, *Letters*, 384.) Colter's extra pay amounted to $179.33, The Act Compensating Lewis and Clark, Donald Jackson, *Letters*, 377-378, n. Colter was paid $377.60, a portion of the amount claimed, on May 28, 1811, after obtaining a judgment against Lewis's estate. L. R. Colter-Frick, *Courageous Colter and Companions*, 123-125, also *Colter, John vs. Hempstead, Edward, Admin*, 1810, Saint Louis, Court of Common Pleas Case Number 38 Folder 009, Missouri Digital Heritage, accessed online. It was the same year the War Department determined that Simmons' contest of payments to Lewis had been unjustified and paid Lewis's estate the amount Lewis was due for reimbursement.

661. Several of the loans are listed in Vardis Fisher, *Suicide or Murder? The Strange Death of Governor Meriwether Lewis* (Athens, Ohio: Ohio University Press), 1962, 64.
662. John Pernier or Peerny to TJ, Feb. 10, 1810, FO. The amount was based upon Peerny's claim. See also TJ to James Madison Nov. 26, 1809, Donald Jackson, *Letters*, 475-476. Lewis Memorandum Book reflects two payments to Peerny, entries, Jan. 1, 1809, and March 6, 1809 "on account," MHS.
663. Frederick Bates to Richard Bates, Nov. 9, 1809, FB 2: 108-112.
664. Frederick Bates to Richard Bates, July 14, 1809. FB 2: 67-73.
665. WC to Jonathan Clark, July 16, 1810, James J. Holmberg, *Dear Brother*, 248-251.
666. His stepson was Clement Penrose. Frederick Bates to Richard Bates, Nov. 9, 1809, FB 2: 108-112. For a background on Penrose, see James J. Holmberg, *Dear Brother*, 200, n 8.
667. Frederick Bates to Richard Bates, Nov. 9, 1809, FB 2: 108-112.
668. Clark also served as Lewis's principal Indian agent for all tribes west of the Mississippi other than the Osage, Jay H. Buckley, *William Clark: Indian Diplomat* (Norman: University of Oklahoma Press, 2008). Bates may have exaggerated Lewis's snubs, or perhaps he and Clark determined that they could not make Bates aware of their actions.
669. Frederick Bates to Richard Bates, Nov. 9, 1809, Frederick Bates, *Life and Letters*, 2: 108-112.
670. Ray V. Denslow, *Territorial Masonry: The Story of Freemasonry and the Louisiana Purchase, 1804-1821* (The Masonic Service of the United States: Washington, D. C. 1925), 17, 40-41, 170-174, including letters,

James Milnor to Br. G. A. Baker, Sept. 10, 1808, and Otho Shrader to James Milnor, Nov. 8, 1808, 176.
671. Ibid., 170-188.
672. Ibid., 182-183.
673. The history is set out in Ray V. Denslow, *Territorial Masonry: The Story of Freemasonry and the Louisiana Purchase, 1804-1821*, ibid. Also, conversations with officers of St. Louis Masonic lodge in 2009.
674. Frederick Bates to Richard Bates, Nov. 9, 1809, FB 108-112.
675. Frederic L. Billon, *Annals of St. Louis In Its Territorial Days*, 90.
676. TJ to ML, July 17, 1808, Donald Jackson, *Letters*, 444. Thomas Fleming, *The Intimate Lives of the Founding Fathers*, 284-286.
677. Zebulon Pike to SW, Aug. 18, 1808, Elliott Coues, *The Expeditions of Zebulon Montgomery Pike*, 1: lxii.
678. Frederick Bates to ML, Nov. 7, 1807, FB 1: 228-233. Wilkinson had recognized that Dickson and Scots trader Aird used the pretext of American citizenship or support to trade in the nations, JW to SW, Sept. 8, 1805, TP 13: 196-204. See also Frederick Bates to John McKinney, March 3, 1808, FB 1: 307.
679. Even prior to Lewis's administration, Pierre Chouteau had worried about the influence of British traders from Canada, Shirley Christian, *Before Lewis and Clark*, 128. Andrew C. Isenberg, "The Market Revolution in the Borderlands: George Champlin Sibley in Missouri and New Mexico, 1808-1826," *Journal of the Early Republic*, Vol. 21, No. 3 (Autumn, 2001), 445-465.
680. Alec R. Gilpin, *The War of 1812 in the Old Northwest* (Michigan State University Press, Lansing: 1958), 195-196.
681. Richard Dillon, *Meriwether Lewis*, 295. R V. S. Pease, "Robert Dickson, the Indian Trader," Aug. 15, 1905, *The Madison Democrat*, in Wisconsin Historical Collections.
682. Acting Governor Pope to the Secretary of War, May 11, 1809, TP 16: 36-37.
683. WC to SW, April 5, 1809, TP 14: 260. Lt. Alpha Kingsley to ML, April 29, 1809, published in *Richmond Enquirer*, June 9, 1809, 3. Fort Belle Vue was later renamed Fort Madison (Iowa).
684. *Richmond Enquirer*, Jun. 9, 1809, 3. WC to SW, April 29, 1809, TP 14: 264-271. House found the fort well secured, ibid., 260 n.

685. Militia Order of Governor Lewis, April 10, 1809, and April 21, 1809, TP 14: 262-263. Extract of Letter from William Clark to friend in Louisville, *The Pittsfield Sun*, May 27, 1809, 2. WC to Jonathan Clark, May 28, 1809, James J. Holmberg, *Dear Brother*, 200-205. Frederic L. Billion, *Annals of St. Louis In Its Territorial Days*, 90. TP 14: 258-259.
686. Frederic L. Billion, *Annals of St. Louis In Its Territorial Days*, 89.
687. A year earlier, a total of fifteen companies mustered in all the districts from spring to November 1808. Louis Houck, *A History of Missouri from the Earliest Explorations and Settlements Until the Admission of the State Into the Union* (R. R. Donnelley & sons Company: 1908), 2: 409-413.
688. Militia Orders of Governor Lewis, April 10, 1809, TP 14: 262-263. Rodolph Tillier to James Madison, April 27, 1809, enclosed in a letter from John Mason to James Madison, June 9, 1809, *The Papers of James Madison Digital Edition*, J. C. A. Stagg, editor (Charlottesville: University of Virginia Press, Rotunda, 2010). Also in LR, Unregistered Series, 1809 Thru 1811, Reel 4. Digital copy, M222/M222-04/M222-04-0191-194, NARA. Thirty years earlier, Tillier thanked Jefferson for his hospitality in Paris, Rodolphe Tillier to TJ, May 1789, FO. Original source: *The Papers of Thomas Jefferson*, vol. 15, *27 March 1789—30 November 1789*, ed. Julian P. Boyd (Princeton: Princeton University Press, 1958), 160.
689. N. Jarrot, *Missouri Gazette and Public Advertiser*, June 28, 1809, 3. For a description of the British agent incident, FB 2: 75, n. 200.
690. *Missouri Gazette*, Jun 28, 1809, 3. The detachments returned by early June and reported that if there had been any unrest, it had been quelled, *Alexandria Gazette*, July 10, 1809, 3, Black Hawk is quoted in Richard Dillon, *Meriwether Lewis*, 312.
691. Meriwether Lewis Memorandum Book, Entry of April 24, 1808, MHS.
692. N. Jarrot, *Missouri Gazette and Public Advertiser*, Jun. 28, 1809, 3. For a description of the British agent incident, see FB 2: 75, n. 200.
693. Frederick Bates to Nathaniel Pope, Oct. 24, 1809, FB 2: 100-101.
694. WC to Jonathan Clark, 24 Nov. 1808, James J. Holmberg, *Dear Brother*, 166-181. Frederick Bates to Richard Bates, July 14, 1809, FB2: 67-73.
695. *National Intelligencer*, June 5, 1809, 3. William E. Ames, "The National Intelligencer: Washington's Leading Political Newspaper," *Records of the Columbia Historical Society*, Washington, D.C., Vol. 66/68 (1966/1968), 71-83.

696. Frederick Bates to James Abbott, July 25, 1809, FB 2: 75.
697. Ibid.
698. *Richmond Enquirer*, May 9, 1809, 4. Rodolph Tillier to James Madison, April 27, 1809, cited above.
699. See Last Will and Testament of Rodolphe Tillier, File No, 0597, St. Louis Probate Court, St. Louis, Missouri, which was written in French. The Will was admitted to probate on the affidavit of Sheriff Jeremiah Connor that the handwriting and signature were Tillier's. The handwriting in the Will does not match the handwriting in a letter from Rodolphe Tillier to Thomas Jefferson dated May 1789 (compare "Penrose"), though the signatures match. See also Rodolphe Tillier, *Translation of a memorial of Rodolphe Tillier's justification on the administration of Castorland, county of Oneida, state of New York* (Thomas Walker, Rome: 1800), which translated Tillier's memorandum into English. Tillier would have used the services of an assistant as a scribe for letters from the factory, but he was a former factor at the time he wrote the letter to Mason. For a letter obviously written by a clerk see, Rudolph Tillier to the Secretary of State, Jan. 12, 1807, TP 14: 78.
700. *National Intelligencer*, May 10, 1809, 3. See also David H. DeJong, "John M. Mason: Superintendent of Indian Trade (October 1807—April 1, 1816)." *Paternalism to Partnership: The Administration of Indian Affairs, 1786-2021* (University of Nebraska Press, 2021).
701. John Mason to James Madison, June 9, 1809, *The Papers of James Madison Digital Edition,* J. C. A. Stagg, editor (Charlottesville: University of Virginia Press, Rotunda, 2010).
702. Founded by French immigrant John Macklot, it was the first shot factory to be built west of Pittsburgh. For the initial news stories, see *Missouri Gazette and Public Advertiser*, Mar 8, 1809, 3 and Nov 16, 1809, 3. "Petition to Congress by John Macklot," Nov. 14, 1808, TP 14: 234-235.
703. *Richmond Enquirer*, May 9, 1809, 4.
704. Rodolphe Tillier Last Will and Testament, April 15, 1810, St. Louis Probate Court File No. 0597. See note 699 for discussion of second Tillier Will admitted to probate.
705. These charges are hinted at in the combination of Secretary Eustis's letter to ML, July 15, 1809, and to SW to WC, Aug. 7, 1809, TP 14: 289-29.

706. SW to JW, June 22, 1809, LS, in reply to Wilkinson's letters of April 20, 23, and 30 and May 29. Tillier's letter was dated April 27. The secretary of war made the allegations in a letter to Lewis on July 15, 1809. The conclusion that Wilkinson made the charges is through process of elimination based upon the secretary's statement that Wilkinson had sent him coded letters on similar topics. I have been unable to locate another source for the additional for Eustis's charges connected with the subagents. Wilkinson had just returned to New Orleans when he sent the letters, *National Intelligencer*, June 2, 1809, 1.
707. SW to WC, Aug. 7, 1809, TP 14: 289-290.
708. Shirley Christian, *Before Lewis and Clark*, 115.
709. SW to WC, Aug. 7, 1809, TP 14: 289-290. See also Ruth A. Gallagher, "The Indian Agent in the United States Before 1850," *The Iowa History and Politics* XIV (1916): 3-55, 27-33.
710. Clark had requested an official list of subagents in 1808, WC to SW, April 20, 1808, Records of the Office of the Secretary of War, Registers of Letters Received, Vol 4., May 8, 1808-Dec. 26-1810, NARA, 62. WC to Jonathan Clark, Nov. 26, 1809, James J. Holmberg, *Dear Brother*, 228-233.
711. WC to SW, April 29, 1809, TP 14: 264-266.
712. WC to Jonathan Clark, Oct. 28, 1809, James J. Holmberg, *Dear Brother*, 216-223. L. R. Colter-Frick, *Courageous Colter and Companions* 304, 394. McFarlane was in the Upper Louisiana as early as June 1808.
713. WC to SW, July 1, 1809, LR.
714. Lewis paid James's brothers Andrew and Lewis as subagents. James also had a brother named "John" in the area (Claim of John McFarlane for late brother James McFarlane, Oct. 12, 1838, Special Files of the Office of Indian Affairs, 1807-1904, Roll 49, File 181, NARA). A "John McFarland" played an important role in the Texas Revolution, but I was unable to substantiate that he was James's brother. James McFarlane to John Breck Treat, Dec. 10, 1808, Edward E. Ayer Manuscript Collection (Newberry Library), accessed online. WC to SW, TP 14: 264-271. If John McFarlane's account of the date of James's death is accurate, the James McFarlane who was alleged to have committed suicide in New Orleans on the eve of the Texas Revolution would not have been the same James McFarlane, *Louisville Daily Journal*, Jan. 18, 1843.

715. Meriwether Lewis Memorandum Book, entries July 1, 1808, and Aug. 13, 1808, MHS. Lewis had been ordered to find minerals the government could exploit before land was sold to settlers.
716. Memorandum of Lewis's Personal Effects, Donald Jackson, *Letters*, 470-474. Jackson discusses the location of the saltpeter caves along the Black River in note 11. Clark told his brother they could offer great value to speculators, WC to Jonathan Clark, 24 Nov. 1808, James J. Holmberg, *Dear Brother*, 166-181 Lewis executed a lease for saltpeter caves on Feb. 23, 1809. TP 2: 60-62. Note the present-day location of Saline County, Missouri.
717. Ibid. WC to SW, April 29, 1808, TP 14: 264-266. Meriwether Lewis Memorandum Book.
718. Reuben, Charles T. Jones, Jr., "George Champlin Sibley: The Prairie Puritan," 65. ML to James Madison Aug 27, 1809, TP 14: 293-312. WC to Secretary of War, Sept. 23, 1808, TP 14: 224-228. Payments to Robinson were protested by the War Department, see W. C. to Jonathan Clark, Nov. 26, 1810, James J. Holmberg, *Dear Brother*, 228-233.
719. David E. Narrett, "Liberation and Conquest," 23-50. Not all men who worked to secure Texas had the same interests, and Robinson's differences with the leaders of the campaign would later surface.
720. John W. Honey to Frederick Bates, Jan. 12, 1809, FB 2: 55-60. George Armistead to Frederick Bates, 30 Nov. 1808, FB 2: 44-45. McFarlane continued to trade with the tribes after Lewis's death, A List of Licenses Issued, FB 2: 201-203. Among other charges against McFarlane were accusations of taking goods from members of tribes by falsely telling them they needed licenses to trade (*Thomas Jones v. Joseph Lewis, Sheriff of New Madrid*, Circuit Court Records, Washington University of St. Louis, Digital Gateway). Note that the attorney for the plaintiff was William O. Allen, who corresponded with Andrew Jackson after Lewis's death. For McFarlane's use of his title, see, James McFarlane to John B. Treat, Dec. 10, 1808, Edward E. Ayer Manuscript Collection (Newberry Library). Clark also reported his title in reports to the War Department.
721. Pierre Chouteau, Jr. to SW, Sept. 1, 1809, Carter, ASP, 14: 312-319. Lewis could argue that the Osage presented one of the significant challenges in the territory. Threats from their rivalries had halted Jefferson's planned expedition by Dunbar and Hunter when an Osage delegation traveled to

Washington to meet with Jefferson to reveal the threat from their rivals, Dan L. Flores, *Southern Counterpart*, 44. And fur trapping was so lucrative on a lawless frontier, it was not considered unreasonable to suspect that rival fur companies would battle each other or more likely, encourage tribes to attack competitors. Manuel Lisa suspected that John Jacob Astor's company would encourage tribes to attack the St. Louis Fur Company trappers. "George Champlin Sibley: The Prairie Puritan," 84-85. The War Department may have interpreted the article differently.

722. A Proclamation, FB 2: 15-16. The District of Arkansas was separated in 1806 by the legislature, but Bates combined it with the New Madrid District prior to Lewis's arrival. In 1808, Lewis obtained approval to separate it to run from all the area north of the $33^{rd}$ degree to the second Chickasaw Bluff and then due west. Louis Houck, *A History of Missouri from the Earliest Explorations and Settlements Until the Admission of the State Into the Union* (R. R. Donnelley & sons Company: 1908), 2: 412. Wilkinson had first proposed prohibiting settlers from traveling beyond the Arkansas Post ostensibly to protect the tribes, JW to SW, July 27, 1805, TP 13: 164-172.

723. WC to TJ, April 29, 1809, TP 3: 264-271.

724. J. Mason to Joseph Anderson, ASP, *Indian Affairs*, IV, 1: 768. Spain had created an earlier Arkansas Post on the Mississippi River in the 1700s. No allowance was planned for the shifting of the river and the buildings did not endure.

725. FB 2: 7, n 1143.

726. In 1809, McFarlane also opened a trading post north at Prairie du Chien (now southern Wisconsin), one that had been approved by the War Department, L. R. Colter-Frick, *Courageous Colter and Companions*, 475-477. The trading post had been authorized. There is nothing in the deposition to suggest that McFarlane was operating a private business contrary to federal policy.

727. As a result, when Lewis turned to U.S. soldiers to help provide security that should have been provided by a militia, some officers refused to cooperate. Richard Dillon, *Lewis and Clark*, 319-320. James McFarlane to William Clark, 20 Feb. 1809, TP 14: 268-269. James McFarlane to ML, Dec. 11, 1808, TP 14: 266-268. Cf George Armistead to Frederick Bates, Nov. 30, 1808, and John W. Honey to Frederick Bates, Jan.

12, 1809, FB 2: 44-45, 2: 54-60. Clement Penrose, a Wilkinson supporter, served as administrator of Hunt's estate a few years later, *Missouri Gazette and Public Advertiser*, Apr. 26, 1810, 3. George Armistead also served as Justice of the Peace for New Madrid, FB 2: 30. Perly Wallis to Frederick Bates, Dec. 18, 1808, FB 2: 45-47, claimed that Armistead acted to prevent the Osage from being attacked.

728. GCR to SW, June 24, 1809, LR, Fooy negotiated drafts for Armistead, Chickasaw Bluffs Factory Ledger, 1806-1808, Memphis State University, Digital Commons, e.g. entry Jan. 31, 1808.

729. Dan L. Flores, *Journal of an Indian Trader*, 27 and n 50. Walnut Hills was located near modern day Vicksburg, Mississippi. Glass was suspected to have been a fence for the robber Samuel Mason from a hardware store he operated, particularly when his life was spared in an infamous killing on the Natchez Trace, Paul I. Wellman, *Spawn of Evil: The Invisible Empire of Soulless Men Which For A Generation Held America In A Spell Of Terror* (New York: The Fireside Press, 1964), 127-130. Robert M. Coates, *The Outlaw Years: The History of the Land Pirates of the Natchez Trace* (The Literary Guild of America, New York: 1930), 157. Like Robert Grinder, Glass's sudden wealth after the death of man was found suspicious. Flores notes that there was no other evidence that Glass was a fence. Christopher Morris notes that Anthony Glass moved into the area during the Spanish Period and that Anthony Glass, Jr. was shown as owning the hardware store in 1831; however, the son could have taken over the father's operation. Christopher Morris, *Becoming Southern* (New York: Oxford University Press, 1995), 107.

730. William C. C. Claiborne to James Madison, August 8, 1808, FO.

731. Dan L. Flores, *Journal of an Indian Trader*, 86-87.

732. John Sibley to SW, May 10, 1809, Register of LR. John Sibley to General John Moran Aug. 26, 1809, Office of Indian Trade, Natchitoches, Sulphur Fork Factory, 1809-1821, LS.

733. Dan L. Flores, *Journal of an Indian Trader*, 88-89.

734. James Aalan Bernsen, *The Lost War for Texas*, 106, citing W. C. C. Claiborne to Col. Cushing, Dec. 29, 1808, *Letter Books of W. C. C. Claiborne*, 4: 279-280 and W. C. C. Claiborne to Henry Dearborn, Dec. 29, 1808, *Letter Books of W. C. C. Claiborne*, 4: 280-281. Bernsen thought the leader of the group could be Reuben Kemper.

735. W. C. C. Claiborne to James Madison, Jan. 1, 1809, *Letters books of W. C. C. Claiborne*, IV: 282-285. He had written that there was nothing to report.
736. Amos Stoddard, *Sketches*.
737. Amos Stoddard to Governor John Sevier, Aug. 30, 1810, Edward E. Ayer Manuscript Collection (Newberry Library), Accessed Online. See also "Letter from Knoxville" in apparent reply in the same collection.
738. Amos Stoddard, *Sketches*, 184.
739. Robert Stoddard, *Autobiography of Amos Stoddard*, 69-70, citing Amos Stoddard, *Sketches*, 185. Because Amos mentioned the flow of the Mississippi, Robert Stoddard surmised that Amos traveled east into Mississippi Territory; however, the Red River is on the west side of the river. Sibley wrote to Stoddard in 1812 and mentioned how Natchitoches had changed since Sibley was there.
740. JW to SW, June 18, 1809, LR. John Brahan to SW (stopped at Colbert' Ferry enroute to Fort Adams, March 29, 1809), CA. Brahan was known to be at Fort Adams in May and June 1809. John Brahan to SW, datelined "Fort Adams," June 10, 1809, LR. He had recruited soldiers for his company from Staunton, Virginia in mid-1807 to 1808 and led them to Fort Southwest Point before then leading them to Fort Adams. See John Brahan to Col H. Burbeck, Aug. 27, 1807, and June 17, 1808, Henry Burbeck Papers, William L. Clements Library, John Brahan to Col. Return J. Meigs, Oct. 2, 1807, CA.
741. John Brahan to Secretary of War, February 10, 1809, LR, enclosing letter from John Smith T to Capt. John Brahan, Feb. 7, 1809.
742. Dick Steward, *Frontier Swashbuckler*, 77.
743. Smith T owned tracts of land east of Knoxville where the U.S. built fort Southwest Point in 1802 (Dick Steward, *Frontier Swashbuckler*, 20). Soldiers moved from that fort to Hiwassee where Brahan was in command. Brahan's letter mentions information Smith T conveyed to Brahan that was not in the Smith T letter, which suggests that there was either a separate letter or that the two met. Because Smith T's letter is dated three days earlier than Brahan's, it is more likely that they met. Brahan could have been expected to use his influence to support the offer, such at Return Meigs, the military agent who had served with him at Southwestern Point, but Smith T would have known more influential people. Brahan

forwarded the letter to the Secretary of War. In February 1809, the War Department was moving troops toward New Orleans in anticipation of an invasion. Smith T's offer could also be seen in light of that action.

744. GCR to SW, July 28, 1809, LR.
745. Ibid. Fort Camp Esperanza, see FB 1: 160, n. 111. For Fort Madison, FB 2: 7, n 114.
746. Walter Overton to SW, June 8, 1808, Records of the Office of the Secretary of War, Registers of Letters Received, Vol 4., April 10, 1808—Dec. 26-1810, NARA, 303.
747. Maury County, Tennessee County Court Minutes, Minute Book 1, entry for March 23, 1809 session. The deed for the assignment of the lot to Russell identifies Gilbert C. Russell as a Captain in the U.S. Army, Maury County, Tennessee, Register of Deeds, Book C-1, p. 92, Sept. 6, 1808. The assignment was proved in open court by the testimony of W. H. Overton.
748. JW to SW (Dec. 1808), LR, requesting that the War Department provide his transportation. JW to SW, datelined Havana, March 5, 1809, Register of Letters Received, Main Series, M22-107.
749. SW to JW, May 4, 1809, LS, *Military Affairs*, M6-107.
750. JW to SW, letters dated April 20, 23, and 30 and May 29, LR. The statement is based on the fact that Eustis told Wilkinson that parties claiming to have authority to act in New Spain had no authority to take action and in letters to Lewis and Clark emphasized that Lewis had not authority to appoint subagents, following Wilkinson's coded and non-coded letters to Eustis. Lewis understood that Eustis made the charge in his reply of July 15, 1809, and absent evidence of charges from other individuals, Wilkinson is the most likely to have sent the charges.
751. For the concern from Washington, see Secretary of State to Governor Claiborne, Oct. 12, 1809, TP 9: 850-852. For list of artillerists, see *The Weekly Chronicle (Natchez Weekly Democrat)*, May 27, 1809, 1. Kira Gayle had Newman's letters translated from the original French. See Francis Newman to Joseph Solis, May 1, 1809, May 19, 1809, July 20, 1809, Kira Gale, *Fifty Documents*, 124-129. See also Kira Gale, *Meriwether Lewis: The Assassination of an American Hero and the Silver Mines of Mexico* (River Junction Press, Omaha 2015), 447. Wilkinson enclosed copies of the letters, in French, in a letter to the Secretary of War, JW to SW, Sept. 3, 1809, LR, Main Series. Officers in the same regiment were

stationed at distant points; however, the significance is that they had mutual contacts and that they reported to the same superior.

752. James Wilkinson to William Eustis, Sept. 3, 1809, LR.
753. W. C. C. Claiborne to Robert Smith, Nov. 5, 1809, Dunbar Rowland, *Letter Books of W. C. C. Claiborne,* 4: 419-423, and *Newman Statement,* Nov. 24, 1809, 5: 18-20.
754. Milton Lomask, *Aaron Burr, 1805-1836,* 302. *National Intelligencer,* June 19, 1809, 3.
755. Dan L. Flores, *Journal of an Indian Trader,* 88-89. W. C. C. Claiborne to Don Benito Perez, July 18, 1809, *Letter Books of W. C. C. Claiborne,* 5: 12.
756. W. C. C. Claiborne to Don Benito Perez, July 19, 1809, Dunbar Rowland, *Letter Books of W. C. C. Claiborne,* 5: 12.
757. Henderson K. Yoakum, *History of Texas,* 1: 163-165. Cf. Ted Schware in, *Forgotten Battlefield,* 31-33, says that Salcedo was beheaded.
758. Ted Schware, *Forgotten Battlefield of the First Texas Revolution* (Fort Worth: Eakin Press, 1985), referring to the Gutierrez diary. Elizabeth Howard West, "Diary of José Bernardo Gutiérrez de Lara, 1811-1812," *The American Historical Review,* Vol. 34, No. 1 (Oct. 1928).
759. William Horace Brown, *The Glory Seekers: The Romance of Would-be Founders of Empire in the Early Days of the Southwest* (The University Press: Cambridge 1906), 218.
760. Frederic L. Billion, *Annals of St. Louis In Its Territorial Days,* 11, 19. John McClanahan gave his account of the expedition in J. McLanahan to Governor Howard, June 18, 1812, Jackson wrote the secretary of state to request his efforts to have the party released as noted in Robert Smith to Andrew Jackson, Nov. 10, 1810, Andrew Jackson Papers, LOC, and reply noted in Harold D. Moser and Sharon Macpherson, and Charles F. Bryan, Jr., eds. PAJ 2: 561. Brahan also sent a letter in support of the party's release. Brahan's letter dated Sept. 20, 1810, is noted in the War Department Register of Letters Received.
761. Thomas Flournoy to James Madison, Oct. 6, 1813, n. 3, FO, Original source: *The Papers of James Madison, Presidential Series,* vol. 6, *February 8—October 24, 1813,* ed. Angela Kreider, J. C. A. Stagg, Jeanne Kerr Cross, Anne Mandeville Colony, Mary Parke Johnson, and Wendy Ellen Perry (Charlottesville: University of Virginia Press, 2008), 676-680. Frank Lawrence Owsley, Jr. and Gene A. Smith, *Filibusters and Expansionists: Jeffersonian*

*Manifest Destiny, 1800-1821* (The University of Alabama Press, Tuscaloosa: 1997), 42-49. Additional filibusters took place at "West Florida" Baton Rouge in 1810 and in East Floridia on the peninsula in 1812 and an attempted revolution was started in Mexico in 1810.

762. Frank Lawrence Owsley, Jr. and Gene A. Smith, *Filibusters and Expansionists*, 42-50.
763. Henderson K. Yoakum, *History of Texas*, 1: 163-165, said that he "died by his own hands" based on a report from one witness. Ted Schware in *Forgotten Battlefield*, 28, says that Magee died from fever based on a report from another witness.
764. William Horace Brown, *The Glory Seekers*, 225-227.
765. *Kentucky Gazette*, May 22, 1810, 3. *The Delaware Gazette*, April 7, 1810, 3. *Richmond Enquirer*, April 20, 1810, 2.
766. ML to Amos Stoddard, Sept. 22, 1809, Donald Jackson, *Letters*, 466-467.
767. David McKeehan to ML, April 7, 1807, Donald Jackson, *Letters*, 399-408.
768. William Eustis to ML, July 15, 1809, Donald Jackson, *Letters*, 456-458. Among the debts submitted were $1,500 to Benjamin Wilkinson as agent for the St. Louis Fur Company, ML to Henry Dearborn, March 7, 1809, Donald Jackson, *Letters*, 450, $940 to Peter Chouteau for presents for tribes for the Mandan Expedition, $1,418.75 and $108 for translating the laws of the territory, L. R. Colter-Frick, *Courageous Colter and Companions*, 318, $29 for a draft on Wilkinson & Price for packhorses for Zebulon Pike's expedition into Mexico in 1806, L. R. Colter-Frick, *Courageous Colter and Companions*, 319.
769. William Eustis to ML, July 15, 1809, Donald Jackson, *Letters*, 456-458.
770. Richard Dillon made this point. Richard Dillon, *Meriwether Lewis*, 324-325.
771. A group that tried to take Texas was indicted for violation of the Neutrality Act in 1815. Henderson K. Yoakum, *History of Texas*, 1: 179-180.
772. ML to William Eustis, Aug. 18, 1809, Donald Jackson, *Letters*, 459-461. Aaron Burr frequently signed his name "A Burr."
773. Ibid.
774. Another possibility is that Lewis stated his intentions to travel to New Orleans only to misdirect anyone who intended to follow him, but Lewis's statement in his letter to Clark from New Madrid that he was already considering changing routes makes that possibility unlikely.

775. Pierre Chouteau, Jr. to Secretary of War, Sept. 1, 1809, Carter, ASP, 14: 312-319.
776. Thomas C. Danisi, *Uncovering the Truth About Meriwether Lewis* (New York: Prometheus Books, 2012), 146-147.
777. Frederick Bates to SW, Sept. 28, 1809, FB, 2: 86-92.
778. Pierre Chouteau to William Eustis, Dec. 14, 1809, Donald Jackson, *Letters*, 479-484, and LR. Chouteau's letter was written in French, along with a translation in English in a handwriting different from the handwriting in his son's letter.
779. ML to William Eustis, Aug. 18, 1809, Donald Jackson, *Letters*, 459-461.
780. Frick, Ruth L. Colter, "Meriwether Lewis's Personal Finances," 16-20.
781. ML to Amos Stoddard, Sept. 22 1809, Donald Jackson, *Letters*, 466-467.
782. *Missouri Gazette and Public Advertiser*, Sept. 13, 1809, 3. The Post Master General to Governor Lewis, March 29, 1809, TP 14: 256-257.
783. The party arrived at the Mandan village on September 24, 1809, *Richmond Enquirer*, Dec 16, 1809, 1.
784. On 22 August, Lewis borrowed $331.45 from merchants Falconer & Comegys who also offered loans based on government paper. Lewis borrowed $175 from Charles Sanguinette on 24 August. *Falconer Comegys vs. Edward Hempstead*, Circuit Court Records Collection, identifier no. ccr1811.01067.004, Washington University at St. Louis.
785. *Peter Chouteau v. Edward Hempstead*, Circuit Court Records, Washington University of St. Louis, identifier no. ccr1811.01072.014 and ccr1809.01073.007.
786. William Eustis to ML, July 15, 1809, Donald Jackson, *Letters*, 456-457. Lewis estimated the amount of his debts as $4,000, ML to William Eustis, August 18, 1809, Donald Jackson, *Letters*, 459-461.
787. Power of Attorney recorded in Deed Book C, page 12, St. Louis Recorder of Deeds. Lodge member Alexander Stuart was also named as an attorney-in-fact.
788. Deed dated Aug. 19, 1809 from ML to William C. Carr, The Meriwether Lewis Papers, Box: OS: La-Le, MHS.
789. L. R. Colter-Frick, *Courageous Colter and Companions*, 323.
790. William C. Carr to WC, Aug. 25 1809, MHS. The term was used at the time to mean "disorganized" rather than mentally unstable, See, SW to ML, July 8, 1808, TP 14: 204.

791. WC to Jonathan Clark, Aug. 26, 1809, James J. Holmberg, *Dear Brother*, 209-214.
792. Lewis and Clark: Settlement of Account, Aug. 21, 1809, Donald Jackson, *Letters*, 462-463, also noted in Vardis Fisher, *Suicide or Murder?* 71, and Ruth L. Colter Frick, "Meriwether Lewis's Personal Finances," 16-20.
793. WC to Jonathan Clark, May 28, 1809, and July 22, 1809, James J. Holmberg, *Dear Brother*, 200-204, and 204-205, respectively. Clark initially planned to travel to Washington if the government would pay his expenses, but his plans became more definite after the War Department denied his reimbursements and after Lewis's death.
794. For comparison, Fortescue Cumming took a trip by ship from New Orleans to Delaware in one month. Clark left St. Louis on September 21 and arrived in D.C. on December 1, three months later.
795. William Carr to William Clark, Sept. 1809, MHS, Identifier number A0289-01391.
796. WC to Jonathan Clark, May 28, 1809, James J. Holmberg, *Dear Brother*, 200-204.
797. Recommendation of William Clark as Governor, April 29, 1809, TP 16: 31-32. It is presumed that the supporters would not have submitted Clark's name without his knowledge. When Clark was suggested as Lewis's replacement after Lewis's death, Clark said that he did not think he would be suited for the position. He later accepted the position as governor of the State of Missouri.
798. See the chapter "River Pirates and the Natchez Trace," Leland D. Baldwin, *The Keelboat Age on Western Waters* (University of Pittsburgh Press: 1941), 116-133.
799. The maps had already been sent to the Secretary of War, and presumably, other sensitive military information had already been passed on as well. Kira Gale made the observation that military couriers frequently split up and sent duplicate information by two sources, similar to the explorers keeping two copies of their journals during the expedition. The practice is logical but she did not cite her source.
800. WC to Jonathan Clark, Aug. 26, 1809, James J. Holmberg, *Dear Brother*, 209-211.
801. Lewis sent furniture to St. Louis prior to his arrival. Frederick Bates to ML, Jan. 26, 1808, FB 1: 266-269. Lewis's Missouri estate administrator sold

three feather beds after his death. *Missouri Gazette and Public Advertiser*, Aug. 16, 1810, 3.
802. Frederick Bates to Nathaniel Pope, Oct. 24, 1809, FB 2: 100-101.
803. John Coburn to WC, Nov. 12, 1809, MHS, L. R. Colter-Frick, *Courageous Colter and Companions*, 381. For Bates's admission, see Frederick Bates to John Coburn, Nov. 2, 1809, regarding the appointment which he had discussed and did not feel he could press until after Lewis's death, FB 2: 104-105. Bates described Coburn as his intimate friend. Coburn was Acting Secretary of the Illinois Territory.
804. Frederick Bates to Nathaniel Pope, Oct. 24, 1809, FB 2: 100-101.
805. Frederick Bates to Richard Bates, Nov. 9, 1809, FB 2: 108-112.
806. John Brown to the President Nov. 20, 1809, and Acting Governor Bates to the President, Nov. 23, 1809, TP 14: 339-342.
807. William C. Carr to Charles Carr, Aug. 25, 1809, William Carr Papers MHS, reprinted in Kira, Gale, *Fifty Documents Related to the Assassination of Meriwether Lewis*, 16.
808. WC to Jonathan Clark, Aug. 26,1809, James J. Holmberg, *Dear Brother*, 209-214.
809. William C. Carr to Charles Carr, Aug. 25, 1809, William Carr Papers, Missouri History Museum.
810. Zadok Cramer, *The Navigator* (Cramer, Spear & Eichbaum: Pittsburgh 1814), 168.
811. This statement is based upon Lewis's signature to the treaty, dated August 31, 1809, the statement of the treaty that Lewis read the treaty to them, and the confirmation of a story in the *Missouri Gazette* that Osage were in St. Louis at the time. Pierre Chouteau, Jr. suggested that McFarlane had brought Osage tribal members to St. Louis at some earlier point and tried to persuade them to travel with him to Washington to finalize the treaty. He claimed that his father was responsible for persuading the Osage to accept the treaty.
812. Undated entry prior to Sept. 1, 1809, Lewis Memorandum Book, MHS.
813. Clark discussed the Aug. 31, 1809, treaty signing in a letter to the Secretary of War on Feb. 20, 1810. He said that Lewis had written the treaty. He did not state specifically that Lewis attended the council on Aug. 31, Letter transcribed in L. R. Colter-Frick, *Courageous Colter and Companions*, 433-436. Lewis's decision to give priority to official duties and his

presiding over the conclusion of treaty negotiations on Aug. 31, 1809, rebuts the theories that his political and financial difficulties had driven him insane by the time he left St. Louis.

814. ML to the President, Aug 27, 1809, TP 14: 293-312. Original of record in NARA, Record Group 107 Records of the Office of the Secretary of War Entry 18 Letters Received, 1800-1889, file number 101-L (5)-1810. The address contains Lewis's handwriting unique "T" and "P" and the "L" in the St. Louis dateline also appears in his hand. The letter was dated the same day that Lewis purchased medicine from Dr. Saugrain.

815. WC to TJ, Feb. 20, 1810, ASP, *Indian Affairs*, 763-767. Clark distinguished the earlier Osage treaty signing through his agent Pierre Chouteau. He did not state that the Aug. 31, 1809 approval was delegated through an agent. Treaty officials also sometimes had an agent read the treaty publicly even when the official was present.

816. Ibid. The ceded land, over fifty million acres would become most of the State of Missouri, much of the State of Arkansas, and part of the State of Iowa.

817. *Missouri Gazette and Public Advertiser*, Sept 6, 1809, 2.

818. Lewis Memorandum Book.

819. Ben Wilkinson to ML, Sept. 1, 1809, Identifier: A0289-01392MSH. William Clark used the term to describe a letter from his brother Jonathan, WC to Jonathan Clark, Sept. 2, 1792, Clark used the term, James J. Holmberg, *Dear Brother*, 19-28. Jefferson used the term in letters to Lewis and close friends.

820. Lewis Memorandum Book, note of Sept. 3, 1809.

821. Lewis Memorandum Book, note immediately above note dated Sept. 1, 1809.

822. WC to Jonathan Clark, Oct. 28, 1809, James J. Holmberg, *Dear Brother*, 216-223. He likely supervised the boats Clark had advertised for in the *Missouri Gazette* that would depart St. Louis about the middle of September. There is a notation in Lewis and Clark's Memorandum Book that St. Louis firm Shreves & Welch agreed to leave St. Louis on Sept. 5 to take pelts to Wheeling for the St. Louis Fur Company. This agreement appears to be different from the terms advertised and must have been a separate shipment. Lewis and Clark Memorandum Book, State Historical Society of Missouri, 39.

823. WC to Jonathan Clark, Oct. 28, 1809, James J. Holmberg, *Dear Brother*, 216-223.
824. One possibility is that Lewis traveled with McFarlane; however, Clark remained in St. Louis until both departed, and Clark wrote that McFarlane's boat was just behind Lewis's.
825. The page prior to the stub of contains Lewis's note to settle with McFarlane when he sees him, notations of giving a deed to Judge Stewart and a note to have his mail delivered to Washington. The note following is his note to deliver a receipt for McFarlane and his notes of his settlement with McFarlane.
826. WC to Jonathan Clark, Sept. 16, 1809, James J. Holmberg, *Dear Brother*, 214-216.
827. SW to WC, Aug. 7, 1809, TP 14: 289-290. For Chouteau's appointment, see *The Secretary of War to Pierre Chouteau*, March 7, 1807, TP 14: 107-108 The Secretary of State Robert Smith on July 8, 1809 refused to reimburse $18.70 for translating Territorial Laws into French for trial. Eustis refused to pay $500 in gifts to Indians. Eustis refused to pay Clark $1,609.91 in hiring subagents. The reimbursement of Lewis' payment to Pierre Chouteau for construction of a furnace was also denied. Lewis had been instructed to determine whether public land contained any valuable salt or lead deposits before selling it. He had paid Pierre Chouteau $81 to build a small furnace for testing the soil. Eustis may have confused that furnace with the one reported in the newspapers to be used to manufacture ammunition. ML to William Eustis, June 16, 1809. Donald Jackson, *Letters*, July 16, 1809, 456-458.
828. WC to Jonathan Clark, Nov. 24, 1808, James J. Holmberg, *Dear Brother*, 166-181.
829. He later responded on September 16 that Governor Lewis would be consulted. SW to WC, Aug. 7, 1809, TP 14: 289-290, n. 59.
830. James House to Col. H. Burbeck, June 9, 1809, Daniel Bissell to Col. Henry Burbeck, Aug. 12, 1809, and James House to Col. H. Burbeck, Jan. 26, 1810, Henry Burbeck Papers, William L. Clements Library. Lewis directed Russell to send House's trunk to Baltimore. House arrived in Baltimore by Dec. 24, 1809, James House to Henry Burbank, Henry Burbank Collection, William L. Clements Library, University of Michigan. House assumed Col. Hunt's command of Fort Belle Fontaine

in Aug. 1808 when Hunt died, Zebulon Pike to SW, Aug. 18, 1808, Elliott Coues, *The Expeditions of Zebulon Montgomery Pike,* 1: lxii. Bissell replaced Captain House as commander of Fort Bellefontaine, Daniel Bissell to Secretary of War, June 16, 1809, TP 14: 276-277.

831. A copy of Lewis's July 8, 1809 letter to the Secretary of War related to protested bills was wrapped together with protested bills in a bundle that a Lewis descendant said that Lewis's brother Reuben had in his possession after Lewis's death. L. R. Colter-Frick, *Courageous Colter and Companions,* 315-317.
832. Frederick Bates to Sec. War Eustis, Sept. 28, 1809, FB 2: 86-92. ML to Peter Chouteau, Sept. 2, 1809, Deed book B, 378 Recorder of Deeds. Referenced in Thomas C. Danisi and John C. Jackson, *Meriwether Lewis* (New York: Prometheus Books 2009), 295, n. 21.
833. A large number of troops had also fallen ill at the Wilkinsonville Cantonment upstream on the Ohio, Matthew Lyon to TJ, Aug. 12, 1801, FO, NARA. Original source: *The Papers of Thomas Jefferson,* vol. 35, *1 August—30 November 1801,* ed. Barbara B. Oberg (Princeton: Princeton University Press, 2008), 74-79.
834. Leland D. Baldwin, *The Keelboat Age,* 89.
835. Norman W. Caldwell, "Cantonment Wilkinsonville," 21.
836. W. C. C. Claiborne to Robert Smith, July 29, 1809, Dunbar Rowland, *Letter Books of W. C. C. Claiborne,* 4: 391-393.
837. Lt. Col. William D. Beall, Deposition, March 21, 1809, ASP: *Military Affairs,* IV I: 278-279.
838. Deposition of Doctor Alexander Macauley, March 21, 1810, ASP: *Military Affairs,* IV 1: 279-280. McCauley also said that the disease caused a number of deaths among the general public, which may explain why Wilkinson was unable to use the emigres to support his efforts in Texas in 1809.
839. Thomas Ashe, *Travels in America, performed in 1806: for the purpose of exploring the rivers Alleghany, Monogahela, Ohio, and Mississippi, and ascertaining the produce and condition of their banks and vicinity* (London: Printed for Richard Phillips, 1808), 2: 242.
840. Antoine Saugrain to Daniel Bissell, June 16, 1809 (enclosed in letter to the Secretary of War) TP 14: 278-279. Dr. Saugrin was a brother-in-law to Dr. John Hamilton Robinson, Ray V. Denslow, *Territorial Masonry,* 41.

841. Mary C. Gillet, *The Army Medical Department, 1775-1818* (Center of Military History, Washington, D.C. 2004), 143. James McFarlane to WC, Feb. 20, 1809, TP 14: 268-269, confirming rain and snow. Compare the testimony of John Chrystie, Deposition, April 24, 1810, ASP: *Military Affairs*, 290, who understood that many soldiers south of New Orleans were suffering from dysentery. His views were not widely published.
842. Norman W. Caldwell, "Cantonment Wilkinsonville," 24, citing Thomas Ashe, *Travels in America*, 3: 93 for a description of the disease at Fort Massac.
843. F. Seip to James Wilkinson, Feb. 15, 1810, ASP: *Military Affairs*, 294-295. Dr. Barton recommended Seip to Jefferson for the Custis-Freeman expedition, Dan L. Flores, *Southern Counterpart to Lewis and Clark*, 59.
844. Mary C. Gillet, *The Army Medical Department, 1775-1818* (Center of Military History, Washington, D.C. 2004), 141. The soldiers' illness in the New Orleans area was unrelated to causes beyond camp conditions, but no one understood that at the time. Lewis would only have known there was unusual widespread fever.
845. W. Eustis to James Wilkinson, April 30, 1809, ASP: *Military Affairs*, 273.
846. Paul Hamilton to Captain David Porter, June 22, 1809, ASP: *Military Affairs*, 274.
847. Claiborne had been very ill with fever. And his wife died from fever in December 1809. J. B. Robertson to Robert Smith, Dec. 3, 1809, *Letter Books of W. C. C. Claiborne*, 5: 21-22, W. C. C Claiborne to Robert Smith, Nov. 5, 1809, Dunbar Rowland, *Letter Books of W. C. C. Claiborne*, 4: 419-423, Claiborne to Sec. State Robert Smith, Nov. 18, 1809, Dunbar Rowland, *Letter Books of W. C. C. Claiborne*, 5: 13-17 For the custom of moving to country during the sickly season, see W. C. C. to TJ, June 9, 1805, *Letter Books of W. C. C. Claiborne*, 3: 86.
848. Charles T. Jones, Jr., "George Champlin Sibley: The Prairie Puritan," 114.
849. TJ to GCR, April 18, 1810, FO, NARA. Original source: *The Papers of Thomas Jefferson, Retirement Series*, vol. 2, *16 November 1809 to 11 August 1810*, ed. J. Jefferson Looney (Princeton: Princeton University Press, 2005), 336.
850. Document signed by ML with promise to pay Dr. Saugrain for medicine, Aug. 27, 1809, Meriwether Lewis Collection, MHS. L. R. Colter Frick, *Courageous Colter*, 514. The due date was listed on list of Lewis's debts,

John Marks Papers, University of Viriginia Archives, but not on the document Donald Jackson transcribed in Donald Jackson, *Letters*, 730-732. Dr. Saugrain was assigned to Fort Bellefontaine, April 26, 1809, about the time that a large numbers of soldiers became ill, SW to James House, April 26, 1809, LS. He was brother-in-law to spy Dr. John Robinson. Rav V. Denslow, *Masonic Pioneers*, 40-41.

851. WC to Jonathan Clark, Oct. 28, 1809, James J. Holmberg, *Dear Brother*, 216-223, GCR to TJ, Jan. 4, 1810, FO.

852. "To the Memory of Governor Lewis," *Missouri Gazette and Public Advertiser*, November 23, 1809, 3.

853. Jon Kukla, *A Wilderness So Immense*, 294.

854. Timothy Flint, *Recollections of the Last Ten Years, Passed in Occasional Residences and Journeyings in the Valley of the Mississippi* (Cummings, Hilliard 1826), 98.

855. Ibid.

856. Ibid., 93.

857. The only boats available to the army to evacuate sick soldiers from New Orleans were gunboats supplied by the Navy and keelboats borrowed from the public. Lt. Col. William D. Bealle, Deposition, 21 March 1810, ASP: *Military Affair*, 278-279. The army had between eight and eighteen boats moored at Fort Adams, Esaias Preble's Deposition, March 16, 1810, ASP: *Military Affairs*, 1810. Amos Stoddard had access to a boat as Military Commandant in 1803, SW to Thomas Cushing, March 1, 1804, TP 13: 16-17. The government purchased a keelboat for the Fort Osage factory in 1808, and it is possible that there would have been a government keelboat available to Lewis, but a government boat was justified for Fort Osage due to the unavailability of other boats in that remote location. The army used boats to transport goods to Fort Osage from Fort Bellefontaine, but the boats could have been for hire and there is no record of any boat or soldiers being requisitioned for the purpose of providing transportation to Lewis. Charles T. Jones, Jr., "George Champlin Sibley: The Prairie Puritan," 32-48. With thanks to Nathan K. Moran for information on public keelboats.

858. Interrogatories Put to Captain John Darington, April 11, 1810, ASP: *Military Affairs*, 284.

## Notes

859. The only boats used at the time were pirogues and flatboats, J. W. M. Breazeale, *Life As It Is*, 252. Though it seems that some references to pirogues included larger keelboats. Map of Nashville 1804 from the notes of then resident Mrs. Temple, showing keelboat landing, map inserted between pages 396-397, A. W. Putnam, *History of Middle Tennessee*. Flatboats did not travel when the water was low, which would not have been likely in September, even though the summer of 1809 was unusually wet. H. E. Hoagland, "Early Transportation on the Mississippi," *Journal of Political Economy*, The University of Chicago Press, Feb. 1911, Vol. 19, No. 2 (Feb. 1911): 117.
860. Lee Sandlin, *Wicked River: The Mississippi* (New York: Pantheon Books, 2010), 15. Timothy Flint, *Recollections of the Last Ten Years*, 103.
861. Lee Sandlin, *Wicked River*, 126.
862. Leland D. Baldwin, *The Keelboat Age*, 66.
863. Ibid., 87.
864. Zadok Cramer, *The Navigator* (1814), 168.
865. Distances in this chapter are taken from *The Navigator* and some of the other travel journals of the time. They are not represented to be exact. River channels changed course over time.
866. Timothy Flint, *Recollections of the Last Ten Years*, 99.
867. Zadok Cramer, *The Navigator* (1814), 170-171.
868. Frederick Bates to Richard Bates, May 31, 1807, FB 1: 135-138.
869. ML to WC, March 15 1807, Donald Jackson, *Letters*, 387.
870. *Missouri Gazette and Public Advertiser*, Oct. 12, 1809, 3. Representation to Congress by Committee of Inhabitants, Oct. 10, 1809, TP 14: 323-327. Also, Petition to Congress by the Inhabitants of the Territory, Referred Jan. 6, 1810, TP 14: 357-362.
871. Henry Marie Brackenridge, *Views of Louisiana: Together with a Journal of a Voyage up the Missouri River, in 1811* (Pittsburgh: Cramer, Spear and Eichbaum, 1814), 125.
872. *Missouri Gazette and Public Advertiser*, Oct. 12, 1809, 3. Smith was to deliver the petition to the next Congress. *Missouri Gazette and Public Advertiser*, Oct 19, 1809, 3.
873. Andrew Jackson's message riders met boats along the riverbanks during the War of 1812.

874. Zadok Cramer, *The Navigator* (1814), 172. In 1802, the Tennessee governor asked the Spanish governor to help control river pirates. For a discussion of the early history of the Chickasaw Bluffs, see, *Beginnings of West Tennessee: In the Land of the Chickasaw 1541-1841* (The Watauga Press, Johnson City, TN 1930), 61-69.
875. *Missouri Gazette and Public Advertiser*, Aug. 16, 1809, 3. Mrs. Dunbar Rowland (Eron Rowland) Dunbar on Indians of Louisiana, *Life, letters and papers of William Dunbar of Elgin, Morayshire, Scotland, and Natchez, Mississippi, pioneer scientist of the southern United States; compiled and prepared from the original documents for the National society of colonial dames in America*, 210.
876. Amos Stoddard, *Sketches*, 210-211.
877. *Missouri Gazette and Public Advertiser*, Aug. 16, 1809, 3.
878. Dr. Thomas Neale. Ray V. Denslow, *Territorial Masonry*, 37.
879. Zadok Cramer, *The Navigator* (1814), 174.
880. In 1801, about 350 to 400 boats were estimated to travel on the river each year. Leland D. Baldwin, *The Keelboat Age*, 37. Boats could travel upstream with use of sails, poles, chains, and oars, ibid., 61.
881. Memorandum of Lewis's Personal Effects, Donald Jackson, *Letters*, 470-474. The package wrapping the silk must have contained a note that the silk was for Julia for the inventory takers to know its purpose. Other likely areas where Lewis bought the items were Fooy's store at Chickasaw Bluffs, and at the crossroads of the Natchez Trace and the east-west trail from Fort Pickering to Mobile, an area that attracted traders about fifteen miles north of the Chickasaw Agency. Lewis could also have purchased them from a peddler on the Chickasaw Trail, on the Natchez Trace or one of his other stops, but he made no record of the purchase. A note in Clark's Memorandum Book provides instructions on dying silk for Julia's dresses.
882. Timothy Flint, *Recollections of the Last Ten Years*, 93.
883. Ibid., 87.
884. Ibid., 247.
885. Hospital boats are mentioned on the Ohio River in Col. Thomas S. Butler's Orderly Book, entry of Aug. 8, 1801, Andrew Jackson Papers, LC and GCR prepared hospital supplies as he moved his recruits down the Mississippi River in 1809, GCR to SW, May 19, 1809, LR.

886. Leland D. Baldwin, *The Keelboat Age*, 89-90.
887. Timothy Flint, *Recollections of the Last Ten Years*, 93.
888. Ibid., 17.
889. Meriwether Lewis Last Will and Testament dated September 11, 1809. The original document signed by Lewis and filed with the court is stored at the Virginia State Library. The handwriting on the front, other than witness signatures, appears to be Lewis's. The handwriting on the back is from clerks of the court. (Note that handwriting expert Gerald B. Richards testified in the 1996 coroner's inquest that the copy of Lewis's Last Will and Testament that he reviewed was not in Lewis's handwriting, but it appears that the copy provided to him for inspection was the copy in the clerk's handwriting that the clerk of the court entered into the official record book rather than an image of the original Last Will and Testament. Prior to the time machine copiers existed, clerks typically wrote a copy of documents filed in their own handwriting in their official record books. The original document does not state where Lewis signed the document. If Russell correctly stated the date that Lewis arrived at Fort Pickering, the travel time would have placed Lewis in the vicinity of New Madrid. The Missouri Historical Society received a certified transcribed copy of the Will as it had already been transcribed by a clerk on the books of the Albemarle County Virginia Clerk's Office in Will Book 5, page 66. (The Meriwether Lewis Collection, MHS). The clerk who transcribed the copy interpreted Peerny's signature as "Geau Peaeny" and that name has been used in writings that relied on the transcribed copy. As stated earlier, Peerny's signature on Lewis's original Last Will and Testament matches his signature on his letter to Jefferson. Lewis's original Will would have been stored by the Clerk until sent to the Virginia State Library for permanent storage, but in both instances described, the Clerk likely sent a transcription of the Clerk's own handwritten copy from the official record book rather than attempting to locate the original.
890. *Missouri Gazette*, Jan 25, 1810, 4. With thanks to Kent Nathan Moran for the discovery. Trinchard's body is entombed in New Orleans.
891. William Carr to WC, Sept. 1809, MHS, Identifier number A0289-01391.
892. Meriwether Lewis Last Will and Testament, Sept. 11, 1809, Virginia State Library.

893. Samuel R. Brown, *Western Gazetteer; Or Emigrant's Directory* (H. C. Southwick, Auburn N.Y. 1817), 206. James Lai Penick, Jr., *The New Madrid Earthquakes* (University of Missouri Press, Columbia and London 1981), 25.
894. Thomas Ashe, *Travels in America*, 1: 296.
895. Henry Marie Brackenridge, *Views of Louisiana*, 129-130. (The traveler found New Madrid to be healthy, but she visited it in early spring).
896. Thomas Ashe, *Travels in America*, 2: 1295-296. For a critical review of Ashe's book from the *Portfolio* see the *Kentucky Gazette*, Oct. 31, 1809, 4.
897. Militia Officers of New Madrid to Governor Clark, undated 1809, TP 14: 270-271.
898. May Sue Anton, *New Madrid: A Mississippi River Town in History and Legend* (Southeast Missouri State University Press: 2009), 34.
899. Louis Houck, *The Spanish regime in Missouri…* (Chicago: R. R. Donnelley & Sons Company, 1909), 2: 331. Later travelers wrote that unhappiness with the U.S. government persisted.
900. Michael Amoureux to ML, May 31, 1807, Donald Jackson, *Letters*, 412-413.
901. Houck, *Spanish Regime in Missouri*, 2: 18, Foley, *History of Missouri*, Georges Henri Victor Collot, *A Journey in North America* (Paris: Printed for Arthus Bertrand Bookseller, 1826). Those conditions were also noted in Louisville on the Ohio as causing yellow fever in summer or the "sickly season." Henry McMurtrie, *Sketches of Louisville and Its Environs* (Louisville: S. Penn, 1819), 140-141. James Lai Penick, Jr., *The New Madrid Earthquakes*, 27 (note the 1794 plat of New Madrid on page 26).
902. Thomas Ashe, *Travels in America*, 3: 134-136.
903. *Missouri Gazette*, Oct. 4, 1809, 3.
904. See note 945.
905. L. R. Colter-Frick, *Courageous Colter and Companion*, 276-281. Larry E. Morris, *The Fate of The Corps: What Became of the Lewis and Clark Explorers After the Expedition* (Yale University Press: New Haven & London 2004), 102. Mary Sue Anton, *New Madrid*, 57-59.
906. Clark said Lewis wrote to him about changing his route, WC to Jonathan Clark, Oct. 28, 1809, James J. Holmberg, *Dear Brother*, 216-223, and in the next letter, Clark asked Jonathan to send him the letter Lewis

mailed to him from New Madrid, WC to Jonathan Clark, Oct. 30, 1809, James J. Holmberg, *Dear Brother*, 224-225.
907. Circular dated Aug. 9, 1809, *Missouri Gazette and Public Advertiser*, Sept. 6, 1809, 2; Sept. 13, 1809, 1. Madison withdrew his repudiation of orders to intercept hostile ships, *National Intelligencer*, Aug. 11, 1809, 2.
908. *Missouri Gazette and Public Advertiser*, Sept. 6, 1809, 2.
909. W. C. C. Claiborne to James Madison, Jan. 1, 1809, Dunbar Rowland, *Letters Books of W. C. C. Claiborne*, IV: 282-285.
910. W. C. C. Claiborne to Robert Smith, Aug. 5, 1808, Dunbar Rowland, *Letters Books of W. C. C. Claiborne*, IV: 399-401. An uprising in Saint-Dominique (Haiti) following Napoleon's attempt to create a foothold in the Caribbean created fear in the Caribbean.
911. Paul F. Lachance, "The 1809 Immigration of Saint-Domingue Refugees to New Orleans: Reception, Integration and Impact," *Louisiana History: The Journal of the Louisiana Historical Association*, Vol. 29, No. 2 (Spring, 1988), 109-141, 116. The French government established a large colony on St. Dominique to raise sugar cane. They brought in black slaves to work the plantations. The slaves rebelled in a bloody revolt to create an independent Haiti, an action that New Englanders compared to the American Revolution, but southern plantation owners viewed as a threat that could inspire their own slaves to revolt. See, Don Hickey, "America's Response to the Slave Revolt in Haiti, 1791-1806," *Journal of the Early Republic*, vol 2, no 4 (Winter 1982).
912. Howard W. Cox, *American Traitor*, 157. Hay and Werner, *The Admirable Trumpeter*, 257.
913. JW to SW, 14 May 1809, and July 2, 1809, LR, Main Series. The regular army consisted of about 2,900 soldiers (3,800 including new recruits) *Pennsylvania Weekly Telegraph*, June 10, 1809: 2, but Wilkinson admitted that one-fourth (which would prove to be more than a third) of those were sick at Terre aux Boeufs, ASP: *Military Affairs* 1: 272. State militias totaled about 657,000. Ibid., 242. The emigres were likely Cuban refugees originally from Haiti that declared its independence from France and then devolved into extreme violence.
914. JW to SW, Aug. 10, 1809, LR, Main Series.
915. JW to SW, Sept. 3, 1809, LR, Main Series.
916. JW to SW, Aug. 10, 1809, LR, Main Series.

917. WC to Jonathan Clark, Oct. 28, 1809, James J. Holmberg, *Dear Brother*, 216-223. The letter had been mailed to Clark at his brother Jonathan Clark's house in Louisville.
918. Clark did not mention that Lewis's letter gave him any concerns as to Lewis's welfare when he mentioned the letter to his brother.
919. *Missouri Gazette and Public Advertiser*, Oct. 4, 1809, 3.
920. Frederick Bates to Richard Bates, Nov. 9, 1809, FB 2: 108-112.
921. ML to Peter Chouteau, Sept. 2, 1809, Deed book B, 378 Recorder of Deeds.
922. Zadok Cramer, *The Navigator* (1814), 173.
923. Thomas Ashe, *Travels in America*, 1: 297, 3: 39. See also Zadok Cramer, *The Navigator* (1814), 178.
924. Francis Trenchard (or Trinchard), 2: 710. Plat of survey by Michael Amoureux of 300 arpens between Lake Gayoso and Mississippi about 3½ miles from Little Prairie in district of New Madrid dated Dec. 23, 1805 and received for record by Soulard on Feb. 27, 1806, Papers of Original Claimants, 1777-1851; First Board of Land Commissioners; U.S. Recorder of Land Titles, Record Group 951; Missouri State Archives, Jefferson City, Missouri. Mary Sue Anton, *New Madrid*, 61.
925. Thomas Ashe, *Travels in America*, 3: 139.
926. Timothy Flint, *Recollections of the Last Ten Years*, 88.
927. Thomas Ashe, *Travels in America*, 3: 142.
928. Zadok Cramer, *The Navigator* (Cramer & Spear, Pittsburgh, 1821), 126.
929. The undated page appears just prior to Lewis's memoranda from 1808, but just after his notes on remedies.
930. Zadok Cramer, *The Navigator* (1814), 185.
931. F. Cuming, *Fortescue Cuming's Sketches of a tour to the western country: through the states of Ohio and Kentucky, a voyage down the Ohio and Mississippi rivers, and a trip through the Mississippi territory, and part of West Florida, commenced at Philadelphia in the winter of 1807, and concluded in 1809* (Pittsburgh: Cramer, Spear & Eichbaum, 1810), 240, 255. But speed depended on a number of factors.
932. Natchez Trace Research Collection, McCain Library and Archives, University of Southern Mississippi, citing, New Orleans Customhouse records moved to National Archives.
933. *Virginia Argus*, Feb. 6, 1810, 3.

934. On June 16, 1805, Lewis ordered soldiers to procure sulfur water to give to a very ill Sacagawea (Lewis entry of June 15, 1805, *The Journals of Lewis and Clark*, Univ. of Nebraska). For comparison, soldiers during the War of 1812 selected campsites based upon the availability of fresh spring or well water.

935. Amos Stoddard to Col. Henry Burbeck, Dec. 10, 1810, Henry Burbeck Papers, William L. Clements Library.

936. Felix Farley's *Bristol Journal*, April 23, 1808, 3.

937. Timothy Flint, *Recollections of the Last Ten Years*, 230.

938. Most river communities probably relied on rainwater stored in cisterns. They would not have had an abundance of stored water in late summer to share with river traffic.

939. Zadok Cramer, *The Navigator* (1814), 149-152.

940. Mary C. Gillet, *The Army Medical Department, 1775-1818*, 141.

941. Interrogatories of Col. Alexander Parker, April 14, 1810, ASP: *Military Affairs* 13: 285-286. Army Surgeon William Upshaw testified that water on the Mississippi was the cause of some of the sickness in camp at Terre au Boeuf, Wm. Upshaw to James Wilkinson, Jan. 3, 1810, ASP: *Military Affairs* 13: 292-293.

942. Leland D. Baldwin, *The Keelboat Age*, 87.

943. Dr. Rush to Capt. Lewis for preserving health. June 11, 1803, Donald Jackson, *Letters*, 54-55.

944. Thomas Trotter, *An essay, medical, philosophical, and chemical, on drunkenness, and its effects on the human body* (London: T. N. Longman, and O. Rees, 1804), 167-168, referenced in, William F. Bynum, *Bulletin of the History of Medicine*, The Johns Hopkins University Press Vol. 42, No. 2 (March-April 1968): 160-185.

945. *The National Intelligencer*, Nov. 27, 1809, 3. The news story was published in Washington soon after Stoddard's arrival in town. A good question is whether boatmen ever attempted to throw sick passengers overboard to prevent the spread of disease likely to kill them and whether someone's attempt at murder could have been defended as the victim's attempted suicide. If Lewis was so feverish that he was unaware of his circumstances, he would not have known what happened.

946. The story appeared in the same issue as Lewis's letter to Stoddard, showing Stoddard to be the source. *The National Intelligencer and Washington Advertiser*, Nov 27, 1809, 3.

947. The account was printed in the same issue as the letter Stoddard had received from Meriwether Lewis and about the same time that Stoddard passed through Washington. *The National Intelligencer and Washington Advertiser*, Nov 27, 1809, 3. Before leaving St. Louis, Lewis had made a note in his Memorandum Book to meet with fort commander Captain Gilbert C. Russell.

948. For comparison, John Honey described obtaining a receipt at the same time that he delivered papers from Frederick Bates to agent John Treat. John W. Honey to Frederick Bates, January 12, 1809, FB 1: 54-60.

949. Zadok Cramer, *The Navigator* (1814), 187.

950. Fooy had been a surveyor when the Spanish occupied the Chickasaw Bluffs. The U.S. Army first built a fort about two miles north of the site of the fort in 1809. It moved the site to higher ground in 1802.

951. F. Cuming, F., *Fortescue Cuming's Sketches of a Tour to the Western Country*, 266-267. Unlike modern barges, Mississippi River barges of Lewis's era were described as several pirogues tied together. This passage states that Fooy ran a barge between New Orleans and Chickasaw Bluffs. Mary Louise Grahan Nazor, "The Indian Trading House on the Chickasaw Bluffs, 1803-1818," *The Tennessee Genealogical Magazine*, Vol 47, No. 4, Winter 2000, 13. Morris S. Arnold, "The Soldiers of Spain in Colonial Arkansas," *Arkansas Historical Quarterly* Vol. 77 Issue 4 (Winter 2018): 305-354, 340. Fooy eventually prospered on the river. By 1816, a traveler wrote his surprise that Fooy's well-appointed house contained fine mahogany furniture.

952. Thomas Ashe, *Travels in America*, 3: 140.

953. Frederick Bates to Albert Gallatin, July 14, 1807, FB, 1: 158-161.

954. John W. Honey to Frederick Bates, January 12, 1809, FB 1: 54-60. Appointments to Civil Offices By Governor Lewis, April 1-September 30, 1808, FB1: 28-31.

955. Andrew Jackson, deed dated Aug. 1, 1797, TSLA. Frances Clifton, "John Overton as Andrew Jackson's Friend," *Tennessee Historical Quarterly*, Vol. 11, No. 1 (March 1952): 23-40.

956. W. C. Smith to SW, Nov. 5, 1809, LR., M221. For the reply, see SW to W. C. Smith Dec. 1, 1809, LS, and SW to Wade Hampton, Dec. 1, 1809, LS.

957. Jon Kukla, *A Wilderness So Immense*, 122. James Ripley Jacobs, *Tarnished Warrior*, 92.

958. Sibley said that officers at Natchitoches were very anti-Jefferson because of the downsizing of the army, John Sibley and Penny S. Brandt, "A Letter of Dr. John Sibley," 387, n. 38.
959. Winfield Scott, *Memoirs of Winfield Scott*, 27. Russell F. Weigley, *History of the United States Army*, 107. But Jefferson called out the militia to support enforcement of his own embargo laws in 1808, ibid., 110.
960. See Howard W. Cox, *American Traitor*, "Conclusion."
961. William Porcher DuBose, B. J. Ramage, "Wade Hampton," *The Sewanee Review*, Vol. 10, No. 3 (Jul. 1902): 364-373, 365.
962. Hay and Werner, *The Admirable Trumpeter*, 183.
963. Rev. John G. Jones, *A Complete History of Methodism*, 381.
964. Russell F. Weigley, *History of the United States Army*, 109.
965. Ibid. The government has already approved sending troops to New Orleans to defend against an invasion from Spain, Defense of the Mississippi Against Spanish Invasion, John Randolph to SW Dec. 18, 1806, ASP: *Military Affairs*, 204. *The Evening Post*, May 29, 1809, 2.
966. H. Dearborn to SW, Feb. 24, 1808, ASP: *Military Affairs*, 228.
967. Howard W. Cox, *American Traitor*, 188.
968. Russell F. Weigley, *History of the United States Army*, 109.
969. Howard Cox, *American Traitor*, 186-192. Cox states his belief that Wilkinson had nothing to do with the directives because he was tied up in a court of inquiry during that period. Others have argued that Wilkinson was too busy in New Orleans in 1809 to concern himself with Lewis. I view the same facts from the perspective that Wilkinson invested much of his life in the army creating a future for himself in New Spain and that he continued to give that objective his priority. Years later, he was still trying to make a place for himself there at the time of his death. Through Wilkinsons many government agents and informants and his influence on Jefferson, he was still capable of influencing War Department policy in 1808.
970. Howard Cox, *American Traitor*, 189.
971. Holman Hamilton, *Zachary Taylor: Soldier of the Republic* (The Bobbs-Merrill Co. New York: 1941), 33-36.
972. Orderly Book of Adjutant General at Fort Adams, Manuscripts, National Archives, Washington, D. C. See also John Brahan to SW, March 29, 1809, CA, written during his stop at Colbert's Ferry.

973. H. Dearborn to James Wilkinson, Dec. 2, 1808, ASP: *Military Affairs*, 272.
974. *The Evening Post*, May 29, 809, 2. *The United States Gazette*, June 1, 1809, 3.
975. *The Charleston Daily Courier*, March 22, 1809, 3, *Kentucky Gazette*, March 28, 1809, 3, *Richmond Enquirer* Jan. 5, 1809, 3. Howard Cox, *American Traitor*, 187.
976. SW to Wade Hampton, et. al, Feb. 17, 1809 and June 2, 1809, June 30, 1809, LS.
977. Ibid.
978. Daniel Bissell to SW, June 16, 1809, TP 14: 276-279.
979. Holman Hamilton, *Zachary Taylor: Soldier of the Republic*, 35-36. Hamilton said, without citing his source, that when Taylor was relieved by William Swan, he traveled to New Orleans where the recruits were stationed and where he became ill. See also *Autobiography of General James Taylor of Newport Kentucky*, 65, University of Chicago and Zachary Taylor Papers, the Trist Wood Papers #800, Southern Historical Collection, The Wilson Library, University of North Carolina at Chapel Hill.
980. K. Jack Bauer, *Zachary Taylor* (Baton Rouge: Louisiana State University, 1985), 7-8. Bauer related a tradition that Taylor contracted yellow fever while serving under Wilkinson in New Orleans. Holman Hamilton, *Zachary Taylor*, 35-36. Hamilton said that Taylor rejoined his company first at New Orleans and became ill there, but his successor Swan commanded his own company at Fort Pickering and led them south when he was succeeded by Russell. Taylor may have commanded his own company at Fort Pickering and became ill there.
981. GCR to SW, June 24, 1809 and July 28, 1809, LR. Swan was also appointed military agent to report to William Linnard, SW by John Smith to William Swann, March 17, 1809, LS. Swan's name was spelled with one "n" in other letters from the Secretary of War. Swan was appointed military agent for the Southern District in December 1809, SW to Wade Hampton, Dec. 18, 1809, LS, and SW to William Swan, Dec. 20, 1809.
982. GCR to R. J. Meigs, April 16, 1809, CA, Russell had been ordered to Fort Adams.
983. GCR to SW, June 24, 1809, LR.
984. W. C. Smith to SW, November, 5, 1809, LR. Russell had planned initially to transport his troops to Fort Adams. GCR to SW, March 11, 1809, LR.

985. Russell F. Weigley, *History of the United States Army*, 113. Howard W. Cox, *American Traitor*, 194-195.
986. SW to JW, July 15, 1809, LS.
987. Russell F. Weigley, *History of the United States Army*, 113-114. Henry Adams, *History of the United States*, 1801-1809, 1071.
988. SW to JW, Sept. 10, 1809, LS.
989. Hay and Werner, *The Admirable Trumpeter*, 300. Randolph to Nicholson, cited in Joseph Wheelan, *Jefferson's Vendetta*, 169.
990. *The American Republic*, Jun 8, 1810, 3.
991. SW to Wade Hampton, Sept. 10, 1809, LS. Wade Hampton to SW, Sept. 30, 1809, LR.
992. SW to JW, Nov 24 1809, LS. Of course, Wilkinson's enemies welcomed the news, *The American Republic*, Oct. 25, 1809, 4.
993. *Trial of Col. Thomas H. Cushing before a General court martial... by Brig. Gen. Wade Hampton, Reported by the late judge advocate* (Philadelphia: Moses Thomas, 1812). *Louisiana State Gazette*, June 15, 1811, 2.
994. *The Palladium*, Dec 16, 1809, 3.
995. SW to Wade Hampton, Dec. 1, 1809, LS.
996. Howard W. Cox, *American Traitor*, 204-205.
997. Richard H. Kohn, *Eagle and Sword*, 179.
998. The subordinate was Col. Thomas S. Butler. Williamson County Minute Book, Vol. 1, 1800-1812, 392, Williamson County, Tennessee Archives. John Overton to Archibald Roane, June 11, 1802, copy in Natchez Trace Collection, Box 4, Folder 5. *Natchez Trace Parkway Survey*, 39. Archibald Roane to John Overton, March 31, 1802, and August 7, 1802. Papers of Archibald Roane, Papers of the Tennessee Governors, TSLA.
999. AJ to Thomas Jefferson, August 7, 1803, PAJ 1: 353-356. PAJ 2: 32-33, n. Thomas Jefferson to AJ, September 19, 1803, PAJ 1: 365.
1000. Robert V. Remini, *Andrew Jackson and the Course of American Empire, 1767-1821* (New York: Harper & Row 1977). AJ to John Coffee April 13, 1804, PAJ 2: 16-18., AJ to George Washington Campbell, April 28, 1804, PAJ 2: 18-19.
1001. GCR to TJ, Jan. 4, 1810, FO. NARA. Original source: *The Papers of Thomas Jefferson, Retirement Series*, vol. 2, *16 November 1809 to 11 August 1810*, ed. J. Jefferson Looney (Princeton: Princeton University Press, 2005), 120-12. Citation abbreviated when repeated.

1002. Elizabeth A. Russell to GCR, Aug. 9, 1809, enclosed in letter from GCR to SW, Aug. 25, 1809, LR. Russell's signature appears on a bond from 1804 in the Jefferson County, Tennessee Court, document cou1804-0006-003, Jefferson County, Tenn. Archives, and matches his signatures on his letter datelined Fort Pickering and his letters to Jefferson. There is no question that the Gilbert C. Russell who served as commander of Fort Pickering in 1809 was the Gilbert C. Russell who lived in Jefferson County, Tennessee in 1804.

1003. The description of the Gilbert C. Russell who led a Tennessee militia company to Natchez in 1803 matches the description of service that the Gilbert C. Russell who later commanded Fort Pickering gave to the Secretary of War. GCR to H. Dearborn, Dec. 4, 1807, LR. Russell confirmed that he began his service as a captain in the Mounted Militia under the U.S. at eighteen and entered the army as an ensign. See also *National Intelligencer* article matching the details of Russell's service, May 7, 1806, 1. Samuel C. Williams, "Tennessee's First Military Expedition," *Tennessee Historical Magazine*, Vol. 8, No. 3 (Oct. 1924): 171-190. Russell spent or incurred obligations for $619.75 for expenses for the expedition. An Act for the Relief of Gilbert C. Russell, TSLA NAID: 210055034 Textual Records, Produced: April 15, 1806. See also *Natchez Trace Parkway Survey*, 81-82.

1004. GCR to AJ, Andrew Jackson Papers, Oct. 20, 1804, Andrew Jackson Papers, LOC.

1005. See GCR to SW, Aug. 8, 1805, and Sept. 10, 1809, Reg. of LR, Russell was at Fort Adams / Loftus Heights in 1805.

1006. Thomas Cushing to SW, Dec. 1807, Register of LR, noting that Russell resigned on Aug. 17, 1807.

1007. GCR to SW, Dec. 4, 1807, LR.

1008. GCR to SW, Aug. 25, 1803, LR, and GCR to TJ, Jan. 4, 1810, FO.

1009. GCR to SW, undated but received April 23, 1808, LR.

1010. Russell was recommended for promotion to 1st Lt. in 1805, SW to TJ, Jan. 11, 1805, FO, but not promoted to 1st Lt. until Nov. 1807, SW to TJ, Nov. 23, 1807, FO. Russell resigned Aug. 17, 1807, Thomas Cushing to SW, Dec. 2, 1807, LR General Orders and Circulars of the War Department, June 28, 1810, NARA, 76. In April, 1808, Henry Dearborn requested Russell be appointed captain, Henry Dearborn to

TJ, April 30, 1808, FO. A later transcription of records at NARA shows his appointment to major in May 1809, but it was more likely 1810. Russell still referred to himself as a captain in January 1810, GCR to SW, Jan. 2, 1810, Register of LR.

1011. Dick Steward, *Frontier Swashbuckler*, 22.

1012. "A brief account of the execution of the six militia men...", Andrew Jackson Papers, LOC Online. The job of executing fellow soldiers was one no soldier wanted and one that could have ended a soldier's career and influence. Jackson must have tasked Russell with the job because Russell owed him a great debt. Russell's father was not a man of influence, because his father relied on him to request help for his brother from the secretary of war and Russell relied on Jackson and later Wilkinson rather than his father for his appointments. Russell had not inherited any property from his father, who was still alive in 1809. Jackson, who was still trying to gain proof that Wilkinson was a spy, could have benefited from placing Russell in Wilkinson's camp. Russell understood that his mission would be to take his soldiers to Fort Adams and Wilkinson's headquarters, but it appears that Russell's plans were changed at the last minute.

1013. It may have been Jackson's plan for Russell to become one of Wilkinson's favorites. But later, during the War of 1812, when Jackson discovered how closely Russell had worked with Wilkinson to make plans to defend New Orleans—the mission Jackson wanted—he threatened to court-martial Russell, AJ to GCR, July 24, 1814, Andrew Jackson Papers. LOC.

1014. Robert J. Meigs to Robert Brent, Sept. 12, 1809, CA. Brahan worked as paymaster until April 1806, when he was transferred to the southern district.

1015. John Brahan to SW, Oct. 10, 1808, LR.

1016. John Brahan to AJ, Nov. 1, 1808, Andrew Jackson Papers, LOC. State of Tennessee to Thomas Overton and John Brahan, 640 acres, Aug. 10, 1807, Bedford County Tennessee Register of Deeds, Book 1808-1809.

1017. Deed Book D, page 70-71, Maury County Register of Deeds, Columbia, Tennessee. Anderson, a more experienced surveyor, certified Walter H. Overton's work.

1018. Return J. Meigs and Timothy Meigs, to Robert Brent, Dec. 6, 1808, Agency Letter Books, CA.

1019. He first traveled to Fort Adams in June 1809. John Brahan to William Eustis, June 10, 1809, LR. James Wilkinson to SW, June 22, 1809, LR.
1020. Return J. Meigs to John Smith, April 18, 1809, Return J. Miegs to William Eustis, Oct. 26, 1809, CA. Circular to the Settlers on Chickasaw and Choctaw Land June 28, 1809, Return J. Meigs, enclosed in Return J. Meigs to John Smith, Chief Clerk, War Dept., Aug. 12, 1809, LR.
1021. Thomas Schroeder Jandebeur, "Thomas Freeman in Madison County: Mississippi Territory, 1807-1810; Alabama, 1820," *The Huntsville Historical Review*, Vol 45, No. 2 (Fall-Winter 2020): 1-51, 26-27, citing Thomas Freeman to Albert Gallatin, Feb. 20, 1809.
1022. Daniel S. Dupre, *Transforming the Cotton Frontier: Madison County, Alabama 1800-1840* (Baton Rouge: Louisiana State University Press, 1997), 27.
1023. A visitor in 1807 first assumed that the inhabitants of the fort had been massacred. Cuming, *Fortescue Cuming's Sketches of a Tour to the Western Country*, 269.
1024. House repeated the rumor that Russell unloaded Lewis's property from the boat, James House to Frederick Bates, Sept. 28, 1809, MHS.
1025. ML to James Madison, Sept. 16, 1809, Donald Jackson, *Letters*, 464-465, original held by MHS, Identifier: D03682.
1026. F. Cuming, *Sketches of a tour to the western country*, 268. The traveler was met at Fort Pickering by Lieutenant Zachary Taylor, future U.S. president.
1027. When Andrew Jackson and his troops visited the fort three years later, they were afforded honors.
1028. GCR to SW, Aug. 25, 1803, LR. Gilbert C. Russell served on juries in Jefferson County, Tennessee from 1802 to 1807, the earliest in the January Term 1802, Jefferson County, Tennessee County Court Minute Book 1, 198. If Russell was truthful about his date of birth, he would have served on a jury as young as sixteen or seventeen years old. If Russell was permitted to enlist in militia service at age 16, he may have been considered emancipated to exercise all other adult rights.
1029. Russell is something of a mystery. He sought reimbursement for spending over $2,000 recruiting soldiers in 1808-1809. He called that amount "an enormous sum," and it would have been for most 23-year-olds. His signature matches the Gilbert Christian Russell from Tennessee who led an expedition of five hundred Tennessee militia and federal volunteers down the Natchez Trace in 1803 under the directions of Jefferson to

assure that Spain would acknowledge the U.S. Louisiana Purchase. That Gilbert C. Russell represented the U.S. in the proceedings in Natchez and remained in the area long enough to oversee the hanging of the notorious Little Harpe bandit in Greeneville. Those feats were remarkable for an 18-year-old. Gilbert C. Russell's letter to Andrew Jackson dated Oct. 20, 1804, suggested that Russell was considering joining the regular U.S. Army and asked for Jackson's help in securing an appointment for him of the position of captain. It appears that Russell was still serving in the Tennessee Militia at Dandridge in 1804. His "joining the army" in 1803, must have referred to his service as a federal volunteer rather than a U.S. Army regular. The Gilbert C. Russell who commanded Fort Pickering is often confused with Gilbert C. Russell, Sr. of Abington, Virginia; however, according to the Fort Pickering commander Gilbert C. Russell's sister's letter enclosed in his letter to the Secretary of War dated Aug. 25, 1809, his sister was named "Elizabeth" and she and the commander's father lived in Jefferson, Tennessee, which was Jefferson County rather than the town of Jefferson due to its proximity to Dandridge. The Gilbert C. Russell, Sr. of Abington, whose date of birth was listed as 1782, did not have a daughter named "Elizabeth." Lewis's brother John Marks gave Russell the polygraph that Jefferson had given Lewis. (Donald Jackson, *Letters*, 473, n 10.) Perhaps the gift was for taking care of his brother in his illness or perhaps he also confused him with the much older Gilbert C. Russell, Sr. of Virginia. See also GCR to SW, Dec. 4, 1807, LR in which Russell's description of his military record matches his service from 1803, and Gilbert C. Russell, Jan. 5, 1835, U.S. Bounty Records, bearing Russell's signature, in which Russell states that he was a Captain in the Tennessee Militia when it marched to Natchez in 1803. The grave marker for Gilbert C. Russell, Sr.'s grave in Mobile, Alabama appears to mix the dates of the birth of the Abington Russell and the service of the Tennessee Russell, but that marker appears to have been a service marker added in the 20th Century. Russell traveled to Washington in December 1807. It is possible that he met Lewis or Jefferson during that trip, but I located no written evidence that he did.

1030. Meriwether Lewis Note, Identifier: A0897-00001, MHS.
1031. GCR to Lewis Marks, April 18, 1813, Lewis Marks Papers, University of Virginia Archives.

1032. GCR to TJ, Jan. 4, 1810, FO.
1033. W. C. Smith to SW, Nov. 5, 1809, LR.
1034. James House to Frederick Bates, Sept. 28 1809, MHS. The hearsay factual additions to Russell's letters would have come from Amos Stoddard, who, in turn, claimed to hear them from the man he met coming from Chickasaw Bluffs, likely James Neelly.
1035. SW to Wade Hampton, Dec. 1, 1809, LS.
1036. Mary C. Gillet, *The Army Medical Department, 1775-1818*, 140. The hospital at New Orleans that she refers to was apparently the one Wilkinson set up when he arrived at Terre au Boeuf. It would have space to care for sixty to eighty soldiers, and it was fully operational by early to mid-September 1809. Deposition of Captain John Darington, April 11, 1810, ASP: *Military Affairs*, 282-283.
1037. Statement of Gilbert C. Russell, Nov. 26, 1811, Donald Jackson, *Letters*, 573-575.
1038. WC to Jonathan Clark, Oct. 28, 1809, James J. Holmberg, *Dear Brother*, 216-223.
1039. See, e.g., Daniel Bissell to Secretary of War, June 16, 1809, TP 14: 276-277 for a general description of buildings at Fort Bellefontaine.
1040. Evidence of Lt. Jacob Jackson, ASP: *Military Affairs* 1: 686-689.
1041. Thomas Ashe, *Travels in America*, 3: 142. Factor David Hogg accused Benjamin Allen, a Chickasaw trader, of using government property to treat his skins for his private business. GCR to SW, Jan. 2, 1810, LR.
1042. The frontier moved west with the Louisiana Purchase. The Secretary of War gave priority to building Fort Bellefontaine at St. Louis and ordered that men could be taken from Chickasaw Bluffs to staff it if necessary. SW to George M. Carmichael, Nov. 7, 1803, TP 13: 10.
1043. GCR to William Eustis, Aug. 26, 1809, LR.
1044. Ibid.
1045. GCR to William Eustis, June 24, 1809, LR. The Secretary of War suggested that all garrisons built in the Louisiana Territory after 1804 be made primarily of blockhouses surrounded by a stockade enclosure, SW to JW, June 28, 1804, TP 13: 27.
1046. W. C. Smith to William Eustis, Nov. 5, 1809, LR. Jay H. Buckley, "A Postmortem Trial concerning Meriwether Lewis's Controversial Death," in John D. W. Guice, ed., *The Mysterious Death of Meriwether Lewis*

(Oklahoma University Press, Norman, 2006), 123-124, quoting Richard Dillon, *Lewis and Clark*, 347. Dillon's description makes it appear that Russell arrested Lewis on frivolous charges, but Russell arrested Smith on charges that Smith considered frivolous.

1047. Thomas Ashe, *Travels in America*, 141.

1048. GCR to SW, Jan. 2, 1810, LR. Smith spent some nights in the home of a widow, which Russell also claimed to be inappropriate. Smith defended that he was caring for the widow of a man who had just died while engaged in a "confidential command" at Fort Adams. W. C. Smith to SW, Nov. 5, 1809, LR. The conditions under which Russell kept Lewis were in stark contrast to conditions described by the 1806 fort visitor. Then, the fort commander invited a traveler and his party to dine with him and served an abundance of fish, venison, squirrel, bear meat, and fruit from the surrounding countryside. So much wine was served that the traveler's companions fell under the tables in a drunken stupor. Thomas Ashe, *Travels in America*, 3: 143.

1049. GCR to William Eustis, Aug. 26, 1809, LR. In September, the War Department advised Russell to begin work on the quarters and wait until the following year to repair the fort, Jon Smith to GCR, Sept. 25, 1809, LS.

1050. Malcolm McGee to Return J. Meigs, Sept. 27, 1808 and David Hogg to Return J. Meigs, Nov. 18, 1808, CA. Note the letter was signed by Malcolm McGee, who could not write and who signed his name with an 'x'.

1051. Reverend Aloysius Plaisance, "The Chickasaw Bluffs Factory and Its Removal to the Arkansas River, 1818-1822, *Tennessee Historical Quarterly*, Vol. 11, No. 1 (March, 1952): 45. His successor John B. Treat died in 1812, James Neelly to Secretary of War, April 30, 1812, LR.

1052. Norman W. Caldwell, "Cantonment Wilkinsonville," 22.

1053. Russell made his defense to Jefferson. GCR to TJ, Jan. 31, 1809, FO. Wilkinson prepared the testimony of physicians in his defense near the same time for his upcoming court-martial.

1054. The Neelly Letter said that Lewis drank alcohol on his trip through the Chickasaw Nation, but the letter was written by John Brahan, who was not present. The January 31, 1810 Russell letter claimed that Lewis drank liquor after he left the fort, but Russell did not witness the act. He said that Lewis admitted to him that he had succumbed to drinking. Jefferson later mentioned that Lewis had recently succumbed to the habit. One of Jefferson's sources would have been Russell's letter; however, there is the possibility that Clark told him that Lewis had been drinking. Clark had received the Suspicious Russell Letters prior to his meeting with Jefferson. Jefferson received Russell's letter after he met with Clark. There is no record that Jefferson ever questioned Clark about whether Russell's statement was true.

1055. Drs. David Peck and Marti Peck opine that Lewis was an alcoholic in their book *"So Hard to Die": A Physician and a Psychologist Explore the Mystery of Meriwether Lewis's Death* (The Marti and David Peck Family Trust of 1992, 2021). I respect their analysis, but I find it more compelling that Frederick Bates did not mention it when he frequently detailed Lewis's shortcomings in his letters to his brother. Like Jefferson's opinion of how Lewis died, the foundation of any opinion as to whether Lewis abused alcohol or can be no more reliable than the unreliable hearsay on which it must rely.

1056. *Missouri Gazette*, Oct. 19, 1809, 3.

1057. GCR to TJ, Jan. 31, 1810, FO. Though Russell said that he kept Lewis confined to keep him from alcohol, a physician might see the treatment as a slow detox for an alcoholic.

1058. Dr. Benjamin Rush, *Effects of the Ardent Spirits* (Exeter, Eighth Printing, 1810), 13.

1059. Thomas Trotter, *An essay..., on drunkenness*, 9, 118, 179, 185. Recent articles argue that Trotter's publication, the first, book-length work on the subject, was not followed as frequently as Dr. Benjamin Rush's published as a pamphlet in 1785 and later as a book in 1810. The point, here is that the similarities in the phrasing with the statements by Bates and Russell and the suggestion that alcoholism could lead to suicide are striking.

1060. Dr. Benjamin Rush, *Effects of the Ardent Spirits*.

1061. Smith's letter has sometimes been interpreted as Smith complaining of Russell's confinement of Lewis, but the secretary of war interpreted it as a complaint of Russell's treatment of Smith. Though Smith wrote with some ambiguity, the secretary's interpretation appears correct. W. C. Smith to William Eustis, Nov. 5, 1809, LR. SW to Wade Hampton, Dec. 1, 1809, LS. Russell brought charges against Smith, in part, for neglecting the medical care of the men at Fort Pickering. Smith was found guilty of that charge and dismissed from service. General Orders and Circulars of the War Department, June 28, 1810, NARA, 57-60.

1062. Amos Stoddard to Col. Henry Burbeck, Dec. 25, 1810, Henry Burbeck Papers, William L. Clements Library.

1063. *Virginia Argus*, Feb. 6, 1810, 3.

1064. GCR to TJ, Jan. 4, 1810, FO.

1065. GCR to SW, Jan. 2, 1810, Register of LR.

1066. TJ to GCR, April 18, 1810, FO. National Archives, Original source: *The Papers of Thomas Jefferson, Retirement Series*, vol. 2, *16 November 1809 to 11 August 1810*, ed. J. Jefferson Looney (Princeton: Princeton University Press, 2005), 336.

1067. Statement of Gilbert C. Russell, Nov. 26, 1811, Donald Jackson, *Letters*, 573-575. Jonathan Williams was selected by Wilkinson to serve on his jury, Howard Cox, *American Traitor*, 228.

1068. The original version has not been located. The only copy known to exist is stored as part of the Jonathan Williams Collection at the Lilly Library at the University of Virginia. The document purports to be a copy because the word "signed" appears to the left of the Gilbert Russell signature copy, which was one method of showing that a document was a copy. In essence, it stated that the original was signed with the name that appears in the copy. The handwriting for the "Gilbert Russell" in the signature, particularly the unique "Russell" is an exact match for the scribe's writing of the same name in a notation below that the statement was given by Gilbert Russell to Jonathan Williams. The scribe wrote the signature. Gilbert C. Russell's signature appears on a commission verdict in the same folder, suggesting that it was written near the same time when Russell was in Fredericksburg. The signature is different and includes Russell's middle initial "C." Historian Donald Jackson discovered the existence of the copy when reviewing the Jonathan Williams Collection, and he included a transcription in this book, *Letters of the Lewis and Clark Expedition*. He correctly transcribed the signature as "Gilbert Russell." Former FBI handwriting expert, Gerald B. Richards, testified to this discrepancy during the 1996 coroner's inquest, James E. Starrs and Kira Gale, *The Death of Meriwether Lewis: A Historic Crime Scene Investigation* (Omaha: River Junction Press, LLC 2009), 126-140, with photos of the signature. He also testified that the signature that purports to be Jonathan Williams was not his. As Richards noted, the signature on the copy is "JWilliams." Williams normally signed his name "Jon Williams." It is possible that the scribe made a significant error on one signature, but significant errors on both signatures is much less likely. The fact that the discrepancy in Russell's signature has not been highlighted is one reason I suggest that for many who have studied the accounts of Lewis's death, the story we think we know may prevent us from seeing facts that would otherwise be clear.

1069. Telephone conversation with Ms. Susan Travis, who claimed to be a descendant of Dr. Smith. She related the family lore that Smith told his family that Lewis was murdered. The hearsay statement is repeated not as evidence that Lewis was murdered, but that different viewpoints arose near the time of Lewis's death.

1070. ML to James Madison, Sept. 16, 1809, Donald Jackson, *Letters*, 464-465. Lewis said that he took some medicine and felt better the following morning.

1071. Timothy Flint, *Recollections of the Last Ten Years*, 240.

1072. Meriwether Lewis personal Memorandum Book, undated entry, MHS. Note also that the Secretary of War ordered the military agent for New Orleans to procure opium as one of the medicines to be used for the troops, SW to William Swan, Dec. 21, 1809.

1073. Compare ML to WC, March 11, 1807, Donald Jackson, *Letters*, 385. ("I took some pills last evening after your departure from which I have found considerable relief and have no doubt of recovering my health perfectly in the course of a few days.") for an example of Lewis's belief in his ability to cure himself with his medicines.

1074. *Missouri Gazette and Public Advertiser*, Oct. 19, 1809, 3.

1075. WC to Jonathan Clark, Oct. 28, 1809, James J. Holmberg, *Dear Brother*, 216-223.

1076. The letter contained a number of strikethroughs and corrections, including a repeat of his closing, which some writers have claimed to be evidence of a deranged mental condition. (See, ML to James Madison, FO, n. 4). But an examination of other letters of the period from Lewis's brothers, military agent Return J. Meigs, and others show similar strikethroughs and connections when writers chose to make their first draft their final draft regardless of corrections.

1077. ML to James Madison, Sept. 16, 1809, Donald Jackson, *Letters*, 464-465. The original letter is in The Meriwether Lewis Collection at the Missouri Historical Society. Based on the digital copy, the letter contains no markings to show that it was received, and the envelope is not known still to exist. According to Dr. John Stagg, former editor of *The Papers of James Madison* at the University of Virginia, Madison did not keep a record that would have verified receipt of the letter. He believes that this letter may have been filed with Madison's personal correspondence rather than official correspondence. Dr. Stagg said that like his predecessor Robert Rutland, he is of the opinion that Madison received the letter (email correspondence with Dr. John Stagg, December 9, 2024). The letter contains several mark outs, which some historians suggest prove that Lewis was ill or not functioning at full capacity. However, other letters at the time written by other correspondents also show similar mark outs, particularly in drafts or when the writer did not take the time to copy the draft into a final version.

1078. Meriwether Lewis Memorandum Book, MHS.

1079. GCR to TJ, Jan. 4, 1810, FO.

1080. For distance at the time, see John B. Treat to William Daly, Oct. 6, 1805, JW to SW, Sept. 8, 1805, TP 13: 232-234. He stated that his letter would go from Arkansas to the Chickasaw Bluffs, then be delivered by an Indian to the Chickasaw Village. The Chickasaw Agency employed Chickasaw riders for mail delivery. Treat's statement that the letter might not reach Daly is unclear whether he thought mail delivery completely unreliable or whether it would have time to reach him at his present location. The location was temporary because Neely attempted to delegate the post office responsibilities to James Allen who lived at McIntoshville, James Neely to SW, Oct. 28, 1809, LR.

1081. Mary Louise Grahan Nazor, "The Indian Trading House on the Chickasaw Bluffs," 13. See also Jerry S. Palazolo, "The Chickasaw Nation, Chickasaw Agency: Two Places, One Post Office," *The American Philatelist* (April 2021), reprint.

1082. SW to Samuel Mitchell, Dec. 9, 1803, enclosed in James Neely to SW, April 29, 1810, LR.

1083. *Natchez Trace Parkway Survey*, 89-93.

1084. Neely's duty as postmaster was confirmed in the letter from William Eustis to James Neely, SW to James Neely, Sept. 18, 1809, and May 26,

1810, Register of LS. His payments to James Allen for duties as postmaster would be disallowed, though prior Chickasaw Agent Thomas Wright had paid Allen as assistant postmaster, Thomas Wright to Col. Return J. Meigs, July 22, 1807, April 18, 1808, July 12, 1808, CA.

1085. Neelly replied on Aug. 9, 1809, that he had just received the appointment forwarded by James Robertson, James Neelly to SW, Aug. 9, 1809, LR.

1086. James Roberson to Genl. [Daniel] Smith, Jan. 22, 1809. LR, Robertson conveyed the message that the Chickasaw wanted David Hogg to be appointed as Chickasaw Agent. Military agent. Return J. Meigs described Hogg as, "ingenious, industrious, temperate, and active," Return J. Meigs to SW, Jan. 27, 1808, CA. Hogg had previously served at Fort Southwest Point, where Brahan had served. See bond SW to David Hogg acknowledging appointment, Nov. 1807, LS and SW to David Hogg acknowledging his appointment by the secretary of war as "agent to their factory or trading house at the Chickasaw Bluffs in the Mississippi Territory," SW, LS, 346.

1087. Neelly acknowledged receipt of the secretary's appointment and instructions from James Robertson at Franklin, TN on Aug. 8, 1809, James Neelly to SW, Aug. 9, 1809, LR, SW to James Neelly. On Aug. 27, 1809, Neelly wrote of his impressions of the Chickasaw Agency on arriving, James Neelly to SW, Aug. 27, 1809.

1088. In April 1809, the annuities were ordered to be delivered to the factor David Hogg at Chickasaw Bluffs, John Smith to _inch Pope, April 4, 1809, LS; SW to David Hogg, July 8, 1809, Ordering that he deliver annuities received to Neelly, LS. SW to James Neelly, July 21, 1809, LS; The annuities were valued at $3,000 and were to be similar to annuities granted in 1808, SW, A Statement of Indian Annuities, LS, *Indian Affairs*, 427. Neelly reported on the tribe's wishes for 1810 based upon their prior experiences, James Neelly to SW, March 17, 1810, LR.

1089. The U.S. government established a trading post at Chickasaw Bluffs in 1802. Presumably, the physical location moved along with the changing garrison locations. J. Mason to Joseph Anderson, ASP, *Indian Affairs*, IV, 1: 768.

1090. See notes 120 and 129 above for a discussion of whether Lewis served as a commander at Fort Pickering in 1797.

1091. The Nicholas Biddle Notes, c. April 1810, Donald Jackson, *Letters*, 497-545, 522.

1092. Mary Louise Grahan Nazor, "The Indian Trading House on the Chickasaw Bluffs," 12-13.
1093. Charles T. Jones, Jr., "George Champlin Sibley: The Prairie Puritan," 63, 66. John Sibley to Henry Dearborn, April 10, 1805, ASP, *Indian Affairs*, VI, 1: 725-743.
1094. Jesse D. Jennings, "Nutt's Trip to the Chickasaw Country," *Journal of Mississippi History*, IX, 1 ([January] 1947): 34-61, 54, quoted in Jonathan Daniels, *The Devil's Backbone* (McGraw-Hill Book Co., Inc. 1962), 132.
1095. So many Chickasaws appeared at the fort to receive their shares in 1806 or 1807, that the secretary of war directed the agent to direct only tribal or clan leaders to appear at the fort to distribute annuities and take the annuities to their clans, SW to Thomas Wright, June 10, 1807. The plan apparently did not work to prevent Chickasaws from appearing at the fort. Mary Louise Graham Nazor, "The Indian Trading House on the Chickasaw Bluffs," 15. The date of the 1810 delivery was October 9, 1810. I have found no record that the agent personally delivered the annuities to the Chickasaw towns.
1096. GCR to SW, Jan. 2, 1810, LR.
1097. Ibid. For Smith's charges, see W. C. Smith to SW, Nov. 5, 1809, LR.
1098. Lanehart's name was also spelled "Leanheart." The United States v. George Leanheart, Nov. 28, 1809 and Nov. 30, 1809, U.S. Dist. Court Records, M1212, and M1315, NARA. The "George Lean" who was noted to have repaired a house at Chickasaw Bluffs, was likely the same person. Mary Louise Graham Nazor, "The Indian Trading House on the Chickasaw Bluffs," 13. The name is spelled "Leanheart" in the caption and "Laneheart" in the body of the minutes in the U.S. District records, Nov. 29, 1809, MF 878 Roll 1, 1215, TSLA. There were several Joseph Van Meters at the time, but if this Joseph was from Virginia, most likely he would have been Joseph Burns Van Meter of Berkley County, now West Virginia. The adjoining Jefferson County was home to the Harper's Ferry arsenal. Author Kira Gale believed that Van Meter was a point man for James Madison, but I do not have any of her supporting information.
1099. See, e.g., Dunbar Rowland, *Encyclopedia of Mississippi History: Comprising Sketches of Counties, Towns, Events, Institutions and Persons* (1907), 2: 177, men held for trial in the Mississippi Territory for coming crimes in the Choctaw Nation.

1100. David Hogg to James B. Waterman, Sept. 21, 1809, datelined Chickasaw Bluffs, recorded in Letter Book of the Arkansas Trading House, 245-246, NARA.
1101. Overton had filed a lawsuit in Wilson County, Tennessee, east of Nashville. The defendant was summoned to appear for a trial on September 24, 1809, but the defendant had not been served and there were no proceedings until November 1809. *W. H. Overton v. John J. Winston*, Loose Records, Wilson Court Records. He would have traveled at a fast rate, but it is possible that he traveled up the Natchez Trace and through Nashville to Wilson County on that date, but it seems more likely he would have known that the defendant has not been served and would not have made the trip.
1102. GCR to TJ, Jan. 4, 1810, FO. Russell said that Lewis had recovered six days after his arrival.
1103. ML to Amos Stoddard, May 16, 1804, Donald Jackson, *Letters*, 189-192. Stoddard also accompanied Lewis and Clark from St. Louis to St. Charles, as ordered by the War Department, for their formal departure. Amos Stoddard to Henry Dearborn, June 3, 1804, Donald Jackson, *Letters*, 196-198. Wilkinson ordered Stoddard to accompany tribal leaders to Washington that were sent to St. Louis thought the invitation the explorers extended from Jefferson. James Wilkinson to Henry Dearborn, Sept. 22, 1805, Donald Jackson, *Letters,* 259-260, James Wilkinson to Amos Stoddard, Oct. 21, 1805, Donald Jackson, *Letters*, 264-265.
1104. ML to Amos Stoddard, Sept. 22, 1809, Donald Jackson, *Letters*, 466-467.
1105. Ibid. Natchitoches was the U.S. main installation on the west side at the Red River. See also John Sibley to Amos Stoddard, April 2, 1812, Robert A. Stoddard, 70, acknowledging that Stoddard had been at Natchitoches sometime earlier.
1106. It was "postmarked" on September 25. "Chickasaw" presumably at the Chickasaw Post Office at Tockshish and then again at Fort Adams on October 4, where it was sent on to Stoddard at Washington, MHS. Excerpts from the Stoddard letter were published in the *National Intelligencer* in Washington on November 27, 1809. *The National Intelligencer and Washington Advertiser*, Nov 27, 1809, 3.
1107. GCR to TJ, Jan. 4, 1810, FO. The letter said that Lewis had recovered, and that Russell detained him by suggesting that he accompany him

once he received Wilkinson's approval. Russell would not have suggested Lewis wait unless Lewis was prepared to depart.

1108. GCR to SW, Aug. 25, 1809, Jan. 2, 1810, LR.

1109. GCR to TJ, Jan. 4, 1810, FO. If Russell sent a written request or received a written reply, a copy has not been found.

1110. Ibid. Russell said that Lewis carried about two hundred twenty dollars in notes and specie including the note for $99.58 that Russell lent Lewis.

1111. James Neelly to SW, Sept. 24, 1810, Records of the Office of the Secretary of War, Registers of LR. The notation of the letter received states in full, "From J. Neelly, Chickasaw Agency, Sept. 24, 1809, advising his draft to the order of David Hogg $100." The letter does not appear in the Letters Received books for the secretary of war, in letter books for Indian Affairs, or in the letter books for the military agent Return J. Meigs. It may have been sent to another department. The notation does not state what the draft was to pay as other Neelly notations generally stated. It could have been to receive cash as suggested in Thomas C. Danisi, "The Real James Neelly: Meriwether Lewis's Caretaker," *We Proceeded On*, Vol. 40 No. 4 (November 2014): 9-26. Previously, Hogg had sent Military Agent Return J. Meigs what he thought to be a forged letter and draft that he was offered supposedly from the former deceased agent Wright and asked for reimbursement of $100. David Hogg to Return J. Meigs, Nov. 15, 1808, CA. He wrote the military agent again in August 1809 to request payment. David Hogg to Return J. Meigs, November 18, 1808 and Aug. 16, 1809, CA. Meigs had thought the draft a forgery and returned it to Hogg, Return J. Meigs to David Hogg, July 19, 1809. Interpreter McGee who wrote the original draft to Hogg and planned to submit it as a claim against Wright's estate. Why Neelly would have paid the reimbursement is unclear unless it was to be charged to his agency accounts, but the amount of the payment is the same and the timing is consistent with the prior request. It is also possible that Neelly issued the draft to purchase horses to pack Lewis's trunks or that he wrote it for funds for his trip to Nashville. Neelly may have issued the draft at the agency and delivered the draft to Hogg when he returned, but the notation of the letter raises the possibility that Hogg followed Neelly to the agency, perhaps as part of the delivery of annuities. If so, Hogg could have been the informant who talked with Stoddard.

1112. Russell would claim that the horses were "loose" suggesting that they may have been taken in as strays, GCR to TJ, Jan. 31, 1810, FO National Archives. Original source: *The Papers of Thomas Jefferson, Retirement Series*, vol. 2, *16 November 1809 to 11 August 1810*, ed. J. Jefferson Looney (Princeton: Princeton University Press, 2005), 191-192. The agency later purchased a bay horse for $100, and had two public horses by September 1807, Thomas Wright to Return J. Meigs, Oct. 1, 1807, CA. And Neelly purchased a horse for public service for $125, Aug. 30, 1809, Records of the Office of the Secretary of War, Register of LR, NARA.

1113. GCR to TJ, Jan. 31, 1809, FO.

1114. Amos Stoddard to Daniel Bissell, *Missouri Gazette and Public Advertiser*, Oct. 19, 1809, 3. Stoddard arrived at Nashville by Sept. 28, 1809. The Chickasaw Agency was about 200 miles from Nashville. If Stoddard traveled 50 miles each day as common for a post rider on the Natchez Trace on horseback, Stoddard would have been in the area of the Chickasaw Agency when Neelly returned to the agency from Chickasaw Bluffs if Stoddard traveled directly from the agency to Nashville. The most-direct path from Fort Adams to Fort Pickering on all maps of the era that have surfaced is the Natchez Trace. At the point on the Natchez Trace closest to Chickasaw Bluffs (near McIntoshville), the Chickasaw Bluffs would have been about 90 miles or one to two days' ride depending upon the urgency. Stoddard would not have been in the "vicinity" of Fort Pickering unless he diverted his journey from a direct route to Nashville to travel toward Fort Pickering. If he traveled toward Fort Pickering, there is no record that he went to the fort.

1115. This assumption is based on the marking of "Chickasaw" as being the post office where the letter was received. There is no record of a separate post office at Chickasaw Bluffs. Mail riders picked up letters from the Bluffs but did not mark them. Similarly, letters mailed on the Natchez Trace were datelined on the first page by the writer, but they were not postmarked from the tavern where they were picked up. The letter was marked at the post officers where the letter was sent in transit. Either Neelly or another courier rode from Fort Pickering to the Chickasaw Post Office by September 25. The post office was eight miles north of the agency. Neelly could have traveled to the agency on September 24 and then to the post office on 25 September. The fact that the letter was sent on to Fort Adams could suggest that Stoddard did not meet Neelly or the postal courier, but it would depend on timing. Stoddard may have arrived after the letter had been sent to Fort Adams. The marking for the Chickasaw on September 25, in any event, indicates that Neelly or a mail courier traveled from Fort Pickering to the Chickasaw Post Office from September 22 to 25 and provides the best written evidence of the identity of the man coming directly from Chickasaw Bluffs, though it does not preclude others.

1116. Amos Stoddard to Daniel Bissell, printed in the *Missouri Gazette and Public Advertiser*, Oct. 19, 1809, 3.

1117. Stoddard would not arrive until about Nov. 10, 1809, or at least, that is the date that the War Department noted receipt of the letter. John Brahan to SW, Sept. 30, 1809, LR.

1118. GCR to TJ, Jan. 4, 1810, FO, NARA. Original source: *The Papers of Thomas Jefferson*, Retirement Series, vol. 2, *16 November 1809 to 11 August 1810*, ed. J. Jefferson Looney (Princeton: Princeton University Press, 2005), 120-122.

1119. See, e.g. JW to SW, July 16, 1809, and Sept. 25, 1809, during the same time period, reporting officer's requests for furloughs.

1120. GCR to TJ, Jan. 4, 1810. Ibid. Though long-barrel pistols were commonly carried by military officers and gentlemen of the period, it not know known exactly what type of pistols Lewis carried. The tomahawk, was described as mounted. Memorandum of Lewis's Personal Effects, Nov. 24, 1809, Donald Jackson, *Letters*, 470-474.

1121. *Mississippi: The WPA Guide to the Magnolia State* (Univ. of Mississippi Jackson Reprinted 1988), 201. The upper Cherokee Trading Trace passed Chickasaw leader Levi Colbert's inn "Buzzard Roost" about seven miles south of the Tennessee River. *The Commercial Appeal*, April 11, 1971, Section 6, 3. *The Life and Dying Confessions of Joseph T. Hare, The Noted Robber...* (D. Rumsey, 1818), 4.

1122. GCR to TJ, Jan. 4, 1810, FO. Russell said Lewis left the fort with two saddles, but he only gave or lent him one. Russell presumably used one saddle to ride one of Lewis's horses to Charlottesville. The second saddle was not one of the items recovered after Lewis's death listed along with the inventory of his effects from his trunks and not mentioned by Lewis Marks as being recovered when recovered Lewis's second horse from

Neelly's wife. John Marks to Reuben Lewis, Jan. 22, 1812, University of Virginia Library, Autograph Vault, Accession Number 9041.

1123. Lewis Memorandum Book, Meriwether Lewis Collection, MHS. Russell acknowledged receiving $241.50 out the $446.90 he claimed was due from Lewis's estate. He expected the remainder to be paid to his attorney. GCR to V. W. Southall, Aug. 18, 1816, Accession No. 9041, University of Virginia. Russell wrote Jefferson that he understood that the note for $99.58 was not found (GCR to TJ, Jan. 31, 1809, FO) but the note was listed on the inventory of items delivered to Washington.

1124. Paul Norton, "One Hundred Years of American Trunk Innovation," *The Journal of Antiques and Collectibles*, online.

1125. Vardis Fisher noted the decisions Lewis would have to take to transport his trunks. Vardis Fisher, *Suicide or Murder?*, 89.

1126. House painted as a hobby, but it is unlikely that Lewis would have gone to the trouble to transport a trunk on the Mississippi River for a friend's amateur paintings or supplies. House's version of Gilbert Stuart's painting of George Washington is held by the Maryland State Art Collection.

1127. James House to Frederick Bates, Sept. 28, 1809, MHS. The letter was sent before Lewis left Fort Pickering on Sept 29. House would not have known that Lewis planned to leave the trunk there. It was also in this letter that House said that he was traveling from St. Louis to Maryland. By comparison, Amos Stoddard's descendants described Stoddard's trunk as a "military chest." Robert A. Stoddard, The *Autobiography Manuscript of Major Amos Stoddard*, 16-17.

1128. Memorandum, Meriwether Lewis to GCR, September 28, 1809. FO, included in GCR to TJ, January 4, 1809. FO.

1129. Ibid., and Meriwether Lewis Memorandum Book, Meriwether Lewis Collection, MHS. Clark shipped bones from the expedition to Brown at New Orleans to place on a ship to send to Jefferson, WC to TJ, June 2, 1808, FO.

1130. Memorandum, Meriwether Lewis to GCR, September 29, 1809, FO, and Lewis Memorandum Book, Meriwether Lewis Collection, MHS.

1131. Memorandum, Meriwether Lewis to GCR, September 29, 1809, FO. Lewis may have trusted Carr, in part, because like Lewis, Carr was born in Albemarle County, Virginia. Frederic L. Billion, *Annals of St. Louis In Its Territorial Days*, 201.

1132. Gilbert C. Russell to TJ, Jan. 4, 1810, FO.
1133. Lewis Memorandum Book. TJ to James Madison, Nov. 26, 1809, Donald Jackson, *Letters*, 475-476.
1134. Freeman said that Lewis's square trunk could not be packed from Nashville and that a smaller trunk was placed inside the larger. The smaller was likely Lewis's portmanteau. William Meriwether acknowledged receiving the long trunk with the smaller trunk (likely the portmanteau) of clothes inside. W. D. Meriwether, May 8, 1810, to an unnamed person for transporting from Richmond a "long trunk of Meriwether that was forwarded to me from Washington enclosing a smaller trunk of clothes and which is at my house." Lewis Marks Papers, University of Virginia Library. Memorandum of Lewis's Personal Effects, Nov. 23, 1809, Donald Jackson, *Letters*, 470-474. A trunk of Lewis's clothes was also located upstairs in the White House after Lewis's death. The trunks will be discussed in Book 2.
1135. Gilbert C. Russell to TJ, Jan. 4, 1810, Jefferson Papers, Memorandum of Lewis's Personal Effects, Nov. 23, 1809, Donald Jackson, *Letters*, 470-474.
1136. Isaac A. Coles to Thomas Jefferson, Jan. 5, 1810, Donald Jackson, *Letters*, 486-487.
1137. WC Memorandum Book. The notes will be discussed in Volume 2.
1138. Russell's Jan. 4, 1810 letter listed the three items, which were also noted on the inventory items Lewis had in his possession after his death. Memorandum of Lewis's Personal Effects, Nov. 23, 1809, Donald Jackson, *Letters*, 470-474. Note that the inventory said that the papers in the portfolio were of no consequence.
1139. The Alexander Wilson account claimed that Lewis called for his buffalo robe and bear skins to sleep. Alexander Wilson to Alexander Lawson, 18 May 1810 (sometimes misprinted as 1811), AW 358-370.
1140. Russell admitted that he arranged for Neelly to transport Lewis's trunks by accepting Neelly's offer, GCR to TJ, Jan. 31, 1810, FO.
1141. House wrote Bates from Nashville on September 28, 1809, that Stoddard told him about hearing rumors of Lewis's attempted suicide as Stoddard was passing near the Chickasaw Bluffs. MHS. The closest Stoddard should have come to Chickasaw Bluffs on the road to Nashville would have been the Chickasaw Agency. A trip to Chickasaw Bluffs would have required a return to the agency to access the Natchez Road, unless Stoddard took

the Cherokee trading trail back to the Natchez Trace; however, there would have been no reason for Stoddard to taken the trail toward the Bluffs and add at least four days to his trip, unless he was going to the Bluffs. He did not state that he went to the Bluffs, and no one claimed to have seen him there. James House to Frederick Bates, Sept. 28, 1809, MHS. Stoddard was in Nashville at that time, because Brahan gave him a letter to deliver to the Secretary of War. See note 1147 below. In 1806, Stoddard requested to take House's position in St. Louis, but the request was apparently denied, Amos Stoddard to Thomas H. Cushing, Nov. 1, 1806, Robert Stoddard, *Autobiography of Amos Stoddard*, 66.

1142. James House to Frederick Bates, Sept. 28, 1809, MHS. Daniel Bissell supported House's application for a furlough because he said he needed a change of scenery for his physical and mental health, Daniel Bissell to Col. Henry Burbeck, August 12, 1809, Henry Burbeck Papers, William L. Clements Library.

1143. Amos Stoddard to Daniel Bissell, portion printed in the *Missouri Gazette*, Oct. 19, 1809, 3.

1144. Those who believe Lewis committed suicide could suggest that the unnamed person who prevented Lewis from taking his own life was Dr. Smith. Russell later charged Smith with being absent from the fort and failing to provide medical care. It would seem a stretch to explain why Smith would have abandoned Lewis's care to travel to the area of the Natchez Trace where he could have encountered Stoddard and why Russell would not have specified the treatment of Lewis in the charges. Because Neelly issued a draft to Hogg datelined Chickasaw Agency, it is also possible that the information could have been Hogg.

1145. James House to Frederick Bates, Sept. 28, 1809, MHS.

1146. *Missouri Gazette*, Oct. 19, 1803, 3.

1147. See letter from John Brahan to SW, Sept. 30, 1809, LR, datelined "Nashville, Tennessee" with "Maj. Stoddard" as the likely conduit written on the cover to the left of William Eustis's name. The words "Public Service" with a possible question mark appear at the top in a different handwriting, but the letter was received in Washington almost 20 days after a letter mailed from Nashville was received and Brahan states in the letter that Stoddard will supply additional information. The Secy of War approved Brahan's furlough until Jan. 1, 1810, provided that Brahan did not receive pay as captain during that period. SW to John Brahan, Nov. 11, 1809, Register of LR, SW.

1148. The date of the receipt of November 10, 1809, was noted on the letter, John Brahan to SW, Sept. 30, 1809, LR. The secretary of war replied to Brahan's letter on Nov. 11, 1809, SW to John Brahan, Nov. 11, 1809, LS.

1149. The *National Intelligencer and Washington Advertiser,* Nov. 27, 1809, 3. The newspaper had already republished news accounts from the Nashville and Lexington newspapers on November 15, but Stoddard provided his own information to the editor about Lewis becoming deranged on the Mississippi River and having to be controlled by people on his boat. Stoddard was ordered to Fort Columbus on Ellis Island, New York, the undated order apparently hand-delivered to him in Washington around November 24, 1809, Register of LS, Order located below letter sent Nov. 24, 1809.

1150. GCR to TJ, Jan. 4, 1810, FO.

1151. GCR to TJ Jan. 4, 1810 and Jan. 31, 1810, FO.

1152. GCR to TJ, Jan. 31, 1804, FO.

1153. Ibid. An alternate interpretation is that Russell could have hired the man who packed trunks holding the annuities to the Chickasaw Nation to also transport Lewis's trunks. But he had not mentioned the annuities in his letter, and Jefferson would not have known what he meant.

1154. Statement of GCR, Nov. 26, 1811, Donald Jackson, *Letters,* 573-575.

1155. WC to Jonathan Clark, Jan. 12, 1810, James J. Holmberg, *Dear Brother,* 233-36.

1156. GCR to TJ, Jan. 4, 1804, FO.

1157. *Missouri Gazette,* Oct. 19, 1809, 3.

1158. GCR to TJ, Jan 4, 1804, FO.

1159. SW to JW, July 15, 1809, LS.

1160. Deposition of Major Electus Backus, April 5, 1810, ASP: *Military Affairs* IV 1: 280-82, Hay and Werner, *The Admirable Trumpeter,* 299.

1161. James Wilkinson, *Burr's Conspiracy Exposed and General Wilkinson Vindicated Against the Slander of his Enemies on that Important Occasion,* 94-99, 181. John Brahan's brother-in-law was also in the army and named "William Tharpe," Mrs. Barton George Lane, "Documentary Evidence Concerning John Brahan," University of Virginia Library. I was unable to find evidence that they were one and the same person.

1162. James Wilkinson to SW, Oct. 18, 1809, printed in *Aurora General Advertiser*, Philadelphia, Pennsylvania, April 27, 1810, 2. John Brahan's brother-in-law "William Tharpe" may have been the same person. See previous note.

1163. James Wilkinson, *Burr's Conspiracy Exposed and General Wilkinson Vindicated Against the Slander of his Enemies on that Important Occasion*, 1811, 97.

1164. Letters from Oct. 6, 1809, Oct. 9, 1809, Oct. 20, 1809, and Oct. 24, 1809, and their datelines or lack thereof, are taken from the index of the Chicago Historical Museum Research Center Online. Note from the index that a letter dated Sept. 18, 1809, from Huntstown that is sometimes identified as being signed by James Wilkinson does not contain his signature and is shown on the index as "Joseph" Wilkinson.

1165. *The Enquirer*, March 2, 1810, 4. The plantation that Brown owned at Chalmette, near New Orleans, was seized and sold to collect his debt to the U.S. *Louisiana State Gazette*, Dec 24, 1810, 2. Brown's plantation would become the battlefield for the Battle Of New Orleans almost five years later as cited in the NPS history for the Chalmette Unit. Brown was appointed by Jefferson. In 1809, the Customs House building was located on what is now Decatur Street and was under construction on what would be called "Customs House Square," Stanley C. Arthur, *A History of the U.S. Custom House, New Orleans* (New Orleans: Works Progress Admin., 1940), 4.

1166. James House to Col. Henry Burbeck, December 24, 1809, Henry Burbeck Papers, Clements Library.

1167. Frederic L. Billion, Annals of St. Louis In Its Territorial Days, 269-270. Clark acknowledged Ben Wilkinson was said to be dead in 1812, Case No. 40, March Term 1812 Clark on behalf of William Clark, v. Jeremiah Connor, L. R. Colter-Frick, *Courageous Colter and Companions*, 96.

1168. James House to Col. Burbeck, Dec. 24, 1809, Henry Burbeck Papers, William L. Clements Library. It is possible that Ben died on the ship transporting the trunk, but House made a point of specifying the ship on which Ben died as if it were a different vessel.

1169. James McFarlane to SW, LR, March 4, 1810, LR.

1170. *The United States Gazette*, April 16, 1810, 4. *Richmond Enquirer*, Apr 20, 1810, 2. Newspapers often reported shipwrecks. I did not find a report of the Dart wrecking during that period. It is possible that the company that owned the ship replaced it if it sank, but I suspect they would have considered it bad luck to give a new ship the name of a ship that sank.

1171. Cornelius Burns Taylor Advertisement, *Missouri Gazette*, Nov. 2, 1809, 3. Risdon Price may have continued in business without Ben Wilkinson's partnership.

1172. Statement of GCR, Nov. 26, 1811, Donald Jackson, *Letters*, 573-575.

1173. John Swain wrote that Lewis entered the Natchez Trace at Lauderdale County, Alabama, suggesting that he took the Cherokee Trace, but he did not reference his source and some facts in his article are incorrect, *The Chattanooga News*, Oct. 10, 1903, 19.

1174. *Nashville Gazette*, Nov 18, 1820, with credit to Mitch Caver for the reference.

1175. Jesse D. Jennings, "Nutt's Trip to the Chickasaw Country," 44.

1176. The Chickasaw Agency house was located at Old Houlka, about two miles south of present-day Houston, Miss. Tockshish was located about five miles north of Old Houlka and about ten miles south of present-day Pontotoc, Miss. The actual site of the post office is presently located in a residential subdivision. At up to fifty miles a day, it would have taken the party two to three days on horseback. If Neely's party was accompanied by Chickasaw driving wagons transporting annuity farm implements and other goods, it would have taken longer. The length of their journey supports the statement in the Neely Letter that the party rested in the Nation a few days before turning north on the Natchez Trace. The letter does not state that the party rested in the eight-mile area known as the Chickasaw Agency. Circumstantial evidence from the text suggests that they did.

1177. Jesse D. Jennings, "Nutt's Trip to the Chickasaw Country," 41, n. 14.

1178. An 1801 Jefferson Peace Medal was discovered in New Albany, Miss. near the Chickasaw Trail (*New Albany Gazette*, unknown date). An intriguing question is whether Lewis could have presented it to an inn host, but more likely, Wilkinson presented it to one of the treaty participants in 1801.

1179. James R. Atkinson, *Splendid Land, Splendid People: The Chickasaw Indians to Removal* (Tuscaloosa, The University of Alabama Press 2004), 193. J. N. Walton to L. C. Draper, Jan. 8, 1883, accessed through www.chickasawhistory.org. Dawson A. Phelps, "Tockshish," *Journal of Mississippi History*, Vol. 78: No. 1 (2016): 69-78.

1180. Mary Louise Graham Nazor, "The Indian Trading House on the Chickasaw Bluffs," 13.

1181. Don Martini, *Who Was Who Among the Southern Indians: A Genealogical Notebook, 1698-1907* (Don Martini: Falkner, MS 1998), 133.

1182. Malcolm McGee (Chickasaw interpreter), Thomas Love (Chickasaw express rider), James Gunn (a Virginia Tory who had settled among the Chickasaw), James Allen (a trader and inn owner at McIntoshville), Thomas McCoy (a weaver in the Chickasaw Nation), Samuel Mitchell (former Chickasaw agent) and John Sphar (a locksmith who performed work for the agency) For John Sphar, see Mary Louise Grahan Nazor, "The Indian Trading House on the Chickasaw Bluffs, 1803-1818," *The Tennessee Genealogical Magazine*, Vol 47, No. 4 (Winter 2000), 13, and Samuel Mitchell to Return J. Meigs, Jan. 8, 1808, CA. For Thomas McCoy, see, Thomas McCoy receipt, July 29, 1805, U.S. Records of the Cherokee Indian Agency, in Tennessee, 1801-1835, Correspondence 1805. For Malcolm McGee, Samuel Mitchell to Return J. Meigs, Jan. 11, 1808, Cherokee Trading, 122-123. The Article appeared in Nashville in the *Democratic Clarion*, Oct. 20, 1809, 3 and in Natchez in *The Natchez Weekly Democrat*, Jan 1, 1810, 4.

1183. The statement was likely sent to the newspapers at both ends of the Natchez Trace with the postriders.

1184. SW to James Neelly, Sept. 18, 1809, Register of LS and James Neelly to SW, Feb. 23, 1810, LR. Neelly later submitted evidence that the prior agent was allotted funds for the post office and suggested that he had also paid Allen for those services. James Neelly to SW, April 29, 1810.

1185. Jo C. Guild, *Old Times in Tennessee*, 101-106. See also *Natchez Trace Parkway Survey*, 70., Cf. Don Martini, *Who Was Who Among the Southern Indians*, 15, noting that the attorney and subagent is often confused with a John L. Allen. Methodist minister Learner Blackman recorded his stop at Allen's house in 1813.

1186. GCR to TJ, Jan. 4, 1810, FO.

1187. Russell said that the packman who "packed the [Lewis's] trunks to the Nation" and that if he had packed the trunks to Nashville, Lewis would not have died. Fort Pickering was in the Chickasaw Nation. The implication is that the packman left the Lewis party near McIntoshville and that Neelly assumed full responsibility for Lewis's trunks from that point. There was also the implication that the packman had been willing to pack Lewis's trunks to Nashville. That interpretation seems logical from all the circumstances; however, scant record does not detail exactly how the packman's services ended.

1188. Gilbert C. Russell to TJ, Jan. 31, 1809, FO.

1189. Russell later wrote Jefferson in his Jan. 31, 1810 letter that Neelly encouraged Lewis to use alcohol, but from the tenor of the letter, that was information that he gleaned through his investigation after Lewis's death.

1190. "Chickasaw Agency," Loose file from NPS, Box 4, Folder 64, Natchez Trace Collection, McCain Library, University of Southern Mississippi.

1191. James Neelly to William Eustis, Aug. 27, 1809, LR. The prior agent Samuel Mitchell had started construction of a new frame house, but it had not been completed when he died. Neelly complained that unless a new Agency House was built or the old one made safe, he probably would incur bills for boarding at another house. The prior agent Thomas Wright chose to board with the carpenter, William Witson, who was working on the agency house. Wright billed the War Department for his lodging cost.

1192. *Travel Diary of Samuel Hastings Stackhouse*, entry of Nov. 25, 1811. His son, James Perry, offered the land where he lived known as "Tocksish" for sale when he moved to Oklahoma in 1837. That land at Section Nine Township Eleven Range Three and Four East was eight miles south of Pontotoc, Mississippi, about five miles north of the agency. *North Alabamian*, June 16, 1837, 3. Hardy Perry provided services for Chickasaw Agent Thomas Wright, Thomas Wright to SW, Jan. 24, 1807, and May, 2, 1808, CA, and probably for his predecessor, Samuel Mitchell.

1193. *Travel Diary of Samuel Hastings Stackhouse*, entry for Nov. 25, 1811. See note 1203 below for the source for Perry's statements.

1194. See The Conrad Prospectus, in John Conrad to ML, c, April 1, 1807, Donald Jackson, *Letters*, 393-397. Copies of the prospectus were sent to prospective purchasers by May 1807, Michael Amoureau to ML, May 31, 1807, Donald Jackson, *Letters*, 412-413.

1195. Letter from Col. M'Kee to General Wilkinson, Feb. 16, 1807, James Wilkinson, *Memoirs of My Own Times*, appendix 81.

1196. John McKee to JW., Feb. 22, 1806, John McKee letters to General James Wilkinson, 1805-1807, Everett D. Graff Collection of Western America, Newberry Library, viewable online.
1197. Malcolm McGee to Return J. Meigs, Nov. 8, 1808, CA.
1198. James Neely to SW, April 16, 1811, LR.
1199. The distance from McIntoshville to the Tennessee Line or "Indian Line" at Grinder's Stand was about 160 miles, or generally, a three-to-four-day ride. The timeline assumes a maximum of fifty miles per day, the distance that non-express post riders were expected to travel on the Natchez Trace.
1200. GCR to TJ, Jan. 31, 1810, FO. In a previous article, I interpreted Russell's statement as his man packed trunks for the Chickasaw annuities; however, the better interpretation is that Russell's man packed Lewis's trunks.
1201. John Bates and John Kincaid receipts to George Gaines, March 31, 1811, Cherokee Trading House Records, NARA, image #'s. 21, 25 and 220.
1202. Statement of Gilbert C. Russell, Nov. 26, 1811, Donald Jackson, *Letters*, 573-575.
1203. Perry's account of Lewis's visit was mentioned by Cincinnati businessman Henry Bechtel in a letter recollecting his life in early 1800's in the Ohio River Valley, Henry Bechtel to Lyman Draper, Dec. 14, 1838, MS. 1 O 81 (4-5), Draper Collection, Wisconsin Historical Society, quoted in part in John Bakeless, *Lewis and Clark*, 413, and Vardis Fisher, *Suicide or Murder?*, 116. Bakeless suggested that Bechtel met a casual traveler who said that he had traveled with Lewis but the "He" in the context of the entire letter was Hardy Perry. Bechtel transported goods down the Ohio and Mississippi. He frequently chose to return home overland on the Natchez Trace and became acquainted with the people who lived along the Natchez Trace. Henry A. Ford and Mrs. Kate B. Ford, comp., *History of Cincinnati, Ohio* (L. A. Williams & Company, 1881), 5, 61, 349.
1204. Three years later, a James S. Neely who claimed to be the Chickasaw Agent's son apparently lived at the Chickasaw Agency. (James Neely to James Brown, May 24, 1812, enclosed in James Brown to Secretary of War, June 11, 1812, LR., NARA, microfilm, M221, Roll 42.) The purported son James S. Neely does not appear in the family genealogy as the agent's son, and it is possible that the agent raised his nephew named "James Neely" as his son, a common practice at the time, e.g.

Andrew Jackson, or that the nephew misrepresented his relationship. He highlighted the word "father" in describing his relationship. In fact, in Nov. 28, 1810, Neely said that a payment from Chickasaw interpreter Malcolm McGee made payable to his nephew James Neelly had been protested, James Neelly to SW, Nov. 28, 1810, LR. That nephew moved to Maury County, Tennessee, and the letter was datelined from Columbia, the county seat. The son or nephew James Neelly's signature is not the signature on The Neelly Letter. Whether the agent was one James Neelly or the other seems to have made no difference in the events leading to Lewis's death.

1205. Jeremiah K. Love, who had worked as a mail rider between the agency and Fort Pickering, worked as an interpreter at the Chickasaw Factory at Fort Pickering. Jeremiah K. Love to SW, April 18, 1808, LR, requesting that Factor Hogg be permitted to hire him as an interpreter; SW to Jeremiah K. Love, April 19, 1808, LS, appointing him as interpreter to the Chickasaw factor; SW to Jeremiah Love and to David Hogg, May 24, 1808 acknowledging Love's appointment as interpreter, LS, and June 23, 1808, LR, stating that he had started work at the factory. Laneheart was found guilty by a Nashville jury that included James Harding, likely Andrew Jackson's friend, and owner of a Natchez Trace inn in Nashville on a farm that Harding later developed into the Belle Meade Plantation.

1206. The Secretary of War honored the draft that Neelly issued to Love but deducted the funds from Neelly's salary because escorting the prisoner was part of his job. SW to James Neelly, Nov. 24, 1809, Register of LS.

1207. One of several references to Chickasaw hospitality was Dr. Rush Nutt's journal from 1805, Jesse D. Jennings, "Nutt's Trip to the Chickasaw Country," 46.

1208. The quote referenced a Mississippi River, regarding names such as "Devil's Backbone," "Devil's Anvil," "Devil's Hole," "Devil's Punchbowl," and "Devil's Tea Table," was "the divinity most religiously propitiated in these dangerous passes." Leland D. Baldwin, *The Keelboat Age*, 70. Similarly, "The Devil's Shoe" was located on the Ohio, "The Devil's Punchbowl" on the Mississippi north of Natchez, and "The Devil's Elbow," on the Mississippi.

1209. TJ to Henry Dearborn, July 12, 1803, FO. National Archives, Original source: *The Papers of Thomas Jefferson*, vol. 41, *11 July—15 November 1803*, ed. Barbara B. Oberg (Princeton: Princeton University Press, 2014), 33-34.

1210. Return J. Miegs to William Eustis, Oct. 26, 1809, CA.
1211. Samuel Mason was known to attack travelers on both water and land. William C. C. Claiborne to James Madison, March 15, 1804, FO, National Archives. Original source: *The Papers of James Madison*, Secretary of State Series, vol. 6, *1 November 1803—31 March 1804*, ed. Mary A. Hackett, J. C. A. Stagg, Ellen J. Barber, Anne Mandeville Colony, and Angela Kreider (Charlottesville: University of Virginia Press, 2002), 589-590.
1212. Willie Blount, Legislative Message, Sept. 26, 1811, *Messages of the Governors of Tennessee, 1796-1821*, ed. R. H. White (Nashville: Tennessee Historical Commission, 1952), 1: 345-352. Chickasaw leader Tuscumby was robbed south of Franklin, Tenn. in 1813 (*State of Tennessee v. John Campbell*, October 18, 1813, Circuit Court of Maury County, loose files, Maury County Archives, Columbia, Tenn.). A company of Andrew Jackson's soldiers returning from the Battle of New Orleans were robbed and nearly killed by bandits.
1213. Rev. John G. Jones, *A Complete History of Methodism*, 86.
1214. The third account attributed to Mrs. Grinder said that he was wearing a blue and white riding coat and that later when his body was found, he was dressed in tattered clothing, apparently opposed to the clothing he was wearing when he arrived, *The Sundbury Gazette, and Northumberland County Republican*, Dec. 7, 1844, 1.
1215. James Neelly to TJ, Oct. 18, 1809, Donald Jackson, *Letters*, 467-468.
1216. JW to SW, Sept. 3, 1809, LR.
1217. *Travel Diary of Samuel Hastings Stackhouse*, entry for Nov. 25, 1811, in private collection.
1218. *Natchez Trace Parkway Survey*, 75-76.
1219. Rev. John G. Jones, *A Complete History of Methodism*, 20.
1220. Dawson A. Phelps, "Tockshish," *Journal of Mississippi History*. Vol. 78: No. 1, Article 6 (2016): 69-78 69-78, 72, citing diary of traveler Francis Bailey in 1797.
1221. Elizabeth Howard West, "Diary of José Bernardo Gutiérrez de Lara, 1811-1812," *The American Historical Review*, Vol. 34, No. 1 (Oct. 1928), 63.
1222. *Natchez Trace Parkway Survey*, 59. A light evening meal, or "supper" was common. George Sibley also discussed the custom of the day.

1223. Jesse D. Jennings, "Nutt's Trip to the Chickasaw Country," 56. Note that some of the distances mentioned in the article are inaccurate.
1224. SW to James Neelly, Aug. 17, 1811, LS.
1225. James Neelly to James Brown, May 24, 1812, Enclosed in James Brown to Secretary of War, June 11, 1812, LR., NARA, microfilm, M221, Roll 42. The Brown's Bottom location is now under a reservoir near New Site, Miss.
1226. GCR to TJ, Jan. 31, 1810, FO. According to Russell, Neelly used the claim of a loan to keep possession of Lewis's pistols and other items.
1227. See, e. g. *Masterson v. Neelly*, Williamson County Tennessee Archives, Franklin, Tennessee.
1228. James Neelly to SW, Sept. 24, 1809, Register of LR.
1229. Elizabeth Howard West, "Diary of José Bernardo Gutiérrez de Lara," 63.
1230. It is possible that Lewis stayed about five miles south at George's brother Levi's inn, W. C. Yates, *Tales of a Tennessee Yeoman* (Franklin, Tenn.: W. C. Yates, 1991), 38.
1231. Elizabeth Howard West, "Diary of José Bernardo Gutiérrez de Lara," 55-77, 63.
1232. James Robertson to Bennett Searcy, May 10, 1794, Paul Clements, *Chronicles of the Cumberland Settlements*, Aug. 25, 1794, 425.
1233. Levi Colbert had partnered with George Colbert when the ferry operated about five miles west before the army moved the wagon road.
1234. *Natchez Trace Parkway Survey*, 72.
1235. Ibid., 88-92.
1236. Newspapers in Natchez and Nashville should also have reported a sighting of Lewis. Their reporting was contingent upon so many variables that the absence of a story about Lewis's travels supports a theory that an effort was made to keep them secret but does not prove it.
1237. Dawson Phelps, "Stands and Travel Accommodations on the Natchez Trace," *The Journal of Mississippi History*, XI: 1 (Jan. 1949), 48. *Natchez Trace Parkway Survey*, 73.
1238. John Brahan to TJ, Oct. 18, 1809, FO.
1239. Rev. John G. Jones, *A Complete History of Methodism*, 69. Jones said that ministers allayed their fears with the belief that God was with them in their work.

1240. Mark Van Doren, *Correspondence of Aaron Burr and His Daughter Theodosia* (Covici-Friede, 1929), 214.
1241. GCR to TJ, Jan. 31, 1810, FO.
1242. SW to Return J. Meigs, Oct. 5, 180_, LS, *Military Affairs*, Dec. 15, 1808-Nov. 12, 1810, 110 (The letter appears to show the date of 1803, but it is registered with letters for October 1809 between letters carrying a similar subject. Also see letter to McRae of same date. Eustis directed those horses be supplied; therefore, it appears that the courier traveled the Natchez Trace to just above Bayou Pierre as directed rather than a river route. The dispatch appears to be the letter from SW to JW, Oct. 5, 1809. The years in all three letters appear as "03" but their placement in the letter book and the mention of directing Daniel Bissell to take boats to Chickasaw Bluffs demonstrate that the year was 1809. Also, the following letter to the Commanding Officers at Chickasaw Bluffs of the same date to move their troops is shown as 1809. The letters appear in the Register of Letters Sent beginning Dec. 15, 1808.
1243. If a pack horse strayed without Lewis's trunks, the party would not have been able to proceed—they would have no way to carry them and they would not have left the trunks in the woods at their camp. It follows, then, that Lewis's trunks were tied to the pack horse that disappeared. James Neelly to TJ, Oct. 18, 1809, FO, and in Donald Jackson, *Letters*, 467-468.
1244. Statement of Gilbert C. Russell, Nov. 26, 1811, Donald Jackson, *Letters*, 573-575.
1245. Whether Cobert intended to show his location as the Tennessee River or in the State of Tennessee, the dateline of "Tennessee" rather than "Colbert's" likely shows his location as north of the river. The letter was postmarked "Nashville," which is persuasive evidence that he was located near or on the Natchez Trace south of Nashville. The post rider would have delivered the letter to Nashville before a separate rider would have taken it to its destination of the Hiwassee Garrison. The postmark date is unclear. Levi Colbert to Return J. Meigs, Oct. 9, 1809, CA.
1246. Local lore held that Neelly stayed overnight at Rippey's Stand, the packhorses carrying Lewis's trunks disappeared. I have found no evidence that Rippey's Stand had been built by 1809 (NPS interview with Hugh Webster, Loose Files). Young Factor's Stand on Factory Creek in what in now Wayne County, Tennessee is a more likely location. It was probably

one of the three stands or inns that a Chickasaw owner built. If Peerny's horse strayed, it would provide an explanation for why Peerny did not arrive at Grinder's Stand at the same time as Lewis, but Peerny would not have been accustomed to walking a wilderness trail.

1247. John Brahan to TJ, Oct. 18, 1809, FO.
1248. Travelers and settlers considered the line the official boundary. It ran along the ridge dividing the waters of the Duck River from the waters of the Tennessee. Samuel Hastings Stackhouse referred to it as "the division line between Tennessee and the Mississippi Territory" Entry Nov. 22, Stackhouse Diary, Andrew Jackson Edmonson referred to it as the "Indian Line." Andrew Jackson, *Journal When a Volunteer Under General Andrew Jackson in 1812-1813*, Mississippi Department of Archives and History, B E24j, 16. Gutierrez referred to it as the "boundary line of the Indian country," Elizabeth Howard West, "Diary of José Bernardo Gutiérrez de Lara, 1811-1812." *The American Historical Review* Vol. 34, No. 1 (Oct. 1928), 64.
1249. John Brahan to SW, 18 Oct. 1809, LR.
1250. See, e.g., Alexander Wilson to Alexander Lawson, 18 May 1810 (sometimes misprinted as 1811), AW 358-370.
1251. *Tennessee Gazette*, 1803, Paul Clements, *Chronicles of the Cumberland Settlements*, 491. The *Gazette* editor blamed local tribes, but robbers frequently disguised themselves as tribal members. *Tennessee Gazette*, May 18, 1803., *Tennessee Gazette*, Aug. 24, 1803, 2.
1252. *Tennessee Gazette*, May 18, 1803, 1 (robbery and murder at Swan Creek) and May 24, 1803, 2 (robbery and murder at Keg Springs).
1253. Archibald Roane to SW, June 9, 1803, Roane Papers, TSLA. *Tennessee Gazette and Mero Advertiser*, May 18, 1803, 1, June 8, 1803, and August 24, 1803, 1. See also Joseph Thomson Hare, *The life and dying confession of Joseph T. Hare: the noted robber who was executed at Baltimore in September last for robbing the mail* (Auburn, New York 1818).
1254. SW to Archibald Roane, July 18, 1803, Tennessee Governor's Papers, TSLA, *Natchez Trace Parkway Survey*, 57.
1255. Note that McKee said that a French Indian countryman was to have called on him to receive the letter for Wilkinson. It is a similar description that a few gave for Thomas Runions. John McKee to JW, Feb. 26, 1807, ASP, Misc., 594.

1256. Runions' family passed down the legend that he was involved with Lewis's death.
1257. People in Nashville warned Alexander Wilson about traveling alone on the Natchez Trace, Alexander Wilson to Alexander Lawson, 18 May 1810 (sometimes misprinted as 1811), AW 358-370.
1258. Dawson A. Phelps and John T. Willett, "Iron Works on the Natchez Trace," *Tennessee Historical Quarterly*, Vol. 12, No. 4 (December 1953), 309-322. Phelps and Willett speculated that McLish's was not in operation prior to Alexander Wilson's trip down the Natchez Trace because he did not mention it, but writers frequently did not mention every inn or site they passed.
1259. Maury County, "Tennessee Court Minutes, 1808-1809," 197, Maury County, Tennessee Archives, Columbia, Tenn. A citizen was later charged with failing to do his duty to mark the road.
1260. Peerny would have been unaccustomed to traveling on foot, and he likely would not have had the shoes or boots for such a walk. It would have taken Peerny too long to walk and arrive the same day as Lewis unless the previous camp was within just a few miles.
1261. A traveler also described them as "tremendous hills," Jesse D. Jennings, "Nutt's Trip to the Chickasaw Country," 44.
1262. With thanks to Tommy Haskins, U.S. Army Corps of Engineers, for the reference.
1263. A posting would have been necessary to enforce a prohibition on trade with the Chickasaw. Alexander Wilson noted that he entered the "wilderness," the name travelers gave to the Chickasaw Nation, when he left Grinders traveling south, and four years later, Andrew Jackson Edmonson made a visual measurement of the distance of "ten steps" between the "Indian line" and Grinder's door, Edmonson, Andrew Jackson, *Journal When a Volunteer Under General Andrew Jackson*, 16.
1264. Descriptions of tavern signs for Kentucky taverns are noted in J. Winston Coleman, Jr., *Stage-Coach Days In The Bluegrass* (University Press of Kentucky, Louisville: 1935), 94.
1265. James Neelly to TJ, Oct. 18, 1809, FO.
1266. Alexander Wilson to Alexander Lawson, May 18, 1810 (sometimes misprinted as 1811), AW 358-370.
1267. See, e.g., TJ to ML, July 17, 1808, Donald Jackson, *Letters*, 444.

NOTES

1268. Alan Pell Crawford, *Twilight at Monticello: The Final Years of Thomas Jefferson* (New York: Random House, 2008), 64. Jefferson was given the privilege of naming the Randolph children, Thomas Fleming, *The Intimate Lives of the Founding Fathers*, 320.

1269. TJ to ML, Aug. 16, 1809, Donald Jackson, *Letters*, 458-459. Jefferson had given a similar ending to his October 26, 1806 letter to Lewis welcoming his return from the expedition,"[the object of this letter] is to assure you of what you already know, my constant affection for you & the joy with which all your friends here will recieve you" but in this ending he added that his affections, which he expressed for other friends, were unalterable, TC to ML, Oct. 26, 1806, Donald Jackson, *Letters*, 350-351. Meriwether Lewis Randolph married Andrew Jackson's grandniece at age 25, and the same year, President Andrew Jackson appointed him Governor of the Arkansas Territory. Randolph died two years later from malaria.

1270. WC to Jonathan Clark, Nov. 16, 1809, James J. Holmberg, *Dear Brother*, 228-233.

1271. References are to Clark's 1809 Journal housed at the Missouri History Museum unless otherwise designated. To avoid unnecessary duplication, the specific dates are not repeated in the notes, but references may easily be located in the journal.

1272. Coleman, J. Winston Jr., *Stage-Coach Days In The Bluegrass* (Louisville: University Press of Kentucky, 1935), 43.

1273. Probably mincemeat pie sweetened with fruit.

1274. Coleman, J. Winston Jr., *Stage-Coach Days In The Bluegrass*, 28.

1275. Ibid., 42-43.

1276. Ibid., 63-64.

1277. James J. Holmberg, *Dear Brother*, 202, n. 1. He had contemplated taking the northern road as a more direct route to Philadelphia and Washington if could justify the trip as official business and obtain reimbursement of travel expenses from the government (WC to Jonathan Clark, July 22, 1809, James J. Holmberg, *Dear Brother*, 204-205.

1278. Based on Clark's statement in his letter requesting that Jonathan send him Lewis's letter. WC to Jonathan Clark, James J. Holmberg, *Dear Brother*, Oct. 28, 1809, 216-223.

1279. WC to Jonathan Clark, October 28, 1809, James J. Holmberg, *Dear Brother*, 216-223.

1280. WC to Jonathan Clark Jan. 12, 1810, James J. Holmberg, *Dear Brother*, 233-236.
1281. WC to Jonathan Clark, Oct. 28, 1809, James J. Holmberg, *Dear Brother*, 216-223. The article may have been the one reprinted in the *National Intelligencer* on November 15, 1809; however, that article added that Lewis was shot.
1282. John Ferling, *Adams v. Jefferson*, 4.
1283. James J. Holmberg points out that "Mr. Shannon" was not the Corps member George Shannon, James J. Holmberg, *Dear Brother*, 219, n. 1.
1284. WC to Jonathan Clark, Oct. 28, 1809, James J. Holmberg, *Dear Brother*, 216-223.
1285. Ibid.
1286. "On April 1$^{st}$ of this year [1806], Daniel Weiseger was granted the right to keep a tavern on Ann Street in the town of Frankfort; this tavern was located where the Capitol Hotel now stands." Register of Kentucky Historical Society.
1287. The inn also known as the "Offutt-Cole Tavern," is still standing.
1288. Clark may also have written this letter from Lexington on Oct. 30, 1809. He simply states, "I have wrote to judge Overton of Nashville about his papers." I am making the assumption that Clark wrote first to his brother before others. Clark does not state who told him that Neelly had gone to Nashville after Lewis's death. Perhaps he encountered the same man the Kentucky newspaper used as a source.
1289. WC to Jonathan Clark, Oct. 30, 1809, James J. Holmberg, *Dear Brother*, 224-225.
1290. Thomas McArthur Anderson, "A Monograph of the Anderson, Clark, Marshall, and McArthur Connection," LOC.
1291. *Kentucky Gazette*, October 17, 1809, 3.
1292. WC to Jonathan Clark, Nov. 8, 1810, James J. Holmberg, *Dear Brother*, 225-228. For a general description of the hotel, see *Kentucky Gazette*, Jan. 2, 1810, 4.
1293. William D. Meriwether to WC, Jan. 22, 1810, Donald Jackson, *Letters*, 489-490.
1294. WC to Jonathan Clark, Nov. 8, 1810, James J. Holmberg, *Dear Brother*, 226-228.

1295. WC to Jonathan Clark, March 8, 1810, James J. Holmberg, *Dear Brother*, 236-241.
1296. *Richmond Enquirer*, Oct. 24, 1809, 3. Description of a Public Dinner held for Thomas Jefferson in Richmond, [21 October 1809]. *Founders Online*, National Archives.
1297. Jack Jackson, *Indian Agent: Peter Ellis Bean in Mexican Texas* (Texas A&M University Press: College Station, 2005), 6-18.
1298. WC to Jonathan Clark, Nov. 8, 1809, James J. Holmberg, *Dear Brother*, 225-228.
1299. John Brahan to SW, Oct. 18, 1809, LR.
1300. John Burke Treat to Frederick Bates, Oct. 31, 1809, FB 2: 103.
1301. Nov. 21, 1809, Jefferson-weather-records.org from the Thomas Jefferson Papers.
1302. James Neelly to TJ, Oct. 18, 1809, FO and Donald Jackson, *Letters*, 467-468.
1303. Col. Return J. Meigs to David Hogg, July 19, 1809, CA.
1304. James Neelly to TJ, Oct. 18, 1809, FO and Donald Jackson, *Letters*, 467-468. For comparison of handwriting, see Neelly's letter accepting his commission, James Neelly to SW, Aug. 9, 1809, LR, and Neelly's report of the condition of the agency, James Neelly to SW, Aug. 27, 1809, LR. Other convincing evidence of forgery is the letter that Neelly wrote to the Secretary of War from the Chickasaw Agency, on the same date, Oct. 18, 1809. That letter bears Neelly's distinctive signature. The letter requested reimbursement of his payment to Jeremiah Love for transporting Lanehart to Nashville, but it did not mention Lewis's death. The distance makes it clear that Neelly could not have been in both locations on the same date. The forgery will be discussed in greater detail in Volume 2 of *Jefferson's Spy*.
1305. James Neelly to TJ, Oct. 18, 1809, FO and Donald Jackson, *Letters*, 467-468.
1306. The Washington, D. C., *National Intelligencer* reported on Nov. 13 that Lewis had died by suicide and on Nov. 15 it reprinted the articles from Lexington that reported Lewis died from three gunshots and cuts to his throat, arms and legs. *National Intelligencer*, Nov. 13, 1809, and Nov. 15, 1809. It is not clear whether the Lexington paper published the same story published in the Frankfort *Argus of Western America* that Clark

read or that the Russellville, Kentucky *The Farmer's Friend* newspaper published on Oct. 27, 1809, which appears to have been based on The Neelly Letter and the *Nashville Clarion* article.

1307. Email correspondence with the Jefferson Library, May 7, 2025. Jefferson maintained a subscription to the *National Intelligencer*, but it appears that he was not prompt in picking up his mail from the post office. The postal service did not offer home delivery of mail. *National Intelligencer*, Nov. 13, 1809, and Nov. 15, 1809.

1308. James Neelly to TJ, Oct. 18, 1809, FO and Donald Jackson, *Letters*, 467-468. Jefferson had been away from home for two weeks (TJ to C. and A. Conrad and Co., Nov. 23, 1809, Donald Jackson, *Letters*, 474-475.)

1309. TJ to James Madison Nov. 26, 1809, Donald Jackson, *Letters*, 475-476. Jefferson also noted in his Memorandum Book that he paid Peerny $10 on Nov. 26, 1809, "to carry him to Washington," Memorandum Books, 1809, Thomas Jefferson, FO.

1310. Sally T. Anderson "Brief Biography of Meriwether Lewis." Autograph Vault, Accession No 9041, University of Virginia Archives.

1311. TJ to James Madison, Nov. 26, 1809, Donald Jackson, *Letters*, 475-476. Lewis did not appoint an executor in the Last Will and Testament that was entered into probate in Charlottesville. Clark had understood from the Suspicious Russell Letters that Lewis had appointed him and William Meriwether to be co-executors, WC to Jonathan Clark, Nov. 26, 1809, James J. Holmberg, *Dear Brother*, 228-233.

1312. This assumes Lewis purchased horses of equal value. He may have purchased a more expensive horse for himself if he had that option. John Pernier to TJ, Feb. 10, 1810, FO.

1313. WC to Jonathan Clark, Nov. 26, 1806, James J. Holmberg, *Dear Brother*, 228-233. Clark had said that he planned to write to Anderson, but there is no evidence that he did other that this letter from Anderson, which could have been a reply to Overton's letter referred to in his Nov. 26, 1806 letter to his brother Jonathan.

1314. WC to Jonathan Clark, Nov. 26, 1809, James J. Holmberg, *Dear Brother*, 228-233.

1315. Ibid.

1316. GCR to TJ, Jan. 4, 1810. FO.

1317. Statement of Gilbert C. Russell, Nov. 26, 1811, Donald Jackson, *Letters*, 573-575. WC to Jonathan Clark, October 28, 1809, James J. Holmberg, *Dear Brother*, 216-223. If this is the same letter Clark said that he received from Lewis from New Madrid, then Lewis changed his travel plans prior to arriving at Fort Pickering. If that is the case, it raises that question why Lewis would have waited until Fort Pickering to notify Madison particularly because Lewis was so anxious to alert Madison that he would be late.

1318. The Last Will and Testament that was admitted to probate does not state where it was signed, but its date of September 11, suggests that Lewis signed it when he was in the area of Little Prairie or New Madrid.

1319. Nevertheless, even if Lewis made the statements, they were not irrational. Lewis may have learned that his sickness at New Madrid had been reported in the newspapers and it was reasonable to assume that Clark could have heard about it before he had traveled too far and that he would come to his aid. Lewis also likely knew that the St. Louis Missouri Fur Company would be sending boats with peltries down the river just behind him. If Lewis lay in a sickbed on the boat, he may have heard other boats coming up from behind and hoped or assumed that Clark or one of his agents was onboard, even he was unaware that McFarlane would be leading them. A little over three years later, Jackson's soldiers would describe hearing other boats coming from behind from long distances on the river. The Suspicious Russell Letters have not been found, and without knowing exactly what they claimed, it is difficult to assess them other than in ways they contradict statements from Russell and their timing.

1320. Kira Gale first mentioned this fact to me. Comparisons of the two letters side by side reveal the similarities of the handwriting. Jefferson could have noticed the similarities if he had taken the time to make the comparison, but that similarity escaped the notice of historians until about 2009.

1321. John Brahan to Thomas Jefferson, Oct. 18, 1809, FO, National Archives, Original source: *The Papers of Thomas Jefferson, Retirement Series*, vol. 1, *4 March 1809 to 15 November 1809*, ed. J. Jefferson Looney (Princeton: Princeton University Press, 2004), 602-604.

1322. James Neely to TJ, Oct. 18, 1809, and John Brahan to TJ, Oct. 18, 1809, FO. John Brahan to SW, Oct. 18, 1809, LR. John Brahan to Amos Stoddard, Oct. 18, 1809, Reuben G. Thwaites, ed. *Original Journals of the Lewis and Clark Expedition*, 1804-1806, New York: Dodd, Mead, 1904-1905, 7: 389.

1323. Joseph Roleson, James Gunn, and Thomas Love, "Minute books of the U.S. Circuit Court for West Tennessee, 1797-1893, and of the U.S. District Court for the Middle Dist. Of Tennessee, 1839-65," RG 21, V. 2, NARA.

1324. Nov. 28, 1809, Final Records Books of the U.S. District Court in Nashville, Vol. 2, 1806-1850, NARA. One grand jury member was Nicholas J. Perkins, who could have been Aaron Burr's captor; however, there was a second Nicholas J. Perkins who served in the Tennessee Legislature.

1325. Nov. 30, 1809, Final Records Books of the U.S. District Court in Nashville, Vol. 2, 1806-1850, NARA.

1326. William Clark, entry of Dec. 6, 1809, William and Clark Memorandum Book, Missouri State Historical Museum.

1327. TJ to Charles Willson Peale, October 6, 1805, Donald Jackson, *Letters*, 260-61.

1328. *Nashville Democratic Clarion*, Oct. 20, 1809, *National Intelligencer*, Nov. 15, 1809, reporting from Lexington, Kentucky, Oct. 28, 1809.

1329. Thomas Fleming, *The Intimate Lives of the Founding Fathers*, 312, 317-318.

1330. John Pernier to TJ, Feb. 10, 1810, FO.

1331. Frederick Bates described the circumstances of Lewis's death as "melancholy," but he had also described Col. Thomas Hunt's death as "melancholy." Frederick Bates to Nicholas Boilvin, Nov. 4, 1809, FB 2: 106-107. A newspaper of the period referred to a boy's death from natural causes as "melancholy." *Pennsylvania Weekly Telegraph*, Oct 14, 1809, 3.

1332. GCR to William D. Meriwether, 18 April 1813, Donald Jackson, *Letters*, 732.

1333. Ibid.

1334. TJ to Gilbert C. Russell, April 18, 1810, FO. NARA. Original source: *The Papers of Thomas Jefferson, Retirement Series*, vol. 2, *16 November 1809 to 11 August 1810*, ed. J. Jefferson Looney (Princeton: Princeton University Press, 2005), 336.

1335. TJ to James Madison, Nov. 26, 1809, LC. TJ to C. & A. Conrad & Company, November 23, 1809, Donald Jackson, *Letters*, 474-475.

1336. WC to Jonathan Clark, Nov. 26, 1809, James J. Holmberg, *Dear Brother*, 228-233.

1337. Wilkinson's aide-de-camp William R. Boote's and General Wade Hampton's likely stops at Grinder's Stand will be covered in Volume 2.
1338. GCR to TJ, Jan. 31, 1809, FO.
1339. He would ask President Madison to order Neelly to send Lewis's trunks to Washington City. TJ to James Madison, Nov. 26, 1809, Donald Jackson, *Letters*, 475-476.
1340. In fact, Hampton suspected that Wilkinson's men were undermining his command, Amos Stoddard to Henry Burbeck, April 4, 1810, Henry Burbeck Papers, William L. Clements Library.
1341. Lindsay Schakenbach, "Schemers, Dreamers, and a Revolutionary Foreign Policy," 267-282.
1342. *National Intelligencer*, Jun 28, 1809, 1. *National Intelligencer*, July 19, 1809, 1.
1343. SW to Wade Hampton, Nov. 7, 1809, LS.
1344. Dumas Malone, *Jefferson the President, Second Term*, 624.
1345. TJ to David Howell, Dec. 15, 1810, FO.
1346. John Bakeless opined that Clark's opinion of Wilkinson "waned" early in his career, but he did not state the basis for his opinion. John Bakeless, *Lewis and Clark*, 54.
1347. ML to Mr. Walker, May 23, 1795, transcribed in L. R. Colter-Frick, *Courageous Colter and Companions*, 303-304. Ms. Frick noted that the tombstone still stands in the Lobbs Run Cemetery near Elarna, Penn. See also Kira Gale, *Meriwether Lewis: The Assassination of an American Hero and the Silver Mines of Mexico*, 32-33.
1348. John Gordon's son Bowling Gordon was one of the leaders in the push. *Nashville Republican*, Jan. 9, 1836, 3.
1349. *Republican Banner*, Oct. 2, 1835, 2.
1350. *Nashville Republican*, Oct. 31, 1835, 3.
1351. *Nashville Republican*, Jan. 9, 1836, 3.
1352. The *Treaty of Guadalupe Hidalgo* was signed February 2, 1848. Funds were approved for the monument two days later. The monument is small by modern standards, but it was large for its time.
1353. The movement was led by Jackson's Company of Spies leader John Gordon's son, Bowling Gordon, who also served as a state legislator. He was joined by Lewis Dillahunty. Gordon served as State Senator for Hickman County, which had been part of Davy Crockett's congressio-

nal district. It was thought to be at John Gordon's Natchez Trace inn where Crockett mounted a tree stump to make what became known as a "stump speech." John Gordon's service as captain of the Company of Spies is noted on his military service records at the National Archives. A copy can be found at the Maury County, Tennessee Archives. A company of spies served as scouts and spies in advance of a movement of troops.

1354. 1848 Public Chapter, 135, Feb. 4, 1848, *Acts of the State of Tennessee*, 1847-48 (Gates and Parker: Jackson 1848). McClean, "Papers Concerning Robertson's Colony in Texas," 1: 76-83. Texas Historical Association.

1355. Meriwether Lewis and William Clark Journal, Dec. 7, 1809, 28, Missouri State Historical Society.

1356. Paul Russell Cutright described the question over Lewis's death in "Rest, Rest, Perturbed Spirit," *We Proceeded On*, Vol 12, No. 1 (March 1986), 7-17, as quoted from *Hamlet*, Act 1, Scene 5.

# INDEX

Adair, James 79, 124
Adams, John 17, 35, 38, 48, 50, 102
Alamo 263
Alaska 22
Albemarle, North Carolina 7, 262
Alexandria 49
Allen, Benjamin 206
Allen, James 227
Ambrose, Stephen xi
American Philosophical Society 45, 47, 58
Anderson, William P. 84, 86, 89, 124, 189, 191, 227, 250, 254
Arikara 118
Arkansas District 107, 140-141, 143-145, 147-148, 157-158, 160, 177, 205, 229, 252
Arkansas Post 140-141, 147, 189, 207
Arkansas River 34, 71, 111, 140-141
Armistead, George 141
Astor, John Jacob 2
Atlantic Ocean 1, 22, 33, 226, 273
Audubon, John James 165
Aztecs 34

Baltimore, Maryland 158-159, 215, 217, 225
Bates, Frederick 100-103, 106-107, 110, 113, 115, 126, 128-131, 134, 138-139, 152-153, 156, 160, 165, 173, 214, 217-219, 225, 252, 262, 266
Baton Rouge 41, 88
Battle of Fallen Timbers 19, 21, 237
Battle of the Alamo 263
Bean's Station 251
Bissell, Daniel 80, 86, 164, 183-184, 217, 219
Black Hawk 133
Blount Conspiracy 44
Blount, William 44
Boote, William R. 182
Bradbury, John 243
Brahan, John 124, 144, 147, 182, 187, 189-191, 212, 217, 219, 227, 239-241, 251-252, 256-257, 259, 266
Bratton, William 170
Breckinridge, Letitia 94, 105

Brown, James  236
Brown, John  45
Brown's Bottom  236
Brown, William  215, 223-224
Bruff, Major James  79, 81-83, 114, 130
Buffalo River  241
Burr, Aaron  xii, 17, 77-91, 96-99, 101, 108, 116, 120-121, 124, 144, 146, 150-151, 171-173, 178, 183, 187, 209, 229, 239, 261, 266
Burr Conspiracy  96-97, 120, 172, 180, 182-183, 186-187, 202, 224
Burrites  87, 90, 99-100, 107-108, 125, 136, 142, 150, 165, 170

Cabanne, Jean  215
Camp Dubois  63
Canada  22, 54, 109, 121, 132
Cape Girardeau  166, 168, 173, 175
Caribbean  22, 100, 170, 181, 202
Carr, William C.  99, 120, 127, 154-156, 168, 215
Charleston  226
Charlottesville, Virginia  5-6, 8, 25-26, 46, 98-99, 154, 243, 253, 257
Cherokee  49, 96, 140, 225, 240
Chickasaw  xii, 24, 34, 49, 51, 70, 81, 87, 140, 144, 167, 178, 189-191, 196-197, 202-207, 210, 213, 216-217, 220, 223, 225-230, 235-242, 252-253, 260
Chickasaw Agency  81, 87, 197, 203-204, 206-207, 210, 220, 226-228, 236, 238-240, 248, 251-253, 260

Chickasaw Bluffs, *see* Fort Pickering / Chickasaw Bluffs
Chickasaw Post Office  204, 209-211, 226
Chickasaw Trail  213, 223, 225-226, 236
Childress, Joseph  133
Choctaw  34, 49, 70, 87-88, 196, 226, 235
Chosen Rifle Company  21, 24
Chouteau, Auguste  64, 73, 101-102, 111, 117-120, 130, 153
Chouteau, Pierre  118, 121, 139-140, 149, 151-154, 157, 160, 173
Christy, William  73, 121
Cincinnati  20, 62
Claiborne, W. C. C.  70, 80, 87, 106, 122-123, 142-143, 145-146, 160-162, 170-171
Clark, Daniel Jr.  42, 44-46, 48-50, 80-83, 171-172, 224
Clark, George Rogers  21, 53
Clark, Jonathan  246-248, 250-251
Clark, Julia  100, 155, 167, 245-247, 254
Clark, Meriwether Lewis  155, 245-247
Clark, William  xi-xii, 1-2, 8, 18, 21, 24, 26, 28, 33, 35-37, 53, 59-65, 67-70, 72-74, 77, 90, 93-95, 99-100, 102, 109-111, 113-114, 117, 119-120, 129-132, 135-140, 149, 154-159, 162-163, 167, 170, 173, 191, 196, 202, 209, 216, 218, 223, 229, 244-252, 254-262, 264, 266

Clinch Mountain 251
Cloverfields 6, 242
Clovertbottom 86
Coburn, John 156
Colbert, George 237-238
Colbert, James 207, 226, 228, 236-237, 257
Colbert, Levi 225, 237-238, 240
Colter, John 129
Columbian Springs 38, 42, 144, 180, 186, 224
Columbia River 102
Columbia, Tennessee 242
Columbus, Christopher 67, 102, 231
Cook, James 7, 67
Corps of Discovery 53, 55, 57-58, 60-65, 67-69, 73, 76, 101, 108, 156, 257
Creek 182
Creoles 121
Crockett, Davy 263
Cuba 145, 147, 170-172, 185, 202, 225
Cushing, Thomas 38

Dailey's Tavern 249
Dandridge, Tennessee 46, 141, 187
Des Moines 131
Detroit 25, 27, 100
Devil's Backbone, The 231, 273
Dickson, Robert 131-132
Dickson, William 58, 80, 190
Dodge, Henry 87, 165
Duck River 241
Dunbar, William 41, 43, 46-47, 166

Eagle Tavern 250
El Camino Real, *see* Spanish Trail
Ellicott, Andrew 43, 45, 47, 50, 58
Enlightenment 9, 73-75
Eustis, William 128, 138, 146, 149-152

Federalist Party 2, 11-17, 35, 44, 47-49, 51-52, 54-55, 78, 89, 100, 102, 141, 179, 181, 186, 261
Févret de Saint-Mémin, Charles Balthazar Julien 266
Fincastle, Virginia 254, 258
Fitzhugh, Dennis 119, 248
Florida 22, 55, 80, 83, 121-123
Folch, Juan Vincente 122
Fooy, Benjamin 177, 202
Forest, The 41, 43-44, 46
Fort Adams / Loftus Heights 38, 40, 43, 49-50, 70, 143-144, 148, 161, 180-182, 184, 186, 188, 190, 207-209, 211, 213, 224, 266
Fort Belle Fontaine 109, 112-113, 131-132, 135-136, 159-160, 183
Fort Belle Vue 132, 135
Fort Clatsop 69, 112
Fort Dearborn 161, 182, 185-186, 213
Fort Greeneville 20-21
Fort Jefferson 166-167
Fort Mandan 67-68
Fort Massac 50, 72, 80, 86, 173, 183, 236
Fort Osage 110, 113-114
Fort Pickering / Chickasaw Bluffs xii, 24, 33, 86-87, 124, 141, 144-145,

158-159, 173-174, 176-179, 183-184, 189, 193-207, 210-211, 213, 215-221, 223, 225-227, 230, 247, 252, 254-255, 258-260
Fort San Fernando De Las Barrancas 177
Fort Southwest Point 46, 187, 189
Fort Washington 20, 36
Fox 96
Frankfort, Kentucky 33, 247-249, 253, 258
Franklin, Tennessee 51, 187, 204, 207, 240, 242
Frazer, Robert 103, 108-109
Fredericktown, Maryland 200
Freeman-Custis Expedition 70-72, 95
Freeman, Thomas 43-44, 47, 69-72, 95, 124, 188, 190-191, 227, 254
French Revolution 8-9, 12-13, 15, 148

Gallatin, Albert 14
Gass, Patrick 102-103, 262
Georgia 6, 25-26
Glass, Anthony 141-144
Glover's Trace 236
Gordon, Bowling 263
Graefenberg, Kentucky 248
Great Lakes 22
Greuze, Jean Baptiste 4, 266
Grinder, Priscilla xii, 243, 252
Grinder, Robert 240-241, 252
Grinder's Stand 229, 240-243, 252, 260, 265
Gulf Coast 22, 34, 180-181, 225

Gulf of Mexico 32, 34, 181
Gunn, James 227, 257
Gunn, John 227
Guntown (now Mississippi) 236-237
Gutierrez, Jose Bernardo 146-147
Gutierrez-Magee Expedition 146

Hamilton, Alexander 10-17, 24-25, 35-36, 48, 50-51, 55, 72, 78
Hampton, Gen. Wade 179-180, 183, 185-186, 247, 261
Harding, John 257
Hare, Joseph 241
Hare, Thomas 234
Harpe Brothers 188, 234
Harper's Ferry 58
Havana, Cuba 145
Hemmings, James 258
Hermitage 85, 190
Hillsboro, North Carolina 227
Hiwassee Garrison 144, 182, 189
Hogg, David 189, 197, 204, 206-207, 210, 237
Hopefield 33, 177
House, Captain James 113, 132, 145, 159, 214-219, 223-225
House, James xiv, 266
House, Thomas 46
Houston, Sam 37
Hunt, Major Seth 114, 121

Illinois Territory 155
Independence River 68

Jackson, Andrew 36, 58, 77, 80-81, 83-87, 89-91, 124, 144-145, 147,

INDEX

178, 186-191, 222, 227, 257, 263, 266
Jackson, Jacob 86-87, 183
Jefferson, Thomas vii-xiii, xvi, 2-3, 5-11, 13-17, 20, 22-24, 26-29, 31-32, 35, 42-65, 68-75, 77-80, 82-90, 93-100, 102, 106, 109-114, 117-118, 121-124, 128-129, 131, 133-135, 138-140, 147-148, 150-154, 157, 162, 174, 179-181, 183, 185-188, 190-191, 193, 199-200, 207, 213, 215, 218, 221, 223, 227, 230, 233, 235-237, 241, 243-245, 247, 250-264, 266, 273
Journals x, 61-62, 64, 68, 74-75, 103, 143, 155, 159, 169, 216, 234, 240, 246-250, 255, 259

Kansas River 62
Kentucky Hotel 250
Kentucky River 248
Kincaid, John 230
Kingston, Tennessee 144, 189

Lanehart, George 207, 226, 230, 257
Lewis and Clark Expedition vii, xi, 1-2, 8, 26-29, 53-54, 56-65, 67-77, 80, 92-95, 97, 102-103, 112, 115, 119-120, 129, 133, 155, 159, 170, 175-176, 201-202, 216, 228-229, 234, 246-250, 255, 257, 259, 262
Lewis County 263
Lewis County, Tennessee viii

Lewis, Lucy (also Marks) 5-7, 9, 15, 19, 127, 154, 162, 167-168, 201, 254, 257
Lewis, Meriwether vii-xiv, 1-11, 13-17, 19-21, 23-29, 31, 35, 41, 44, 46, 48-49, 52-54, 56-77, 80, 87, 90-103, 105-115, 117-122, 124-125, 127-141, 145, 147-179, 182-183, 186-188, 190-211, 213-221, 223-231, 233-244, 246-266, 270, 273
Lewis, Reuben 119, 138-139
Lewis, William 5-7, 60, 127, 243
Lexington, Kentucky 33, 155, 249-251, 258
Lisa, Manuel 101, 106, 119-120, 132
Little Prairie 174
Locust Hill 5
Loftus Heights, *see* Fort Adams / Loftus Heights
Los Angeles 34
Louisiana Purchase 50, 54-57, 69, 79, 96, 187, 263, 267
Louisville, Kentucky 61, 119, 246-248
Love Inn 226
Love, Jeremiah 220, 227, 230, 237-238
Love, Thomas 227, 257

Mackenzie, Alexander 54
Madison County (now Alalbama) 190-191
Madison, James 16, 123, 131, 133, 135-136, 138-139, 145, 149-150,

433

154, 157, 173, 200-204, 208, 259, 261
Magee, Augustus 146-147
Mandan 67, 93, 117-124, 135-137, 148-151, 153, 261
Mandan Expedition 119-121, 123-124, 135-137, 148-151, 261
Marks, Captain John 6, 254, 257
Mason, John 136-137
Masons 25-26, 130, 166
Mason, Samuel 234, 241
Maury County, Tennessee 124, 145, 242, 263
Maury, Rev. Matthew 7, 56
McClallen, John 71, 73
McCoy, Thomas 227
McFarlane, Andrew 16
McFarlane, James (killed in Whiskey Rebellion) 15-16
McFarlane, James (Lewis's subagent) 138-141, 143, 148, 153, 156-160, 162, 173, 177, 194, 196, 223, 225
McFarlane, Lewis 16
McGee, Malcolm 227
McIntosh, John 226
McIntoshville 203, 207, 213, 226-230, 235-236, 257
McKeehan, David 149
McKee, John 37, 70, 81, 87, 229
McLanahan, Josiah T. 124, 147, 261
McLish, John 241
McLish's Stand 241-242
Meriwether, Nicholas 6
Meriwether, William 6-7, 203, 255
Mexican-American War of 1848 263-264

Mexico 34, 70, 72, 79-80, 89, 122, 136, 171, 251
Michaux, André 54
Miranda Expedition 81, 84, 147, 151, 261
Miranda, Francisco de 81, 83-84, 261
Miró, Esteban 33-34
Mississippi River 2, 22-26, 28, 31-34, 37-38, 41-44, 49-50, 53-54, 56, 58, 61, 63, 72, 80, 83-84, 86-88, 96-97, 113, 117, 136, 141, 143-144, 154, 157-158, 160-170, 172, 174-175, 177, 179-180, 183-187, 193-194, 201-202, 208, 217, 224, 229, 234, 237, 242
Mississippi Territory 41-42, 69, 88-89, 183, 191, 213
Missouri River 28, 53, 56, 61, 63, 65, 71, 73, 81, 94, 120
Mitchell, Samuel 228
Mobile (now Alabama) 225
Monongahela River 16
Monticello 5-6, 8, 243-245, 251-253, 257, 264, 271
Morgan, Gen. Daniel 14, 16
Morgan, George 169

Nacogdoches 37, 42
Napoleon 4, 7, 22, 35, 50, 54, 122, 266
Nash, Ira 121
Nashville, Tennessee 49, 51, 58, 80, 83, 85-86, 90, 124, 144-147, 173, 182, 184, 188, 190-191, 195, 199, 202, 207, 209-211, 213-217, 219-220, 226-228, 230, 235,

238, 241-243, 247-251, 253-254, 256-257, 263
Natchez 25, 34, 41-44, 46, 58, 70-71, 87-88, 141-143, 161, 168, 182, 187-188, 190, 213, 224, 226-227, 233-235, 238-239, 241
Natchez Trace viii, 70, 81, 141, 143, 146, 187-188, 204, 207, 209-211, 213, 217, 225-227, 230-242, 246, 252, 263, 266
Natchitoches 42-43, 71, 109, 113, 122, 139-140, 142-147, 208-209, 224
Natchitoches River 46
Neelly, James xii, 199, 204-205, 207, 210-211, 220-221, 225-230, 234-243, 249, 251-253, 256-259
Neutrality Act of 1794 44, 83, 90, 136, 151, 261
New Madrid 33, 86-87, 107, 167-170, 173-174, 196, 202-203, 247, 250
Newman, Francis 145-147, 171
New Mexico 32, 69, 121
New Orleans 22, 25-26, 31-34, 37-38, 42-43, 49, 52, 70, 79-82, 85, 87-88, 106, 122-123, 145-147, 152, 154, 158, 160-161, 164, 167, 170-173, 175, 180-181, 183-185, 187-188, 195-196, 202-204, 213-215, 223-225, 261
Newport, Kentucky 85
New Spain 32, 37, 41-42, 44-47, 64, 79, 109, 121-123, 137-138, 140, 144-146, 148, 151, 171-172, 182, 216, 251, 263

New York City 78, 83
Nolan, Philip 29, 41-43, 45-47, 79, 146, 251
Northwest Passage 27, 50, 54, 62-63, 69

Ohio River 20, 25, 28, 50, 61, 80, 86, 166-167, 169
Old Houlka 226
Ordway, John 170
Oregon 53, 63
Orleans Territory 43, 80, 106, 122, 187, 203
Osage 64, 93, 96, 101, 109-114, 118, 131, 135, 139-141, 149, 153, 156-158, 160, 173, 229, 237
Overton, John x, 83, 124, 144, 146, 178, 189, 206, 249-250
Overton, Thomas 189
Overton, Walter H. 144-145, 147-148, 189, 207

Pacific Ocean 8, 27-29, 53-56, 62-63, 67, 69, 76, 94, 228, 273
Paris, France 6, 8, 12, 54
Patterson, James 124, 147, 191, 261, 263
Patterson, J. Nelson 263
Patterson, Nelson 124, 263
Peale, Charles Willson 4, 92, 95, 266
Peale, Rembrandt 266
Peerny, Jeau (written by Jefferson as "John Pernier") 100, 128-129, 163, 165, 168, 203, 215-216, 220, 237, 241-242, 251-256, 258-259
Penrose, Clement Biddle 112

Pernier, John, *see* Peerny, Jeau
Perry, Hardy 228, 230, 236
Philadelphia, Pennsylvania 6, 25, 45, 57-58, 70, 94-95, 97, 112, 133, 226-227, 237
Pike, Zebulon 26, 71-72, 120, 122, 139
Pike, Zebulon Sr. 72
Pittsburgh, Pennsylvania 15, 24-25, 38, 59
Platte River 120
Preston, William 105, 127
Price, Risdon H. 114-115, 130, 158, 225

Quasi-War 25

Randolph, John 31, 88-90, 181-183, 185
Randolph, Meriwether Lewis 244
Randolph, Thomas Mann 188, 258
Red River 47, 55, 70-72, 84, 141-143, 145, 148, 158, 208-209, 221
Republican Army of the North 147
Republican Party 2, 8, 11, 16-17, 35, 48, 77, 89, 96, 101-102, 141, 179, 186-187
Revolutionary War 11-12, 14-15, 21-22, 41, 79, 166, 179, 262
Richmond, Virginia 89-91, 97-98, 150, 250, 253
Rio Grande River 55, 123, 263, 273
Robertson, Bonley 203
Robertson, James 238, 248-249
Robinson, Dr. John 72, 113-114, 130, 139-140, 147, 159

Roleson, Joseph 257
Romanticism 9, 74-75, 95, 151
Runions, Thomas 241
Rush, Dr. Benjamin 58, 176, 198-199, 201
Russell, Gilbert C. xii, 5, 124, 141, 145, 148, 158, 177, 182, 184, 187-191, 193-203, 205-211, 213-218, 220-221, 223-225, 227-230, 237, 239-240, 242-243, 254-256, 258-260
Russellville 246

Sabine River 71, 82, 146
Sac 96, 131-133
Sacagawea 68
Salcedo, Mauel Maria de 146-147
San Antonio 34, 42, 146
Santa Fe 34, 50-51, 55, 62-63, 65, 69-73, 77, 79, 81, 83-84, 95-96, 100, 113, 120-124, 135, 139-140, 144, 147-148, 150-151, 155, 159, 178, 183, 186, 191, 221, 256, 261, 263-264
Santa Fe Trail 113, 124
Saugrain, Dr. Anthony 162
Sauk, *see* Sac
Scott, Winfield 8, 14, 77, 89-90, 98, 179
Shannon's, Mr. (a tavern) 248
Sheheke 93, 117-118, 120, 123, 136, 154
Shelbyville, Kentucky 247
Sibley, Dr. John 42-43, 71, 113, 139, 141-143, 147-148, 189, 224, 261
Sibley, George 113-114, 162

Simpsonville, Kentucky 247
Sioux 110
Smith, John (Ohio Senator) 117
Smith, Reuben 124, 147
Smith's, Mr. (a tavern) 247
Smith T, John 82, 87, 107-109, 124, 136, 144, 147, 165-166, 172, 177, 189, 191, 213, 261, 263
Smith, W. C. 178, 195, 197-200, 206-207, 217
Spanish Trail 37, 42
Sphar, John 227
St. Augustine, Florida 227
Staunton, Virginia 25-26, 182, 256
St. Charles (now Missouri) 65
St. Francis 139, 158
St. Francis River 139-140
St. Genevieve 25, 87, 109, 114, 124, 144, 165-166, 169, 173
St. Louis 2, 25, 62-65, 73-74, 79-82, 87, 89, 93, 96, 98-103, 105-106, 108-110, 112-115, 117-123, 127, 130, 132-136, 139-141, 148, 152, 154, 156-168, 173, 177, 183, 188, 193, 202, 208-209, 215, 217-219, 225, 243, 245, 247-248, 252
St. Louis Lodge No. 111 130
St. Louis Missouri Fur Company 2, 118-121, 123, 135-136, 154, 158, 163, 247-248
Stoddard, Major Amos 38, 42, 63-65, 70, 80, 85, 109, 111, 128, 143-145, 148, 166, 175-176, 199-200, 208-211, 216-220, 238, 243, 257
Stuart, Gilbert 266

Swan, Capt. William 184, 195
Swan Creek, Tennessee 241

Taylor, Zachary 182-184
Temple, Jonathan and Eleanor 246
Tennessee River 236-237, 239, 241
Terre aux Boeuf 184, 224
Texas 32, 42-47, 50, 55, 62, 71, 80, 82-84, 96, 100, 107, 121-122, 124, 139-141, 143-148, 150-151, 155, 158-160, 178, 183-186, 191, 208, 221, 229, 251, 256, 261, 263-264
Texas Revolution 263
Tharp, Capt. William 224
Tick Creek 248
Tillier, Rodolphe 109, 112-113, 115, 130, 134-138, 148-150, 153
Tockshish's Stand 227
Treat, John B. 229, 252
Trinchard, F. S. 168, 174
Trotter, Dr. Thomas 176, 198-200
Trough Spring 246-247
Trunks 108, 155, 159-160, 163, 165, 186, 191, 194, 201, 210, 214-216, 218, 220, 223-225, 227, 229-230, 234-235, 238, 240, 242, 245, 247, 249-250, 254, 256

Van Meter, Joseph 207, 257

War of 1812 11, 132, 189, 234
Washington, D.C. / Washington City 28, 44, 49, 57, 82, 85, 90, 93-94, 108, 113, 122, 133-134, 137-139, 145-146, 148-152, 154-159, 162, 166, 171-173, 176, 181, 183-186,

188, 191, 201-204, 208-211, 213, 217, 219-221, 225, 230, 239, 245, 249, 252-254

Washington, George xiv-xv, 2, 6, 12-13, 15, 19, 21-23, 25, 31-32, 34, 43, 49, 52, 57, 63, 227, 235, 237, 264, 266

Wayne, General Anthony 19-20, 24-25, 32, 35-36, 48, 52, 180, 186, 237

Wescott, Robert 79, 87, 108

Wesinger House 248

Whiskey Rebellion 12-14, 16-17, 138, 262

Whiteside, Jenkins 254

Wilkinson, Benjamin 114-115, 117-122, 124, 130, 132, 136-137, 151, 158, 162, 223-225

Wilkinson, General James xii, 20, 24-25, 27, 29-39, 41-53, 56, 58, 63, 65, 68-72, 76-85, 87-91, 95, 99-101, 107-115, 120-122, 124-125, 130, 132, 134, 137-139, 141-142, 144-153, 156, 158-159, 161-162, 170-173, 177-191, 195, 197-198, 200-202, 204, 209, 211, 221, 224-225, 229, 235-237, 243, 260-262, 266

Wilkinson, James Biddle 71

Wilkinsonville 51

Wilson, Alexander 70-71, 95

Winnebago 132

Wirt, William 97-98

Wyandot 25

Yellowstone River 68

Young Factor's Stand 238

Yrujo, Carolos Martinez de 54, 68

# ABOUT THE AUTHOR

Tony L. Turnbow has studied the history of the historic Natchez Trace and the circumstances of Lewis's death for more than 40 years. In 1996, he served as the alternate juror on an official coroner's inquest into the circumstances of Lewis's death in 1809. He has written about Lewis's death in *We Proceeded On*, the journal of the Lewis and Clark Trail Alliance. In 2009, he wrote and produced a full-length play, *Inquest on the Natchez Trace*, that recreated an 1809 inquest setting to give voice to witness statements about Lewis's death.

Mr. Turnbow practices law in Franklin, Tennessee. With a Bachelor of Arts and a concentration in southern U.S. history from Vanderbilt University and a Juris Doctorate from the University of Tennessee College of Law, Mr. Turnbow has continued to use his training to explore the primary history of the old Natchez Trace. He previously authored the nonfiction *Hardened to Hickory: The Missing Chapter in Andrew Jackson's Life* about Andrew Jackson's fight with the general and spy at the center of this book. He also wrote a young adult historical fiction series, *Fighting Devil's Backbone*, about land pirates on the Natchez Trace.

Mr. Turnbow has appeared in television productions that explored the circumstances of Lewis's death, and he frequently speaks to groups about the history of the Natchez Trace.

www.ingramcontent.com/pod-product-compliance
Lightning Source LLC
Chambersburg PA
CBHW030332230426
43661CB00032B/1389/J